PERFORMANCE MANAGEMENT SYSTEMS AND STRATEGIES

PERFORMANCE MANAGEMENT SYSTEMS AND STRATEGIES

Dipak Kumar Bhattacharyya
Director
Camellia School of Business Management

Pearson

Associate Editor–Acquisitions: Nitin Valecha
Associate Editor–Production: Amrita Naskar

ISBN 978-81-317-5422-1

First Impression, 2011
Seventeenth Impression, 2024
Eighteenth Impression, 2025

Published by Pearson India Education Services Pvt. Ltd, CIN: U72200TN2005PTC057128.

Head Office: 1st Floor, Berger Tower, Plot No. C-001A/2, Sector16B, Noida 201301 U.P., India.

Registered Office: Featherlite, 'The Address' 5th Floor, Survey No 203/10B, 200 Ft MMRD Road, Zamin Pallavaram, Chennai - 600044.
Website: in.pearson.com, Email: companysecretary.india@pearson.com

Compositor: White Lotus
Printed in India at Sai Printo Pack Pvt Ltd

Dedicated to Tapodeep, Sudip and Sutapa,
the three masterminds who always monitor my performance.

Contents

Preface

Among all human resource management functions, today, performance management is considered the most crucial, as only through this developmental function, an organization can sustain in the long run. Moreover, performance management systems provide essential inputs to organizations to take crucial HR decisions, and also help organizations to align their business goals with the performance of the people. Understanding performance management systems and strategies, therefore, has now become important for management students (specializing in HR) and HR professionals.

Against this backdrop, the objective of this book is to develop skills and competencies of HR students and professionals to understand the nitty-gritty of performance management systems and strategies. This book intends to provide extensive theoretical knowledge with practical overtones to the students, and application-based knowledge to the professionals to help them successfully implement performance management systems and strategies. With such comprehensive knowledge and practical skills, HR students would be able to develop their capabilities as future managers to manage performance in any organization. As managers, HR students will be able to derive maximum advantage to successfully develop the people of the organization through effective feedback and by adopting appropriate strategies to align the people with the business of the organization. They would be able to effectively measure and rate the performance of the people and scientifically base their strategic HR decisions like promotion and rewards, training designs, sustaining an environment of motivation and effective work culture for mutual benefit of the people and the organization, etc. Organizations also in the process can emerge as winners in a competitive environment. Successful performance management practices in organizations, apart from nurturing a motivating work culture, bring in effectiveness, efficiency, quality, productivity, innovation and profitability. This book will provide the students and the professionals with an insight into all these.

Chapter 1 deals with the meaning of performance management, history of human resource management function, its development in India, performance management as HRD function, history of performance management, performance management as a management tool, philosophy, benefits, processes of performance management, performance objectives, standards, dimensions, domains and ethics.

Chapter 2 introduces the concept of performance planning, its definitions, process, contents, model of elements and standards of a performance plan, process of transition from individual performance plan to group performance plan, performance role clarity, alignment of strategic plans with performance plans and strategy realization through performance plans.

Chapter 3 deals with performance appraisal, its meaning and definitions, role of appraisals in performance management, importance of performance appraisal, objectives of performance appraisal, reasons behind the failure of performance appraisal, steps and characteristics of performance appraisal system, performance appraisal design, approaches in performance appraisal, types and methods of performance appraisal, concepts and methods of potential appraisal, biases of performance appraisal and diagnosis of poor performance.

Chapter 4 discusses performance management review, introducing its definitions, process of employee development through performance review, types, steps, benefits and structured process of performance review, performance counselling, etc.

Chapter 5 introduces performance management systems, explaining the definition and concept of performance management system, its benefits and steps, importance, features, processes, dimensions, conceptual framework, relations with organizational strategy and social perspectives, performance consulting, role of performance consultants, pillars of managing performance, performance management theatre, annual stock-taking of performance, e-performance management, etc.

In chapter 6, the concept of strategic performance management has been introduced, along with its definition, evolution, characteristics, generic strategies, performance and strategy linkage, purpose of performance management strategy, process of performance management strategy and components of strategic performance management process, strategy and performance management cycle, linkage between individual performance and strategy, benefits of strategic performance management, advantages and disadvantages of strategic performance management, strategic performance management and the balanced scorecard, strategic performance management and metrics, environmental threats and risks, etc.

Chapter 7 discusses competency-based performance management systems, deliberating on definitions of competency, managerial skills and competencies, skill inventories, multi-skilling, skills for the new millennium, developing competencies for effective performance management, competency identification and assessment process, competency mapping, steps to introduce competency-based systems, developing competency models, HR competencies, elements of performance-based competencies and competency dictionary.

Chapter 8 talks about performance-based compensation, introducing its concepts, process of design, job evaluations, incentives, benefits, performance-related pay, compensation broadbanding, designing compensation through skill-based programmes, competency-based pay, performance guide charts, performance-based executive compensation, calibration of executive compensation to performance, performance measurement in executive incentive programmes, etc.

Chapter 9 elaborates on performance-based career planning, career development and succession plans. The chapter helps us to understand the interrelation between career planning, career development, succession planning and the performance management function of an organization. Also the chapter elaborates on the process of career planning, process of career development, importance and significance of succession planning and the process of strengthening internal supply of manpower through career planning, career development and succession planning.

Chapter 10 deals with team performance management, explaining the definitions and concepts of team, principles of team performance management, methodology of team performance, approaches to change team behaviours, work wheel and team performance, measuring and managing team performance, different stages of teamwork and team-building exercises.

Chapter 11 introduces the concept of performance measurement process and then goes on to talk about the various tools and techniques like balanced scorecard, HR scorecard. The chapter provides detailed guidelines for developing balanced scorecard and HR scorecard for an organization.

Chapter 12 elaborates on performance management and mentoring, introducing its definitions and concepts, characteristics, differences, benefits, types, ethical guidelines, culture, etc.

Chapter 13 discusses performance measurement using various quantitative and statistical tools. For effective performance measurement, the chapter at the outset highlights on the importance of selection of performance measurement criteria, integrated performance measurement systems, statistical methods of performance measures, performance measures through ranking and rating, scales for evaluation of performance measures, performance matrix and models, key performance indicators, performance measures through productivity indices, etc.

Chapter 14 introduces the readers to the basics of international performance management, discussing its structure and strategy, expatriates' performance management, effect of culture, performance management in international assignment, globalization and international performance management practices, compensation and international performance management practices, etc.

Chapter 15 details the process of performance audit, human resource accounting, audit and valuation, detailing various concepts, structures, steps, methods and techniques.

Chapter 16 deliberates on the delicate aspects of ethical and legal issues of performance management, its concepts, perspectives, objectives, benefits, dilemmas, etc.

Chapter 17, the final chapter of the book, discusses the various contemporary issues of performance management, organizational improvement tools as drivers of performance management systems, business process reengineering, lean management and culture, Toyota production system, total quality management, six sigma, quick response manufacturing, etc.

Special Pedagogic Features of the Book

The book has been written keeping in view the primary needs of the students and professionals so that they can get first-hand exposure to theories and practices. Performance management is the most important area of human resource management function, as organizations can sustain in competition only through improved performance of employees. A comprehensive text on this subject, keeping up with the all-India syllabi, therefore, is required. So far, our focus was on performance management books that dealt with some specific areas. But with this comprehensive text, I am sure students and professionals will get immensely benefitted. The book is written in simple business language with proper fusion of theories and examples from the corporate world (including case studies, exercises, etc.) The readers will find this book extremely useful in developing their knowledge and practical insight into performance management systems and strategies. The key features of the book are mentioned below:

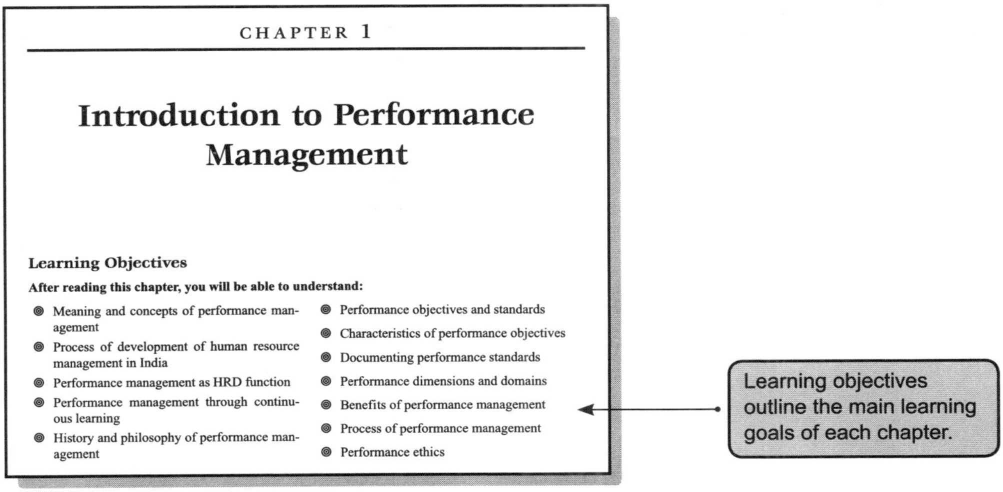
CHAPTER 1

Introduction to Performance Management

Learning Objectives

After reading this chapter, you will be able to understand:

- Meaning and concepts of performance management
- Process of development of human resource management in India
- Performance management as HRD function
- Performance management through continuous learning
- History and philosophy of performance management
- Performance objectives and standards
- Characteristics of performance objectives
- Documenting performance standards
- Performance dimensions and domains
- Benefits of performance management
- Process of performance management
- Performance ethics

Each chapter begins with a relevant small case example.

Marico's Performance Management

Marico is a leading Indian group in consumer products and services in the global FMCG market. Marico markets well-known brands such as Parachute, Saffola, Sweekar, Hair & Care, Nihar, Shanti, Mediker, Revive, Kaya, Sundari, Aromatic, Fiancee, and HairCode. Marico's brands and their extensions occupy leadership positions with significant market share in most categories—coconut oil, hair oils, post-wash hair care, anti-lice treatment, premium refined edible oils, niche fabric care, etc. Marico is present in the skin care services segment through Kaya Skin Clinics (48 in India and the Middle East), the Sundari range of Spa skin care products (in the USA and other countries), and also through a recently acquired nascent soap franchise (in India and Bangladesh). Products and services in hair care, skin care, and healthy foods. Marico is consistently consolidating its market share in the Indian FMCG market. With its prime brands like Parachute and Saffola, Marico could achieve a 20 per cent growth in its sales revenue. Today Marico has become a conglomerate. All this Marico could achieve because of its strong brand identity and its strategy to add value to existing products and services.

Exhibits inside the chapters provide a wide variety of figures, illustrations and other documents to prepare the students for real life challenges.

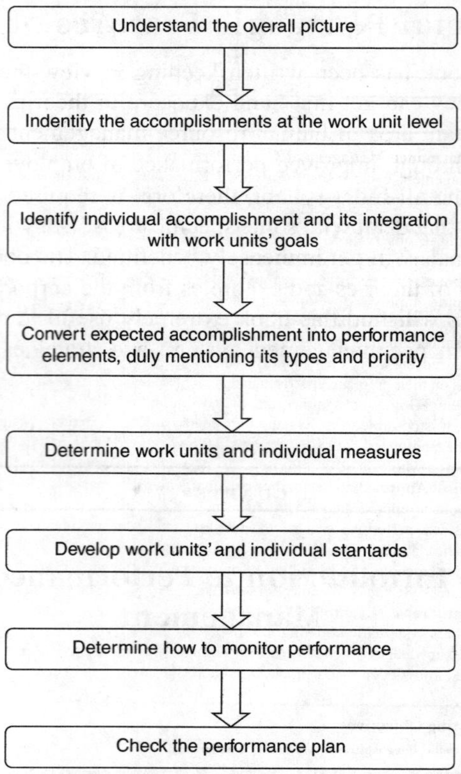

Exhibit 2.1 *Employee Development Programme*

SUMMARY

Performance management is the strategic HRD function which develops organizational capability to sustain in competition. The age-old use of performance management was to validate compensation design and other HR-related decisions like promotion, demotion, transfer, etc. With the realization that people are the only sustainable drivers of achieving organizational excellence, the performance management focuses have shifted towards HRD activities like identification of training needs, providing performance feedback directly to employees to enable them to make an informed choice about their career development opportunities, etc. This chapter first analysed the process of development of human resource management functions, and then delineates from the discussion the process of development of performance management functions. Being the introductory chapter, to set the premises, the chapter elaborates on the process of development of the concepts to help the readers to appreciate its genesis. Among others, the chapter also elaborates on the history of performance management, its philosophy, methods and techniques of setting performance objectives and standards, benefits of performance management, its domains and dimensions, and finally the ethics of performance management.

Being the introductory chapter, it sets the premise for the other chapters of the book. All important aspects of performance management have been covered in a nutshell in this chapter.

Each chapter ends with a summary of the key issues discussed in the chapter.

KEY WORDS

Performance Management Cycle: Performance management cycle starts from core job descriptions and reinforced with strategic plans. It translates to performance development, performance appraisal, observations and feedback, and reformulating the performance standards. This cycle continues, as performance management is an ongoing employee development function.

Performance Management Philosophy: Performance management philosophy basically espoused the values and beliefs of the organizations on their embraced performance management systems. Going through the performance philosophy, it is possible to understand the specific roles of the employees, their superiors and the organization as a whole.

Holistic Approach to Performance Management: A holistic approach to performance management considers performance management is a 'strategy which relates to every activity of the organization set in the context of its human resources policies, culture, style and communications system'.

Continuous Leaning: Continuous learning ensures systematic updating of employees' skills and knowledge, experience sharing through structured knowledge management approach, sharing of information through various transparent communication mediums, etc. The basic thrust for continuous learning is to help the employees to develop and achieve the results, to prepare for the change, and nurture compelling work culture.

Individual Performance Domain: Individual performance domain focuses on individual performance management to achieve results and goals with some performance standard. These results and goals are recorded and referenced during a performance appraisal process. Ongoing training and development is provided as needed. Ideally, the supervisor and employee exchange ongoing feedback during the appraisal period to enhance the individual's performance.

Mission Performance Domain: Mission performance domain identifies the purpose of the organization, based on the changing business focus and customers' expectations. The mission provides overall direction, and performance targets when aligned with the mission helps in achieving the cherished goals and objectives of the organization. Depending on the changing business focus, organizations redefine their mission and accordingly performance requirements of the people also get changed.

Key words highlight the important concepts addressed in each chapter.

General review questions are meant to help students revisit the key concepts discussed in a chapter.

GENERAL REVIEW QUESTIONS

1. Discuss the history of performance management functions. In what way does the process of development of performance functions get influenced by the history of human resource management and HRD functions?
2. Explain the concept of performance management cycle. Using the performance management cycle, how can you justify that performance management is a continuous process?
3. Do you consider performance management as a management tool? Develop your answer with justification.
4. What is philosophy of performance management? How performance management philosophy is determined?
5. Explain the concept of performance objectives and standards. How do performance objectives and standards help in performance management process?
6. Explain the process of developing performance standards collaboratively.
7. What are the important characteristics of performance standards?
8. Explain how performance management can benefit an organization.

Critical review questions test the students' ability to apply their learning to real life situations.

CRITICAL REVIEW QUESTION

12. Your organization is a world-renowned knowledge process outsourcing company, mainly catering to the billing functions of global organizations. You have been recruited by your company to perform the outsourced jobs of one of the leading IT Company, based in the USA. This company has over 50,000 employees in their payroll. Billing and employees' claim form processing is part of your major duty, which as a team leader you do with five graduates who are reporting to you. The job is absolutely protocol bound and requires your mandate (acceptance or non-acceptance) instantly. Accuracy in decision and speed of work both are essential parts of your and other team members' job. Identify what could be your performance domains and dimensions. Develop your answer with specific examples.

Use of case studies from companies like Mono India, Infosys, TCS and Proctor and Gamble to help students build application-based knowledge.

CASE STUDY

Linking Performance to the Bottom Line: The Approach of Mono India

The Mono India, an Indian conglomerate with more focus on FMCG products, operates globally with 59,000 workforces in their payroll. The company manages each product line as strategic business units (SBUs). For absence of commonality in product lines, SBUs do not compete with each other. The company follows a matrix structure, making each employee reportable to two bosses. FMCG SBU head, Mr Pratap, has a high reputation for achieving the consistent growth for last 5 years. Mono India strategically locates their manufacturing units keeping in view the market proximity. Accordingly, the company located their 16 Indian units spread across 14 states and 2 union territories in India. Market in unrepresented states and union territories are controlled from manufacturing units that are close to them.

CASE STUDY

Valuing Human Resources—The Infosys Way

The human resource accounting concept was pioneered by the Indian public sector companies. It was first introduced by two public sector majors, i.e., Bharat Heavy Electricals Limited (BHEL) and Steel Authority of India Ltd (SAIL) in the 1970s. At Infosys, the concept was started in the year 1995–96. Infosys basically utilized the Lev & Schwartz Model of human resource accounting. Later with the

Acknowledgements

Writing this book would not have been possible without the support and cooperation of my family, friends and colleagues. I gratefully acknowledge the support and cooperation of my wife and children, N. R. Datta, Chairman and Managing Director of Camellia Group; Partha Pal, Deputy Director (Academics); Aveek Bhattacharyya, Business Development Head of Camellia Group; my friends and colleagues at the Camellia School of Business Management; Prof. Sudipti Banerjea, my mentor at the University of Calcutta; and all my students of Camellia Business School, Indian Institute of Social Welfare and Business Management, and various other institutes where I was earlier engaged. Finally, I congratulate the team at Pearson Education for bringing out this book in its best possible form.

I would welcome suggestions and comments from my readers and friends at dkbhattacharyya@yahoo.co.in.

DIPAK KUMAR BHATTACHARYYA

About the Author

Dr Dipak Kumar Bhattacharyya is a Ph.D. from the University of Calcutta and has been engaged with teaching and research at postgraduate level management programmes for more than 20 years. Dr Bhattacharyya also has about 15 years of experience in industry in HR-related functions. Presently, he is the Director of the Camellia School of Business Management, Kolkata. Earlier, he was the Dean of the Indian Institute of Social Welfare and Business Management (IISWBM), Kolkata; and also served as the Director of the Institute of Engineering and Management, Kolkata and All India Management Association – Centre for Management Education, New Delhi. He has also been a visiting professor at XLRI, Jamshedpur and IIFT, Kolkata. He is actively involved in teaching, research, training and consulting. He has authored several books on HR and management and also published more than 100 research papers in various journals of national and international repute.

CHAPTER 1

Introduction to Performance Management

Learning Objectives

After reading this chapter, you will be able to understand:

- Meaning and concepts of performance management
- Process of development of human resource management in India
- Performance management as HRD function
- Performance management through continuous learning
- History and philosophy of performance management
- Performance objectives and standards
- Characteristics of performance objectives
- Documenting performance standards
- Performance dimensions and domains
- Benefits of performance management
- Process of performance management
- Performance ethics

Performance Management Culture

To ensure performance culture in the largest public sector bank in India, based on shared understanding, clear purpose and results based on accountability, some action plans have been drawn by the bank. Earlier, the bank used to follow job descriptions, and managers and executives followed such mandates to achieve business objectives. However, the changing business scenarios demanded more flexibilities in performance, requiring managers and executives to be multi-skilled and deliver more in line with the pre-set key result areas (KRAs). KRAs in the bank are decided based on the finalized business objectives at the top, and hence at the individual level, managers and executives hardly get any flexibility to alter KRAs. The entire performance management functions in organizations have been entrusted to the specially developed cell, under one senior-level manager. The cell operates under the Strategy and Policy Group of the Bank. It implements and monitors the performance management functions in the organization, and, based on its review, the Strategy and Policy Group of the Bank recommends appropriate human resource development (HRD) or organizational development initiatives. Recently, based on such practices, the bank has been able to redesign its working systems and practices, focusing more on the creation of a compelling performance culture in organizations.

INTRODUCTION

Performance management is now considered as the most crucial and strategic HRD function to enable organizations to sustain in competition. Traditionally, however, performance management was more for validating compensation design decisions and to initiate other HR measures like promotion, demotion, transfer, etc. With the realization that people are the only sustainable drivers for achieving organizational excellence, performance management perspectives have changed, and today it encompasses crucial HRD activities like identification of training needs, providing performance feedback directly to employees to enable them to make an informed choice about their career development opportunities, etc. This chapter first analyses the process of development of human resource management functions and then delineates from the discussion the process of development of performance management functions. As it is the introductory chapter, it sets the premises by elaborating on the process of development of the concepts thereby helping the readers appreciate its genesis.

HISTORY OF HUMAN RESOURCE MANAGEMENT FUNCTION

Human resource management as a profession gained acceptance with the incresed spate of globalization and rising complexities of business. Before we understand the subject of performance management, it is important to understand the context with the incidence of human resource management functions. Human resource management as a subject of study has its roots dating back to 4000 B.C. (Chaldeans' incentive wage plans). Since then, it has been practised in different civilizations. However, here we are more concerned with the recent history (Bhattacharyya, 2006).

Before the industrial revolution, working processes and systems involved close relationships between mentors and apprentices. The focus was more on learning a particular trade. Apprentices (commonly known as trade apprentices) even used to stay in the shop (workplaces) or at the mentor's house to learn the craft from the master craftsman. The relationship between mentors and apprentices were not bound by wages only. It was more on a mutual share of efforts—good or bad and long and perpetuating. The system was more a replication of the *Gurukul* system of learning prevalent in ancient civilizations like India. However, we also get some opposing views of employer–employee relationships during these days. In some countries, the status of labour was extremely low and the relationships between employers and employees were characterized by slavery, serfdom and the guild system. Barring slavery, which was based on negative incentive system, serfdom and the guild system were more a structured approach to the management of human resources. Serfdom was based on positive incentive system, whereas the guild system involved master craftsmen (the owner), the journeyman (the traveling workers) and the apprentice. In fact the guild system was the beginning of human resource management practices, involving selection, training and development of workers, and emergence of collective bargaining over wages and working conditions (Bhattacharyya, 2009).

With the beginning of the industrial age, i.e., the shift from guilds and home-centred production to steam-driven factories, the working relationships had changed, requiring workers to perform the same repetitive tasks. The assembly line systems of production further made this process more mechanized, requiring workers to put in physical labour. With the division of labour, the work processes were fragmented, requiring each worker to perform specific tasks. The skill requirements being very low, skill interchangeability among workers was high, which made it possible for workers to perform most of the jobs in the factories. This can be better understood from the example below.

Tea manufacturing or processing is an age-old industry in India and other countries like Sri Lanka, Kenya and China. For obvious reasons, e.g., raw material sourcing (green tea leafs), tea manufacturing units are mostly adjacent to tea gardens. Tea workers or tea tribes are a cult, and they learn these jobs not through institutional systems, but rather acquire it through generations and also so through practice. With tea gardens being mostly located in remote areas, tea workers and other tea officials like executives and managers need to stay in adjacent housing colonies. A work breakdown analysis of tea manufacturing indicates involvement of the following activities:

- Withering of tea leafs, which can be done in open or closed troughs. The withering time varies depending on the variation in ambient temperature. While in open troughs it may take up to 14 hours, in closed roughs, depending on the nature of environmental conditioning, it may take 2 to 6 hours. The ambient temperature can be verified taking the reading of the industrial thermometer. The progress of withering needs to be measured from time to time through visual checking. Both the under- or over-withering of leaves lead ultimately to quality problems.
- Crush–tear–curl (CTC) operation—This operation is done using CTC machines. Workers attached to this operation are required to put withered leaves in the mouth of CTC machines and carry the outputs to the adjacent fermenting bay.
- Fermenting—This operation requires spreading of CTC outputs on the fermenting bays to allow the formation of coppery colour. The fermenting time again depends on the temperature and varies from 1 to 2 hours.
- Drying—The fermented leaves are then put in dryers to get the final output. The drying operation is considered critical as rework on over- or under-dried outputs may not ensure the desired quality level. During the drying operation, supervisors need to check the quality through visual inspection to adjust the driers.
- Spreading—After collection of the dried outputs, it needs to be spread on a tarpolin, till the temperature becomes normal.
- Grading—Tea output in a day accumulates together. Grading operation segregates the tea depending on the size of the granules. After tea tasting, pricing is done at the factory level and accordingly packed.

All these operations are simple and can be done by any worker, the skill sets being interchangeable. In the tea industry, the absenteeism rate among workers is very high, which compels the organization to rotate workers through different jobs to continue production activities. However, in modern organizations, the scope of skill interchangeability may not always be possible because of complexities of technologies and manufacturing processes.

Subsequent to the industrial revolution, a new economic doctrine, i.e., laissez faire, intensified the competition among organizations. The transition from home-centred to factory-centred mass production, along with the competition, deteriorated the employer–employee relationship. This exposed the need for a more structured approach to the management of employer–employee relations.

Reviewing the history, it is observed that great thrust had been given to personnel management functions by business expansion, labour strategies and higher wage rates during World War I (1917). Before this, the thrust was more on labour welfare to ensure that workers are not exploited in organizations. This was because of the movement of social activists, political parties and trade unions of different countries who were putting pressure on their respective governments to come out with legislations pertaining to labour so that they are protected and given their due rights and privileges. Labour welfare officers were statutorily appointed to ensure safeguarding the interests of workers. Thus, many of these activities had been initiated then for welfare and paternalism. Labour welfare officers then had no managerial role. However, the devastating effect of the world war necessitated urgent reconstruction of the economy. At organization level, there was immediate need to augment productivity. Labour welfare officers, because of their closeness to workers, were given the additional role of personnel management so that they could effectively motivate people to contribute more for enhancing productivity. The great depression of 1920–21 thereafter threw many personnel men out of jobs, and this created a disillusion for this profession. A number of literatures came up around the world during 1920–22, dealing with different areas of personnel administration and by 1923, it was considered that the profession had reached a stage of maturity, as organizations started giving importance to this profession, recognizing its imperativeness like other core functions—production and marketing (Bhattacharyya, 2006).

Human resource management, as a profession, therefore, gradually evolved with the attitudinal change of the people, and so also with the emergence of various employment laws and regulations. All these cascaded to a major shift in sociological trends. With the global acceptance of human resource management as a profession, it is now recognized as the complex, dynamic configuration of four major drivers, i.e., strategy, people, technology and the processes for any organization.

From the records, we find that the beginning of institutionalized personnel management function was started at the National Cash Register Co. (NCR). At the NCR, a major strike and subsequent lockout took place in 1901. In this battle, the workers suffered tremendously. The company president, John H. Patterson, then decided to improve worker relations forming the personnel department to manage workers' grievances, discharges, safety and other employee-related issues. The personnel department also kept track of legislations and court decisions and trained the supervision on various legislative practices.

Thus, tracing the history, we find that personnel function derived from the introduction of welfare and charitable activity. Initially welfare was perceived as a moral duty and later welfare was considered as precondition of industrial efficiency. The second development sprung from the employers' endeavours to cope with the challenges of trade unionism. The third phase of development could be attributed to the development of the concept of humanization of work.

Factors which are responsible for the development of this profession in a phased manner from a world perspective can be listed as follows:

- Rapid technological changes throughout the world, which had a great bearing upon personnel functions as it fundamentally changed the relationship between people and work.
- Increased competition at home and abroad. Such competition virtually reduced the profit of the organization to the level of production cost. The free movement of technology from one country to another does not allow any production process to monopolize any particular technology.
- The rise of consumerism, government protection, so also international competition, developed the necessity to maintain quality and price, which completely redressed the opportunity to follow the traditional production method.
- Social changes are also taking place at a fast pace. Business function is no longer a mere profit multiplying one. Organizations, being a part of society, also have to fulfill certain responsibilities towards society.
- Political development also restructured trade unionism. Trade unionists are no longer a mere wage bargainer.
- Structural changes in employment (more oriented towards white collared jobs, gradual decline of unskilled jobs) and changes in sector distribution of employment (more geared to tertiary or service sectors) also brought a great challenge to the employers.

For personnel management functions, all these challenges had a great impact. The alienating and de-humanizing effect of repetitive and monotonous tasks, in the wake of technological advancement, is a universal phenomenon. Effective utilization of human resources under this technological environment is the prime challenge before today's personnel functions.

PROCESS OF DEVELOPMENT IN INDIA

The history of evolution and growth of personnel management in India is not very old. The Royal Commission on Labour in 1931 for the first time recommended the abolition of Jobbers Systems and the appointment of labour officers to deal with the recruitment and to settle their grievances. The Factories Act, 1948, made it obligatory for industries to appoint labour welfare officers. Today personnel management function in India encompasses all professional disciplines like welfare, industrial relations, personnel administration, HRD, etc.

The general functional areas of personnel vis-à-vis HR professionals can be grouped under five major heads as below:

- Determining and staffing for employment needs
- Measuring performance and developing employee potential
- Preserving effective employee–management relationships
- Uncovering and resolving employee problems
- Anticipating and coping with organizational changes

The new changes have extended the functional horizon to many. From a legalistic approach, it has extended to human relations; from a mere passive factor of production, employees are now perceived as human resources. The functional demand, therefore, encompasses many areas like management by anticipation, more use of work teams by small group activities/quality circles, practising total quality management culture, etc.

Human Resource Development As a Separate Personnel Discipline

So far, our discussion has centred on personnel functions. At this stage, we will delineate HRD as a separate discipline of personnel management. But before we go into the details of HRD functions, a brief understanding of the historical process is considered necessary to appreciate the importance of HRD functions in today's organizations.

It is believed that Kurt Lewin's (1947) studies of behaviour of small groups and setting up of national training laboratories are the beginnings of the HRD profession, which till late 1940 was the domain of psychiatrists, psychologists, counselors and nurses, and furthered the concept of human relations training and the experiential approach. Participants in training groups (T-groups) effectively identified problems, acquired the skills and also actively collaborated in the problem solving process. Training group leaders, unshackling their traditional role of instructors, became facilitators and focused on how the individual relates to and interacts with other individuals and with groups and got them trained on leadership and its influence, handling conflict, expressing feeling, giving and receiving feedback, competition and cooperations, problem solving, and increasing awareness on oneself and one's impact on others.

In 1969, the Handbook of Structured Experiences for Human Relations Training was published by university associates giving structured experiences with guidelines for training and development. The subsequent publication of handbooks for group facilitators in 1972 and 1973 furthered the process of developing training and organization development vis-à-vis HRD as a recognized area of professional endeavour, delineating HRD as a new profession encompassing personnel function.

Performance Management As an HRD Function

Performance management as a sub-set of human resource management function focuses on facilitation support to employees for their individual and overall organizational development. Traditionally, organizations used to focus on age-old command-and-control models to exert the desired level of performance from the employees. However, modern performance management practices altered such percepts and consider people as assets, and like any other asset, people also have the potential to add future value. This obviously shaped the HRD dimension of performance management function, making it a long-term or strategic function of management. It is strategic, as alignment of individual performance with the business objectives of organizations ultimately leads to the achievement of strategic intents. It is strategic as organizations, through effective performance management, can focus on continuous development of human resources to sustain in competition. It facilitates in not only achieving the business results co-creating the performance goals, but also facilitates in preparing employee development plans matching with the long-term goals of the organizations. All these made performance management, in the strictest sense, an HRD function.

In Figure 1.1, we have illustrated the performance management cycle, which starts from core job descriptions reinforced with strategic plans and goals, which translates to performance development, performance appraisal, observations and feedback, and reformulating the standards of performance. This cycle continues, as performance management is an ongoing employee development function.

Job Description

Job description is a systematic process of collection, analysis and documentation of the important facts about the job. Through job descriptions we name a job, i.e., establish the job identity. Job descriptions facilitate in implementing strategic plans, translating the organizational vision to mission and then initiating the desired strategic initiatives to achieve the mission through well-defined goals and

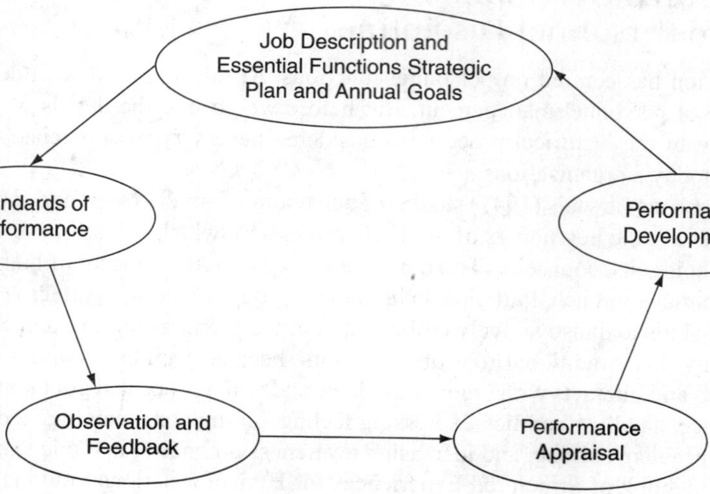

Figure 1.1 *Performance management cycle*

objectives. From a performance management point of view, job descriptions help in recruiting the right fit through adequate profile matching and also extend support to develop performance standards. Across organizations, we find commonality in job title; hence a well-structured job description also facilitates in benchmarking the performance, matching with the best performances nationally and internationally. Thus, job descriptions provide the basis for job-related selection procedures and thereby also help in setting performance standards and, subsequently, in performance benchmarking within and outside organizations. For these reasons, job description is construed as the first stage of performance management cycle of any organization.

Standards of Performance

Performance standards are documented guidelines for excellent performance of any job. To gain acceptance from the employees, organizations prefer to develop performance standards collaboratively. However, this may not be feasible for every job. For example, performance protocol or standards for a complex research and development job may require the organizations to conform to the laid down guidelines that are externally determined, which naturally squeezes the power of the organizations to decide the performance standards. Whatever be the manner of deciding performance standards, communicating the same to the employees is very important. For newly recruited employees, organizations prefer to familiarize performance standards through induction programmes. Individual-level performance is compared with the documented performance standards to measure the extent of employees' performance achievement. Standard job descriptions also set the initial premise for standards of performance. These apart, performance standards are determined based on industry practices, benchmarked data, etc.

Observation and Feedback

Observation is performance monitoring to measure the deviation from the performance standards and to initiate the corrective actions. Feedback is sharing the performance levels achieved by the employees. Both observation and feedback are important ingredients of the performance management process. Performance feedback is observable and verifiable work-related behaviours, actions, statements and results. With the feedback, employees can understand their performance gaps and can accordingly improve to deliver better performance in future. Organizations can also take important HR decisions using the performance feedback.

Performance Appraisal

The performance appraisal process summarizes, assesses and develops the work performance of employees based on the objective assessment of performance-related information. We have several methods of performance appraisal and have discussed these in a separate chapter. Most of the organizations focus on teamwork. This has now made 360-degree assessment of performance more important. This method even requires customers to evaluate employees' performance.

Performance Development Plan

Organizations with performance development plans develop the quality of the workforce to make them the enablers for organizational growth and development. Performance development plans need to be reinforced by continuous learning; professional growth; sustaining employee performance to meet or exceed expectations; enhancing job- or career-related skills, knowledge and experience; making employees understand the change; and, finally, motivating employees. Performance development plans may be considered at each stage of the performance management process.

Performance Management Through Continuous Learning

To develop a performance culture in organizations, it is important for the organization to focus on continuous learning. Continuous learning ensures systematic updating of employees' skills and knowledge, experience sharing through structured knowledge management approach, sharing of information through various transparent communication mediums, etc. The basic thrust for continuous learning is to help the employees to develop and achieve results, to prepare for the change and to nurture a compelling work culture. In a globally competitive business environment, employees of organizations must have up-to-date information about the new technologies, about the market and customers, about the nature and type of effectiveness in their current jobs, etc.

DEFINITIONS AND CONCEPTS OF PERFORMANCE MANAGEMENT

Performance management, per se, is a cyclical process. Organizations manage performance with two-fold objectives: to assess the employees' performance and to develop the employees' performance. Both these objectives help organizations to achieve strategic intents, i.e., achievement of organizational objectives. The process encompasses setting of performance objectives for the organizations as a whole, which is then cascaded to divisional-, departmental- and individual-level performance objectives. After setting these performance objectives, the process requires rating of employees' performance against the pre-set performance goals, objectives or standards, and deciding of future employees' development programmes to improve the performance. Through the performance rating or assessment, organizations can map the performance gap, identify the employees' potentiality and accordingly develop employees' capabilities through competency development, i.e., knowledge, skill and abilities (KSA). With the positive behavioural skill change or renewal, employees become good performers and accordingly organizations can enjoy the sustainable competitive advantages. Therefore, performance management can immensely benefit organizations, irrespective of their size, locations and geographical dispersion.

Based on the above introductory discussions, we can summarize the essential features of performance management systems as follows:

A holistic approach to performance management as given by the Institute of Personnel Management in 1992 produced the following definition of performance management: 'A strategy which relates to every activity of the organization set in the context of its human resources policies, culture, style and communications systems. The nature of the strategy depends on the organizational context and can vary from organization to organization.'

Interpreting this definition, we can identify the following important activities of performance management:

- Communicating vision to all employees
- Translating vision to mission
- Converting mission to overall objectives of the organization

- Setting departmental and individual performance targets that are related to overall objectives
- Converting such targets in terms of measurable outputs
- Developing the formal appraisal procedure and systems
- Linking performance to pay, wherever it is essential (particularly for senior managerial employees, performance-based pay is more applicable)
- Conducting formal performance reviews to track the progress towards achieving the targets
- Using the review process as the basis to identify training, development and reward outcomes
- Evaluating the performance holistically to improve organizational effectiveness

The Institute of Personnel and Development (CIPD) in 1998, based on the survey and series of practice-based case studies, could come to the conclusion that performance management is a continuous process rather than an annual activity (Armstrong and Baron 1998). Performance management through the process of shared understanding not only helps in achieving the organizational objectives, but also facilitates in developing the employees. A comprehensive definition of performance management can be drawn after Briscoe and Claus (2008), as follows:

'Performance management is the system through which organizations set work goals, determine performance standards, assign and evaluate work, provide performance feedback, determine training and development needs and distribute rewards.'

Latham et al. (2007) considered performance management as a continuous process, while the performance appraisal as an even at discrete time intervals. Sparrow (2008) argues that performance management emphasizes an open and honest communication between managers and individuals and the development of trust-based relationships.

Reviewing all the above definitions of performance management, therefore, we can define it as a continuous process of developing individual employees through evaluation of their contributions towards achieving organizational goals, and giving feedback and initiate appropriate HR actions, including design of training and development programmes, deciding rewards, promotions, transfer, etc. However, with the emergence of teamwork, this concept is changing, as in the corporate world team-based performance is now more emphasized rather than individualized performance.

HISTORY OF PERFORMANCE MANAGEMENT

Historically, the concept of performance management was developed to authenticate the process of wage determination. Also, organizations traditionally used performance management to drive the behaviours of employees to get specific outcomes. However, such a rewards-driven approach to performance management could not be sustained in knowledge-intensive organizations. Moreover, traditional organizations have also started becoming knowledge intensive for technology-intensive manufacturing processes. The focus of performance management has gradually shifted towards promoting the learning and development of the reinforced work environment. It became a process of continuous development of employees to sustain organizational competitive advantages. Such perceptive change in performance management was more evident in organizations worldwide from the 1980s. It was at this time that organizational performance became a major issue for achieving productivity and for sustaining competitiveness through prudent utilization of human and other resources. Today's organizations, using scientific performance management systems, not only track individual employee's performance, but also align such performance with the overall organizational performance to meet business objectives.

Some of the key driving factors for the development of scientific performance management systems are:

- Strategic dimensions of human resource management functions
- Integrated approach to develop the competencies of employees to understand how its employees are currently performing
- Identification of those employees that contribute most, or least
- Undertaking a thorough assessment of the training needs of its employees
- Setting development plans for employees
- Designing compensation packages
- Ensuring transparency over performance in the workplace
- Providing a framework to document issues relating to performance
- Assessing future career development requirements, etc.

Historically, performance management systems became more scientific after the introduction of decision support systems in the 1970s. In the 1980s, executive information systems were introduced, which got more structured with the introduction of computer-integrated business intelligence systems in the 1990s. Along with these improvements, new management concepts like customer relationship management (CRM), technology-integrated advanced management techniques, planning, reporting and the concept of corporate performance management (CPM) (Gartner, 2001) were introduced. All these together then became the basis of strategic planning in organizations. CPM or business performance management describes the process, methodologies, metrics and systems needed to manage the performance of an organization. The main characteristics of CPM include complete integration, automating data processing, support of collaboration, analytical insight and focusing on exceptions. The important steps in CPM are strategic planning, score carding, budgeting, forecasting, consolidation and business intelligence.

Gradually, performance management systems have been institutionalized and today it is embraced in all organizations worldwide as a development tool to ensure the organizations' sustenance in a competitive world. Using different performance metrics, it is now possible to assess the present state of business and, accordingly, draw business plans, budgets, etc., along with the necessary employee development interventions.

PERFORMANCE MANAGEMENT AS A MANAGEMENT TOOL

Performance management is the most critical management tool to improve overall organizational health. By recruiting the best fit, organizations cannot sustain in the long run, obviously for gradual redundancies of skill, knowledge and competencies. As a management tool, performance management ensures managers and employees possess the requisite skills and do whatever they ought to, conforming to the performance standards. But developing performance systems and enforcing its uses as critical management tool autonomously may not work, as an individual's willingness to perform is all the more important. This brings into focus the relationships between the managers and their employees. An integrated performance management system that establishes the linkage between the people and the organization can also account for relationship issues and effectively operate to get the desired results.

Performance management as a management tool, therefore, manages the business, shapes individual behaviour and directs employees' behaviour to achieve strategic aims. Mohrman and Mohrman (1995) emphasized, 'performance management is managing the businesses'. Tracing history, we observe, over the years, performance management from the traditional HR domain, slowly transformed to a business process, duly aligning activity with strategic goals. It directs people and controls the flow of training and reward.

PHILOSOPHY OF PERFORMANCE MANAGEMENT

Etymologically, philosophy is 'loving wisdom', and when we relate it to performance management systems, it means the critical evaluation of all the facts of an experience. Critical evaluation means assessment that is free from bias or prejudice. Hence, performance management philosophy means a value-based approach to evaluate the performance of employees.

> Hughes Communications India Ltd (HCIL) is a subsidiary of Hughes Communications Inc., USA, and is the largest satellite service operator in India. HCIL's philosophy of performance management is 'what gets measured, gets assessed and what gets assessed, gets enhanced'. HCIL appraises employee performance on an annual basis, giving credit for their achievements and setting targets for the forthcoming year. HCIL has developed a balanced policy that is both objective and holistic in its approach. HCIL's HR team facilitates the appraisal process and also trains senior personnel in assessing individual performance. It shares a reciprocal relationship with various processes facilitating continuous improvements in areas such as selection, career planning, goal setting, reward schemes and culture building. Assessments in HCIL are not just for improvement and development, but are also well recognized and rewarded.
>
> *Source*: Adapted from: http://www.hughes.in/about/about_hughes.htm

Professionally managed organizations always emphasize on developing performance management systems based on their perceived performance management philosophy. To develop employees to deliver their best is all along the motto of all professionally managed organizations. Through well-crafted performance management systems, organizations ensure that people are geared for success and ultimately help organizations to achieve their business goals. An Indian MNC starts its performance management system with its hiring process. It invests time to understand the prospective employees' goals, capabilities, career expectations, etc. Once the new recruits cross such successive hurdles, they ultimately become the right fit for the job and become part of a high-performing team. The structured performance management systems enable their employees to get clear feedback and incentives, based on performance results, and also to get a clear direction about the next performance cycle. Performance management philosophy for the company, therefore, is to develop an organized system of evaluation that communicates mutual performance expectations, monitors results of work activities, collects and evaluates performance that determines achievement of goals, and uses performance information for important decisions and also for allocating resources.

From the foregoing discussions, it is clear that performance management philosophy basically espouses the values and beliefs of the organizations on their embraced performance management systems. Going through the performance philosophy, it is possible to understand the specific roles of the employees, their superiors and the organization as a whole. For example, we can understand how the embraced performance management philosophy of any organization aligns the efforts of managers and employees with the goals of the organization, from the following specific roles:

- Employees irrespective of their hierarchical levels must feel responsible to communicate their performance with the managers. They must actively participate while framing their development plan and extend all support to deliver their best to achieve the organizational goals.
- Managers must develop performance targets for their employees through mutual discussion, recognize the performance of employees, and guide the employees to improve their performance, extend the resource support, and take them through rigorous training and development programmes. The underlying philosophy here is to develop people and to harness their potential.
- The organization must feel responsible to design and develop a transparent performance management system. To make the performance management system operational, the organization must also develop the skill and ability of managers and truly make them the enablers to drive change in the organization through effective performance management systems.

Thus, the espoused values and beliefs of effective performance management system, when positive, can motivate employees to deliver their best. Any high-performing organization can achieve excellence and sustain in competition. The espoused philosophy of performance management systems translates to job behaviours, job responsibilities and performance goals.

OVERVIEW OF PERFORMANCE MANAGEMENT

Modern performance management systems emphasize the facilitation model of leadership. With the recognition of people as the only sustainable resource for competitive advantage and subsequent institutionalization of practices like linking employees' performance to the strategic intents of the organizations, performance management practices have now been recognized as a high priority human resource management function. As a process, performance management provides an opportunity for mutual discussion on the development goals of employees and organizations and designs a feasible plan to achieve such decided goals. This process not only helps organizations to grow and achieve excellence, but also provides opportunities to successfully respond to changes. The new model of performance management lays emphasis not only on achieving the goals, but also increases the sense of responsibility in people who embrace it in their day-to-day work systems. For example, a customer-centric organization needs to focus on a service culture, which even extends to functioning at the operations level. Performance management systems, therefore, need to be tracked with the customer-centric approach and team rewards based on valuing the customer services.

Performance management, therefore, among others, emphasizes on managing, supporting and developing human resources at all levels within the organization. It systematically monitors individual and team performances, rewards the person who delivers his or her best and takes corrective or remedial actions for those who lack in their performance. For effective performance management results, organizations need to develop the people through continuous learning.

In such a refocused approach of performance management, a manager's involvement in performance management is ensured through the following course of actions:

- To establish specific job assignments.
- To write job descriptions, assign responsibility for strategic initiatives, develop and apply performance standards.

- To discuss job performance with the employees and provide feedback on strengths and weaknesses, as may be needed.
- To conduct periodic performance evaluation to improve the performance and employees' developmental goals.

With the above overview on performance management, it is now clear that performance management is one of the critical development functions for organizations.

PERFORMANCE OBJECTIVES AND STANDARDS

Performance objectives and standards are the most common methods to define the basis for measuring performance results. Using these objectives and standards, managers can provide specific feedback to describe the gap between the expected and actual performance. For every job position, it is desirable to define the performance objectives and standards to track the results of employees' performance. A finer distinction between the performance standards and objectives can be made: while standards are more related to job-task completion and can be tracked to the individual-level performance, objectives are more aligned with the overall organizational performance, leading to the achievement of business goals. Both objectives and standards are useful when, in addition to being written down and verifiable, they are SMART.

- S = Specific
- M = Measurable
- A = Attainable
- R = Relevant
- T = Timely

Specific—Performance objectives and standards must spell out the actions and results that are expected to be accomplished.

Measurable—It must be measurable to track the degree of accomplishment. For ease in measurement, it is often recommended to design quantitative measures like ratios, percentages, counts, etc. Some performance measures are, however, difficult to quantify. In our chapter on performance management research, we have explained different tools and techniques used for both qualitative and quantitative performance management.

Attainable—Setting of performance objectives and standards must be realistic, i.e., achievable or attainable, within the given resource constraints. Often organizations deliberately assign stretch targets to put pressure on individual employees. But this may not always be the right approach, as employees may feel over-stressed and underperform. From industry practices, it is evident that the performance level of employees less than 55 per cent is considered to be poor. Those who perform within 55–70 per cent are considered to be performers who meet expectations. With a performance level of 70–100 per cent, employees exceed expectations, and beyond 100 per cent employees are considered to be star performers. This, therefore, exemplifies how industry rates performance.

Relevant—Individual goals, objectives and standards need to be aligned with the unit, departmental and overall organizational missions. Missions define the purposes and from the purposes, people get the directions. Mission-aligned performance standards and objectives, therefore, help in achieving business results.

Timely—While deciding on performance objectives and standards, it is necessary to spell out the time frame, i.e., time within which the employees are expected to deliver the set results. Goals and objectives are annual; hence performance targets also need to be annual. However, for better tracking of results, performance monitoring is done at short intervals to ensure achievement of performance targets.

Performance Objectives and Standards—Comparative Analysis of Advantages and Disadvantages

The advantages and disadvantages outlined in Table 1.1 can give guidance on when to use objectives or standards or both.

Characteristics of Performance Objectives

Performance objectives are framed to define the future state of achievement which allows the organization to succeed and to create value. The future state of achievement for any organization is directly linked with the overall mission and objectives of the organization. When the mission and overall objectives of the organization change, its future state of achievement also changes, and so also the performance objectives of the employees. We can list the following characteristics of performance objectives:

- Performance objectives are mutually agreed targets, which employees are expected to achieve during a performance assessment cycle.
- Performance objectives cannot be separated from the job of employees; rather it forms part of the job.
- Performance objectives are the 'ends', hence they provide directives to employees to achieve the results and to focus on the resources.

Table 1.1 *Advantages and disadvantages of performance objectives and standards*

Performance Objectives	Performance Standards
Aligns organizational objectives to employees' objectives.	Focus on job duties.
Specific to individual, as the KRAs even for the employees doing similar nature of job may vary, depending on the employees' performance track record.	Can be made applicable to all employees doing similar nature of duties.
Facilitates communication between the employees and the managers.	Facilitates communication specific to job or duties.
Focus on future.	Makes the performance measurement process very clear.
Flexible.	Standards are job specific.
It can be used for all employees, but more applicable for those whose scope of responsibilities is wider with the mix of routine and non-routine nature of work.	More suitable for protocol-bound or standard-specific jobs, as deviations may lead to non-performance. Hence, standards are used for routine nature of jobs only.
More focused on annual results rather than routine aspects of jobs.	Too much focused on tasks.
To make the objectives realistic may be flexible.	No flexibility.
More challenging to the employees.	Not challenging, as employees are required to perform protocol-bound jobs.
Needs to be consistent with culture.	Needs to conform to work practices.

It is always desirable to develop performance objectives through mutual discussion, negotiation, compromise and agreement. Although differences between objectives, targets and goals can hardly be made, based on the scale and time, some distinctions can be made. By setting the performance goals, both the organizations and the employees plan for the results. By identifying objectives, organizations become more specific in quantifying the goals and focus on overall effectiveness and efficiency at the individual, departmental and organizational level. This is ensured through alignment of performance objectives with the mission, and setting of objectives in a collaborative process, to elicit commitment and responsibilities from the employees.

Some Examples of Performance Objectives

From organizational practices, we can highlight some of the examples of performance objectives as under:

- Complete the in-house training programme schedule by 1 October 2010.
- Reduce telephone expenses by 15 per cent within the first half of the fiscal year.
- Identify three new cost-effective vendors for supply of raw materials by the end of FY 2010.

To generate ideas for performance objectives, we can raise the following questions:

- What can employees do to improve the overall effectiveness?
- To what extent can employees' efforts to meet the objectives during the appraisal period help us to achieve results?
- What needs to be done to improve the quality of service?
- What refinements need to be made in operations by the process of new introduction or elimination?
- What do the employees need to do to optimize resources, modify systems, change priorities and update skills?
- What do employees need to do to meet the demand of the customers?

Points to Be Considered for Developing Performance Objectives

Consider the following points while developing the performance objectives for any organization:

- Set short-term goals with a long-term perspective. Objectives are generally set for periods of a year or less, which ultimately cascades to long-term gains.
- Identify critical performance issues and the possible bottlenecks to meet the same.
- Never underestimate resource needs.
- Ensure flexibility to bring changes in the performance objectives.

STANDARDS OF PERFORMANCE

Performance standards are written statements to describe the job well. It is a benchmark for evaluation of work, as it defines the process of meeting or exceeding performance expectations. Performance standards are developed in collaboration with the employees. To new employees, performance standards are adequately explained to guide them the way they need to perform the job.

Written or documented performance standards become more like a standard operating procedures (SOP), which provide guidelines to employees, clarify what are expected from them, and what are the essential functions and related tasks. Therefore standards of performance become a common understanding, become the basis for performance appraisal, ongoing feedback and performance counseling.

Organizations follow different approaches while developing the written performances. A directive approach to develop performance standards requires managers to write the standards for employees. After writing and developing the standards, the same is then shared with the employees and their doubts, if any, are then clarified. On the contrary a collaborative approach to performance standards requires managers and the employees to develop the standards through mutual discussion and agreement. Being mutually decided, the commitment from the employees to achieve the results is also unusually high.

Whatever may be the approach followed to develop performance standards, it is important to explain the process to those who are concerned and ensure that they understand it in its entirety. While writing or developing the standards, it is also necessary to refer to job description, vision, mission, goals and the objectives of the organization, and the desired model of performance evaluation. To guide the employees in the process of achieving the performance standards, it is also essential to document the desired pattern of behaviour expected and the minimum acceptable performance for the task or function.

Some of the principles followed by organizations while developing performance standards are:

- Relate performance standards to employees' job requirements.
- Write performance standards in clear language, describing specific behaviours and actions that lead to meeting the expectations.
- Incorporate measurable or verifiable features in performance standards.
- Detail performance expectations in terms of deadlines, cost, quality, quantity, customer satisfaction, degree of initiatives, innovativeness in suggesting process changes, or in any other areas of activities, which can be traced back and verified.
- Determine the acceptable margin for error.
- Determine the specific conditions for meeting the performance expectation.

The above principles can also be construed as important guidelines for developing performance standards.

Relating Performance Standards to the Hierarchical Level

Depending on the hierarchical level, performance standards vary and even at times become complex. With the level 1 hierarchical level (top level of the organization), performance standards become more general. Let us examine the following examples:

Level	Description
Level 1	Simple description of general expectation. Example: Task Description: Processing of tea. Standard: Segregate made tea as per quality, price and batting order in auction market. Example: Task Description: Finalize business plans. Standard: Finalized Business plans need to be submitted by agreed-upon date.

Level 2 Simple description of specific expectations.

Example: Task Description: Processing of tea.
Standard: Grade made tea and complete the grading process within 1 hour of drying.

Example: Task Description: Develop business plans.
Standard: Submit developed business plans one week before the deadline for finalization.

Level 3 Description of specific expectations and success indicators.

Example: Task Description: Processing of tea.
Standard: Dry fermented tea leaves ensuring zero case of over- or under-drying through constant monitoring of output and the temperature of driers.
Task Description: Develop business plans.
Standard: Produce business plans in accordance with the format and submit it to the departmental heads two weeks before the deadline for finalization.

Level 4 Description of specific expectations, success indicators and conditions, if any.

Example: Task Description: Processing of tea.
Standard: Ferment or oxidize CTC leafs to the correct extent, keeping pace with the variation of ambient temperatures.

Example: Task Description: Develop business plans.
Standard: Prepare business plans as per the format and submit the same three weeks before the deadline of finalization.

Checklist for Performance Standards

After developing the performance standards, we can test its effectiveness based on the following checklist:

- Are the standards realistic, attainable and consistent?
- Are the standards specifying the minimum acceptable level of performance?
- Are the standards candid about the specific actions or results, which the employees are expected to accomplish?
- Are the standards measurable and verifiable?
- Are the standards in consonance with the organizational goals?
- Are the standards challenging?
- Are the standards clear and unambiguous?
- Are the standards dynamic?

Benefits of Performance Management

An effective performance management system provides multiple benefits for the organizations, which ultimately cascades to improved top line and bottom line results.

- Firstly, it focuses on key objectives and priorities for the organization, aligning with the management by objectives and the organizational strategy as a whole. Obviously people in the organization get clarity and shared vision and mission to put their efforts in the correct direction. This also ensures optimization of resource utilization, as people can avoid wastage of their efforts pooling all these to the right direction.
- Secondly, performance management acts as self-motivating for the employees as they get a clear picture about what they contribute to the organization and how their contributions relate to the

organization's success. Organizations also provide the required support to the employees, helping them to achieve the results.

- Thirdly, it allows organizations to monitor how they function as a whole, as it emphasizes on the achievement of targets assigned to the individuals. The monitoring process helps in identifying the performance gaps and thus acts as an important control device to intervene and improve.
- Fourthly, it helps organizations to align their important HR decisions like promotion, increment, transfer, training, manpower planning, etc.
- Fifthly, based on the performance track of employees, organizations can also draw their plans and frame strategies to stay ahead of competitors.
- Finally, it also helps organizations to fulfil their commitments to different stakeholders, as all people working with them try to meet their assigned tasks and responsibilities.

PROCESS OF PERFORMANCE MANAGEMENT

The performance management process indicates the way performance management systems in any organization are implemented. The process outlines the sequence of actions taken to achieve the intended goals. Performance management process in any organization tries to achieve the following objectives:

- To link work efforts of employees with the vision, mission and objectives of the organization. Fulfilling this objective, it is possible to make both the employees and the organization understand how the job performance contributes to the organization.
- To set clear performance expectations for giving clear directions to the employees on what they need to do to achieve their goals. Performance expectations are the summation of results, actions and behaviours.
- To focus on employees' efforts, eliminating the wasteful jobs. This ensures productive use of the work of employees.
- To link the performance to the employees' career development, so as to enable them to understand how meeting of the performance expectation and exceeding the expectations can help them to grow within the organization.
- To ensure performance monitoring on a regular basis. The process of monitoring includes coaching, feedback and giving flexibility to employees, so that they can build their capabilities.
- To make performance evaluation an ongoing process. The frequency, however, will depend on the nature of the organization and the degree of competition.

Thus, the effective performance management process, backed by adequate planning, can mutually benefit the organization and the employees. For such reasons, performance management is considered to be one of the key processes of an organization. The performance management process is also construed as a cycle, which varies with the changing business needs of the organization. It plans, checks and assesses employees. Through the process of planning, organizations develop performance goals to properly direct the employees' efforts. Checking is done through the process of review of goals, matching with the employees' performance achievements. Even at this stage, organizations need to reframe their objectives, for obvious shift of the initial planning premises. At the assessment stage, employees' performances are compared against the expected objectives, using appropriate assessment tools or techniques.

To develop an effective process of performance management, organizations require an ongoing 'dialogue' with their people. It requires sustained efforts to develop the right organizational attitude to manage the performance, so that it improves the overall functions of the organization. Important processes, therefore, can be listed as follows:

- Make sure that employees understand the objectives and priorities of the organization.
- Help people to focus on their efforts rather than acting on hunches.
- Justify the benefits (to people) so that they can manage and improve their performance.
- Help the people to deliver the results through extending appropriate support.
- Align the organizational reward systems with performance management.

PERFORMANCE DOMAINS

Performance domains are based on the focus of an organization on performance measures. Based on the type of measurement or measurement criteria, we can have the following performance domains:

- Mission
- Process
- Critical performance sub-systems
- Individual

Mission performance domain identifies the purpose of the organization, based on the changing business focus and customers' expectations. The mission provides overall direction, and performance targets when aligned with the mission help in achieving the cherished goals and objectives of the organization. Depending on the changing business focus, organizations redefine their mission and accordingly the performance requirements of the people also get changed.

Process performance domain can be understood, first understanding the concept of the process itself. The process is a series of steps required to produce a product or service. For example, quality efforts focus on process performance domain. A defined process cuts across various sub-systems. Market research, new product development, new product design, customer service, financial planning and management, each follow a process. Designing a performance management based on the process requirements helps the organization to achieve results in each processes and sub-processes.

Critical performance sub-systems performance domain defines internal performance sub-systems that always directly connect to the internal environment, and frequently with the external environment (the mission domain always interacts with the external environment). These sub-systems differ from processes in that processes cut across multiple performance sub-systems. Examples include:

- Programmes (implementing new policies and procedures to ensure a safe workplace; or, for a non-profit, ongoing delivery of services to a community)
- Products or services to internal or external customers
- Projects (automating the billing process, moving to a new building, etc.)
- Teams or groups organized to accomplish a result or an internal or external customer

Individual performance domain focuses on individual performance management to achieve results and goals with some performance standard. These results and goals are recorded and referenced during a performance appraisal process. Ongoing training and development is provided as needed. Ideally, the supervisor and employee exchange ongoing feedback during the appraisal period to enhance the individual's performance.

PERFORMANCE DIMENSIONS

Performance dimensions indicate broad categorization of employees' behaviours and actions, which form the basis of performance assessment. For example, strong networking ability is one of the important performance dimensions of marketing people to achieve results. Thus, performance dimensions relate job and the work with those peripheral attributes, possessing which employees' can deliver their best. Usually organizations decide the performance dimensions outlining the range of behaviours that employees need to possess and demonstrate while accomplishing their job roles. We may not have any universality in performance dimensions, as these are specific to job and so also the nature of the organization. Nevertheless, we still find some commonality in performance dimensions, across jobs. These are:

- Strong interpersonal skills
- Customer service orientation
- Teamwork
- Effective communication
- Valuing diversity
- Analysis and problem-solving
- Decision-making and results orientation
- Adaptability
- Fostering a safe and secure environment

Once performance dimensions are identified and clearly defined, it is for the organization to communicate the same to the employees and help them to understand what it constitutes. Better communication to employees would be possible, when identified performance attributes are explained using some rating scales. For example, the degree of interpersonal skill required can be explained using a 5-point scale, where 5 denotes the highest and 1 the lowest. For marketing and human resource functions it may be 5, or at least 4 (depending on the level of hierarchy), while for the operations and finance functions, such requirements may not be so high.

Let us now list some of the performance dimensions.

TEAMWORK DIMENSIONS

- Employee's ability to solve problems with alliances
- Ability to work cooperatively and respectively with co-workers
- Ability to use diplomacy and tact when interacting with others
- Ability to diffuse tension
- Ability to manage conflict
- Ability to collaborate and foster collegial cooperative attitudes
- Ability to share knowledge and information

After identification of performance dimensions for effective teamwork, we then use the appropriate rating scale to assess an employee's performance.

Here, it is appropriate for use to differentiate between the performance dimensions and competencies. Performance dimensions are the actions that employees are supposed to take to perform the job. Competency, on the other hand, is the cluster of KSA that describes a general trait that an employee has or should have to perform a job. While competencies relate to the individual, performance dimensions relate to the job.

PERFORMANCE ETHICS

Abuse of performance management systems is a violation of ethics. It not only indicates poor focus on corporate governance, but also creates an unhealthy work environment, where every employee feels demoralized. Reduced performance and productivity, and employees' dissension even ultimately weakens the organizational competitive strength. It is necessary to ensure transparency in performance evaluation process, and communicate to employees, whose interests get prejudiced for any performance aligned decisions like promotions, transfer, salary raise or increments, training, etc. Some organizations even ask the poor performers to quit. Violation of ethics in performance management systems may not always be deliberate for the managers. It may be just for their self-understanding of the process in absence of any guidelines. Managers often feel they are skillful and knowledgeable enough to rationally use the performance management process. Ethical performance management practices require managers to help the employees to understand how their contributions mutually benefit them and so also the organization.

Often we misconstrue that legal compliance is synonymous to ethical conformance of performance management systems. This may not be true. For example, clarity, and so also mutuality of expectations, can lead to higher performance. Both of these do not require legal compliance, but critical ethical aspects of performance management.

SUMMARY

Performance management is the strategic HRD function which develops organizational capability to sustain in competition. The age-old use of performance management was to validate compensation design and other HR-related decisions like promotion, demotion, transfer, etc. With the realization that people are the only sustainable drivers of achieving organizational excellence, the performance management focuses have shifted towards HRD activities like identification of training needs, providing performance feedback directly to employees to enable them to make an informed choice about their career development opportunities, etc. This chapter first analysed the process of development of human resource management functions, and then delineates from the discussion the process of development of performance management functions. Being the introductory chapter, to set the premises, the chapter elaborates on the process of development of the concepts to help the readers to appreciate its genesis. Among others, the chapter also elaborates on the history of performance management, its philosophy, methods and techniques of setting performance objectives and standards, benefits of performance management, its domains and dimensions, and finally the ethics of performance management.

Being the introductory chapter, it sets the premise for the other chapters of the book. All important aspects of performance management have been covered in a nutshell in this chapter.

KEY WORDS

Performance Management Cycle: Performance management cycle starts from core job descriptions and reinforced with strategic plans. It translates to performance development, performance appraisal, observations and feedback, and reformulating the performance standards. This cycle continues, as performance management is an ongoing employee development function.

Performance Management Philosophy: Performance management philosophy basically espoused the values and beliefs of the organizations on their embraced performance management systems. Going through the performance philosophy, it is possible to understand the specific roles of the employees, their superiors and the organization as a whole.

Holistic Approach to Performance Management: A holistic approach to performance management considers performance management is a 'strategy which relates to every activity of the organization set in the context of its human resources policies, culture, style and communications system'.

Continuous Leaning: Continuous learning ensures systematic updating of employees' skills and knowledge, experience sharing through structured knowledge management approach, sharing of information through various transparent communication mediums, etc. The basic thrust for continuous learning is to help the employees to develop and achieve the results, to prepare for the change, and nurture compelling work culture.

Individual Performance Domain: Individual performance domain focuses on individual performance management to achieve results and goals with some performance standard. These results and goals are recorded and referenced during a performance appraisal process. Ongoing training and development is provided as needed. Ideally, the supervisor and employee exchange ongoing feedback during the appraisal period to enhance the individual's performance.

Mission Performance Domain: Mission performance domain identifies the purpose of the organization, based on the changing business focus and customers' expectations. The mission provides overall direction, and performance targets when aligned with the mission helps in achieving the cherished goals and objectives of the organization. Depending on the changing business focus, organizations redefine their mission and accordingly performance requirements of the people also get changed.

GENERAL REVIEW QUESTIONS

1. Discuss the history of performance management functions. In what way does the process of development of performance functions get influenced by the history of human resource management and HRD functions?
2. Explain the concept of performance management cycle. Using the performance management cycle, how can you justify that performance management is a continuous process?
3. Do you consider performance management as a management tool? Develop your answer with justification.
4. What is philosophy of performance management? How performance management philosophy is determined?
5. Explain the concept of performance objectives and standards. How do performance objectives and standards help in performance management process?
6. Explain the process of developing performance standards collaboratively.
7. What are the important characteristics of performance standards?
8. Explain how performance management can benefit an organization.

9. What are the important performance domains? How do performance domains relate to performance dimensions?
10. Explain the concept of performance ethics. Give your answer relating it to some organizational practices.
11. Short Notes:
    (a) Collaborative performance standards
    (b) Teamwork dimensions of performance
    (c) Critical performance sub-systems
    (d) Behavioural aspects of performance
    (e) Observation and feedback

CRITICAL REVIEW QUESTION

12. Your organization is a world-renowned knowledge process outsourcing company, mainly catering to the billing functions of global organizations. You have been recruited by your company to perform the outsourced jobs of one of the leading IT Company, based in the USA. This company has over 50,000 employees in their payroll. Billing and employees' claim form processing is part of your major duty, which as a team leader you do with five graduates who are reporting to you. The job is absolutely protocol bound and requires your mandate (acceptance or non-acceptance) instantly. Accuracy in decision and speed of work both are essential parts of your and other team members' job. Identify what could be your performance domains and dimensions. Develop your answer with specific examples.

REFERENCES

Armstrong, M. and A. Baron (1998), *Performance Management: The New Realities* (London: CIPD).

Bhattacharyya, D.K. (2006), *Human Resource Management*, 2nd edition (New Delhi: Excel Books).

Bhattacharyya, D.K. (2009a), *Organizational Behaviour* (New Delhi: Oxford University Press.

Bhattacharyya, D.K. (2009b), *Human Resource Development* (Mumbai: Himalaya Publishing).

Briscoe, D.B. and L.M. Claus (2008), 'Employee Performance Management: Policies and Practices in Multinational Enterprises', in P.W. Budwah and A. Denisi (eds), *Performance Management Systems: A Global Perspective* (Abingdon: Routledge).

Gartner (2001), Corporate Performance Management, http://www.gartner.com/it/page.jsp?id=597910, accessed on 19th September, 2009.

Institute of Personnel Management (1992), *Performance Management in the UK: An Analysis of the Issues* (London: IPM).

Latham, G., L.M. Sulsky and H. Macdonald (2007), 'Performance Management', in P. Boxall, J. Purcell, and P. Wright (eds), *Oxford Handbook of Human Resource Management* (Oxford: Oxford University Press).

Lewin, Kurt (1947), 'Frontiers in Group Dynamics', *Human Relations*, 1(1): 5–42.

Mohrman, S.A., S.G. Cohen and A.M. Mohrman (1995), *Designing Team Based Organization: New Forces of Knowledge World* (San Francisco, CA: Jossey Bass Publishers).

Sparrow, P. (2008), 'Performance Management in the UK', in A. Varma, P.S. Budwar, and A. Denisi (eds), *Performance Management Systems: A Global Perspective* (Abingdon: Routledge).

FURTHER READING

Bhattacharyya, D.K. (2007), *Human Resource Research Methods* (New Delhi: Oxford University Press).

Boyett, Joseph H. and Henry P. Conn (1988), *Maximum Performance Management: How to Manage and Compensate People to Meet World Competition* (London: Gland bridge Publishing Ltd.).

Burke, R.J (1978), 'Characteristics of Effective Employee Performance Reviews and Development Interviews: Replication and Extension', *Personnel Psychology*, 31: 903–19.

Byham, W.C. and G.C. Thornton (1986), 'Assessment Centers', in R.A. Berk (ed), *Performance Assessment: Methods and Applications* (London: The Jones Hopkins University Press).

Cardy, R.L. and G.H. Dobbins (1994), *Performance Appraisal: Alternative Perspectives* (Cincinnati: South-Western Publishing Co.).

Frazier, G.L. and R.D. Howell (1983), 'Business Definition and Performance', *Journal of Marketing*, 47: 59–67.

Kane, J.S. and C.E. Lawler (1979), 'Performance Appraisal Effectiveness: Its Assessment and Determinants', in B.M. Straw (ed), *Research in Organizational Behavior* (Greenwich: JAI Press).

Longenecker, C.O. and D.C. Ludwig (1990), 'Ethical Dilemmas in Performance Appraisal Revisited', *The Journal of Business Ethics*, 9: 53–61.

CASE STUDY ON PERFORMANCE MANAGEMENT SYSTEMS

In studying performance management systems, it is imperative to understand corporate practices. Here we have discussed about an important case with far-reaching implications on performance management issues. Students are advised to carefully go through the case and understand the performance management issues. Get any doubts clarified from your instructor.

What Is a Case?

A case is a short description, in words and numbers, of an actual management situation. A typical case consists of number of pages of prose description with some quantitative materials (figures), exhibits, organization charts, graphs or tables. The use of cases for advanced management education started at Harvard University in 1908.

What Is a Case Study?

Case study is a systematic way of helping students to learn from experiences. Such studies are intended to serve as the basis for class discussion and not as an illustration of either good or bad management practices. They are not intended to be a comprehensive collection of teaching material. They provide a useful backbone to a programme of study.

Steps of a Case Study

- Read the case carefully and note down all the material facts and identify the problem(s).
- Mention the area of management to which the main problem relates. It is possible that the problem may overlap other areas as well, which may demand simultaneous solution. The total view of the situation should not be lost.
- Place yourself in the position of management and view the case situation and the case problem.
- The analysis should be from a managerial angle—unbiased and objective.
- List out various possible alternatives and then prioritize on the basis of comparative superiority and feasibility.

- Select the best alternatives and state the same as your decision.
- Indicate an estimate of outcome including the possible side effects, if any.

Case Study Techniques

Case study method is basically a qualitative analysis pertaining to an organization. In some cases, however, where quantitative details about the organization are available, case study may also provide certain insights to operational details of case problems scientifically. Normally case study method focuses on organization or at best two or three homogenous or competing organization (for benchmarking) unless it is a cross-organizational study to authenticate any management practices or approves or disapproves any assumptions to establish certain theories. Case study requires in-depth analysis of some situations and study on their inter-relationship in an organization. Important characteristics of case study methods can be listed as follows:

- In case study method, one can choose to study a single organization or social unit or more. One may even confine his focus only on certain areas or situations of the sample organization. To illustrate if the purpose is to review an organization's strategy, one may critically examine, the vision, mission, goals, objectives, strategies, action plan and policies, and document his/her observations.
- Case analysis is done very intensively focusing on some limited identified areas rather than exhaustively. Such studies may be longitudinal in nature for drawing correct inferences.
- Even though perennially case study method is considered a qualitative analysis, we can also do quantitative analysis and interpret the organizational issues, when such details are available. For example, we can analyse the resource allocation strategy of an organization in terms of cost–benefit analysis. Similarly, efficacy of a compensation strategy can be studied comparing outsourcing vis-à-vis employment on permanent payroll.
- In case analysis, we always attempt to establish a casual relationship between various factors couching qualitative and quantitative information. To illustrate effective CRM may be co-related with increased market share. Employee motivation may be related to productivity.
- Case analysis is a direct approach and, therefore, requires analytic rigour and experience.
- Case study unleashes the best management practices and therefore significantly contributes in enriching the theories. For example, benefit of 'direct participation', which is a strategy to use collective wisdom of the people to develop a response capability toward some targeted goals of the organization, would not have been known to the world, unless the practices of 'CHEVRON', the petroleum giant, were brought into the limelight by researchers.

Despite its advantages, case analysis may often suffer from the problem of generalization and unless properly structured may also vitiate the purpose of learning.

Important Guidelines

There is no single correct solution even for a specific management problem. Logical thinking in line with the accepted basic principles and practices (processes) of management is what which is judged and assessed by the examiner.

Questions which are given at the end of each case study suggest the line of enquiry; hence study the questions carefully.

A case with questions at the end is known as close-ended case study. But there are also cases which may not have questions at the end. These are open-ended cases. A case solution is done duly identifying the problems and issues and providing answers to those problems.

Mere restating the facts of a case report without any meaning should be avoided.

CASE STUDY

Performance-based Incentive Systems of Modern Bank of India

The CEO of a national-level private sector bank, Modern Bank of India, which is growing very fast, always nurtures the view that HR people themselves are poor in managing behaviour of people in his organization. He feels that over the years, his HR is instrumental in demotivating people, as they failed to retain the result-oriented employees, causing huge manpower-replacement cost to the organization. Besides, employees feel that the performance management system is too complicated, and focuses only on achievement of quantitative targets, rather than on the other positive aspects of employees, who largely feel that they are instrumental in taking their organization to a new height, with focus of customer satisfaction and developing organizational loyalty. Business target achievement, fixing a stretch goal and forcing employees to accept the KRAs, without listening to them, may have helped in achieving the short-term goals, but such achievements far outweighed the losses when good performers left the organization in less than two years. As per policy, immediately after recruitment the organization is to train the new recruits through a month-long induction programme, and allow them to understand the jobs for the next two months, without setting for them any specific targets for achievement. All these add to the costs for the company. The CEO laments that every employee replacement costs them directly two times the annual salary paid to an employee, and indirectly it costs even more, as value addition differs between existing individual employees and replacement employees. Average value-addition potentiality of marketing executives (at current discounted values), assessed by the organization, using the learning curve theory, taking the employment span to be of 10 years, five years before indicated a figure of Rs. 25 lakhs. Five years down the line, the figure is Rs. 15 lakhs. The CEO justifiably argues that what HR is doing is to recruit on a piece-meal basis, rather than considering the long-term effect.

In one of the corporate level meetings, with all functional heads present, the CEO was blunt in accusing the HR department, telling 'lets accept that our HR department is an utter failure. Our HR department still considers employees just another input into the process. There is no effort to make our employees a partner in the organization.' The CEO then asked the HR people to put up a detailed performance-driven compensation plan, which will help the organization to optimize the compensation cost and at the same time will reduce the attrition rate, thereby increasing the motivation level of employees.

The HR manager accordingly prepared the plan which is as follows:

Variable pay component in executive compensation in India has now been increased to almost 50 per cent from 20 to 30 per cent, only a few years back. Without linking it to company performance alone, a three-tiered structure has now emerged, that is, the variable pay is linked to company performance, team performance and individual performance.

Our company's annual turnover today is Rs. 1000 crore. We have 900 marketing executives with the current rate of staff turnover at 15 per cent. The number of marketing executives with a tenure of more than five years with the company is 115. The number of marketing executives over 40 years of age is only 60.

The benchmarked annual salary data in comparable private sector banks in the country for marketing executives is Rs. 6 lakhs (considering the cost to the company), while our organization today pays Rs. 6.25 lakhs. Our organization believes in pay equity and follows broad banding while designing base pay. The calculated wage cost to annual sales is 20 per cent.

An employee-motivation survey carried out by the HR department of the organization indicated that 30 per cent of the marketing executives feel that they are underpaid, 50 per cent feel that they are getting the competitive benchmarked salary, while the rest 20 per cent feel that they are getting more than the market rate. In response to a questionnaire item, requiring executives to point out what should be their perceived percentage of salary rise, which they feel will motivate them, the replies suggested that an incentive plan needs to be designed, which corroborates with the Scanlon Plan explained below.

This plan relates compensation cost ratio to the total sales value to measure effectiveness of performance. As per this plan, an incentive bonus will be payable to marketing executives, based on the percentage reduction in the marketing executive to sales ratio, comparing the base period and assessment period.

The HR manager believes that following this plan will not only ensure optimization of compensation cost of marketing executives (whose variable component of compensation is now linked with individual performance achievement) but also foster teamwork and develop a culture of togetherness, which will have enduring effect on marketing executives' motivation and retention.

Question for Discussion

Imagine you are the CEO of the bank. Critically review the proposal of the HR manager and comment whether this proposed incentive plan would really ensure motivation and increased retention of marketing executives of the company. Give justifications in support of your answer.

Tentative Case Solutions

Introduction

The case critically examines the incentive scheme of Modern Bank of India, a national-level private sector bank in India. The CEO of the bank is dissatisfied with the HR managers. According to the CEO, the HR department is not skillful at motivating the employees, besides following poor human management procedures, the effect of which is seen in the high attrition rate the bank is witnessing. The CEO believes that the present HR performance measurement systems lay too much emphasis on the quantitative aspects and not on the qualitative aspects. The business target achievement unit is fixing a stretched target and focuses only on KRAs. This approach, the CEO feels, has lead to the fulfillment of the short-term goals/objectives albeit at the cost of long-term goals. It has been observed that employees are leaving the organization after completing their two years with the company and on account of their attrition; the company has to bear additional costs in terms of recruitment, training of new employees, etc. In light of the above facts, the CEO has asked the HR department to come up with a performance-driven compensation plan which can increase employee motivation thereby reducing the high attrition observed.

The New Incentive Plan

The new incentive plan has the following features:

- Introduction of variable pay component in executive compensation.
- Three-tier structure for variable—company performance, team performance and individual performance.

Scanlon Plan has to be followed for incentive pay. This plan helps the management to tap the ingenuity of employees as a means of improving production.

Analysis

The analysis shows the following points:

The new plan will help curtailment of attrition as the new compensation plan will increase the bank's employee's pay packet to 6.25 LPA (lakhs per annum) against the industry benchmark of 6 LPA.

The tangible outcome of the policy is already known where a survey was conducted amongst the employees to judge their reactions towards the proposed performance appraisal system. As part of the survey, it was observed that a majority of the employees considered the revised salary figures as either competitive or were satisfied.

The Scanlon plan is effective. A quick analysis reveals that as the ratio of marketing executives to sales decrease, the bank will be able to save more money. Hence this plan helps the bank to increase the sales and reduce the employees. This plan will also help the bank to increase the team culture and improve the performance.

Recommendations

The following recommendations are suggested:

- The real causes of discontent amongst the employees shouldn't be implicitly assumed. It is very likely that salary is just one reason of the high attrition. Hence, it is imperative that some form of survey or informal discussions be conducted between the senior management and the employees to undercover their real sources of dissatisfaction.
- It is the responsibility of the management to ensure that working hours of the employees is kept to industry standards only.
- For enthusing motivation, the HR managers should conduct assign challenging roles to employees based on their capabilities. This would at least ensure work satisfaction amongst the employees.
- Upgradation of the bank's technology which will help in improving the employee productivity.

Role Play Exercises for Performance Management

Performance management requires, among others, frequent counseling sessions with the employees. In such sessions, managers share the performance feedback and also suggest possible ways and means to employees to develop. For those who perform below the expectation levels, such counseling sessions also help the employees to identify their weaknesses and understand the imperativeness to develop them to match with the level of expectations. Many organizations use it as a morale-boosting way and means, while some use it negatively to show the non-performers the exit route. Whatever may be the purposes, managers need to master the art of counseling. Role play exercises help in reaching to the level of perfection to performance counseling.

From the script below, do this Role Play, writing the dialogues both for the Manager and for the Graduate, the focal theme of which is Praise and Develop.

Brief for the Manager

You are the Manager of a Development Department whose task is to plan, organize and control layout and equipment changes in the manufacturing division of the company. One of your staff, a graduate engineering, aged 24, has just completed a project to install a new layout of conveyors, sorters and packing machines at the end of a line producing small plastic bottles. This has been highly successful. The Manager of the line and the staff working on it are all pleased with it and prefer it to the original layout.

Now is the time to talk to your young graduate, show how pleased you are with this project and its conclusion, and try and discover which areas are ones in which further help, training and development of skills are required.

Brief for the Graduate

You have been working for one year in this Development Department whose task it is to plan, organize and control layout and equipment changes in the manufacturing division of the Company. You have just completed a project to install a new layout of the conveyors, sorters and packing machines at the end of a line producing small plastic bottles. This has been highly successful. The Manage of the line and the staff working on it are all pleased with it and prefer to the original.

Your boss has asked to see you. You hope he is as pleased as you are with the outcome of this project. If you get the chance you would like to become involved in an automation and computerization project next. You have heard that the main line producing the shrink wrapped 6-pack of half-litre bottles is due to be automated further later this year. You would like to do that. The most difficult issue during this last project was negotiation with several different companies for the purchase of the conveyor equipments—their salesmen were fairly aggressive and you found it difficult to deal with them.

(Hints: Remember you have to confine your discussion within the ambit of the scripts). This role play requires two characters. It is better to practice also the role reversals. Role Play facilitates the development of the following skill sets:

- Questioning skills
- Listening skills (including summarizing and reflecting)
- Establishing rapport
- Controlling conversations
- Understanding of body language
- Giving and receiving feedback
- Objective setting
- Gaining agreement and commitment
- Structuring the meeting
- Observation, interpretation and judgement
- Identifying training/development needs
- Reconciling individual and organizational needs

Non-participants in a role play can fill up a structured observation sheet as under. This will help them to develop analytic skill. However, in turn, all must participate in a role play.

Role Play Observation Sheet

Note both positive and negative observations.

Points to consider	Examples and their effects
Opening Putting at ease Venue, Seating, Formality Clarity—was the purpose explained?	
Middle Sensitivity, use of questions, listening Control of pace Structure and direction Body language; approach and style Rapport and agreement Who is doing all the talking?	
Editing Outcome, feelings at the end, acceptance or agreement Summary	
Overall effectiveness Was the aim achieved?	

CHAPTER 2

Performance Planning

Learning Objectives

After reading this chapter, you will be able to understand:

- Definitions and concepts of performance planning
- Performance planning process
- Development and contents of a performance plan
- Process of developing employee performance plans
- Eight-step model of elements and standards of a performance plan
- Preparing the performance development plan
- Transition from individual performance plan to group performance plan
- Performance plan and role clarity
- Creating strategic plans and its alignment with the performance plans
- Strategy realization essential elements through performance plans

Aligning Strategy with the Performance Plans

The strategy alignment and implementation, rather than strategy content, differentiates organizations. Measurement is the key in transforming and maximizing employee performance and productivity. Organizations like General Motors, Armstrong World Industries, Inktomi, and Cisco Systems Inc. could successfully link their strategies with their performance plan and performance management systems.

With the emergent need to improve the performance to survive the onslaught of Japanese automobile majors, General Motors Europe (GME) developed a balanced scorecard, encompassing all the functions and operations of the organization. In all the 8 business units and 12 functions, the company introduced the balanced scorecard. According to Martin Shotbolt, leader of General Motors Europe's Information Systems and Services Change Management Team, 'overall, scorecard adoption has strengthened strategic performance management because it has helped all operating units across GME to focus on and understand how their performance and capabilities impact on business strategy'. High-performance capabilities of GME could help the company to sustain their global market leadership. Performance management systems could push its competitive standards, and contribute to critical success areas by reorienting of strategic planning, priorities, and management. In the process, performance management systems of the company could drive the corporate goal of value creation for employees, customers, and shareholders.

INTRODUCTION

Performance management cycle starts with the process of reviewing employees' performance against the organizational performance expectations. At the beginning of the performance management cycle, it is important to review with employees the performance expectations of the organizations. Such a review must also consider the behavioural aspects, as an employee's behaviour also reflects on their performance. Review of employees' behaviour is important as it helps to assess the way the job is done, employees' propensity to teamwork, interpersonal communications, attitude towards subordinates' development, etc. The review exercises also set the premises for future performance expectations from the employees. In many organizations, it is often observed that outstanding performers are attitudinally bad, and often exhibit disruptive behaviour, which ultimately creates a difficult situation in the work place. People who are subordinate to such employees feel unhappy and even take harsh decisions to leave the organization. Such attrition ultimately affects the organizational performance. On the contrary, good performers with positive behaviour for their helpful attitude can benefit the organization creating a compelling culture to perform. Therefore, during the performance planning itself, it is important for the organizations to assign weights to behavioural and target-achievement aspects, as the behavioural syndrome decides the performance outcome, if not the performance output. Performance review processes, therefore, take stock of behavioural and the performance results, and accordingly provide the feedback to the employees. Performance feedback needs to be given to employees on an ongoing basis. The purpose is to give the message to the performance laggards and help them to develop their performance. With the balanced scorecard, nowadays, it is possible to give real-time performance feedback to employees, and even employees on their own can self-assess their contributions in achieving the organizational objectives. Also, employees enjoy self-pride in understanding the gravity of their contributions. Giving effective performance feedback to a great extent depends on the way it is provided to the employees. Good managers make this feedback process a two-way communication. Some managers fear adverse performance feedback to employees will increase their dissension, and they may even feel demoralized, which may exert adverse impact on their future performance. But with the role of a performance facilitator, when managers help the employees to understand their performance gaps, and also show them the way it can be improved, even under performers can churn out to become good performers. Many organizations, therefore, provide training to their managers to successfully provide their performance feedback to employees. With ongoing candid performance communication (two-way), organizations achieve better results. It makes the performance management system more effective, and ultimately contributes to develop a compelling culture of performance.

PERFORMANCE PLANNING PROCESS

Performance management is the systematic process of planning, monitoring, developing, rating, and rewarding good performance. Planning sets performance expectations and goals for the individuals and groups, keeping pace with organizational objectives. Performance plans for employees explain what employees need to do to accomplish their jobs successfully. It consists of written and documented performance elements, which form the basis of performance management. For group or team performance, critical performance elements are difficult to document. Although individual members of the group need to accomplish the critical performance elements, group performance consists of achieving group goals. Group goals are an aggregation of individual level critical and non-critical performance standards.

Performance elements explain what the employees are required to do and how well they have to do it to achieve the desired level of performance. Effective performance elements and standards are those which are understandable, measurable, attainable, fair, and challenging. Performance elements can be critical, non-critical, and peripheral or additional elements.

Critical performance elements are those that are most important, without which employees' overall performance become unacceptable. Non-critical performance elements are those that are not critical but assume importance while we summarize the performance results. Additional performance elements are not used even when we summarize the performance results. For example, non-critical performance elements being accounted in performance summarization could be the overall performance impact, such as behavioural elements, interpersonal relations, sincerity and dedication to work, etc. In contrast, additional performance elements which are not even considered while summarizing performance results are those like employees' volunteerism to new work assignment, propensity to acquire new skills and self develop, etc. Based on the study of accomplished critical, non-critical, and additional performance elements of employees, we can understand the potentiality and use these as inputs to succession planning.

Involvement of employees in the performance planning process ensures employees' understanding of the goals of the organization, and also employees get clarified on their job roles, the rationale behind such job roles, and the process of accomplishing them. Through the performance planning process, the organization also clarifies elements and standards of performance appraisal. Job elements and standards are so designed, so that it becomes measurable, understandable, verifiable, equitable, and achievable. Critical job elements make employees accountable for their work assignments. Non-critical and additional job requirements also form the basis of job performance. As the performance plans are drawn on the current premises or assumptions, any change in the planning premises ultimately affects the performance plans. It is for this reason that performance plans need to be flexible enough to keep pace with the changes. Such flexibility ensures adjustment of performance expectations. Organizations also experience a wide performance variation in individuals and groups. When such variations are on the positive side, it may be required to upwardly revise the performance expectations and standards both for the individuals and the groups. On the contrary, when individual employees and their groups consistently deliver less than the performance expectations and standards, organizations may require making downward adjustments of performance plans.

I could experience two such cases in the corporate world. In the first case, a leading private life insurance company, Birla Sun Life, could get almost 80 per cent of the business from one of their managers within 3 months, leaving achievement of 20 per cent business targets in the next 9 months. Private insurance companies set performance targets much on the higher side, and assume achieving more than 60 per cent of the targets tantamount to a very good performance level. In this case, periodic performance review could help the company to understand the high-performance potentiality of one of their managers. The company accordingly took the opportunity to upwardly revise the performance targets for the subsequent three quarters (9 months), rewarding such managerial talent. The result was good; the manger could generate more business, much higher than the previously set performance targets.

In the second case, Kitchen Appliances, a Videocon unit, had to declare temporary suspension of work for producing more colour televisions (CTVs) much ahead of their time schedule. The company produces CTVs independent of market demand. Temporary work suspension benefits the company in terms of saving the labour cost (as a significant percentage of their workers are from outsourcing vendors) and other variable overheads. Also, the company could rage the price war, as adjustment of saved costs reduces the price of CTVs.

Thus, a flexible approach to performance plans can benefit the organizations and the individuals as they can make best use of their talents and increase their rewards.

Monitoring is the next phase of the performance planning process, which facilitates the continuous measurement of performance to provide feedback. Employees and their groups can track their contribution to reach the performance goals of the organizations. At the individual level, monitoring involves reviewing the performance progress with the employees against job elements and standards. Ongoing monitoring helps the managers to understand how well employees are performing in meeting the pre-decided performance standards and the underlying problems in performance standards, if any, for making necessary changes. Unrealistic performance standards lead to complications, as employees get demotivated when they deliver far less than their assigned targets. Systematic monitoring and adjustment of the performance plans can eliminate such problems.

Developing is the other important aspect of performance plan. Through performance review, employees' developmental needs can be assessed, and the gap, if any, can be suitably addressed. Focus on employee development can enhance employees' capacity to perform. Organizations through different developmental plans, such as training, job rotation (to expose employees' to new skills), creating assistant-to positions, and improving work processes, can develop employees. With such developmental opportunities, employees can strengthen their job-related skills and competencies, and perform better in their work places.

Performance rating is a summarization of employees' performance. It tracks performance variation, if any, over different time periods and accordingly identifies best, average, and poor performers. While best performers are rewarded through pay hike and promotion, average and poor performers are taken through a series of development programmes to put them back on track of the high-performing group. In performance appraisal, rating means evaluating employee or group performance against the elements and standards in an employee's performance plan and assigning a summary of rating. For organizations, a report on performance rating helps in the adjustment of business plans.

Rewarding is recognition of employees both individually and as members of the group to give credence to their performance. It motivates good performers and an organization can also get the opportunity to retain the talented employees. When they observe their fellow top-performing colleagues get rewarded, average and poor performers feel inspired to improve their performance. With positive expectations, employees perform better. Organizations make their rewarding and recognition programmes ongoing, rather than waiting for their performance cycle to end. It requires adoption of a flexible pay plan and so also the flexible HR policies.

> R. Rogers, L. Miller, and J. Worklan (1993) in their landmark study on *Performance Management: What's Hot—What's Not* (Development Dimensions International and the Society for Human Resources Management) could identify that effective performance planning, among others, is one of the essential prerequisites for the success of performance management systems in any organization. While feedback and coaching is the heart of effective performance system, performance planning shows the organization as well as the individual employees the goals and its link with the organization. The study indicated that with a sense of ownership and involvement, when aligned with performance plans, performance results get better.

DEVELOPMENT AND CONTENTS OF A PERFORMANCE PLAN

To develop a performance plan, we first focus on individual level performance requirements, rather than the performance requirements of groups and the organization as a whole. Hence, the steps for developing a performance plan are drawn using the employee performance requirements that relate more to individual employee-level performance. However, following such steps, we can cascade the performance efforts requirement for the groups and the organizations as well. Such cascading effects on groups and organizational performances may not always be possible for all types of jobs. For example, one research and development (R&D) professional may develop several prototypes for consumer durables, but marketing and operations people may adopt those which they feel fit to the customers' requirements and have an operational feasibility. In the consumer electronics industry, to withstand the competitive pressure, most of the organizations separate their R&D activities and allow their employees to innovate products independent of market demand. This is to woo the customers to new designs and gain market leadership. Michel Porter (1985) named this as product differentiation strategy to fight against competition. Hence, performance consideration of the R&D professionals in an organizational context is limited only to those whose ideas effectively translated to new designs resulting in market success.

Thus, application of performance plan steps, drawn at the individual employee level, may not always work, as the nature of performance may not be traceable to organizational performance in its entirety, though it may fulfil the individual employee-level performance requirements.

Keeping in view the above constraints, we can draw the following steps to develop the contents of a performance plan:

1. Review organizational goals to associate preferred organizational results in terms of units of performance, that is, quantity, quality, cost, or timeliness. Organizational goals are often established during strategic planning. Performance management translates these to results that vary depending on the nature of jobs, in terms of quantity, quality, timeliness, or costs. Results are the primary outcome in terms of products and services, or any other that we desire to achieve in the performance process. Therefore, examples of results can be a percentage increase in sales, the extent of impact on the stakeholders, and so on. In other words, we can define results as the expectations through performance. Premise of the results are the goals, as they set the performance expectations. While setting the goals, organizations need to be 'SMART', that is, specific, measurable, acceptable, realistic to achieve, and time bound (meeting the deadline). For example, the organization's overall goal may be to increase its profit by 30 per cent by the end of the next financial year. To achieve this goal, organizations need to devise the performance expectations, cascading it to various sub-goals for each constituent part of the organization. For example, an organization having multiple product lines may distribute such an overall goal of achieving 30 per cent growth in profitability to different product lines at varying degrees. The high revenue–generating product line may get a sub-goal of achieving 50 per cent more in their sales, while the least revenue-generating product line may get the sub-goal of achieving 10 per cent more in sales.
2. In step 2 of the performance planning process, we need to specify the desired results. These results vary with respect to different performance domains. For example, at the operation level employees may be expected to produce high-quality items, while a marketing team may be expected to render best customer services. In step 2, therefore, we cascade over goal or sub-goals into specific performance results.
3. In step 3, we align performance results with the organizational results. This is to ensure performance results contribute to the overall organizational goal achievement. Hence, organizations look for answers to the following questions:
    a) Are the employees able to trace how their contributions fit to the achievement of overall organizational goals?

b) Are the employees able to understand what organizational goals they are pursuing?
c) Are the employees aware of how they need to pursue organizational goals?
d) Are the employees able to understand what could be the most productive way to pursue the goals?
e) Are the employees able to understand how their contribution to organizational goals will be measured?

4. In step 4, we need to prioritize the specific performance actions, sub-goals, or goals, assigning some weight to each criterion. To better understand, some organizations may also assign numeric values to each criterion. Professionally managed organizations who prefer performance-based recruitment indicate these through structured mapping, assigning weights or numeric values. Assigned weights or numeric values help employees prioritize their actions and also decide the required time per criterion. For example, a marketing manager's time allocation may be weighted as follows:

   a) 70 per cent of time to develop new market opportunities
   b) 10 per cent of time in analysing customer feedback
   c) 10 per cent of time in planning
   d) 10 per cent of time in scanning competitors' information

5. In step 5, performance evaluation measures are identified. Performance measures may be quantity, quality, timeliness, innovativeness, or cost. For a factory worker, performance measures may be quantity produced conforming to quality and cost-effectiveness in a given time frame. For an HR manager, this may be reducing employees' grievances within a week at the most, and saving the cost of arbitration or legal suits. For an R&D scientist, this may be developing a given number of prototypes within a given time at optimum costs. The biggest challenge for the managers is to identify the appropriate performance measures. It requires thorough understanding of performance domains and their relations with the goals or sub-goals. Again, selection of measurement tools requires special attention as these need to be valid and reliable.

6. Identify specific measures more precisely. For some performance domains, we need to be more precise to be able to accurately measure employees' contributions. For example, development of prototypes by R&D scientists can be further precised, prototypes that can be used and adopted in commercial runs. For example, a developed prototype may not be suitable for fitment trial and subsequent production run in the absence of required plants and machineries, or it may not be customer satisfactory.

7. Identify performance standards or the level of performance for accurate evaluation. Performance standards clarify the level that is expected to be achieved by the employees while they deliver results. For example, if the performance standards for R&D scientists is to develop 10 effective prototypes (effectiveness in terms of cost optimization, production feasibility, and customer acceptance) and one R&D scientist achieves the development of 12 prototypes, then this performance is termed 'exceeds expectations'. When it is just 10, it is termed 'meets expectation', but if it falls short of 10 then 'does not meet expectation'.

8. Document the performance plan indicating the expected results, performance measures, and performance standards. A documented performance helps both the managers who evaluate the performance as well as the employees who deliver them.

After developing the performance plans, with all the above stated details, organizations need to extend the necessary resource support to achieve the expected results. Resource support does not indicate only the fund allocation; it even extends to employee development programmes through training, coaching and mentoring, regular performance monitoring, feedback, and performance counselling. While documenting the performance plans, it is important to make employees understand them as well.

PERFORMANCE PLANNING STEPS

We have already understood the process of developing the contents of performance plans. The following performance planning steps can ensure the effectiveness of the same:

- Establish performance goals that are objective, quantifiable, and measurable.
- Describe the resource requirements to meet these goals.
- Document indicators to measure the performance.
- Align individual employee-level performances with organizational goals.
- Rate performance as per documented procedures in the performance plan.

PROCESS OF DEVELOPING EMPLOYEE PERFORMANCE PLANS

Traditionally in some organizations, performance plans are developed based on employees' job descriptions. This, however, cannot lead to achieving the expected results, as it elaborates only the activities and not the performance accomplished. Activities in isolation cannot be aligned to organizational goals. Here are a few examples.

Job Description:

Human Resource Manager—Work requires exceptional skill in managing people, recruiting and motivating them, designing suitable compensation, planning of manpower retention and redundancy, designing suitable training programmes, managing organizational change through development, and finally managing the performance of employees.

Major Duties and Responsibilities

Manage employee grievances.
Extend support to line function for managing people.
Recruit or source people who match with organizational requirements.
Identify suitable reinforcers to motivate people.
Design competitive and cost-effective compensation plans.
Ensure employee retention through various innovative practices.
Effectively manage a manpower redundancy programme.
Design training programmes, emphasizing more on in-house programme delivery.
Manage organizational change through appropriate organizational development initiatives.
Develop and administer a suitable performance management system.

EIGHT-STEP MODEL OF ELEMENTS AND STANDARDS OF A PERFORMANCE PLAN

So far we have reviewed performance plans, focussing only on activities. Here we will focus on performance plans that establish elements and standards duly addressing the accomplishments which lead to the achievement of organizational goals. This eight-step model is based on organizational practices, and for each successive step, the inputs come from the previous step.

Step 1: Understand the Overall Picture

This initial step requires consideration of overall organizational goals and objectives, rather than considering employees' job descriptions while developing the performance plans. This is done collecting information on the general outcome of the strategic plan of organizations. Organizational strategic plans also outline the goals and objectives (goals are the subjective targets while objectives are the quantitative targets) and the quantifiable and measurable performance goals. Alignment of employee performance plans with the strategic plan of the organization ensures a holistic consideration of all aspects providing the overall picture. Employees' achievements of goals at every stage integrate with the overall goals of the organization and in the process fulfil the organization's strategic intents. In other words, the general outcome goals of the strategic plan cascade to the specific or output-oriented performance plan, making performance plan a subset of the organization's strategic plan.

Step 2: Identify the Accomplishments at the Work Unit Level

This step determines the accomplishments (i.e., the products or services) at the unit level. Organizational units may be a strategic business unit (SBU), a product line (representing a bundle of similar types of products, such as detergents of Hindustan Unilever), a division, or a product mix (representing a single product, that is, a single type of detergent of Hindustan Unilever). Through adoption of appropriate measures, organizations determine the nature of accomplishments expected from the work units to develop the performance plan accordingly.

Step 3: Identify Individual Accomplishments and Their Integration with the Work Unit Goals

Here we consider the performance elements that include individual and group assignments and responsibilities. Using a role-result matrix (represented in a table duly identifying the expected results from the unit level employees that lead to the accomplishment of results at the unit level), we list the unit's products or services and the members' accomplishments for each job position in terms of quantifiable and verifiable performance elements. It is important to understand that role-result matrix is not intended to document the activities (verbs); it specifies the accomplishments of unit level employees who lead to the achievement of results at the unit level.

Step 4: Convert Expected Accomplishments into Performance Elements, Duly Mentioning Their Type and Priority

In this step, we need to identify specific elements of the performance plan and assign weights as well as priorities. We may have a number of job elements in a performance plan for an employee, but all may not be equally important. Elements with highest priority and weights are known as critical elements. In each job position, at least one critical element needs to be present. We may also have non-critical and additional performance elements. All such elements are clearly spelt out and accordingly get reflected in the performance appraisal format.

> **Identifying Critical Elements of a Job**
>
> To understand which element of a job is critical, the following issues need to be clear:
>
> Does it relate to individual performance?
> Does it affect the performance of the work unit?
> Does non-performance on this element seriously impede the work?
> Does the element take maximum time of the employees?

Step 5: Determine Work Unit and Individual Measures

After identifying critical, non-critical, and additional performance elements in the earlier step 5, we determine how to measure their performance. Measures explain the work unit's work process. Here again we focus on general measures and specific measures.

Step 6: Develop Work Unit and Individual Standards

With the identification of general and specific measures for the performance elements, at this stage we establish the standards. Standards for the elements form the basis of performance appraisal programmes.

Step 7: Determine How to Monitor Performance

Performance monitoring not only indicates measurement of performance but also feedback to employees. Although performance appraisal may be at a specific time interval, performance monitoring should be an ongoing and informal process, primarily to keep the employees on track. In the performance plan, such detailing helps implement the structured process. To ensure that performance monitoring is effective, organizations need to focus on following aspects:

- Decide the nature of data to be collected. Data collection may be through complete enumeration or based on a sampling method.
- Decide the time interval of data collection, the onus of data collection, and the custodian of such data.
- Study all the existing performance reports to design the feedback reports.
- Design feedback tables, graphs, or matrix wherever necessary.
- Ensure the feedback process is instantaneous and automatic.

Step 8: Check the Performance Plan

The final step examines the efficacy of the performance plan based on the following checklists. These checklists cannot be construed as final and all inclusive, rather they are tentative. In many organizations, performance requirements need to conform to regulatory requirements. However, the checklists presented below can be used as a template to understand the degree of effectiveness of a performance plan.

- Check whether the critical elements are truly critical. (Ensure this is based on the understanding that failure on the critical element makes the overall performance of employees unacceptable.)
- Decide the range of acceptable performance. (Ensure this making performance action quantifiable, observable, and verifiable.)
- Decide whether the assigned performance standards are attainable. (Ensure this deciding the degree of attainability of performance standards.)
- Decide whether the attainable standards are challenging. (Ensure this assessing the degree of efforts that employees need to put to reach this performance level.)
- Decide the degree of fairness of the standards. (Ensure this comparing the performance expectations in similar job positions.)
- Understand whether the performance standards are applicable. (Ensure this by assessing the possibility of measurement of performance and data collection.)
- Understand whether the performance standards can be understood by the employees. (Ensure this avoiding any ambiguity in detailing the performance standards.)
- Understand the flexibility of elements and standards of performance. (Ensure this by making the performance plan adaptable enough to the changes in the goals, objectives, and strategies of the organization.)
- Understand whether the measurement is possible at each level of job element, that is, exceed the expectation level, meet the expectation level, good in meeting the expectation level, average in meeting the expectation level, and poor in performance achievement. (Ensure this by developing a scale assigning a numeric value to each such performance level.)

A flow chart of all the above steps is presented in Exhibit 2.1.

PREPARING THE PERFORMANCE DEVELOPMENT PLAN

Performance development plans are prepared after setting the performance standards. Performance standards are decided as a part of the ongoing process of observation and feedback. It is the final element of the performance appraisal process. Based on the performance development plans, organizations and employees initiate action for organizing education or development opportunities. While developing the performance development plan, it is necessary to discuss training, education, or development opportunities with the employees, identify the steps to be taken, and document the strategy to accomplish the objectives. Such documentation should include the following:

- A description of the specific steps to be taken.
- Names of those who will assist the employee.
- End dates for the completion of the plan's objectives.
- A statement of how the successful completion of the plan's objectives will be appraised.

Performance management itself is considered as an employee development function. Based on the performance appraisal results, organizations draw employee development programmes to meet the

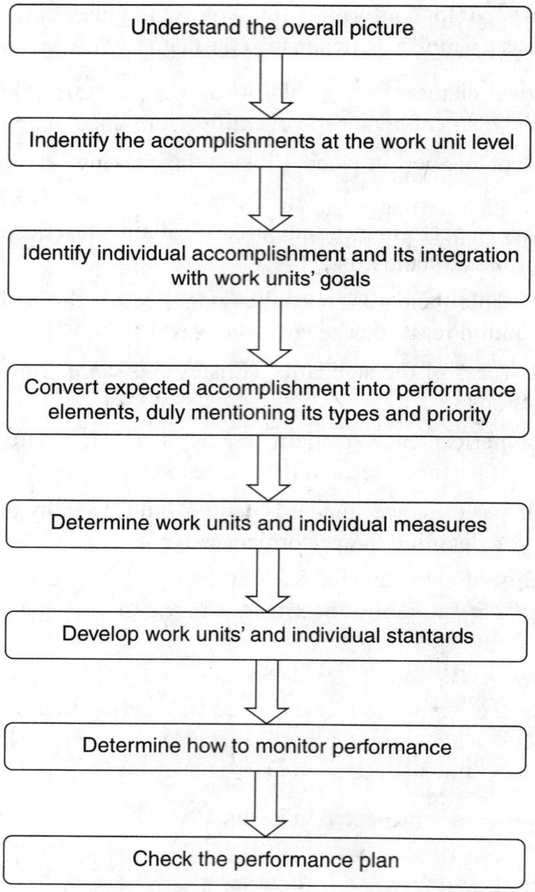

Exhibit 2.1 *Employee Development Programme*

performance gaps and to enhance the existing performance level. Employees also can give inputs about their chosen development path, keeping pace with the organizational goals.

TRANSITION FROM INDIVIDUAL PERFORMANCE PLAN TO GROUP PERFORMANCE PLAN

Instead of focussing on individual job performance, W. Edwards Deming (1982) suggested to focus on improving the organizational productivity and quality. That individual level performance plan and its subsequent review cannot always relate to organizational productivity has been extensively studied in several organizations, and the results have authenticated this. Traditionally, those receiving the evaluations are the most dissatisfied with the review. Deming's observations were tested by Ford Motor Co., and it was observed that individual level performance plan and its evaluation was a major barrier to continuous organizational improvement and quality performance. Ford Motor's introspection revealed that company resources were being squandered on excessive internal competition, that the system was not getting to the root causes of problems, and that work was being redone unnecessarily. In all of those situations, Ford shifted to teamwork, revamping its performance review system to emphasize on developing teamwork to meet customer needs.

Thus, as the old model for performance reviews does not lead to productivity and quality improvements, it must change. If companies really want everyone to relentlessly pursue quality and productivity improvements, they must change not only the performance evaluation process, but also the reward system.

According to Deming, the sources of variability in a performance review system cannot be understood by looking only at individuals. Variability sources may be people, information, equipment, materials, and methods. Also, variability may emerge for the interaction among all these sources. Therefore, evaluating individual performance and accordingly rewarding the good performer cannot ultimately lead to the overall improved performance of the organization. Based on this assumption, Deming suggested following a line of actions to balance the individual and group performance plans:

Focus on the right issues: In the individual performance plan, the boss is the key customer. Hence, focussing on the boss's requirements or pleasing the boss himself by default can bring the results, in terms of rewards. Introducing multi-rater feedback or 360-degree performance review also cannot settle this impasse. Thus, organizations need to balance the focus, highlighting also on group performance plans, making employees feel the importance of their contribution to the group. A group-focussed performance plan would be possible when performance standards for both the individual and the group are developed, making people feel responsible for achieving the group goal. For example, if the individual goal of a hotel's marketing team member is to develop a delicious menu (as a Chef), the group goal may be ensure its optimum pricing. A marketing group or team in a hotel needs to be cross-functional, that is, represented by employees from different divisions apart from marketing. From that perspective, a hotel chef also is a part of the marketing team. The real test of a team is to get driven by a common goal. Thus, performance plan for a group or team can also be simultaneously developed, without, however, impairing the individual level performance plans.

Setting the right goals: While developing a performance plan, we often set goals without understanding the root causes of the problems. We try to make a judgement with certain behavioural statements or opinionated questions, such as 'effective participation in teams', 'meet the deadlines', 'aptitude to learn', 'accept responsibility for mistakes', and so on. These are known as 'organizational citizenship behaviours', but are certainly not able to capture actual results of problem solving nor improve the performance. Hence, it is important to set goals, accomplishment of which requires teamwork. For example, improving productivity through teamwork is more important than individual performance goals.

Using the right measures: Use of quantitative performance measures being focussed on the evaluation issue at a point of time becomes more a post-mortem function for individual performance plans. A group performance plan can focus on continuous process improvement, without giving any cognizance to past practices and goal achievements. Hence, while choosing the right measures for a performance plan, it is important for the organizations to design the measures for the group performance plan.

Concentrating on the right kinds of criteria: In individual performance plans, often we fail to establish a link between the actual productivity, quality, and rewards (which may be in the form of increased compensation, promotion, and bonuses). Assuming achievement of increased productivity and quality culminates in improved bottom-line (profitability) of the company, which essentially requires teamwork; organizations often select the criteria that lead to improved financial results.

Thus, the transition from an individual performance plan to a group performance plan would be possible when organizations address the above four points.

PERFORMANCE PLAN AND ROLE CLARITY

Role clarity in performance plans helps us achieve higher teamwork. This is, obviously, so that employees understand what is expected from them and which aspects of the job are important. Also, employees can understand the job's evaluation process. Therefore, role clarity becomes the key driver to employee performance. Without role clarity, employees fail to understand their job requirements, which ultimately leads to performance-related problems. This makes role clarity an important prerequisite for effective performance planning, and job expectations and performance measures clear with focus on the goals for each person or work group. Role clarity also helps employees better understand the way work should be done. With increased freedom and authority, employees feel more committed to work and organizations and get the best to meet their strategic intents. Hence, it is necessary to differentiate role accountabilities both horizontally and vertically. We can illustrate the components of role clarity as in Exhibit 2.2

To check whether adequate role clarity exists or not, we need to consider the following points:

- Does every member of the team have a documented job description?
- Does every employee understand the process of measurement for their performances?
- Do employees match with their job role in terms of their knowledge, skills, and abilities?
- Do employees understand how their performance relates to the organization's achievement of strategic goals?

Superior's understanding (Job roles)	Self understanding (Employee's understanding of the job roles)
Others' understanding (Expectations from the job role)	Reality (Execution of job roles)

Exhibit 2.2 *Components of role clarity*

ROLE DESCRIPTIONS TEMPLATE

Name of the company: Ignite

Name of the officer: S.K. Juneja
Position: Chief Operating Officer

Department: Knowledge Process Outsourcing

Purpose of the role (broad description of why the role exists): Develop and implement an operational philosophy consistent with Ignite's long-term strategy.

Ongoing accountabilities: These are a breakdown of the purpose of the role into key elements. They should be in enough detail to provide clarity on what the individual will be called to account for on the role. Accountabilities are not time bound, or as specific and detailed as goals, objectives, or task lists.

1. **Manufacturing philosophy:**
   Develop a consistent manufacturing philosophy.
   Develop a manufacturing systems strategy.
   Implement the strategy in every plant.
2. **New product strategy:**
   Develop a new product strategy based on inputs from marketing and sales.
   Analyse the capacity, investment, and resource requirements for implementation.
   Recommend the strategy for implementation.
3. **Engineering processes:**
   Develop an engineering framework for Ignite locally and worldwide to ensure consistency among different engineering systems.
   Implement consistent engineering processes.
4. **Budgeting framework:**
   Develop a timely and effective operational budget process (each facility producing its own budget to be rolled up into larger budget).
   Ensure consistency across various manufacturing facilities.
   Ensure adherence to the budget.
5. **Supplier relationship strategy:**
   Develop a relationship management strategy between Ignite and its global commercial supplier base.

Implement the supplier relationship strategy.

Scope of role (resource limits)

To be determined:

Financial authority

Binding authority

Level of manageable exposure

CREATING STRATEGIC PLANS AND THEIR ALIGNMENT WITH THE PERFORMANCE PLANS

Without going into the details of various types of organizational strategies, we need to focus on Porter's (1980) generic strategies, which yield competitive advantages for the organizations. Cost leadership, product differentiation, and focus are the three generic strategies suggested by Porter. He suggested that to ensure long-term profitability, organizations need to make a choice between one and more of the generic strategies. The concept of strategy–performance relationships has its origin in the theory of industrial organization (IO), pioneered by Bain (1956) and Mason (1939). At the outset, it is important to understand that strategy–performance relationships still continue to be debatable issues. For example, McGee and Thomas's (1986, 1992) studies could not establish any link between strategy and performance. Studies by Davis and Schul (1993) and Zahra (1993) could establish a link between strategy and performance and could also show how such a link gets influenced by the situational variables. Most of the researches on strategy–performance relationships leverage on the generic strategies of Porter (1985).

Without going into the details of empirical validity of having linkage of strategy with the performance or not, we will now focus on organizational practices. Operationally, strategy–performance relationships may be influenced by the organization's reward practices. We have evidence of studies on organizational strategy, human resource (HR) practices, and performance (Balkin and Gomez-Mejia, 1987; Hambrick and Snow, 1989; Lawler, 1986a, 1986b; Ulrich and Lake, 1990; Waldman, 1994; Zingheim and Schuster, 2000). All these studies suggest that the organizations should adopt those human resource practices which can complement and support the organizational strategy. More specifically, the reward system should be aligned to motivate employee performance that is consistent with the firm's strategy; attract and retain people with the knowledge, skills, and abilities required to realize the firm's strategic goals; and create a supportive culture and structure (Galbraith, 1973; Kilmann, 1989; Nadler and Tushman, 1988). Alignment of the reward system with organizational strategy helps to determine organizational effectiveness. Becker and Gerhart (1996) suggest that the human resource system can be a unique source of competitive advantage, especially when its components have a high degree of internal and external fit. Another review by Gomez-Mejia and Balkin (1992) contends that the old model of compensation (with pay structures based on job analyses, descriptions, specifications, and classifications) is no longer effective in today's business environment. They conclude that modern organizations must align their reward system practices with their organizational strategy in order to achieve higher levels of performance at both the individual and organizational levels.

Using Porter's (1985) generic strategies as the basis, we can now list the process of linking performance plans with the organizational strategy in line with the following approaches.

Using the product differentiation strategy, organizations can encourage individual employees to innovate and either develop the new products or bring changes in the existing ones. With specific reward practices, aligned with the individual performance levels, it is possible for the organization to achieve such strategic intents. With cost leadership strategy in line with specific reward practices, organizations can encourage employees to explore cost reduction and control and assume higher responsibility and authority to achieve higher levels of performance. Using this strategy, a better fit can be possible when organizations select the group-based incentives instead of individual incentive plans. Similarly with cost leadership, strategy firms can focus on improved customer service, as customers can also be the beneficiary for the firm's cost-effectiveness. With product differentiation strategy, organizations can emphasize on improved customers services, creating a unique niche. Employees need to be creative to pursue such a strategy. Rewarding creativity firms can achieve higher perceived levels of organizational performance.

In the backdrop of above discussions, therefore, it is possible for us to conclude that the senior management team must come together to review, discuss, challenge, and finally agree upon the strategic direction and key components of the performance plan. Without genuine commitment from the senior team, successful alignment of performance plan with the organizational strategy is unlikely. Good performance measures identify the critical focus points for an organization and reward their successful achievement. When used to guide an organization, performance measures can be a competitive advantage as they drive alignment and common purposes, focussing on everyone's best efforts at the desired goal. But defining measures can be tricky. Teams must continue to ask themselves, 'If we were to measure performance this way, what behaviour would that motivate?' For example, if the desired outcome is world-class customer service, measuring the volume of calls handled by representatives could drive the opposite behaviour.

Cascading the strategies through individual level performance plans is essential for achieving organizational success. Cascading is best possible when the organizations get armed with the strategic map, operational definitions, and the overall organizational strategic performance measures. In each functional area, we create our own map of success and define our own specific performance measures. In the 1990s, Sears cascaded its strategic plan to all of its stores through local store strategy sessions involving all employees. The plan was shown graphically by a strategy map, and reinforced through actions such as the sale of financial businesses, for example, Allstate. Online performance measures helped store managers to gain feedback on their own performance, and also let them share best practices with other managers. Alignment of strategy with performance plans can be both a macro- or micro-level organizational issues. Macro-organizational issues are large-scale, system-wide issues that affect many people within the organization. Galbraith and Kazanjian argue that there are several major internal subsystems of the organization that must be coordinated to successfully implement a new organizational strategy. These subsystems include technology, reward systems, decision processes, and structure. As with any system, the subsystems are interrelated, and changing one may impact others.

Technology is an inclusive term. It includes knowledge, tools, equipment, and work methods that are embedded with the goods and services produced by an organization. While selecting the technology, it is important for every organization to consider its strategic fit. When technology fits with the strategy of an organization, it helps in strategy implementation, and thus achieves the performance goals. To illustrate, when organizations try to achieve excellence in quality to gain competitive advantage from their competitors, they strategically make a choice of such a technology that can contribute to the production of superior quality goods as well as to the rendering of superior quality services. Similarly, when the organizations pursue the low-cost strategy, emphasis is given on adopting a technology-intensive production process to reduce labour costs. From another perspective, organizations may consider effective use of the existing technology, restructuring their production process, and boosting employees' morale and motivation to better perform with the effective mix of extrinsic and intrinsic motivational reinforces, such as innovative compensation, reward systems, and incentive plans. On the other hand, recognition of commendable performance inculcates the sense of achievement through intrinsic reinforcement. Both can successfully help in achieving the strategic intents. Apart from the individual level motivation, organizations also emphasize on divisional and department level motivation adopting profit and gain sharing strategies. Many organizations adopt the system of incentive payment to employees on quarterly, 6-monthly, or annual basis, based on the division and department level performance and also on the performance of the overall organization. Likewise, by introducing the system of shared decision making, organizations can enhance the employees' commitment in achieving the performance plans. Shared and so also the distributed decision-making processes help the organization make the midterm adjustments in performance plans that may consider upward or downward revisions, adjusting the resource allocation plans accordingly.

Like the strategy-fit technology, a strategy-fit organizational structure also helps the organization to successfully implement the performance plans. The structure of an organization establishes the link between the people and their jobs, between the individual level jobs and the departmental jobs, and between the departmental jobs and the organizational jobs as a whole. The organizational structure also establishes a formal pattern of interaction and coordination between different individuals at different hierarchical levels. Many research studies authenticated that a strategy-fit organizational structure achieves better performance results. Different types of organizations have different natures of strategic focus. For example, a functional structure of an organization helps in cost optimization cross-utilizing the services of the functional experts. A divisional structure on the other hand optimizes the resources focussing on specialized machines and equipments and so also the production process. A matrix structure optimizes the utilization of employees' services across the departments.

In implementing performance strategy, micro-organizational issues are also important. Such issues consider behavioural aspects of strategy implementation. Employee behaviour within the organization is the major determinant for achieving the strategic intent. Also, strategy implementation is largely influenced by the culture and the general propensity of employees to resist the change. Globally, it is also observed that the culture-fit strategy enhances the degree of employees' voluntariness to cooperate and implement the new strategy. The culture of any organization evolves over a period of time and culture is the configuration of values, actions, and beliefs that are nurtured by the employees of the organization.

While choosing the appropriate strategy, organizations also consider various information inputs, particularly to validate their decisions for change. It requires managers to carefully analyse and evaluate the information to set the strategic premise and to explore various strategic alternatives to finally select the best in terms of its cost-effectiveness and feasibility in implementation. Also, a participative approach to strategy framing increases the degree of employees' acceptance of new strategy and its successful implementation. A participative approach reduces the resistance to change. To successfully manage the change, it is desirable for the managers to understand the frame of reference that persuades the employees to resist the change.

STRATEGY REALIZATION: ESSENTIAL ELEMENTS THROUGH PERFORMANCE PLANS

Alignment of performance plans with the business goals of the organization starts when annual performance plans or work plans are drawn. Merely restating the organizational goals, without laying down the process of its measurement with reference to the performance goals, cannot truly help in strategic alignment of performance plans. It is necessary for the organizations to make use of certain metrics to determine the performance against the goals. Some of the suggestive line of actions for strategic alignment of performance goals is presented below:

- Establish the job element that directly relates to the organizational goal and include clear, credible measures of performance quality, quantity, timeliness, and/or cost-effectiveness.

- Include employee and customer perspectives in the mandatory supervisory element and standard.
- Make employees accountable for at least one critical performance element, which when not achieved may not lead to the accomplishment of organizational goals.

To achieve excellence in business performance and results, most of the organizations worldwide initiate to align their strategies with their performance management systems. Organizations adopt strategies to achieve their defined goals and objectives. A well-developed strategy map for any organization gives the sense of direction to all cross sections of organizational members. Linking such strategies with the individual performance goals in the form of KPA (key performance areas) and KRA (key result areas) benefit the organization to reap a competitive advantage through the high performance level of organizational members.

Alignment of strategies with the people working in organizations could be best possible relating processes, systems, and relationships to the performance management systems (PMS) of the organizations. Such strategy-aligned PMS facilitate organizations not only to transform the people cascading the strategic objectives, but also to facilitate effective utilization of corporate strategy, and in the process get more from the employees. To do this effectively, it is important for the top management of the organizations to be committed and involved with the process, including understanding the organization's visions, mission, strategy, values, and life cycles. Using a balanced scorecard, organizations can pursue their strategy to get a unique edge in a competitive market.

Before alignment of strategies with the PMS, it is important to identify, analyse, and prioritize the core business processes and key customers. Effective analysis and definition of key customer requirements ensure shortlisting of critical business drivers and measures, which can then be cascaded to individual employees' goals and objectives (against the identified key drivers), and a well-drawn scorecard can provide a measurement tool, with which the company can identify the gaps between their plans and execution. Thus, an effective balanced scorecard of any organization should align their strategy with their performance management systems, identifying their business process and definable customer requirements.

Human resource practices of the organizations are also aligned and integrated to business strategy to ensure congruence and synergy within the organization. This requires a systematic and holistic approach in ensuring that business strategy policies for managing human capital are all aligned with baseline targets for all workgroups, teams, and individuals. A strategy-linked incentive system is used for rewarding performance. Team-based rewards are instituted to avoid individual 'free-rider' problems. By doing so, people transformation can truly take place.

Personal scorecard measures and targets must be meaningful and directly related and attributable to each individual employee. Job competencies are integrated into personal scorecards, translating the same into non-financial goals and appropriate standards of behaviour. In the process, personal scorecards can also function as job descriptions and performance contracts.

> Cisco Systems Inc., a worldwide leader in Internet infrastructure, has the quality of leadership that is a critical success factor in enabling the organization to tackle current business challenges in addition to those as yet unseen opportunities. Stephen Thoma, Leadership and People Development Manager at Cisco Systems Europe, Middle East, and Africa, emphasizes: 'Our continuing mission is to incubate all the passion and principles of leadership we have developed so they can be incubated in every level of the organization as an implicit way of doing things. If we were to lose these "baked-in" qualities and the capacity to reinvent ourselves, frankly we'd lose everything'.

Despite the untoward experience of many organizations, it is possible to turn strategies and plans into individual actions to exert the best performance from the employees. The problem arises in translating strategies into action plans. For example, if the organization adopts new market development and customer retention strategies to achieve the objective of 20 per cent market growth, without suitable action plans, employees may feel directionless, as they may fail to understand how to address these strategic intents. Effective strategy implementation is possible with motivational leadership, elaborating the action plans with the clarity of strategic intent and emotional contracting.

SUMMARY

Performance planning in organizations is primarily a discussion process through which organizations try to reach an agreement on the key jobs and responsibilities of individual employees. Effective performance planning helps in developing a common understanding of the organizational goals and objectives, facilitates identifying the set of competencies that individual employees need to demonstrate while doing their job, and finally creates the appropriate individual development plan. Performance planning thus is considered as the important precursor for effective performance management systems in organizations. With a clear operating charter, individual employees can assign priority in their jobs and feel responsible to fulfil the organization's expectations. The process of performance planning starts with the identification of key job responsibilities of the individual employees, the degree of competencies that the organizations expect individual employees to demonstrate, and finally the performance deliverables. At this stage, employees also need to be communicated the performance measurement criteria, and how their performance deliverables can be tracked with the overall organizational goals and objectives. Such strategic alignment of the individual performance with the organizational performance helps the individual culminate the sense of responsibilities and channelize their efforts in fulfilling them. Therefore, effective performance planning increases the organization's productivity.

With the opening vignette and organizational caselets, this chapter discusses performance planning and its process, the development and contents of a performance plan, its steps and processes, its model of elements and standards, its transition from the individual to organizational level, the guidelines for checking the performance plans, the performance plan and its role clarity, and finally the alignment of performance plans with the strategic plans of the organization. The chapter concludes with a real-life case study on performance planning. Wherever possible, the chapter discusses theories related to the organizational practices.

KEY WORDS

Critical Performance Elements—Critical performance elements are those that are most important, without which employees' overall performance become unacceptable.

Monitoring—Monitoring facilitates the continuous measurement of performance to provide feedback. Employees and their groups can track their contribution to reach the performance goals of the organizations. At the individual level, monitoring involves reviewing the performance progress with the employees against job elements and standards.

Rewarding—Rewarding is recognition of employees both individually and as members of the group to give credence to their performance. It motivates good performers and an organization can also get the opportunity to retain the talented employees. When they observe their fellow top-performing colleagues get rewarded, average and poor performers feel inspired to improve their performance. With positive expectations, employees perform better.

Personal Scorecard—Personal scorecard measures and targets must be meaningful and directly related and attributable to each individual employee. Job competencies are integrated into personal scorecards, translating the same into non-financial goals and appropriate standards of behaviour. In the process, personal scorecards can also function as job descriptions and performance contracts.

Micro-organizational Issues—Micro-organizational issues pertain to the behaviour of individuals within the organization and how individual actors in the larger organization view strategy implementation. Implementation can be studied by looking at the impact organization culture and resistance to change has no employee acceptance or motivation to implement the new strategy.

Role Clarity—Role clarity in performance plans helps us achieve higher teamwork. This is, obviously, so that employees understand what is expected from them and which aspects of the job are important. Also, employees can understand the job's evaluation process. Therefore, role clarity becomes the key driver to employee performance.

GENERAL REVIEW QUESTIONS

1. What is performance planning? How it is carried out in organizations?
2. Explain the steps involved in developing the contents of a performance plan.
3. Explain how job description helps in developing employee performance plans.
4. Discuss the eight-step model of elements and the standards of a performance plan.
5. Develop checklists to measure the degree of effectiveness of a performance plan.
6. Explain the transition process from an individual performance plan to a group performance plan.
7. Explain how performance plan is influenced by the concept of role clarity.
8. Discuss how effective performance plan can help in strategy realization.
9. Short Notes:
   (a) Performance plans
   (b) Non-critical performance elements
   (c) Performance elements
   (d) Performance domains

CRITICAL REVIEW QUESTION

10. Visit any organization of your choice and explain how their performance plans align with their strategic plans. Develop your answer with some background information of your chosen organization.

REFERENCES

Bain, J.S. (1956), *Barriers to New Competition* (Cambridge, MA: Harvard University Press).

Balkin, D.B. and L.R. Gomez-Mejia (1987), 'Toward a Contingency Theory of Compensation Strategy', *Strategic Management Journal*, 8: 169–82.

Becker, B. and B. Gerhart (1996), 'The Impact of Human Resource Management on Organizational Performance: Progress and Prospects', *Academy of Management Journal*, 39(4): 779–801.

Davis, P.S. and P.L. Schul (1993), 'Addressing the Contingent Effects of Business Unit Strategic Orientation on Relationships between Organizational Context and Business Unit Performance', *Journal of Business Research*, 27(3): 183–200.

Deming, E.W. (1982), *Out of the Crisis* (Cambridge, MA: Massachusetts Institute of Technology Center of Advanced Engineering Study).

Galbraith, J.K. (1973), *Economics and the Public Purpose* (Harmondsworth: Penguin).

Galbraith, J. and R. Kazanjian (1986), *Strategy Implementation: Structure, Systems and Process*, 2nd ed (St. Paul, MN: West).

Gomez-Mejia, L.R. and D.B. Balkin (1992), *Compensation, Organizational Strategy, and Firm Performance* (Cincinnati, OH: Southwestern Publishing Company).

Hambrick D.C. and C.C. Snow (1989), 'Strategic Reward Systems', in C.C. Snow (ed), *Strategy Organizational Design and Human Resource Management* (Greenwich, CT: JAI Press), pp. 929–64.

Kilmann, R.H. (1989), *Managing Beyond the Quick Fix: A Completely Integrated Program for Creating and Maintaining Organizational Success* (San Francisco: Jossey-Bass).

Lawler, E.E., III (1986a), *High Involvement Management* (San Francisco, CA: Jossey-Bass).

Lawler, E.E., III (1986b), 'Reward Systems and Strategy', in J.R. Gardner, R. Rochlin, and H.W. Sweeney (eds), *Strategic Planning Handbook* (New York, NY: Wiley).

Mason, E.S. (1939), 'Price and Production Policies of Large-Scale Enterprises', *American Economic Review*, 29(1): 61–74.

McGee, J. and H. Thomas (1986), 'Strategic Groups: Theory, Research and Taxonomy', *Strategic Management Journal*, 7(1): 141–60.

McGee, J. and H. Thomas (1992), 'Strategic Groups and Intra-industry Competition', *International Review of Strategic Management,* 3, 77–98.

Nadler, D. and M. Tushman (1988), *Strategic Organization Design* (Glenview, IL: Scott Foresman).

Porter, M.E. (1980), *Competitive Strategy* (New York: Free Press).

Porter, M.E. (1985), *Competitive Advantage* (New York, NY: Free Press).

Ulrich, D. and D. Lake (1990), *Organizational Capability, Competing from the Inside-Out* (New York, NY: John Wiley & Sons).

Waldman, D.A. (1994), 'Designing Performance Management Systems for Total Quality Implementation', *Journal of Organizational Change Management*, 7(2): 31–44.

Zahra, S.A. (1993), 'Environment, Corporate Entrepreneurship, and Financial Performance: A Taxonomic Approach', *Journal of Business Venturing*, 8(3): 319–40.

Zingheim, P.K. and J.R. Schuster (2000), 'Total Rewards: Pushing the Pedal to the Metal', *The Journal of Business Strategy*, July/August, 21(4): 15–17.

FURTHER READING

Bhattacharyya, D.K. (2006), *Human Resource Management*, 2nd edition (New Delhi: Excel Books).

Bhattacharyya, D.K. (2009), *Organizational Behaviour* (New Delhi: Oxford University Press).

Bhattacharyya, D.K. (2009), *Human Resource Development* (Mumbai: Himalaya Publishing).

Kaplan, R.S., and D.P Norton (1996), *The Balanced Scorecard: Translating Strategy Into Action* (Boston, MA: The Harvard Business School Press).

Lawler, E.E., III, S.A. Mohrman, and G.E. Ledford, Jr. (1995), *Creating High Performance Organizations: Practices and Results of Employee Involvement and Total Quality Management in Fortune 1000 Companies* (San Francisco, CA: Jossey-Bass).

Morgan, B.S., and W.A. Schiemann (1999), 'Measuring People and Performance: Closing the Gaps', *Quality Progress*, 1: 47–53.

Peters, T., and R. Waterman (1982), *In Search of Excellence* (New York, NY: Harper & Row).

Quinn, R. and D. Mills (1985), 'Planning with People in Mind', *Harvard Business Review*, July–August, 63: 97–105

CASE STUDY

Linking Performance to the Bottom Line: The Approach of Mono India

The Mono India, an Indian conglomerate with more focus on FMCG products, operates globally with 59,000 workforces in their payroll. The company manages each product line as strategic business units (SBUs). For absence of commonality in product lines, SBUs do not compete with each other. The company follows a matrix structure, making each employee reportable to two bosses. FMCG SBU head, Mr Pratap, has a high reputation for achieving the consistent growth for last 5 years. Mono India strategically locates their manufacturing units keeping in view the market proximity. Accordingly, the company located their 16 Indian units spread across 14 states and 2 union territories in India. Market in unrepresented states and union territories are controlled from manufacturing units that are close to them.

Confectionary Division of Mono India is the sole FMCG product line that enjoys more than 50 per cent of the market share in India. The corporate strategic plan of the company envisages annual incremental growth of not less than 5 per cent in a fiercely competitive confectionary market in India. Mr Pratap literally needs to develop a performance plan with a participative approach and shared vision of 'do or die'. As SBU head, he manages all activities of the confectionary division. Every employee of the SBU clearly understands what they need to achieve and why. Mr Pratap understands that achieving a 5 per cent market growth can only be possible when employees at their individual level deliver a minimum of 10 per cent more. In the confectionary business, Mono India strategically follows a maximum 6-month product life cycle with two primary objectives: to prevent aping by the competitors and to remain ever competitive with product differentiation. Mono India's operation team has a great market demand. Competitors hire them with an increased salary primarily to ape the formulations. The R&D unit of the company targets a minimum of 10 acceptable flavours of Tiffin cakes and biscuits. Every new item comes with value addition without price increase. To customers it becomes a winning steal.

The marketing team always endeavour to create news in the market. A new product launch is preceded by road shows, school functions, and shelf-space occupying in retail outlets. This is to create a compelling pressure for consumers to buy the product. With smart adaptable workforces, Mono India is able to sustain in the competitive marketplace. The winning zeal of the employees is rewarded to perpetuate the process of high performance. New Vice-president Marketing at the corporate level, however, now critical about this approach of making employees just preoccupied with the hitting the numbers to meet their performance objectives. His major concern is that the company is unable to sustain the befitting culture, which often flouts the on-the-job behaviour of employees. Analysis of customer complaints revealed that the marketing team hardly attends the low-profile retailers, obviously for their small order bookings. Segmentation analysis could cluster the retail outlets, showing an alarming representation of the company's products in small retail outlets, resulting in less visibility of the company's new biscuits and cakes. These small outlets sell their competitors' products. Alternative biscuits and cakes at the customers' end are still accepted when they do not get the choice of selecting Mono's range of products. Moreover, many Indian customers are not informed buyers of biscuits and cakes. Many buy it out of impulses. They buy it as they see it.

Vice-president Marketing now desires to bring changes in the performance planning process, making it clear that reaching the bottom-line results alone cannot help the company to sustain in the long run. He expects every employee of Mono India to drive home this message that effective performance achievement is possible when a balance is struck between linking employees' objectives to the corporate strategy and developing appropriate behaviours. He suggests the following steps to facilitate this new process of performance planning:

1. Define the corporate culture as a driving force for the growth of the organizations.
2. Determine the expectations from the employees, including the way they should do their jobs, serve their customers, deal with their peers, and so on.
3. Determine which performance behaviours are important to the organizational success.
4. Understand how employees' performance will be measured.
5. Prioritize employees' performance objectives.
6. Align employees' performance objectives horizontally to develop the sense of collaboration.
7. Design a performance plan which incorporates the following key components:
    a) Employee surveys (360-degree survey)
    b) Individual development plan
    c) Regular performance reviews

Question: Critically evaluate the line of action of VP-Marketing of Mono India.

CHAPTER 3

Performance Appraisal

Learning Objectives

After reading this chapter, you will be able to understand:

- Meaning and definitions of performance appraisal
- Role of appraisals in performance management
- Process and method of performance appraisal
- Importance of performance appraisal
- Objectives of performance appraisal
- Reasons for failure of performance appraisal
- Steps and characteristics of the performance appraisal system
- Performance appraisal design
- Approaches in performance appraisal
- Types and methods of performance appraisal
- Concepts and methods of potential appraisal
- Biases of performance appraisal
- Diagnosis of poor performance

Transformation of TCS

To make employees responsive to internal and external factors and change their mindsets and build capabilities, TCS always focusses on empowered decision-making and inculcates a sense of ownership. It views change as an ongoing process and quickly responds to changes, to remain globally competitive, revisiting organizational structure, practices, and decision-making practices. Adjustments against IP (industry practice), SP (Service practice), and GM (geography matrix) always continue as an ongoing exercise. In fact TCS always senses it in advance. Perhaps for this reason, TCS for the first time in India envisaged the need to designate a Chief Transformation Officer (CTO). Through their learning programme, it always ensures people capability development, which facilitates continuous mutation of organization structures, both meeting the changing employees' aspirations and customer delight. A glaring example of TCS concern about the organization structure is evident from their recent change to matrix structure, only to keep pace with the external front. Organizational changes often cannot succeed only with internal initiatives. TCS engaged an outsider, who acts as a change agent bringing fresh perspectives in the organization.

Involvement of everyone in the process of transformation, clearly making transparent the key concerns—why change, why now, what it means, where it will take the company, and what it means to everyone—provides a cascading effect and makes the process a great success through voluntary participation of employees. TCS's organizational transformation model encompasses strategic planning, change management, and alignment with project management to create business value. A performance measurement system with an economic value-added (EVA) approach provides a framework to align corporate values with the performance of the constituent business units and the individual employees attached therewith.

INTRODUCTION

Performance appraisal is one single important tool which helps in deciding training requirements for an organization and reinforces training activities to balance the team efforts ensuring proper allocation of activities among different members of the group. In human resource management, performance appraisal is the most crucial area of activity. Through periodic performance improvement, organizations can continue to sustain their competitive advantage and identify non-performers, get rid of them, and rationalize the manpower requirement. Performance means the degree or extent with which an employee applies his skill, knowledge, and efforts to a job assigned to him and the result of that application. Performance appraisal means analysis, review or evaluation of performance, or behaviour analysis of an employee. It may be formal or informal, oral or documented, open or confidential. However, in organizations, we find formal appraisal systems in documented forms. It is, therefore, a formal process to evaluate the performance of the employees in terms of achieving organizational objectives. Like any other function, performance appraisal is also an important management activity.

DEFINITIONS

Performance means the degree or extent with which an employee applies his skill, knowledge, and efforts to a job assigned to him or her and the result of that application. Tracey (1998) defined performance as 'a basic instructional method in which the trainee is required to perform, under controlled conditions, the operation, skills, or movement being taught'. Performance appraisal is defined as a process of evaluating employees to understand how well they do their jobs according to performance standards (Dessler, 2000). After an employee has been selected for a job, has been trained for it, and has worked for a period of time, his or her performance should be reviewed. Traditional performance appraisal relies on economic reward and the threat of punishment to motivate employees to reach a desired performance. But this concept does not hold true anymore. Today, performance appraisal is used for developmental and motivational purposes in the organizations. Performance appraisal is not a standstill evaluation activity, but a dynamic process which should be viewed as follows—planning the employees' performance and evaluation, and improving the performance of the employees. This process brings the new concept—performance management (Kaynak, 2003). Performance management is essential for today's organization to integrate the management goals and employee performances. It is a system for integrating the management of organization and employee performance in order to support and improve companies' or organizations' overall business goals (Williams, 1988).

ROLE OF APPRAISALS IN PERFORMANCE MANAGEMENT

Performance management is a continuous process, although its appraisals are periodic activities. Thus, as a process performance management is a dynamic process, although its evaluation or appraisals are static. With this, we understand performance appraisals as subsets of performance management. On the other hand, performance management is not possible without performance appraisal. It helps organizations assess where they stand vis-à-vis their competitors in terms of effectiveness in performance. Appraisals do not just reduce the individual performances into some quantitative data, they measure and rate the individual performances with one another, and in the process facilitate in taking performance-related decisions, such as employee development, promotion, transfer, compensation design, etc. more objectively. Using a well-calibrated measurement scale, such comparisons can also be made across the functions and hierarchical levels. We have discussed about such measurement scales in Chapter 13. In this backdrop, the role of performance appraisals in performance management can be summarized as under.

Performance appraisal leads to increased performances at the individual and organizational level. When the performance appraisal system in any organization fails to meet this objective, we need to re-look into the performance appraisal systems. Decreased level of performances can be attributed to defective performance appraisal systems. This occurs when appraisals are linked to rewards and a smaller number of employees get the reward. Those who do not get rewarded feel de-motivated. This occurs primarily for expectations' mismatch. It is for this reason that performance appraisal systems need to be properly integrated with more than one objective such as positive approach to employee development, mentoring and counselling, rewards, promotion, etc. Psychologically, people nurture a negative attitude to performance appraisals when they are rated poor. The primary role of performance appraisal systems, therefore, is to focus on positive developmental aspects of the people and the organization as a whole.

Similarly, the role of performance appraisal systems should be to make the performance management process more effective and productive. The appraisal systems must help managers manage their performance. Line managers must see it as a tool to improve employee performance. They must not feel overwhelmed when it helps only in tracking the poor performer and taking actions against them. Rather, they must consider its developmental aspects—future performance improvement through training and competency building. The next important role of performance appraisal systems, therefore, is to focus on developing the positive understanding of managers and to make them nurture that attitude which culminates in building the confidence in employees to embrace it as a tool for their improvement.

PROCESS AND METHODS OF PERFORMANCE APPRAISAL

In our preceding discussions, we have already focussed on the performance improvement and developmental aspects of appraisal systems. To design an effective performance appraisal system, which can help to achieve the above role, managers and the organizations, *per se*, need to follow the process as categorized below:

- Understand what to measure duly listing the job criteria and its expected level of standard.
- Determine the frequency of appraisal. In a competitive market, rather than making it an annual event, it is always desirable to review or appraise the performance at short intervals.
- Identify the appraisers and train them to feel confident about the process of appraising.
- Provide feedback to help employees understand their strengths and weaknesses.

After designing performance appraisal systems, it is necessary to select the appropriate appraisal techniques. Several appraisal techniques, such as supervisors, subordinates, peers, customers, self-appraisal, multi-source feedback, etc. have been suggested by different scholars (Schuler, 1995; Mathis and Jackson, 1994; Casio, 1995). Organizations, however, need to choose those that can better address their requirements. Also, it is necessary to choose more than one appraisal method to understand the accuracy of measurement and its reliability and validity.

Although organizations tend to formalize performance appraisal systems, keeping pace with the administrative and developmental needs, often it becomes a more rigid process of employee evaluation. Employees may feel dissatisfied primarily for single source performance feedback. Obviously, this requires developing of multi-source feedback systems, such as 360-degree appraisal systems. According to Lepsinger and Lucia (1998), 'The 360-degree feedback process involves collecting ideas about a person's behavior from the person's boss or bosses, direct reports, colleagues, fellow members of project teams, internal and external customers, and suppliers'. The 360-degree appraisal is also known as 'multi-rater feedback, multi source feedback, full-circle appraiser, multi-dimensional evaluation, and upwards feedback appraisals'. This method provides better feedback and performance information of the ratees can be collected from different stakeholders who in course of the ratees' work got influenced in one way or the other. Hurley (1998) also recommends this feedback method for the obvious feasibility of collecting more comprehensive performance information.

In performance management systems, we have many appraisal methods to evaluate the performance of employees. These methods have been discussed separately. Fisher, Schoenfeldt, and Shaw (1996) categorized such methods in three groups, that is, comparative appraisals, behavioural appraisals, and output-based appraisals.

PURPOSES OF PERFORMANCE APPRAISAL

A performance appraisal programme can serve multiple purposes to benefit both the organization and the employee. The following performance objectives are more generic in nature, and for their obvious universality can be made applicable to all types of organizations.

- To give opportunity for regular interaction between the employees and their managers or supervisors to mutually decide the performance standards.
- To equip managers or supervisors for effective identification of the strengths and weaknesses of employees' performance.
- To empower managers and supervisors to identify and recommend specific employee development programmes that can contribute to competency development and improved performance of employees.
- To align performance appraisals with the rewards and other important human resource management decisions.
- To make available important performance-related information of employees, which can be the basis for future business plans of the organization.
- To facilitate organizational control.
- To make this system an important vehicle for mutuality between the employees and the organization. With mutual goals both the employees and the organizations can develop.
- To make employees' understand their job role and functions.

- To act as a mechanism to increase communication between employees and their managers or supervisors.
- To provide opportunities to employees for self-regulated performance control. Organizations do this using performance scorecard, dashboards, balanced scorecard, etc.

Whatever may be the purpose of performance appraisals, they can be categorized into either administrative or developmental needs. While the administrative needs are organizational, developmental needs are both for the employees and the organizations. Administrative needs are more specific to meet the requirements of human resource management activities and decisions such as compensation, promotion, transfer, lay-off, human resource planning, job evaluation, recruitment validation, and so on. Also, other important administrative needs of performance appraisal are the feasibility of documenting the human resource management actions, as when employees feel prejudiced, that is, the decisions as against their interest, they can challenge the organization in a court of law.

Developmental needs of performance appraisal focus on individual employees' development through training and other competency development initiatives which contribute to improve the future performance of employees. Individual development is facilitated by the performance feedback. Appraisal feedback becomes the basis for discussion on the strengths and weaknesses of employees and accordingly focus can be given on the performance improvement. Through such discussions, employees' performance problems, if any, can be eliminated focussing on the need-based training and development programmes. With renewed skills and knowledge, employees then achieve high performance, and can look forward to future growth potentiality. A developmental approach to appraisal requires managers to nurture positive job behaviour.

Some of the administrative or developmental needs of performance appraisal systems are compensation administration, feedback, recognition, documentation for HR decisions, identification of poor performers, HR decisions on retention and termination, complying with the legal requirements, decisions on transfer and promotion, identification of training needs, HR planning, organizational development needs identification, recruitment validation, evaluation of HR systems, etc.

We can further summarize the purposes and objectives of the performance appraisal process in any organization as:

- To identify and define the specific job criteria. Many organizations at the beginning of the year set key performance areas (KPS) or key result areas (KRAs) for employees, based on mutual discussions.
- To measure and compare the performance in terms of the defined job criteria. KRAs and KPAs are also designed so they help measuring job performance in quantitative or qualitative terms.
- To develop and justify reward systems, relating rewards to the employees' performance.
- To identify the strengths and weaknesses of employees and to decide on proper placement and promotion.
- To develop suitable training and development programmes for enriching performance of employees.
- To plan for long-term manpower requirements and to decide upon the need for organizational development programmes, duly identifying the change areas for overall improvement of the organization.
- To identify motivational reinforcers to develop communication systems and also to strengthen superior subordinate relationships.

IMPORTANCE OF PERFORMANCE APPRAISAL

The above purposes also define the importance of performance appraisal. The primary importance of performance appraisal is to reinforce important people-related decisions such as promotion and transfer, training and development, compensation and reward, human resource planning, organizational development, etc. We have already discussed about these in the preceding text. However, the degree of importance varies between organizations. For example, continuous employee development may be the priority for one organization, while taking important human resource management decisions may be the priority for another. Apart from the primary importance listed above, performance appraisal also motivates, communicates, and strengthens superior–subordinate relationships, decides on KRA/KPA, and improves the overall performance of the organization.

OBJECTIVES OF PERFORMANCE APPRAISAL

Objectives of performance appraisal are embedded their purpose and importance discussed above. Here again we need to understand that organizations fulfilling the purpose of performance appraisal systems attain certain objectives. Such objectives of performance appraisal systems are remedial, developmental, innovative, and motivational.

- Remedial objectives help in correcting the low performance behaviour of employees through different HR actions. While some of the HR actions may be punitive, such as reduction in pay, transfer, and even termination, some others may be developmental.
- Developmental objectives of performance appraisal systems enable employees to grow in their present and future jobs. Such objectives are met first through identification of training needs and then the administration of such training to improve the employee's performance. It even extends to career development in the form of promotion.
- Innovative objectives facilitate discovering the ways to deal with new jobs and also streamlining the process of doing the existing jobs.
- Motivational objectives of performance appraisal are rewards, motivation, effective communication, and better interpersonal relations.

REASONS FOR FAILURE OF PERFORMANCE APPRAISAL

Often we find in organizations performance appraisal systems defeat the purpose of achieving their intended purposes and objectives. There may be numerous causes of such failure, but mostly it occurs as the top management fails to share information and extend support. These failures of performance appraisal can be attributed to ambiguous performance standards, rater bias, lengthy process of form filling and documenting, and wrong selection of performance criteria. At times, the appraisal process itself may be conflicting. A reward-aligned performance appraisal may conflict with the administrative and developmental needs. This is particularly evident when rewards are limited only to a few good performers. Those who do not get rewarded feel de-motivated. Some other reasons for the failure are attributed to managers' lack of skill and competency, absence of feedback systems, and lack of resource support.

Also the performance appraisal process becomes a source of conflict for both the managers and the employees, often for its annual frequency. In true sense, in such cases, employees get performance feedback only after a year, which delimits their eagerness to correct and develop. This problem can be avoided by making the appraisal at short intervals and providing feedback to employees on a continuous basis.

Another important reason for the failure of performance appraisal systems is employees' perceived disbelieve in the system. Such a syndrome can be attributed to organizational practices, as organizations often make it a process of compliance rather than meeting the needs to change and develop. With its cascading effect, employees also consider it as perfunctory and play the passive role. This can be mitigated with appropriate performance planning right at the beginning.

STEPS TO PERFORMANCE APPRAISAL

Irrespective of the methods applied for performance appraisal, its steps follow more or less a set pattern, which are as follows:

- Establishment of performance standards. This is done mostly while developing a job description.
- Communication of standards to the employees.
- Measurement of performance.
- Comparison of performance with the job standards.
- Discussing the appraisal results with the employees.
- Initiating the corrective action, where necessary.

CHARACTERISTICS OF AN APPRAISAL SYSTEM

Performance appraisal systems need to be accepted by all. It is important at the outset to understand the distinction between the performance evaluation and appraisal. Patten (1982) defined performance evaluation as the objective assessment, that is, more emphasis on quantitative assessment of performance, while performance appraisal is more holistic, as it considers both the objective and subjective assessment of the employees' performance. In line with Patten, therefore, we can define performance appraisal as the configuration of 'feed, development and assessment'. As a process, performance appraisal, therefore, focusses on the job of employees, the work environment prevalent in the organization, and the employee as a person. All these factors are interrelated and interdependent. To ensure effective performance appraisal, it needs to be employee specific, subjective, objective, and so also more focussed on employees' problem-solving abilities. Also, it is important to make the appraisal system more specific to the job performance, rather than other peripheral traits such as personality, which may or may not influence on the job performance of employees.

PERFORMANCE APPRAISAL DESIGN

Effective performance appraisal design is the important precursor for its success. All the reasons for its failure, mentioned earlier, can be suitably addressed by designing an effective performance appraisal system. Some of the important considerations in designing a performance appraisal system are as follows:

Goals: Organizations set the performance goals through the job description and structure the same through mutual discussion and acceptance both by the managers and the employees. While job description sets the basis, the performance premise is set by the business goals of the organizations. Hence, the process of mutual decision and acceptance of performance goals need to be aligned with the business goals of the organizations.

Reliability and consistency: Effective performance designs need to be reliable and consistent. This is ensured through objective and subjective rating and by producing consistent and reliable measurement criteria.

Clear and unambiguous format: The appraisal format must be practical and simple to achieve its basic functions. Long and complicated formats are not only time consuming, they often create ambiguity in interpreting the useful information.

Frequency of appraisal should be regular and routine-bound: Instead of making the appraisal process an annual event, it should be a continuous process giving feedback to employees on a regular basis. This would enable employees to self-regulate their performance and organizations to initiate the necessary corrective actions.

Open and participative: Employees' involvement in designing the performance appraisal systems makes it more effective as they feel committed to it. Through open and transparent performance review interview or meeting, they can draw their future plans and adopt suitable strategies to improve future performances. Such participation not only enhances the commitment to deliver, but also inculcates a sense of belonging.

Performance rewards: This should the essential part of performance appraisal systems. Performance rewards may be both positive and negative. Often organizations make it discretionary. This makes the performance appraisal process more ineffective.

Noticeable, impersonal, and timely feedback: Feedback to employees will not serve any purpose, unless it is made in compliance with all these objectives. Noticeable feedback requires communication of information to the employees about the appraisal process. Impersonal feedback is possible when the rating is free from bias and errors. Timely feedback, on the other hand, requires real-time sharing of performance information with the employees.

Relevance and responsiveness of performance appraisal: The performance appraisal system not only establishes clear performance goals, it also ensures assignment of job role to the individual employees and the work groups. It means the appraisal system should aim at specific job needs and job roles of individual employees as well as their work groups; otherwise it lacks its orientation.

Commitment from the top: Effective design of performance appraisal systems also requires involvement and commitment from the top. When an organization mandates performance-based HR decisions, the top management cannot be discretionary; else it loses its sanctity.

Although there may be other areas of concern for effective performance design, compliance with the above, by and large, can substantially reduce the performance-related problems, and make it more effective to achieve the intended objectives of the organizations. Craig, Beatty, and Baird (1986) suggested an eight-stage performance appraisal process for its effective designing. These are listed below, as our preceding discussions are more inclusive in this respect.

- Establishing standards and measures.
- Communicating job expectations.
- Planning.
- Monitoring performance.
- Appraising and documenting performance.
- Feedback.

- Decision making.
- Development of performance.

However, the core of any appraisal system is communication, which may be upward or downward.

APPROACHES TO PERFORMANCE APPRAISAL

To appraise the performance of employees, organizations adopt various approaches. Performance appraisal per se is a multistage process. In line with Einstein and LeMere-Labonte (1989) and Monga (1983), such approaches can be listed as under:

- **Intuitive approach**—With this approach, managers appraise the employees' performance on the basis of their perception and external behaviour.
- **Self-appraisal approach**—This approach appraises the employees with standard common format.
- **Group approach**—This approach appraises employees' group performance by a.
- **Trait approach**—This approach focusses on appraisal of employees' performance on the basis of dimension of multiple traits such as personality, integrity, honesty, dependability, punctuality, and so on.
- **Result-based approach**—Here appraisal is done in terms of measurable performance, comparing against the mutually decided expected performance targets of employees.
- **Behavioural approach**—This approach appraises the behavioural parameters demonstrated by the employees in the course of their performance.

TYPES AND METHODS OF PERFORMANCE APPRAISAL

Different methods of performance appraisal are followed in different organizations to achieve the above objectives. Since some methods of performance appraisal are complicated and call for adequate knowledge in quantitative techniques, many organizations follow traditional methods of appraisal while others consider modern methods as the basis for evaluating their employees' job performance.

Traditional Methods

Traditional methods of performance appraisal may be categorized broadly under the following heads:

Straight Ranking Method

This is the oldest and simplest method of performance appraisal by which employees are tested in order of merit giving some numerical rank and placed in a simple group. Such grouping separates employees under each level of efficiency, which may vary from most efficient to least efficient. Since it is a blunt quantification of performance, it does not account for behavioural parameters and only considers an individual employee's level of efficiency in relation to others. For such obvious deficiency, this system does not provide a scientific basis for performance appraisal of employees.

Paired Comparison Techniques

This is a somewhat better method of performance appraisal as each employee is compared with others in pairs at a time. For each performance trait, an individual employee's performance is tallied with others

Table 3.1 *Trait reliability of person rated*

As compared to	A	B	C	D	E
A	×	−	−	−	−
B	+	×	−	+	−
C	+	−	×	−	−
D	+	−	+	×	−
E	+	+	−	+	×

in pairs and the rank order is decided. This system is not suitable in those cases where the number of employees is usually high. For better comprehension, Table 3.1 presents a comparison on trait reliability.

Man-to-Man Comparison

Under this method, certain factors are selected for analysis, such as leadership, initiative, interpersonal relationship, etc., and a scale is designed by a rater for each such factor. After rating such factors separately, aggregate performance of an individual employee is decided and is also given a scale. Likewise, an individual employee is considered with others. This method is somewhat a factor comparison method and widely used in job evaluation. Since developing a uniform rating scale is a complicated task, this factor is not much in use for performance appraisal of employees by the organizations.

Grading Method

Under this method, certain features worth understanding the performance of an employee are identified. Such features may be leadership, communication power, analytic ability, job knowledge, etc. The raters mark/rate such features according to a scale and match employees' performance compared to his/her own developed grade definition. For example, A, B, C, D, E types of grade definitions for each feature may be developed by a rater to indicate: A = Very Significant, B = Significant, C = Moderate, D = Average, E = Poor. Such types of grading are of much use for selecting an employee or grading him or her in written examinations.

Graphic or Linear Rating Scale

A graphic rating scale is a continuous scale to enable a rater to mark the performance of an employee along a continuum. The scale offers a list of areas related to job performance, and the managers are required to rate those areas assigning a numerical score. There may be a number of scales to relate to certain jobs or performance-related dimensions, such as job knowledge, responsibility, or quality of work. The continuum of scale may range from high to low, good to poor, most to least, very significant to insignificant, and so on. Typically, such a scale may have five to seven points, or even less, depending on the dimensions of measurement. In a printed form, performance factors are arrayed, and the rater needs to rate those factors giving a numerical value relating the same to the achieved performance level of employees using a continuous scale. The method, therefore, enables quantification of performance scores and a subsequent statistical analysis. However, this method cannot help in making a rating cluster for obvious differences in the job characteristics. Hence, the results obtained through this scale may not always be objective. The appraisal scores are subject to various interpretations of raters, and its reliability and validity is often questioned. Despite such limitation, this scale is one of the simplest and most widely used methods of performance appraisal.

For its simple and wide use, organizations design their own graphic rating scale, satisfying certain conditions and characteristics as under:

- Clear definition of performance dimensions.
- Behaviourally anchored scales to enable the raters to make an objective rating of the observable characteristics.
- Avoidance of abstract traits such as honesty, integrity, and loyalty.
- Brief and unambiguous way of presenting the performance dimensions. At times points or anchors need to be chosen in a way that can be easily understood. For example, to describe the leadership quality, we can use terms such as team leader, middle of the run, task master, people centric, and country club, instead of outstanding, very good, good, average, and poor.

A graphic rating scale can standardize the performance appraisal systems in an organization, despite its susceptibility to rating errors. For example, performance of employees can be rated uniformly across performance levels. This leads to a halo effect. Central tendency error may occur for the lack of variation or differences in ratings, as people tend to be rated as average. Contrarily, leniency error occurs when the raters tend to rate employees very high. Finally, the extreme performance error may occur in this scale when the raters rate the employees unduly very harsh.

Example of Graphic Rating Scale

<table>
<tr><td colspan="4">Graphic Rating Scale
This scale appraises five generic job dimensions. You are required to appraise the performance of employees putting a (√) mark against each performance dimension in the appropriate column, as may be deemed fit by you.</td></tr>
<tr><td rowspan="2">1. Job Knowledge: Understands the job and can implement such understanding to improve the job.</td><td>Require Guidance
☐</td><td>Understand the job
☐</td><td>Have exceptional understanding of job
☐</td></tr>
<tr><td colspan="3">Remarks: Employees with exceptional understanding of the job are rated as exceptionally good in risk taking</td></tr>
<tr><td rowspan="2">2. Job Initiative: Capable to generate new ideas and a self-starter.</td><td>Lacks initiative
☐</td><td>Takes initiative
☐</td><td>Exceptional in taking initiative
☐</td></tr>
<tr><td colspan="3">Remarks: When employees are rated as exceptional, they are capable to take initiative and can generate new ideas.</td></tr>
</table>

3. *Job Application:* Application minded on job.	Poor in job application ☐	Capable in job application ☐	Exceptionally capable in job application ☐
	Remarks: With exceptional job application capability employees can always take new job challenges.		
4. *Work Quality:* Perfect and precision minded in job execution.	Poor in perfection and job precision ☐	Conforms to job protocols ☐	Always conforms to high job perfection and precision ☐
	Remarks: Employees with high level of perfection and precision always conform to the quality.		
5. *Work Volume:* Degree of capability in achieving the job targets.	Poor capability to achieve job targets ☐	Capable to meet the performance targets ☐	Capable to deliver more than the performance targets ☐
	Remarks: With high capability, employees can achieve more job targets.		

Forced Choice Description Method

This combines objective and subjective judgement on an individual employee's performance against each rating element. Positive and negative phrases are given asking the rater to indicate the applicability of such phrases as objectives in describing the employee whose performance is rated. The method does not involve any discussion; it just forces the assessors to choose the best- and worst-fit statements from a group of statements. Score value is pre-assigned against each such statement and the same is not revealed to the assessor. This is done primarily to eliminate bias and compare the standards of performance. For its obvious complexity, this system is not very popular. Moreover, the system becomes redundant when the appraisal process involves personal interview.

Forced Distribution Method

This is a method to evaluate employees' performance according to a predetermined distribution scale. The distribution is a form of comparative evaluation in which an evaluator rates subordinates according to a specified distribution. Unlike ranking methods, forced distribution is frequently applied to several rather than only one component of job performance. For example, under such a method, the rater may be asked to distribute 5 per cent of the total employees on top of the scale, indicating their superior performance and promotability; 10 per cent may be put immediately under this level, indicating their good performance and future promotability. The proportions of forced distribution may vary. Instead of specifying the rating in percentage terms, top management often asks the raters to categorize employees into top, middle, and bottom levels of distribution. This method of performance appraisal can eliminate rating errors, such as the errors caused by leniency and central tendency. However, the method itself may be prone to rating errors, as it forces discriminatory ranking of employees, even in cases when performances may be similar. Particularly while rating a small group of people, who might have performed equally well, the method may require discrimination, resulting in some good performers being ranked at the bottom of the graded continuum. Because of such in-built problems, the method loses its wide acceptance.

Checklist Method

It is a process of assessing employees' performance, compiling yes/no responses. The assessor is furnished with a checklist of pre-scaled descriptions of behaviour, which are then used to evaluate the employees being rated (Monga, 1983). The scale values of the behaviour items are unknown to the assessor, who has to check as many items as she or he believes describe the work being assessed. The final rating is done by averaging the scale values of the items by the HR department based on such assessment. The method, therefore, is not an objective method of appraisal and also not free from bias.

Free Easy Method

This is an open-ended qualitative appraisal of employees' performance, giving an opportunity to the rater to put down his/her impression in subjective form on important job factors. The method involves a written appraisal report of employees' performance, in terms of job behaviours and/or results. The subject of an essay appraisal is justification of pay, promotion, or termination decisions, but essays can be used for developmental purposes as well. Since it is descriptive and essay type, it is likely to be biased by judgemental errors. Also, these appraisals are to a large extent unstructured and open-ended; therefore, more susceptible to rater bias.

Critical Incident Method

This method measures employees' performance in terms of certain 'events' or 'critical incidents' instrumental for success or failure on the job. Such critical incidents are identified by the rater after in-depth study of employees' working. As negative incidents get more focussed and recording incidents demands utmost care, it is not free from defects. In this method, a supervisor describes critical incidents giving details of both positive and negative behaviours of the employee. These are then discussed with the employee. The discussion focusses on actual behaviour rather than on traits. While this technique is well suited for performance review interviews, it has the drawback that the supervisor has to note down the critical incidents as and when they occur. This may be impractical and may delay the feedback to employees. It makes little sense to wait 6 months or 1 year to discuss a misdeed, a mistake, or a good display of initiative.

Work Standard Approach

In this technique, management establishes the goals openly and sets targets against realistic output standards. These standards are incorporated into the organizational performance appraisal system. Thus, each employee has a clear understanding of their duties and knows well what is expected of them. Performance appraisal and interview comments are related to these duties. This makes the appraisal process objective and more accurate. However, it is difficult to compare individual ratings because standards for work may differ from job to job and from employee to employee. This limitation can be overcome by some form of ranking using pooled judgements.

Group Appraisal Method

This is an evaluation of an employee by multiple judges. The immediate supervisor of the employee and a few others discuss the performance standards and then evaluate the performance of the employee. The greatest advantage of this method is that it is relatively free from bias even though it is time consuming.

Field Review Method

This type of review is conducted by the HR Department by interviewing the supervisor of an employee to understand the subordinate employees' performance. Normally for such type of an appraisal, the appraiser, that is, the representative of the human resource department, gets equipped with certain questions and, more in the form of an informal interview, asks those questions about the employees whose performances are to be reviewed to their respective supervisors. HR department can identify areas of inter-assessor disagreement and understand the uniformity of performance standards. The method is considered more valid and reliable, although a little time consuming. Since this process of appraisal is an indirect method of appraising the performance, it may not always reflect the true performance level of the subordinate employees. Such an interview is always having a sensitizing effect on the interview, whose responses may be some opinionated generalization. Moreover, this method keeps the key managerial personnel always busy. Despite such defect, the process being simple and possible to administer and centralize the task of performance appraisal function, most of the organizations prefer to have this type of appraisal for down-the-level employees. Since individual assessors differ in their standards, they inadvertently introduce bias in their ratings. To overcome this assessor-related bias, essay and graphic rating techniques can be combined in a systematic review process.

MODERN METHODS

The traditional methods of performance appraisal, discussed above, suffer from a major limitation for their obvious emphasis on assessing individual performance or task, considering it as an isolated factor. To eliminate such narrow and partial approach, the newer techniques of performance appraisal have been developed and are widely practised by the organizations, particularly for managerial and supervisory employees. Some of the modern techniques are discussed here.

Appraisal by Results for Management by Objectives

Management by objective (MBO) is a comprehensive management approach that is adopted for performance appraisal and so also for organizational development. It is a systematic and organized approach to focus on achievable goals and to attain the same by maximizing available resources. It increases organizational performance aligning organizational goals and employees' objectives throughout the organization. Ideally, it provides a strong input for employees to identify their objectives, and the time frame by which they must meet such objectives. MBO-based performance appraisal system is also in-built with the performance tracking and feedback processes.

The method was first documented by Peter Drucker (1954) in his book *The Practice of Management*. In the 1990s, when MBO was used for performance appraisal only, its primary focus was on developing objective criteria for evaluating the performance of the individuals. Identification of common goals is jointly done by the managers and the employees of an organization. After such identification, each individual's major area of responsibilities is defined. Such defined responsibilities become the basis for evaluating the performance of the individual employee.

Most of the organizations emphasize on developing key result areas (KRAs) through MBO exercise, as this approach necessitates joint meetings of the supervisors and the employees to define, establish, and set goals or objectives which the individual employees would achieve within a prescribed time limit (mostly it is the form of yearly targets). Such an exercise also establishes ways and methods to measure performance. Goals are mostly work related and career oriented and are integrated with overall organizational objectives. Periodic evaluation of employees' performances is done in terms of goals, and if required goals may be revised. MBO also calls for superior–subordinate interactions and a supportive role of the supervisor (which as well includes counselling/coaching).

The method being result oriented, it seeks to measure employee performance examining the extent to which predetermined work objectives can be met. Usually the objectives are established jointly by the supervisors and subordinates. An example of an objective for a sales manager might be: Increase the gross monthly sales volume to Rs X by 30 April. Once an objective is agreed, the employee is usually expected to self-audit, that is, to identify the skills needed to achieve the objective. Typically they do not rely on others to locate and specify their strengths and weaknesses. They are expected to monitor their own development and progress.

Advantages

The MBO approach overcomes the problems of trait-based approaches to performance appraisal as it concentrates on actual outcomes. When the employee meets or exceeds the set objectives, then he or she is considered to have delivered an acceptable level of job performance. Employees are judged according to real outcomes, and not on their potential for success, or on the subjective opinion of their abilities. The guiding principle of the MBO approach is that direct results can be observed. The method recognizes that it is difficult to dissect the entire complex and varied performance elements, as the employees cannot be broken into constituent parts. But putting all these parts together, we can directly observe and measure the performance, as it culminates to an overall performance level in terms of target achievements.

Disadvantages

Despite many advantages of MBO methods of performance appraisal, primarily in terms of employees' sense of autonomy and achievement, it can often lead to unrealistic expectations of management. Management often sets targets based on MBO and imposes the same on employees without a participative approach and reality checking. Thus, clarity of purpose, the biggest strength of MBO could be the source of weakness also. A flexible approach to organizational objectives (necessary for organizational survival) often needs to be imposed on employees very rigidly, leading to non-achievement and employees' frustration. Variable objectives may even confuse employees. Again the method being emphasizes more on tangible goals, intangible goals like morale, good interpersonal relations, commitment to the job, etc., are often ignored. Moreover, MBO exercise is too time and money consuming. Peter Drucker himself said: 'It's just another tool. It is not the great cure for management inefficiency.... Management by Objectives works if you know the objectives, 90% of the time you don't'.

MBO in Practice

According to Drucker, managers often get bogged with the 'activity trap'. This often takes them away from the core objective issues of the organization. Designing a performance system with an MBO approach put the managers and the employees on the right track. While the employees get their clear direction, managers can concentrate on other important strategic issues.

MBO is extensively used by world class organizations. At Intel, the MBO process follows sequences as under:

- Start with a few well-chosen overriding objectives.
- Set subordinates' objectives that fit in with your overriding objectives.
- Allow your subordinates to set their own key results to enable them to meet their objectives.

At Microsoft, MBO helps in preventing competing missions and objectives, and is also used for setting objectives.

Canon Production System (CPS) uses MBO at all hierarchical levels to emphasize on managing results.

STEPS FOLLOWED IN MBO IMPLEMENTATION

From our foregoing discussions, it is clear that MBO embeds in the organization-wide goal setting and appraisal processes. To implement MBO, we need to follow certain steps as under:

- Decide the organizational goals based on the organization-wide plan.
- Cascade the organizational goal to departmental goals.
- Discuss and allocate departmental goals.
- Define expected results.
- Review the performance and measure the results.
- Provide feedback.

Wal-Mart, using the extensive participative approach, that is, involving people in the goal setting process, manages the performances of their associates using MBO.

Assessment Centre Method

An assessment centre approach of performance appraisal evaluates the behaviour of people using several exercises and games, observations, and interviews primarily simulating the real-life situations. It also uses multiple observers for evaluation. Several evaluations are pooled in a meeting where the assessors reach a consensus on the evaluation report of each participant of the assessment process. Assessment centre reports can be subjected to statistical tests and validation and can also be used for the purpose of recruitment and selection. In each assessment centre, the number of participants may vary from 5 to 20. More than 20 participants in one assessment centre may create a problem. The term 'assessment centre' is used to indicate extended assessments in a single centre or a venue.

This method emphasizes on testing candidates in a social situation by a number of assessors, using a variety of criteria (which may be a paper-pencil test, interviews, in-basket exercise, business game, role playing incident, or a leaderless discussion). The assessors or evaluators are drawn from experienced executives, working at different levels of management. Under this method, performances of employees are evaluated both individually and collectively. This method is useful in measuring interpersonal skills, organizing and planning abilities, creativity, resistance to stress, work motivation, decision-making powers, and so on in performance management.

The assessment centre approach (ACs) is used extensively for selection and development (Thornton, 1980). Typically, it assesses the performance behaviours of people relating the same to several performance dimensions. This is done through simulation. The method enjoys more validity and reliability. Content validity (Sackett, 1987), criterion-related validity, construct validity, etc., of ACs have been well established in several research studies.

Uses of Assessment Centres

- Recruitment and selection.
- Promotion and other rewards.
- Identification of leaders.
- Identification of self-directed team members and followers.
- Potential appraisal.
- Identification of training and development.
- Matching competent people for jobs.
- Organizational development.
- Skill/competency development.

Human Asset Accounting Method

This method attaches money value to people employed with the organization. The process estimates the goodwill value of people or human resources, based on measurement of some variables. Such variables can be either key variables or intervening variables. Key variables are organizational policies and decision-making styles, strategies, skills of people, etc. Intervening variables are those that strengthen the key variables to achieve the desired level of performance. They are loyalties, attitudes, motivations, interpersonal relations, communication, and so on. Measuring such variables can quantify human assets, which are otherwise difficult. To measure individual performance, this method is not much in use. However, for collective measurement of performance, this method can be effective. We have discussed this method in chapter on Human Resource Auditing and Performance Management.

Behaviourally Anchored Rating Scales (BARS)

This method helps in measuring and improving job performance more accurately. For each performance area, some standard statements are provided. These are then put on the scales in BARS. While developing such BARS, group discussions are conducted to identify significant job dimensions that need to be evaluated. BARS may be of different types for different job dimensions. Normally they are presented vertically with scale points ranging from five to nine. Because of its behavioural orientation, it is considered as the most useful techniques of performance appraisal. Moreover, this system provides an opportunity to both the appraisee and the appraiser to interact and participate in developing standards for each performance area. This system being time-consuming and painstaking, despite its advantages, organizations try to avoid it.

Behaviourally anchored rating scales (BARS) are developed with some effective or ineffective behavioural statements. We call it behaviourally anchored as it represents a continuum of descriptive behavioural statements whose value ranges from the least to the most effective. Steps for designing BARS are as follows:

- Document the important performance dimensions of job or jobs.
- Identify some critical incidents that explain effective and ineffective behaviour.
- Relate identified effective and ineffective behaviour to the required performance dimensions.
- Assign numerical values to each such performance dimension.

Behavioural Observation Scales (BOS)

Behavioural observation scales are the frequency ratings of critical incidents pertaining to workers' performance. Latham and Wexley (1977) developed BOS, as they perceived that both the graphic rating scales and BARS require supervisors to make vague judgements. Managers here rank the list of critical performance-related desired or undesired work issues or incidents based on the number of occurrences. Using a five-point scale, such frequency of behaviour can be measured. For example, a scale as follows may be of use:

- Never
- Rare
- Sometimes
- Often
- Very often

> Some examples of BOS may be listed as:
> Workers' absence from workplace increases our loss of man-days ________
> Workers never require their work to be supervised ________
> Employees like their self-development opportunities ________
> Bad workmanship causing high rate of rejection in our organization ________

Mixed Standard Scales

Mixed standard scale (MSS) helps us measure good, average, and poor performance referring to specific job-related behaviours. Depending on the performance dimension, its uses differ. For example, for a marketing person, customer relations and knowledge about market intelligence could be the important

Table 3.2 *Mixed standard scale*

Please indicate whether the individual's performance is better than (+), equal to (0), or worse than (–) each of the following standards:

1.	________	Generally agrees and cooperates with others (equal to: in COOPERATION)
2.	________	Lacks supervisory skills and poorly handles employee-related issues (worse than: in LEADERSHIP)
3.	________	Makes use of good judgement while solving problems and provides useful alternatives (equal to: in PROBLEM SOLVING)
4.	________	Highly cooperative and also motivates others to feel cooperative while doing jobs (better than: in COOPERATION)
5.	________	Not so good at solving problems, giving judgements, and anticipating potential difficulties (worse than: in PROBLEM SOLVING)
6.	________	Effectively directs, coordinates, and motivates employees to deliver their best (better than: in LEADERSHIP)
7.	________	Displays skills in supervising, encouraging productivity, quality, and development of employees (equal to: in LEADERSHIP)
8.	________	Displays defensive attitude towards others while executing the job (worse than: in COOPERATION)
9.	________	Anticipates problems and trouble-shoots the problems proactively (better than: in PROBLEM SOLVLING)

performance dimensions. But in the case of a finance manager, such performance dimensions vary. MSS primarily focus on mapping the concrete observable job-related behaviours, based on which simple judgements of performance management–related issues can be made. The unique feature of MSS is that it measures performance-based examples of behaviour from three dimensions, that is, good, average, and poor. Thus, each performance dimension has three statements whereas MSS needs nine statements: three for each of the statement to measure effective or ineffective job-related performance behaviours. For getting better results, MSS is randomly mixed as it substantially reduces the rater errors.

This method, therefore, evaluates traits with three specific descriptions of each trait. These descriptions indicate performance levels conforming to each trait. Questions are randomly arranged deliberately to prevent any rating bias. Characteristically, therefore, this scale is essentially a trait approach to performance appraisal, where measurement is done on the basis of comparison in three dimensions, indicating better than, equal to, or worse than to measure the level of performance. An example of a mixed standard scale is given in Table 3.2.

Behavioural Checklist Method

Under this method, the rater checks the standard behavioural statements indicating some of the performance dimensions. This method is perhaps the oldest technique of performance appraisal, but rating being two-dimensional, somewhat like yes/no, its reliability and validity is often questioned. It is more applicable to map the employees' developmental needs. When it is used to describe the behaviour of the subordinates, rather than rating, the results are better. It is a major operational difficulty to develop the proper instruments and to relate the same to the employees' performance criteria. A behavioural statement may indicate both the effective or ineffective job-related behaviours. Let us examine the following randomly chosen behavioural statements:

- Attends to customers' complaints after logging the complaints.
- Talks to the employees when they are agitated.
- Always prefers those job assignments that provide learning opportunities.
- Takes decisions only after facts and figures are gathered.
- Never manipulates company's information to woo customers.
- Plans before starting of a job.
- Prioritizes work assignments based on the boss's mandates.

THE 360-DEGREE APPRAISALS

This appraisal method is now largely in use throughout the world. It requires performance feedback from all important stakeholders of the organization, such as the ratee himself, his superiors, peers, other team members, customers, and suppliers. Apart from its effectiveness in reporting performance, this method also ensures total employee involvement (TEI) and employee empowerment. It reduces the error of a subjective evaluation system in an organization.

The 360-degree Feedback

Suman Dubey, General Manager (Operations) in a KPO outfit, knew he was a demanding boss. During a 360-degree feedback from his subordinates, he was in for a shock. The subordinates did not stop at saying he was a hard taskmaster, they even called him a 'cold and uncaring individual'. Dubey was dumbfounded when he realized that not appreciating people and not tempering his criticism were having a rundown effect on his subordinates. Today, he says, 'When people are doing well, I take care to tell them about it. I am more open in my discussions. The results have been amazing: Team work is up and lead times are down.'

Ms Subha, Head of Human Resources at a call centre, was surprised to know that colleagues thought she had no sense of humour. She'd been one of the first people to laugh at herself in college. Her rueful reaction to this feedback was, 'I do have a sense of humour but, evidently, I've become very good at hiding it. I guess that needs to change.'

These two are examples of people who have been affected by 360-degree feedback. Also known as multi-rater feedback, full-circle appraisal, and group performance review, this feedback system has today become a very popular tool for employee appraisal worldwide. It involves collecting feedback on an individual's behaviour and the impact of that behaviour from his boss, colleagues, and fellow members of project teams, internal and external consultants/customers, and direct reports.

However, 360-degree can be considered in an organization only when the following are true for an organization:

- The organization is not able to meet challenges that come its way because of increased competition or global expansion.
- People in the organization feel the need to change their behaviour to combat increasing competition and to progress in their careers, but are unsure about what and how to change.

- There is no formal system in place through which people receive information on what others think about their behaviour.

The 360-degree feedback is not a package that can be delivered by a given date; it is a process that needs to be implemented in steps. Before implementing the 360-degree feedback, it should be designed to support a corporate strategy or goal.

- Every employee should understand what it is and how it works.
- Employee development should be high on your company's agenda, and employees should believe that the organization and manager would support feedback processes.
- Sufficient resources should be available to ensure that the integrity level of the process is high.
- The staff should be trained in the process.
- Employees must trust that the information would be used for developmental purposes and should be willing to receive and give feedback.

Most companies implement the 360-degree feedback in stages. It is a good idea to start with a small group of employees, using them as a tool to gain maximum value from the total experience. Apart from performance appraisal, the 360-degree feedback is also used to bring cultural change in the organizations and for organizational development.

POTENTIAL APPRAISAL

The potential appraisal is a future-oriented appraisal to measure the potentiality of an employee for future higher positions. It helps in succession planning and is a holistic approach to study wholesome qualities of an employee with a given intellect, personality, and character. Industry practices apply two widely used approaches for potential appraisal, that is, helicopter and whole person qualities. The helicopter method tries to measure the potentiality of a person on large as well as specific issues. The whole person qualities method measures the wholesome qualities/potentialities of a person with a given set of variables. Potential appraisal data is extremely useful for career planning, as the latent abilities of an individual can be captured and matched with the future role and responsibilities. However, in India, we do not have documented practices on potential appraisal in the corporate world. Potential appraisal is carried out using methods such as self-appraisals, peer ratings, management by objectives (MBO), psychometric tests, simulation exercises, case analyses, and leadership exercises.

As this appraisal process identifies the hidden talents and skills of a person, which even the person may not know, we also call it future-oriented appraisal. Some organizations, however, consider potential appraisal as an integral part of performance appraisal. The obvious justification here is using the results of potential appraisal to review the future performance standards, and also to use such inputs for succession planning. Despite such practices, we need to appreciate the differences between the two. For example, in performance appraisal, the criterion used is the achievement of assigned goals; on the other hand in potential appraisal, based on the current level of performances, employees' skills are assessed to understand whether such skills can make some major differences in future job roles and responsibilities.

Using a structured potential appraisal form, we can judge the potentiality of an employee. The appraisal form in such cases needs to cover the following important areas:

- Indication of improved performance areas.
- Degree of accomplishments of the present target.
- Overall performance rating of employees.

- Areas of development for skills, knowledge, competencies, and qualities.
- Possible steps taken by the employee to improve performance and career development .
- Training requirements for the employee.
- Process of updating knowledge on the job- and subject-related areas.

Overall rating of employees is done on critical behavioural characteristics such as decision making, sense of independence, job confidence, ability to handle stress, interpersonal skills, leadership ability, level of motivation, ability to handle conflict, etc.

Techniques of Potential Appraisal

Techniques of potential appraisal are decided by the organizations. However, using a single technique may not always be reliable. Some of the techniques of potential appraisal are as follows:

- Self-appraisals
- Peer appraisals
- Superior appraisals
- MBO
- Psychological and psychometric tests
- Management games such as role playing
- Leadership exercises, etc.

Self-appraisal requires the employees to give their own performance feedback. Employees autonomously rate their own performance on various parameters, spell out their training needs, if necessary, talk about their degree of accomplishment, strengths, and weaknesses, and so on. While filling the performance format, employees need to be honest, objective, nurture positive attitude, cover each and every aspect of performance, and seek future responsibilities. Other approaches such as peer appraisals, superior appraisals, and MBO have already been discussed. The other methods have been covered in the chapter on Performance Management Research.

COMPONENTS OF THE APPRAISAL FORMAT

We cannot have an appraisal format that can address all performance requirements. However, any generic appraisal format essentially contains key performance areas (KPAs), a self-appraisal, a performance analysis, performance ratings, and counselling components. Essentially, the appraisal format needs to aligned with the objectives of the performance appraisal system, and generate information on all the important aspects, mentioned above. We have already appended one standard performance appraisal format at the end of this chapter.

DIMENSION OF PERSONAL ATTRIBUTES

In performance appraisal, we measure many generic qualities and attributes of an individual performer, while we account for the achievement of targets. While the achievement of targets is measurable and traceable, attributes, traits, and other general qualities are difficult to assess, unless its exact

Table 3.3 *Personal and demonstrated personality traits*

Personal Qualities	Demonstrated Performance Qualities
Adaptability: Ability to adjust with new or changing situations or persons. *Appearance and bearing:* Possess good bearing and appearance. *Decisiveness:* Ability to quickly decide. Dependability: Ability to consistently accomplish allocated jobs autonomously. *Drive and determination:* Ability to vigorously and resolutely execute a job. Ingenuity: Ability to creatively solve unforeseen problems. *Initiative:* Ability to take action independently. *Integrity:* Ability to honestly perform in all dealings. *Loyalty:* Ability to be faithful and willing to support all stakeholders of the organizations. *Maturity:* Ability to balance the situation befitting with the age and seniority. *Stamina:* Ability to sustain stress and strain and perform successfully. *Tenacity:* Ability to face the odds and difficulties. *Verbal expression:* Ability to communicate with clarity. *Written expression:* Ability to communicate in writing with clarity.	*Professional knowledge:* Ability to apply professional knowledge and achieve the highest standard of performance. *Administration:* Ability to optimize resources. Responsibility for staff development: Ability to develop people through training. *Foresight:* Ability to plan beyond present needs. *Delegation:* Ability to feel responsible and exercise guidance and supervision to people down the hierarchy. *Motivation:* Ability to feel self-motivated and motivate people down the line and exert the desired results. *Morale:* Ability to sustain morale both for self and for others down the line. *Control:* Ability to exert control over people down the line and gain their confidence.

Source: Adapted from Monga (1983).

understanding is spelt out to the assessors. It is for this reason that we need to understand the meaning of personal qualities and the demonstrated performance qualities. In line with Monga (1983), we can draw such a list of personal qualities and demonstrate them as in Table 3.3.

BIASES IN PERFORMANCE APPRAISAL

In organizations, performance appraisal often suffers from the crisis of errors or biases. Such errors or biases can be primarily attributed to the lack of objectivity of the raters or the assessors. Organizations need to reduce such errors, else the purpose of performance appraisal gets defeated. Broadly, we can categorize performance errors/biases as follows:

- The halo effect and horn effect.
- Leniency error (loose rater).
- The error of strictness (tight rater).
- The central tendency error.
- The recency effect.
- The contrast error.
- The similarity (similar-to-me) effect.

The Halo and Horn Effect

Solomonson and Lance (1997) defined the halo effect as 'the influence of a rater's general impression on ratings of specific ratee qualities'. In other words, the rater gives the subordinates good grades although the performances are not at the expected level. Here raters get influenced by one or the other qualities of the ratee, even when his/her performances are not up to the mark. For example, less absenteeism, timely attendance, and obedience of a particular ratee may influence the raters to give high performance score, irrespective of the level of actual performance. Often personal likings or dislikings of the raters overlook the poor performances. Lefkowitz's (2000) studies found that positive regard for subordinates relates to higher halo effect.

Horn effect is the opposite of halo effect. Here the rater rates the ratee poor despite the ratee's higher level of performance. It means that because of the rater's perceived negativity of any behavioural traits, the ratee scores poor in the performance appraisal, irrespective of their level of performances. Uyargil (1994) proposed some solutions to reduce the halo and horn effects in performance appraisals, such as raters' training and directing raters' to provide some proof of events, that justify his/her high or poor rating.

The Leniency Error

This common appraisal error occurs when the appraisers feel scared of their strenuous relationship with the subordinates for giving poor rating. Such fear propels them to give a high rating, which causes leniency error. Jawahar and Williams' (1997) study indicated that performance rating for pay raises or promotions are more prone to leniency error. However, performance ratings for employees' development and feedback are less likely to suffer from leniency error. Raters who are more prone to leniency error are known as loose raters.

The Error of Strictness

This type of error is just the opposite of leniency error. Here the raters are known as tight raters, as they always rate performances of the subordinates poorly. Often such types of raters pre-decide the rating score, for example, a maximum of 80 per cent for top performers, between 70 per cent and 80 per cent for very good performers, between 60 per cent and 70 per cent for good performers, and so on. Based on such pre-decided rating scores, they rate their subordinates. According to Kaynak et al. (2005), such raters suffer from the problems of losing their positions when employees get the highest rating. Also they try to show that they are the best.

The Central Tendency Error

Some raters instead of over (lenient) or under (strictness) rating give an average score to all performers, despite actual performance variations. They prefer to rate the employees in the middle of the scale. According to Dessler (2000), such errors occur as the rater is less acquainted with the ratees, and giving an average score is the best option to commit any judgemental mistake. Also these types of raters often believe performance appraisal is a waste of time; hence, the average rating is the best bet.

The Recency Effect

Most of the organizations carry out the performance evaluation function annually or biannually. Such long time gaps between appraisals create the problems, as the rater looses performance-related information. The rater then tries to find information directly related to the value of performance. In this process, the rater gets more inclined to the ratee's latest behaviour irrespective of their actual performances. This ultimately leads to errors due to recency effect. Such errors can be minimized by keeping an ongoing record of performance, and accounting the same for the whole performance period. It is also important to remember that some ratees deliberately perform very high with the approaching of the appraisal time, to get the benefit of high rating for the errors due to recency effect.

The Contrast Error

Objective performance rating is possible when the rating is done based on the pre-decided established standards. However, often the rater rates the employees' performance in relation to other employees, forgetting the established performance standards. In this process, the contrast errors occur. Here the performance score or the appraisal grade of the ratee gets affected with the rating of the other, who has been rated just before. Uyargil (1994) recommends a random appraisal of employees to avoid such errors. It means that instead of assessing employees in the same nature of jobs and grades sequentially, to avoid the contrast error, the assessors may assess employees simultaneously, picking them from different groups or clusters.

The Similarity Effect

While assessing the performance of the ratees, often the appraisers suffer from the propensity of overrating those ratees who are similar to them in terms of personality, behaviour, or background (Pulakos and Wexley, 1983). Some ratees may deliberately induce the raters to commit this type of error, aping their behaviours, tastes, and preferences. Their demonstration pleases the raters and consequently they get the best rating. Raters training can reduce such performance rating bias.

Whatever may be the nature of performance bias or errors, it is difficult to eliminate the same altogether; however, it is possible to minimize it. Accordingly, organizations need to adopt a suitable line of actions to minimize the performance bias or performance rating errors.

REDUCING PERFORMANCE ERRORS

We have already explained a different nature of performance bias and errors. To reduce such errors, organizations adopt various alternative forms of performance assessments, such as direct observations, open-ended questions, essays, consolidation of views from multiple raters, and so on. Such measures improve the reliability of standard tests mentioned earlier. Various studies indicate that training can substantially reduce the rating errors. Studies by Latham, Wexley, and Purcell (1975), Jaeger and Busch (1984), and Pulakos (1986) could authenticate it. Training programmes for the raters focus on familiarization with the measures, making the raters understand the sequence of operations, and the process of interpreting the normative data.

Another approach to reduce the performance rating errors is the selection of appropriate judges/raters. Hambleton and Powel (1983) recommended certain criteria for the selection of performance judges/raters. These are considerations of demographic variables, forming the panel of raters with the representation of experts and people from the interest groups, etc.

Organizations also make use of statistical techniques to measure the degree of performance bias/ rating errors. Rater effect is measured computing the difference between a rater's average with the average of all ratings. When the rater effect is zero, we consider non-existence of systematic bias in the performance scores. Other statistical techniques to measure the performance errors/bias recommended by Houston, Raymond, and Svec (1991) are least squares regression, weighted least squares regression, and the imputation of the missing data. Ordinary least squares regression fits where the observed rating is viewed as the sum of the candidate's true ability, a rater effect, and random error. Weighted least squares regression is used where each rater's score is weighted by a measure of the rater's consistency. Finally, imputation of missing data method is appropriate where actual data of the performers could not be evaluated. The imputation approach is most appropriate when each rater evaluates only a few candidates. The weighted regression approach is most appropriate when variations are expected in rater reliability.

DIAGNOSING POOR PERFORMANCE

To fix the problem of poor performance in organizations, we need to diagnose the causes. Poor performance may be either for lack of ability or for poor motivation level. Incorrect diagnoses of poor performance can lead to problems, as based on these organizations initiate corrective actions. Suppose poor performance of an individual employee has been diagnosed as 'lack of effort', against the real issue of 'lack of ability', and you as his/her manager now exerts pressure to perform. Such wrong diagnoses and initiations of corrective action can only aggravate the problems. 'Lack of ability' to perform is traceable with the following points:

- Difficult tasks.
- Low aptitude, skill, and knowledge of employees.
- Lack of improvement opportunities over time.

To enhance the ability employee performance, organizations carry out series of actions:

- Taking stock of the existing resource support, and wherever necessary giving such support.
- Providing additional training.
- Considering redeployment (shifting the employee to a new job in an of area interest).
- Finally, even if it does not work, getting rid of the employees.

IMPROVING MOTIVATION

Poor performance of employees may be attributed to low motivation. In such cases, organizations need to take appropriate actions such as inculcating a motivating work environment, mutual setting of performance goals, support for performance improvement, and instituting the provisions for performance feedback. With all these, organizations can create a performance improvement plan for employees. Typical performance improvement plans, among others, again require mutual discussion and agreement between the employees and their managers. Once this is achieved, 80 per cent of the performance improvement plan can be materialized, as employees with their participation enhance their commitment to improve the performance. All the causes of poor performance are intertwined; hence, solving one problem leads to the solution of another problem. Let us take the example of low morale and motivation.

This problem, when it interferes with the performance of employees, can be avoided to a great extent by involving employees in the goal setting process.

SUMMARY

Performance appraisal reinforces the human resource management function in an organization. In this era of technological change and global competitiveness, organizations are constantly required to renew and update the skill of their people or else they are likely to encounter the problem of manpower obsolescence, which among others, will call for frequent downsizing or rightsizing. While performance appraisal updates organizations to take a stock on their skill inventories, training helps to address the skill gap. Performance appraisal as a process serves both the administrative and the developmental purposes of organizational decision making. Important HR decisions, such as promotion, transfer, termination, compensation aspects, etc., are categorized under an administrative category. Developmental decisions pertain to improve and develop the employees' performance, focussing on need-based training, and other employee developmental programmes.

We have various traditional and modern tools for performance appraisals. In this chapter, we have discussed all these. Organizations can make best use of all these methods to measure the performance of their employees. As no single technique can be the panacea to measure all types of performance, also a single measurement cannot truly unearth the performance issues, it is always recommended to use multi-rating approach. In this chapter, we have also discussed issues to correct the performance problems of employees recommending methods such as motivation and participation of employees in the goal setting process.

KEY WORDS

Developmental Needs of Performance Appraisal—Individual employees' development through training and other competency development initiatives that contribute to improve the future performance of employees. Individual development is facilitated by the performance feedback. Appraisal feedback becomes the basis for discussion on the strengths and weaknesses of employees and accordingly focus can be given on the performance improvement.

Performance Goals—Organizations set the performance goals through the job description and structure the same through mutual discussion and acceptance both by the managers and the employees. While job description sets the basis, the performance premise is set by the business goals of the organizations.

Intuitive Approach—This approach rates employees' performance based on their perception and external behaviour.

Trait Approach—This approach requires evaluation of employees' performance based on the observed dimensions of personality, integrity, honesty, dependability, and punctuality.

Mixed Standard Scale (MSS)—Mixed standard scale (MSS) helps us measure good, average, and poor performance referring to specific job-related behaviours. Depending on the performance dimension, its uses differ. For example, for a marketing person, customer relations and knowledge about market intelligence could be the important performance dimensions.

Group Appraisal Method—This is an evaluation of an employee by multiple judges. The immediate supervisor of the employee and a few others discuss the performance standards and then evaluate the performance of the employee. The greatest advantage of this method is that it is relatively free from bias even though it is time consuming.

GENERAL REVIEW QUESTIONS

1. Define performance appraisal. Briefly state its importance and objectives. What are the steps you would like to follow for appraising the performance of a managerial employee?
2. What is the different performance appraisal systems followed in an organization? Select at least five methods and briefly discuss their strengths and weaknesses.
3. A traditional performance appraisal system emphasizes on assessing the individual performance as an isolated factor. Briefly discuss the newer techniques of performance appraisal, critically reviewing the shortcomings of traditional systems.
4. Discuss the effectiveness of MBO and BARS in a performance appraisal. Develop KRAs for an HR manager and identify five important performance criteria for assessing the performance on a six-point behaviourally anchored rating scale.
5. Critically review the performance appraisal system in India. Elaborate your answer visiting at least two organizations.
6. Develop a standard performance appraisal form for supervisors in an organization, selecting at least 10 factors for review. Recommend your proposed development plans for such supervisors based on your review.
7. Explain different types of biases in performance appraisal. How can such biases be reduced?
8. Short Notes
   (a) Human asset accounting method
   (b) Assessment centre method
   (c) Field review
   (d) Critical incident method
   (e) Key performance areas

CRITICAL REVIEW QUESTION

9. A traditional performance appraisal cannot help an organization measure the potentiality of employees. These seriously impede the succession planning and the future career development of employees. Visit an organization which successfully manages a potential appraisal system and develops a critical report about its effectiveness in the said organization.

Exhibit 3.1 *Managerial appraisal review form*

Appraisal Period: From **To:**

I. Personal Data:

Name	**Designation**	**Grade**
Personal No. **Date of Birth**	**Department**	**Division**

Academic Qualifications	Years of Experience in Present Organization
Professional Qualifications	
Professional Membership	Outside Present Organization
Date of Retirement	Date of Last Promotion
II. Appraisal	

II. A. Important Points

1. Assess the employee on his performance in his present position only.
2. Try not to allow personal prejudices influence your appraisal. The rating should be as objective as possible.
3. Assess the ratee on his performance during the whole year. Do not allow isolated incidents or recent instances to bias your assessment.
4. Assess each factor independently, uninfluenced by the rating on the other factors.
5. Assess the ratee on all factors.
6. The rater and reviewer must initial in ink in the box against the most appropriate rating in each case.
7. All entries in this form should be handwritten and legible.

II. B. General Performance Factors

Please initial in the box against the appropriate rating.

Factors	Rater	Reviewer		Degree
1. *Knowledge of the Job* All round knowledge of the job including concepts and techniques required and their application; know-how of the latest trends, developments, and innovations in the field of work.			Excellent	Exceptional mastery of all phases of work. Has up to date knowledge of his field.
			Good	Thorough knowledge of the job.
			Satisfactory	Adequate knowledge of the job for the position he is occupying.
			Unsatisfactory	Poor knowledge of his job.
2. *Planning of Work* Scheduling of one's assignments in order to meet deadlines; setting of well-defined targets; concentration on task priorities; ability to anticipate problems and take corrective action.			Excellent	Highly effective in setting goals and prioritizing them. Anticipates problems and takes corrective action.
			Good	Effective in meeting tough deadlines most of the time.
			Satisfactory	Usually effective in meeting routine schedules.

			Unsatisfactory	Is indifferent to planning and cannot meet deadlines.
3. *Abilities to Achieve Results* Utilization and productivity of subordinates and resources; target achievement; follow-up system and coordination with departments; coping with sustained work pressures; quick response to special jobs without letting routine matters suffer; keeping superiors and subordinates informed about relevant jobs, problems, and results.			Excellent	Highly effective in organizing resources and getting extraordinary results.
			Good	Achieves superior results and is able to withstand work pressures and crises.
			Satisfactory	Achieves normal results expected of him through good organization and follow-up.
			Unsatisfactory	Does not use available resources; does not achieve expected results.
4. *Sense or Responsibility* Ability to handle given assignments independently or with minimum supervision; degree of chasing or control required from superiors; setting of self targets and their completion; seeking information on problems; willingness to take a decision or do a job without passing the buck.			Excellence	Very high sense of responsibility; can handle assignments independently; displays rate initiative and drive.
			Good	Is willing to shoulder greater responsibilities than the job demands; displays considerable initiative.
			Satisfactory	Takes on responsibilities of his job and copes with routine problems. Takes routine decisions.
			Unsatisfactory	Does assigned tasks reluctantly; requires constant direction and supervision.

5. *Maintaining Discipline* Sense of organizational discipline and ability to maintain it in the work force; punctuality; on-the-job presence; setting of personal example to subordinates; firmness in dealings with subordinates; standards of cleanness, safety, and housekeeping in the work place; willingness to accept the consequence of unpleasant decisions made by superiors.			Excellent	Maintains high standards or organizational discipline and sets personal examples to his men.
			Good	Achieves above average standards of discipline, safety, and housekeeping; is committed to decisions of superiors.
			Satisfactory	Meets and maintains expected standards of discipline and punctuality.
			Unsatisfactory	Is not punctual and is noted for unscheduled absences; talks loosely about superiors.
6. *Getting Along with People* Clarity and effectiveness in communicating with superiors, peers, and subordinates; handling of conflicts, levels of maturity in dealing with bosses and peers, ability to take feedback and correct oneself; skill in influencing others without arousing antagonism; caring attitude towards colleges and subordinates.			Excellent	Has a marked ability for fruitful interaction with people.
			Good	Is highly effective in understanding, relating, and communicating with people.
			Satisfactory	Has the ability to communicate with people and influence them for good performance.
			Unsatisfactory	Finds it difficult to relate with bosses, peers, or subordinates.

7. *Teamwork and Cooperation* Ability to work with colleagues, peers, and other departments; kind of participation in meetings; degree of involvement in team project; willingness to share one's resources with others in the department if needed; seeking and offering peer assistance; degree of sensitivity to group feelings and response.			Excellent	Highly productive and successful in working with colleagues and peers.
			Good	Positive participation and integration with team.
			Satisfactory	Adequate commitment and contribution to team efforts. Notable peer collaboration.
			Unsatisfactory	Does not function as a team member. Goes all out for himself. Tends to disrupt rather than contribute to team efforts.
8. *Identification with the Company* Sense of identification with the company's values and interests; concern for satisfaction of clients/ customers' needs; pursuit of excellence in performance; concern for cost reduction through optimum utilization of men, materials, or equipment; concern for preservation of company's property.			Excellent	Thoroughly identifies himself with the company's values and interests and transmits them to peers and subordinates.
			Good	Is involved with and loyal to the company's interests; has a high sense of belongingness to the company.
			Satisfactory	Shows necessary concern for company's values and interests.
			Unsatisfactory	Low commitment to company's interests. Talks loosely about the company and has no belongingness to it.
9. *Development of Subordinates* Ability to guide subordinates in their work assignments; delegation of work; steps taken for training and development of subordinates; ability to get them to accept the challenge of higher responsibilities or targets.			Excellent	Gives very high priority to development of subordinates.

			Good	Takes positive steps for subordinate development such as training and job enrichment/enlargement.
			Satisfactory	Shows concern for development of subordinates; is able to motivate them.
			Unsatisfactory	Has no interest in the development of his subordinates.
10. *Approach to Problem Solving* Ability to seek alternative ways to solve a problem or meet a deadline within the rules of the company; flexible and practical approach; ability to cope with unusual problems and situations; generation of original ideas and enduring solutions to problems.			Excellent	Is extremely resourceful and has practical and original skills to solve problems.
			Good	Is flexible in approach and successful in finding solutions to many unusual problems.
			Satisfactory	Is able to find solutions to routine problems; is receptive to new ideas
			Unsatisfactory	Is upset when problems come; fails to solve them.

III. A. Training Plans

Please tick below selectively, the type of training courses that you think will help improve the ratee's performance.

1. Technical (please specify the area)
2. Functional (please specify the area)
3. Computers
4. Management Training
   (a) General management programmes
   (b) Total quality management
   (c) Problem solving skills
   (d) Communications skills

(e) Leadership skills
(f) Interpersonal/behavioural skills
(g) Value engineering
5. Any other (please specify)

III. B. Development Plans

What are your plans to develop the ratee (e.g., special assignments and increased responsibility)?

I have seen my performance appraisal for the year...... and it has been discussed with me with respect to my performance and development plans.

Date................... **Signature of the Ratee**

IV. Checklist of Observable Behaviour

Please go through each of the items listed below. Whenever the item description distinctly tallies with the observable behaviour in the ratee, tick in the column marked 'Yes'. If it is not so, please tick in the column marked 'No'. This checklist is not an assessment of performance. It is used for developmental purposes.

Sl. No.	Description	Yes	No
1.	Pay attention to documentation. Is systematic in record keeping for future references.		
2.	Is clear and concise in written communication.		
3.	Has the capacity for self-analysis and correction of his weaknesses.		
4.	Has the aptitude for systematic and methodical work. Is patient with minute details.		
5.	Makes positive attempts to update himself in his professional field and learns new things.		
6.	Does not accept substandard work.		
7.	Does not lose heart in spite of failures or setbacks.		
8.	Has a sense of humour.		
9.	Promotes healthy industrial relations in his department or work place.		
10.	Is skilled in organizing complex activities.		
11.	Is trustworthy. Does not let down colleagues for personal gain.		
12.	Has the courage of his convictions. Expresses dissent when he is convinced of a different approach to the task or problems.		
13.	Respectful of elders and superiors. Polite. Does not hurt colleagues or subordinates.		
14.	Finds it very easy to get to know people and get along with them.		
15.	Clear in his verbal communication. Is seldom misunderstood. Can convey his thoughts precisely and clearly.		

V. Confidential Rating of Overall Performance

Please initial in any one of the following:	
The individual has achieved an exceptionally high standard of performance. In significant areas of responsibility, he has exceeded expected standards. Performance is consistently excellent.	Outstanding
The standard of performance has been consistently above aggregate; and in several areas, responsibilities were discharged so as to merit favourable comments rather than mere satisfaction.	Superior
The individual has performed well by and large and to the satisfaction of his superior.	Satisfactory
Not up to the minimum requirements of the position.	Unsatisfactory

This employee has worked under my supervision.

From ____________

To____________

Signature of the Rater Date:____________
Designation
Department

Signature of the Reviewing Authority Date:____________
Designation
Department

Exhibit 3.2 *Strengths and weaknesses of different performance appraisal methods*

Methods	Strengths	Weaknesses
Appraisal by objectives (MBO etc.)	It provides a quantitative measurement of performance that is verifiable. Quantification of performance being objective, subjectivity in analyses can be avoided.	Appraisal being result oriented, it is not suitable for determining the potential.
	Weakness performance area can be quickly identified, thus it provides a meaningful basis for improving the performance.	Individual performance area being different, it does not facilitate peer comparison.
Graphic rating	It is a simple and popular method.	Highly subjective and unreliable.
	It facilitates peer comparison, therefore, it provides an objective basis for decision on remuneration, rewards, and promotion.	Being subjective, weighting of factors may be necessary for improving the quality of analysis.
	Certain common criteria may be provided for improving the quality of comparison.	It does not provide facility for feedback and employee development.

Exhibit 3.2 *(continued)*

Methods	Strengths	Weaknesses
Essay type	Its proper use can provide quality information which can help in taking meaningful decisions for placement, promotion, and development.	It requires good writing ability. Appraisers should have the power to take mature judgements. Being subjective, inter-employee comparison is difficult.
Critical incidents method	Being highly objective, it provides factual data on employee's performance and behaviour.	Since performance is analysed on incidents, it tends to be fragmentary.
	Usually helps in improving the communication and development of employees.	It cannot be a method independent of evaluation.
	It is useful as a supportive evaluation.	It does not provide any basis for comparison.
Forced distribution	It is free from any bias and is uniform in standards.	It cannot be an independent method of appraisal. It is better used as a control instrument. Not suitable for communication and employee development.
Straight ranking method	It is simple and helps in taking decisions on salary progression and promotion.	It does not provide feedback and also cannot be used for large groups and interdepartmental comparisons.

Exhibit 3.3 *Behaviourally anchored rating scale*

Guide to Performance Appraisal					
Assessment Criteria	**A**	**B**	**C**	**D**	**E**
Quality	Leaps tall buildings in a single bound	Must take a running start to leap over tall buildings	Can only leap over a building with no spire	Needs some improvements	Cannot recognize building at all, must less jump
Timeliness	Is faster than a speeding bullet	Is as fast as a speeding bullet	Not as fast as a speeding bullet	Would you believe a slow bullet?	Wounds self with bullet
Initiative	Is stronger than a locomotive	Is stronger than a bull elephant	Is stronger than a bull	Shoots the bull	Smells like a bull
Adaptability	Walks on water consistently	Walks on water in emergencies	Washes with water	Drinks water	Passes water in emergencies
Communication	Talks with God	Talks with the Angel	Talks with himself	Argues with himself	Loses the arguments

Exhibit 3.4 *Typical potential appraisal form*

Appraisal of Potential 2009–2010

Employee Name:______________________________

Department:______________________________

Job Title:______________________________

Immediate Reporting Boss:______________________________

Please complete the following appraisal of potential for your employees. This appraisal focusses on those tasks or responsibilities which are beyond the scope of their assigned performance roles. In other words, this appraisal can track the extent of employees' capability in delivering at the 'exceeds expectation level'. While appraising the potential of employees, it is necessary to examine the management by objective concepts, and accordingly focus on the following assessment areas:

- Determine results expected in the coming year
- Determine proposed target dates
- Establish target dates
- Analyse previous years' goals and objectives
- Establish new goals for the next year

Apart from capturing the above information to assess the potentiality of employees, it is also necessary to discuss the assessment results with the concerned employees.

Please examine the following questionnaire template and based on your perception, identify what skills, knowledge, talents, and qualities must be reinforced for improving the potentialities of your employees.

To what extent the concerned employee tries to achieve excellence in his/her work and prepare himself/herself for more responsibility?	
Based on your assessment, what development programmes would you recommend for the employee?	
What should be the next desired level position for the employee?	
What specific performance results impress you to recommend such a position?	
Do you think such performance results are better than the level of standards in comparable positions?	
Describe how well performance results were achieved compared to the standards of the job position.	
Critically evaluate the methods and the approaches followed by the employee while doing the job. (Particularly examine the outcome or effect of his/her performance results, such as is he/she more autocratic in getting the work done by the people reporting to him? Are his/her subordinates executing the job in good spirits? What is the motivation level of subordinates?)	
In which performance areas do you feel the employee should improve?	

Exhibit 3.5 *A simple MBO appraisal form*

Name		**Job/Role**	**Date**
Key job area	Objective/target to be achieved	What data is needed for performance indicators?	What training/learning needs may be needed?
1.			
2.			
3.			
4.			
5.			
Progress Review Dates			
Notes on Achievements/Progress (at date)			

REFERENCES

Bhattacharyya, D.K. (2007), *Human Resource Research Methods* (New Delhi: Oxford University Press).

Casio, W.F. (1995), *Managing Human Resources,* 4th edition (New York: McGraw-Hill).

Craig, S.E., R.W. Beatty and L.S. Baird (1986), 'Creating a Performance Management System', *Training and Development Journal*, April issue: 38–42; May issue: 74–79.

Dessler, Garry (2000), *Human Resource Management* (New Jersey, NJ: Prentice-Hall).

Drucker, P.F. (1954), *Practice of Management* (New York, NY: Harper).

Einstein, W.O. and J. LeMere-Labonte (1989), 'Performance Appraisal: Dilemma or Desire?', *Sam Advanced Management Journal*, 54(2): 26–30.

Fisher, C.D., C.F. Schoenfeldt and J.B. Shaw (1997), *Performance Appraisal: Human Resource Management*, 3rd edition (Boston, MA: Houghton Mifflin).

Hambleton, R.K. and S. Powell (1983), 'A framework for Viewing the Process of Standard Setting', *Evaluation and the Health Professions*, 6(1): 3–24.

Houston, W.M., M.R. Raymond and J.C. Svec (1991), 'Adjustments for Rater Effects', *Applied Psychological Measurement*, 15(4): 409–21.

Hurley, Simon (1998), 'Application of Team-Based 360° Feedback Systems', *Team Performance Management*, 4(5): 202–10.

Jaeger, R.M. and J.C. Busch (1984), 'The Effects of a Delphi Modification of the Angoff-Jaeger Standard Setting Procedure on Standards Recommended for the National Teacher Examination' (paper presented at the annual meeting of the National Council on Measurement in Education, New Orleans, LA).

Jawahar, I.M. and C.R. Williams (1997), 'Where All the Children Are Above Average: The Performance Appraisal Purpose Affect', *Personnel Psychology*, 50: 905–25.

Kaynak, H. (2003), 'The Relationship between Total Quality Management Practices and Their Effects on Firm Performance', *Journal of Operations Management*, 21: 405–35.

Latham, G.P. and Kenneth N. Wexley (1977), 'Behavioural Observation Scales for Performance Appraisal Purposes', *Personnel Psychology*, 30(2): 255–68.

Latham, G. P., K.N. Wexley and E.D. Purcell, 1975, 'Training Managers to Minimize Rating Errors in the Observation of Behavior', *Journal of Applied Psychology*, 60, 550–555.

Lefkowitz, J. (2000), 'The Role of Interpersonal Affective Regard in Supervisory Performance Ratings: A Literature Review and Proposed Causal Model', *Journal of Occupational & Organizational Psychology*, 73: 67–85.

Lepsinger, R. and D. Lucia (1998), 'Creating Champions for 360 Degree Feedback', *Training and Development*, (February) 52: 49–52.

Mathis, R.L. and J.H. Jackson (1994), *Human Resource Management* (Min/St. Paul, MN: West Publishing).

Monga, M.L. (1983), *Management of Performance Appraisal* (Mumbai: Himalaya Publishing House).

Patten, T.H., Jr (1982), *A Manager's Guide to Performance Appraisal* (London: Free Press).

Pulakos, E.D. (1986), 'The Development of Training Programs to Increase Accuracy on Different Rating Forms', *Organizational Behavior and Human Decision Processes*, 38: 76–91.

Pulakos, Elaine D. and Kenneth N. Wexley (1983), 'The Relationship among Perceptual Similarity, Sex, and Performance Ratings in Manager-Subordinate Dyads', *Academy of Management Journal*, 26(1): 129–39.

Sackett, P.R. (1987), 'Assessment Centres and Content Validity: Some Neglected Issues', *Personnel Psychology*, 40, 13–25.

Schuler, R.S. (1995), *Managing Human Resources* (St. Paul, MN: West Publishing Company).

Solomonson A. and C. Lance (1997), 'Examination of the Relationship between True Halo and Halo Effort in Performance Ratings', *Journal of Academic Applied Psychology*, 82(5): 665–74.

Thornton, G.C. (1992), *Assessment Centers in Human Resource Management.* Reading, MA: Addison-Wesley.

Thorton, G., III (1998), 'Psychometric Properties of Self-Appraisal of Job Performance', *Personal Psychology*, 33(2): 263–71.

Tracey, W.R. (1998), *The Human Resources Glossary* (Washington, DC: St. Lucie Press).

Uyargil, C. (2004), 'Yetkinliklere Dayal nsan Kaynaklar Yönetimi – E itim Notlar, Tükiye Bankalar Birli i Kütüphanesi, Istanbul, Turkey.

Williams, R. (1988), *Performance Management* (London: Thomson Learning Press).

FURTHER READING

Bernardin, H.J. and R.W. Beatty (1984), *Performance Appraisal: Assessing Human Behavior at Work* (Boston, MA: Kent Publishing Company).

Bernardin, H.J. and E.C. Pence (1980), 'Effects of Rater Training: Creating New Response Sets and Decreasing Accuracy', *Journal of Applied Psychology*, 65: 60–66.

Boland, Tony and Alan Fowler (2000), 'A Systems Perspective of Performance Management in Public Sector Organizations', *The International Journal of Public Sector Management*, 13(5): 417–30.

Burke, R.J. (1978), 'Characteristics of Effective Employee Performance Reviews and Development Interviews: Replication and Extension', *Personnel Psychology*, 31: 903–19.

Dearborn, D.C. and H.A. Simon (1958), 'Selective Perception: A Note on the Departmental Identification of Executives', *Sociometry* (June): 140–48.

Grote, D. (1996), *The Complete Guide to Performance Appraisal* (New York, NY: American Management Association).

Keany, T. and A. Mcgann (1975), 'A Comparison of Behavioral Expectation Scales and Graphic

Rating Scales', *Journal of Applied Psychology*, 60: 695–703.

Landy, F.J. and J.L. Farr (1983), *The Measurement of Work Performance: Methods, Theory and Applications* (New York, NY: Academic Press).

Meyer, H.H., E. Kay and R.P. French (1965), 'Split Roles in Performance Appraisal', *Harvard Business Review*, 65(1): 123–29.

Nisbett, R.E. and T.D. Wilson (1977). 'The Halo Effect: Evidence for the Unconscious Alteration of Judgments', *Journal of Personality and Social Psychology*, 35: 450–56.

Oberg, W. (1972), 'Make Performance Appraisal Relevant', *Harvard Business Review* (January–February): 61–67.

Rao, T.V. (1985), *Performance Appraisal Theory and Practice* (New Delhi: Vikas Publishing House).

Reilly, R.R. and McGourty (1998), *Performance Appraisal in Team Setting* (San Francisco, CA: Jossey-Bass).

CASE STUDY—1

Training Milieu

Veriphone India in Bangalore is a software development company that has a turnover of Rs 200 crore. It employs 400 persons.

The company is professionally managed. The management team is headed by a young dynamic Managing Director. He expects performance of high order at every level and more so at the supervisory and managerial levels. However, the junior level vacancies are filled up by different types of trainees in the company.

The company offers a 1 year training scheme for fresh computer engineers. During the first 6 months of the training, the trainees are exposed to different functional areas. This is considered to be the core training for this category of trainees. By the end of the training, the trainees are identified for placement against the available or projected vacancies. Then, further training in the next quarter is planned according to individual placement requirements. During the last quarter, the training will be on-the-job. The trainee is required to perform the jobs expected of him after he is placed there.

The training scheme is broadly structured keeping in mind the training requirements of computer engineering graduates. The company has a reasonably good system of manpower planning. The intake of trainees is generally planned on the basis of project requirements.

Mr Anuvab Rao joined the company in the year 1999 after his B. Tech. degree from a reputed institute. He was taken as a trainee against a projected vacancy in the CAD/CAM division.

In Veriphone, the areas of interest for a trainee in CAD/CAM are few. Moreover, since Mr Anuvab Rao specialized in CAD/CAM in his B. Tech., his training was planned for the first 3 months only. Thereafter, he was put for on-the-job training in the CAD/CAM department. He took interest and showed enthusiasm in his work there. The report from his divisional head was quite satisfactory.

The performance of the trainee is normally reviewed once at the end of every quarter. During this review, the training manager personally talks to the trainees about their progress, strengths, and shortcomings.

At the end of the second quarter, the training manager called Mr Rao for his performance review. He appreciated his good performance and told him to keep it up. A month later, Mr Rao met the training manager. He requested that his training period be curtailed to 7 months and that he be absorbed as a regular computer engineer. He argued that he had been performing like a regular employee in the department for the last one quarter. As such, there was no justification for him to be put on the training any more. Further, he indicated that by doing so, he could be more effective in the department as a regular engineer. He would gain seniority as well as some monetary benefits as the regular employees were eligible for many allowances, such as conveyance, dearness, house rent, education, and so on, which was a substantial amount compared to the stipend paid to him as a trainee.

The training manager turned down his request and informed him that it was not the practice of the company to do so. He told him that any good performance or contribution made by the trainees during the training period would be duly rewarded at the time of placement on completion of 1 year of training. Further, he told him that it would set a wrong precedence. Often some trainees were put on the job much earlier than the normal period of three quarters for several reasons.

Thereafter, Mr Rao's behaviour in the department became different. His changed attitude did not receive any attention in the initial period. However, by the end of third quarter, his behaviour had become erratic and unacceptable. When he was asked by the division head to attend to a particular task, he replied that he was still a trainee and such tasks should not be assigned to a trainee. According to him, those jobs were meant to be attended by full-time employees and not by trainees.

The divisional head of CAD/CAM division complained to the training manager of Mr Rao's behaviour and he was summoned by the training manager. During the discussions, Mr Rao complained that while all the remaining trainees were having a comfortable time as trainees, he was the only one who was put to a lot of stress and strain; the department was expecting too much from him. He felt that he should be duly rewarded for such hard work; otherwise, it was not appropriate to expect similar work output from him.

The training manager tried to convince him again that he should not concentrate on rewards and that as he was a trainee, his sole concern should be to learn as much as possible to improve his abilities. He advised him that he should have a long-term perspective rather than such a narrow-minded approach. He also informed him that his good performance would be taken into account when the right occasion arose. He warned him that he was exhibiting a negative attitude. His demand for earlier placement was illogical and that he should forget this as he had already completed 8 months and had to wait only for 4 months. He advised Mr Rao that the career of an individual had to be seen on a long-term perspective and that he should not resort to such child-like behaviour as it would affect his career and image building in the company.

Mr Rao apparently seemed to have been convinced by the assurance given by the training manager and remained passive for some time. However, when the feedback was sought after a month, the report stated that he had become more troublesome. He was called again for a counselling session and was given two weeks time to show improvement. At the end of those two weeks, the training manager met the CAD/CAM division head to have a discussion about Mr Rao. It was decided that he be given a warning letter as per the practice of the company, and accordingly, he was issued one.

This further aggravated the situation rather than bringing any improvement. He felt offended and retaliated by thoroughly disobeying any instruction given to him. This deteriorated the situation more and the relationship between the division head of the department and the trainee was seriously affected.

In case of rupture of a relationship, normally the practice was to shift the trainee from the department where he was not getting along well to some other department so that he would be tried and could have another lease for striking a better rapport. But unfortunately, in the case of Mr Rao, there was no other department to which he could be transferred, since that was the only department where his specialization could have been put to proper use. By the time he completed his training, he turned out to be one who was not at all acceptable in the department for placement as his behaviour and involvement were lacking. In view of this, the divisional head recommended that he be taken out of that department. When Mr Rao got information about it, he was thoroughly depressed.

One of the primary objectives of the training department is to recruit graduates who have good potentials and train them to be 'effective' persons, in different departments. They are taken after a rigorous selection process that includes a written test, a preliminary, and a final interview. During the training period, their aptitudes, strengths, and weaknesses are identified.

Their placements in departments are decided primarily on the basis of their overall effectiveness. Here is a case of a person who was hardworking in the beginning but turned out to be a failure at the end. The training manager was conscious of this serious lapse and was not inclined to recommend his termination. But at the same time it was difficult to retain a person whose track record was not satisfactory. He still felt that a fresh look be given to this case but he was unable to find a way out. He was then faced with the dilemma whether or not to terminate Mr Rao's services.

Questions:

1. Where did the things go wrong?
2. Who is responsible for this episode?
3. Should the training manager concede to his demand for appropriate placement?
4. What are the open options for the training manager other than the termination of Mr Rao's services?
5. Did the divisional head of CAD/CAM handle the trainee properly? How could he have put Mr Rao back onto the right track?

CASE STUDY—2

Aligning Performance Management with Employee Development

The knowledge-intensive IT-enabled service (ITeS) organizations in India, which primarily serve the international clients, could realize, in a competitive market, that the survival mantra is to exceed the customers' expectations. Among others, it requires people to develop their competencies, renewing their knowledge and skills. In ITeS, skill and knowledge life cycles are short and unless it is constantly renewed, people become redundant. Replacing people with the hiring of new skill sets is not only expensive but also at times raises performance questions. New hires take time to deliver the results, and the opportunity costs in the process get increased.

Realizing such operational difficulties and cost over-runs, the management decided the introduction of personal development programmes for employees known as 'SHARP EDGE'. Every employee gets the performance feedback in a quarterly performance review meeting with their seniors, who explain the changing skill sets in their verticals and how they can develop such skill-sets with in-house training supports. The performance review meeting among others also highlights on their skill compatibility based on the degree of interchangeability. 'SHARP EDGE' programmes are integrated with the long-term business needs of the organization, and allow credit points to the employees who acquire the new skill sets. Learning or acquisition of skills could only be established when employees obtain an external certification after in-house learning and implement successfully their learned knowledge in their changing work process. Credit points help the employees in career advancements and pay rise in annual performance reviews.

Institutionalizing the 'SHARP EDGE' helped the company retain the manpower and substantially reduce the costs of manpower redundancies. Over and above, the company could stay ahead in competition.

Question: Identify a similar software for e-performance management and mention its features and operational details, including the benefits that the user organization can derive from it.

CHAPTER 4

Performance Management Review

Learning Objectives

After reading this chapter, you will be able to understand:

- Definition and concept of performance review
- Different aspects of employee development through performance review
- Different types of performance review
- Concept of performance review meeting
- Different steps in performance review
- Benefits of performance review
- Structured performance review process
- Performance counselling
- Different phases of performance counselling

Rationalizing Performance Review Through Forced Ranking

To make the performance review process compatible with the organizational requirements, we often make use of forced ranking. As performance assessment tool, forced ranking can only be effective when employees and the organizations understand each other. Many organizations use forced ranking as a reengineering tool, particularly for right-sizing employees. Obviously for this reason, forced ranking is misconstrued. It is recommended to use forced ranking as a performance review tool only when organizations deliver results above the industry standard. It, therefore, facilitates reaching the exceeded expectation levels of performance. In reality, forced ranking calls for continuous performance improvement, and in that way discards the traditional performance review process. It resembles Deming's assumption that performance review per se cannot solve the performance problems or improve the performance unless we embrace it as a system. Context and orientation aspects of performance review systems integrate the individual development and the achievement of personal, group, and organizational goals. Wipro, the Indian conglomerate, could embrace such a multidimensional performance review mechanism to achieve the personal, group, and organizational goals. Rather than making performance review process the backbone of compensation reviews, Wipro also emphasizes on the economics of scale. In its true sense, Wipro could embrace the performance review process as a system. Thus, forced ranking per se is not bad; rather, it helps the employees to self-assess where they stand vis-à-vis the best industry performance results.
Adapted from: http://www.gtcs.com

INTRODUCTION

The success of the organization depends on employees' performance and how they develop over the period of their tenure with the organization. Performance reviews can help in developing both the individuals and the organizations. For organization, we do not have any end to the level of excellence. Hence, apparently well-run organizations also need to look at the future and plan for the best performance of employees, so that they cascade to overall organizational performance. To compete, sustain, and grow, the performance review requires the organization and its employees to adapt and adjust to the changing environment of business. In the process, performance review develops organizational capabilities to compete, making available the best-talented people for work. In Chapter 3, we have already elaborated the performance appraisal systems, which is synonymous with the performance review systems. However, the performance appraisal or performance evaluation as a concept is often construed as an in-built critical look to the assessment of employees' performance. Hence, in this chapter we have focussed on performance review, more as a standalone concept, keeping in view the industry practices. Various performance measurement tools discussed in Chapter 3, therefore, have not been repeated here.

It is often debated as to whether the term 'performance reviews' should be used. It is rather better to use the term 'performance previews'. Performance previews do not look back but forward. Employees' performances are noted but on real-time basis. Performance previews do not just look into the behaviour, but also into the future that must occur before the performance happens. Performance previews' premise is that the performance-related behaviour occurs regularly, rather than as a bi-annual or annual event, as in performance review.

Any organization that subscribes to the concept of performance preview is forward-thinking and focusses on retention of high-performing workers relying on collaborative teamwork. Such organizations focus on coaching and teamwork to achieve synergy. Thus effective performance preview requires coaching, not directing.

A standard performance review is usually done annually in any organization. However, to enforce performance control, often organizations may conduct performance review with less frequency, say, half yearly, quarterly, monthly, and even with an ongoing review system; empowered by a balanced score card or e-performance management systems, it could be even on a daily basis. Such ongoing performance review systems can be better termed as performance preview. It not only gives immediate feedback to the employees, but also reinforces organizational capability to respond to the environmental changes.

For the purpose of this book, however, we have used the terms performance review and performance preview interchangeably.

DEFINITION

Performance review is an ongoing process to document expected results, standards of performance, and evaluation of the employees' performances. Performance review also tracks the progress towards achieving the results, assesses how well the performance results are achieved, provides suggestions, and so also gives the guidelines to follow the suggestions to improve future performances, etc. It is ongoing, as organizations need to remain watchful on workers' performances, rather than focussing only on isolated performance issues. It means, it focusses on the holistic evaluation of performances. Also, the performance review process requires organizations to collect information, and such information gathering cannot be just a one-time affair. Every employee's performance curve goes up and down; hence it cannot be assessed unless it is continuous. The review process involves a formal discussion about an employee's development and performance. It is also known as a planning process, as it involves setting up a plan of action for the next period and reviewing what has been achieved in the last period. Some of the factors considered in performance review are work conduct, key performance indicators, work plans, roles and responsibilities, position descriptions, training/learning, and financial and non-financial compensation. Traditionally, formal performance review is conducted once a year. However, some organizations conduct it on a quarterly or half yearly basis. There may be, however, midterm review in between the formal annual review. Performance review is a two-way process, between the reviewer and the reviewee. Some systems use multiple 'raters', particularly 360-degree systems where managers, subordinates, colleagues, and co-workers provide input to the review process. Most organizations use paper-based systems, although some use computer-based systems. A good performance review system helps both individuals and organizations. Formal reviews should mainly document the decisions and actions that occur on a regular basis. There should be 'no surprises'. A formal discussion should review what both parties have been discussing informally. Therefore, performance review is an analysis of an employee's work habits undertaken at a fixed point of time to determine the degree to which stated objectives and expectations have been reached. Performance review is not a stand-alone process. It encompasses the training and development function while addressing the need for achieving organizational growth.

A comprehensive performance review of any organization focusses on the following aspects of employees' development:

- Developing employees' capabilities to master the job-specific skills.
- Making employees aware of the organizational policies and workplace regulations.
- Helping employees deliver the results meeting the deadlines.
- Culminating the employees' willingness to volunteer for new job responsibilities.
- Developing employees' ability to take an initiative.
- Making employees work well with others.
- Developing employees' communication skills.
- Helping employees master the time-management skills.

Similarly, some of the negative performance factors of employees are also unearthed and appropriate actions are taken by the organizations. Such negative factors are:

- Dissuading employees to frequently remain absent from duties.
- Persuading employees to reduce the absence from workstations, either by leaving the workplace early or by stretching the lunch break.
- Restricting mis-utilization of organizational resources.
- Straightening employees to refrain from misbehaving with others.

On the other hand, the positive effect of performance review in fact can develop employees' problem-solving capabilities, and make them more spontaneous to get the things done and work as a team.

SCOPE OF PERFORMANCE REVIEW

Depending on the nature of the organization, the scope of performance review varies. Commonly, however, the scope of performance review encompasses the following aspects:

- Job performance—Considers meeting goals and developing mutually decided standards.

- Working relationships—This aspect focusses on maintaining professional relationships with co-workers, subordinates, and managers.
- Core job skills—Emphasizes on the normative aspects of job, including its skill and competencies.

Performance review, therefore, tries to address all the above aspects, and in the process ensures organizational effectiveness. However, while we review the performance, it is important to agree on the key performance indicators, the nature of information and its sources to measure the performance indicators, post-review discussions with the employees, the design of need-based training, mentoring, etc.

TYPES OF PERFORMANCE REVIEW

Approaches to performance review widely vary in organizations. Many consider it as an ongoing process, while some organizations consider it as a special event and hence conduct it to achieve some specific purpose.

Probationary review: It is the general trend to hire employees on probationary terms, may be for a period from, 6 months to 1 year, on satisfactory completion of which they are confirmed. It is intended to ensure that employees are the right-fit with the organization in terms of performance; also it facilitates recruitment validation. If the employees are unable to perform up to the expected standards, organizations can persuade them to leave. This process has legal mandates. Probationary review, therefore, assesses employees' performance during their period of probation, based on which they are either confirmed or released from the organizations.

Rehiring review: Often employees may voluntarily leave the job, or organizations to right size, or on poor performance count, may ask them to leave. Even after such employment cessation, employees may be rehired. At this time, organizations make use of the rehiring review. The process in this case is more or less like probationary review, as in this case also rehired employees' performances are reviewed for subsequent confirmation of their employment or termination.

Self-review: Self-review requires employees to review their own performance. The process involves answering certain questionnaire items that is followed by a performance interview. Often a self-review system is integrated with the organizational performance review process, so as to get the right feel about the employees' own performance. In a multi-rating process, this is one of the important areas of review. It helps managers to correctly track the employees' performance and effectively discuss the performance aspects with the employees.

Peer-review: Often peer-review, like the self-review, forms a major part of the normal review process. Employees' self-assessment may not often provide us the right performance picture. This can be better validated by peer-review, i.e., review of their performance by their colleagues. The purpose and sanctity of the performance review process may often get defeated by peer-review, as employees may practise mutual appreciation and make it an issue of bargain.

PERFORMANCE REVIEW MEETING

A performance review meeting takes place between the managers and the employees. In such a meeting, managers assess the performance of the employees, such as the attainment of agreed-upon goals, overcoming difficulties in achieving the goals, if any, etc. Both the managers and the employees work together in such a meeting. Some organizations call it performance appraisal or performance evaluation meeting. The frequency of such a meeting depends on the organizational performance review cycle, which may be half yearly, yearly, or even in shorter time cycle. A meeting in shorter time spans, say monthly or quarterly, enforces performance control, as organizations can understand from beforehand the line of action they need to take or initiate to resolve the problem. Therefore, through comprehensive two-way discussions, the performance review meeting benefits organizations by tracking the performance, documenting the difficulties in performance, initiating the corrective action, and drawing the future mutually agreed performance goals. Also in this process, it helps in identifying employees' developmental needs, and accordingly designing the training and development programmes, so that the organizations remain competitive with knowledge, skill, and competency renewal.

STEPS IN PERFORMANCE REVIEW

Performance review is the most important part of the total performance management system and process. It entails discussions between the managers and the employees to assess the degree of performance achievement, identify the training and development needs, and draw the action plan for future performance improvement. For such an obvious range of activities, the performance review process goes through different stages and in every stage we need to follow certain steps. Such stage-wise steps are documented below.

Before the Performance Review

- Develop the time schedule for performance review and the venue for review discussion. Performance review meeting or discussion essentially should be conducted during the working hours of working days. Many organizations overstretch their performance review meeting and even conduct the same during the weekend breaks, etc.
- Understand the job descriptions of employees to clearly assess the expectations from the employees that were decided during the performance planning.
- Study employees' self-assessment reports.
- Study the supporting documents for employees' performance.
- Make sure that the review meeting maintains two-way communication channel, so that the employees can open up during the review process.
- Advise employees to come prepared with all supporting documents during the review process.

During the Performance Review

- Guide employees with specific feedback on the performance, which helps them to prioritsze with performance goals decided during the performance planning, and to understand the performance area, where they have excelled the expectations or failed to meet them.
- Make sure that the employees are able to share their self-evaluation and understand where they are right or wrong.
- Make employees understand their developmental needs.
- Ensure mutual agreement on setting the targets for future performance improvement.
- Ensure mutual agreement on development goals.
- Provide clarity in explaining the performance review process, answering any question from the employees, if any.

- Understand the degree of organizational support and identify the area, where it went wrong.
- Complete the performance review process, obtaining signature from the employees.

After the Performance Review

- Ensure that the employees get a copy of their performance review report.
- Keep record of the performance review report.

Thus, an effective performance review process requires strict adherence to certain steps at different stages. During the review process, managers need to minimize interruptions, creating a positive and collaborative environment for discussions. Employees should feel enthused and volunteer for participation. The task requires specific managerial skills, such as listening, use of clear and unambiguous language during discussions, positive attitude to answer employees' calls, and finally closing the discussion with a positive node of encouragement.

Despite the above-mentioned structured steps, performance review goes wrong for certain errors, which we have already documented in Chapter 3. Such errors are halo, horns, first impression error, recency, leniency error, severity, central tendency, clone error (when the rater rates high finding compatibility of behaviour and personality in the ratees), and spillover error (propensity to rate lower for poor performance track records during the earlier period). To reduce such performance errors, it is desirable to document the performance rack of employees on a continuous basis, and also advise the employees likewise.

BENEFITS OF PERFORMANCE REVIEW

Performance review *per se* is the important subset of the performance management process. Hence, success of performance management systems and processes highly depends on effective performance review. In fact, designing of effective performance review systems is winning halfway through managing the performance of employees. Some of the important benefits of performance review can be listed as under:

- Helps in strategic improvement of employees' performance.
- Facilitates in compensation design and planning.
- Validates compensation increase or decrease (particularly in cases of incentives, etc.) in employee-specific cases.
- Validates decisions on promotion, demotion, transfer (with or without relocation), etc.
- Helps in identification of training and development needs of employees.
- Helps in employees' career planning and development.
- Helps in succession planning.
- Provides valuable inputs in reviewing HR policies, procedures, and strategies.
- Helps in reviewing the job description.
- Guards against legal battles on employees' claim.
- Keeps check on wrongful HR decisions pertaining to dismissal, demotion, and transfer prejudicing employees' interests.
- Extends support for resource planning for the future.

◎ Gives inputs to competency mapping.

◎ Rationalizes strategy framing for the organization.

With all these benefits, organizations can truly embrace their capability and remain competitive in their respective areas of business. Managers need to make the performance review process as stressless as possible and promote its benefits.

STRUCTURED PERFORMANCE REVIEW PROCESS

Every organization adopts a structured approach to their performance review process. Now it is almost customary for the organizations to start the performance review process with the self-appraisals of employees. Employee self-appraisals are preferably completed 2–3 weeks before the formal performance review process starts. With these inputs, managers initiate the performance review discussions firstly defining the major areas of responsibilities (preferably four to five). To do this, managers can first identify the critical success factors that can address the core job requirements of employees. This can also be done based on the job description. Depending on the identification of major areas of responsibility, evaluation criteria and performance standards are decided. Secondly, performance competencies, skills, and behaviours are documented based on shared understanding. Thirdly, the overall assessments are made and the level of employees' performance is graded as per the performance rating scale. Fourthly, employees' development plans are drawn keeping in view the need for closing the performance gaps, enhancing the job skills and performance plans, as well as employees' career advancement plans, their potentiality exploration, etc. This done, employees' performance goals and expectations for the coming performance cycle is drawn.

Typical formats used for each such area is presented in Exhibits 4.1 and 4.2.

Likewise, for every area of performance review, it is possible for the organization to design the structured format for better documentation of the review results.

Exhibit 4.1 *Major areas of responsibility*

Major areas of responsibilities/goals	Observed achievements and areas for improvement	Outstanding above expectations Meets expectations below Needs improvement

Exhibit 4.2 *Performance competencies and their related skills and behaviours*

Competency areas	Observed competency areas and suggestions for improvement	Outstanding above expectations Meets expectations below Needs improvement
Feel responsible for the jobs: Evident from employees' interest in accurate and timely completion of the assignments, concern for self-achievement of goals and the goals of the department, as well as the organization as a whole. Such competencies are also evident from employees' propensity to effective handling of multiple responsibilities		
Customer focus: Evident from employees' dedication to meet and even exceed the expectations (both explicit and implicit) of internal and external customers, degree of understanding customers' needs beforehand, and gaining the trust and respect		
Problem solving ability and creativity: Evident from employees' ability to identify and analyse the problems, ability to develop alternative and cost-effective solutions, and creative troubleshooting of problems		
Collaboration/teamwork: Evident from employees' ability to maintain harmonious work relationships with all stakeholders, propensity to demand, and share information, positive attitude to share resources, workplace diversity, and show respect for others		
Interpersonal skills: Evident from effective communication to persuade others to get the results, i.e., achievement of goals		

Performance Counselling

It is a process of advising employees, listening to their problems, and enabling them to find satisfactory solutions on their own. Performance counselling as a process helps subordinates to analyse their performance objectively. It helps in identifying training and development needs and also ensures improvement in the future performance of an employee.

Primarily performance counselling attempts to help an employee in the following ways:

- It helps an employee to understand his/her strengths and weaknesses. More effective counselling sessions even enable employees to make their independent SWOT analysis, i.e., strengths, weaknesses, opportunities, and threats.
- Since good performance counselling believes in giving feedback information about the employees' behaviour, hence their performance, it helps in improving the professional and interpersonal competence of employees.
- It helps in setting goals, formulating an action plan for further improvement of employees.
- It helps the employees identify different alternatives for dealing with problems.
- A good performance counselling session being supportive and empathetic, it helps employees feel encouraged to openly discuss their aspirations, conflicts, and problems.

CONDITIONS FOR EFFECTIVE PERFORMANCE COUNSELLING

Conditions for effective performance counselling may be listed as follows:

- A climate of mutual trust, confidence, and openness needs to be ensured at the outset.
- Climate should be such that it can ensure subordinates' free participation in the review process and also in their giving the correct feedback. This is important, as counselling is not a one-way process of communication, rather a two-way traffic.
- The focus of performance counselling is on employee development. Employee development should not be considered isolated from other issues of performance appraisal, i.e., remuneration and rewards, promotion, motivation, etc.

DIFFERENT PHASES OF PERFORMANCE COUNSELLING

There are different phases of the performance counselling processing. They are as mentioned below:

Rapport Building: This is the initial phase of performance counselling. Managers who are entrusted for performance counselling, at this beginning stage, try to gain acceptance, inculcating confidence in the minds of employees whose performance is being reviewed. Without this, employees may not listen and support the counselling process. It requires open and transparent sharing, listening to the problems, and empathy.

Exploration: In this phase, apart from visiting the employees and creating a climate of openness, the counsellors help the employees to understand their SWOT. The success of this phase lies in making the employees discover all these on their own and at the same time initiate remedial measures independently.

Action Planning: Specific plans and actions for the development of employees are identified at this phase of performance counselling. The counsellor helps the employees to implement such action plans for effective results. For making such action plans acceptable, some counsellors prefer to develop the action plans exposing employees to a series of brainstorming sessions. This process enables the employees to develop the action plans independently.

PERFORMANCE COUNSELLING PROCESS

Firstly, the counsellor should be an excellent listener. He should pay attention to the ideas, feelings, and sentiments of the person being counselled. This enables the counsellor to understand and analyse the subordinate's concern. The effectiveness of a performance counselling session, therefore, depends on the efficiency of asking questions. The questions should be framed in such a way that they should try to seek constructive suggestions from the subordinate, should be open-ended and empathetic, but should not be critical or appearing as if the intention of the counsellor is to test or evaluate the subordinate person.

Secondly, the performance-counselling process should ensure communication of feedback to the subordinates in such a manner so as to evoke a constructive response from them. Since, giving a negative feedback is embarrassing, feedback should always be descriptive and non-evaluative. It should be focused on the behavioural attributes rather than on the subordinate himself. Feedback should be made more data based and suggestive. It should be continuous and verifiable.

COUNSELLING INTERVIEW

Before beginning the counselling session, the counsellor needs to study the subordinate's job responsibilities, his education, training and experience, job performance, and his past jobs. He should make adequate planning of the discussion and the issues involved, and determine the developmental need for discussion with the employee.

The interview should be sincere, informal, and friendly. The counsellor should explain the purpose of the discussion to the interviewee and also emphasize on the issue that the interview is essentially a two-way communication. The subordinates should be encouraged to discuss their appraisals. The counsellor should focus on the strong points and encourage the subordinates to suggest their developments. It is essential for the counsellor to reach an agreement on development plans and also to summarize the points discussed in the session at the end of the interview. He should make record of plans mutually agreed upon in the interview. See Exhibit 4.3 for more details.

Exhibit 4.3 *Employee performance review format*

<table>
<tr><th colspan="2">Employee's Name</th><th>Title</th></tr>
<tr><td>Date</td><td>Grade</td><td>Date in current position</td></tr>
<tr><td colspan="3">Major areas of responsibilities:</td></tr>
<tr><td colspan="3">Has there been any change in employee's job during the period of evaluation? Yes/No
If Yes, mention the types of change and the reasons thereof:</td></tr>
<tr><td colspan="3"></td></tr>
<tr><td colspan="3">Evaluation criteria of major areas of responsibilities: Mention the degree of the employee's perfo rmance criteria with respect to the identified factors documented above.</td></tr>
<tr><td colspan="3"></td></tr>
<tr><td colspan="3"></td></tr>
</table>

Evaluation criteria—rating definitions:
Define your five-point rating scale to measure the degree of performance (you may use the following rating scale as reference):
1—Unsatisfactory
2—Below normal
3—Normal and expected
4—Very good
5—Exceptional

Performance factors (indicative list)					
A. Quality of work					
1. What is the quality of the employee's technical skills?	1	2	3	4	5
2. Does the employee maintain awareness of changes in technical areas and respond to those changes?	1	2	3	4	5
3. Does the employee correct errors or question inconsistencies in work assigned?	1	2	3	4	5
4. Does the employee organize work to make the job easier and the supervisor's job easier?	1	2	3	4	5
5. Is the work accurate and timely?	1	2	3	4	5
Rater's comments:					
B. Quantity of work					
1. Does the employee manage work efficiently?	1	2	3	4	5
2. Are speed and consistency of output, time utilization, and results satisfactory?	1	2	3	4	5
Rater's comments:					
C. Interpersonal relationships					
1. How does the employee work with others? Can the employee receive assignments from several people, judge or resolve priorities, and maintain good working relationships with those involved?	1	2	3	4	5
2. Does the employee obtain cooperation from others?	1	2	3	4	5
3. Is help offered to others during slow periods?	1	2	3	4	5
4. How effectively does the employee address and resolve conflict/problem situations with others?	1	2	3	4	5
5. How are dealings with outside contacts handled?	1	2	3	4	5
Rater's comments:					
D. Initiative and self-reliance					
1. Is the employee able to take action without direction, i.e., what is the extent of supervision required?	1	2	3	4	5

2. Does the employee seek out new and better ways of accomplishing a task? Does the employee seek out new responsibilities?	1	2	3	4	5
Rater's comments:					
E. Dependability					
1. Is the employee generally willing to change plans in order to meet deadlines?	1	2	3	4	5
2. Does the employee accomplish all tasks within the proper time frame?	1	2	3	4	5
3. Is work complete and thorough, eliminating the need for close review?	1	2	3	4	5
4. Is closer review of work required during the pressure periods?	1	2	3	4	5
5. How much knowledge of the supervisor's work and department functions does the employee have?	1	2	3	4	5
6. In the supervisor's absence, can this knowledge be applied to ensure that matters are tended to or are referred to the proper person for action?	1	2	3	4	5
7. Are such factors as attendance, punctuality, time off, adherence to institution policies, and procedures satisfactory?	1	2	3	4	5
Rater's comments:					
F. Summary assessment					
Taking all the performance factors and evaluation criteria into consideration and realizing that some of the factors are more significant to acceptable performance than others, how would the employee's overall performance be summarized during this evaluation period?	1	2	3	4	5
Rater's comments:					

Employee input (optional)

Any activities and/or accomplishments completed during the evaluation period that the employee feels were of significant value or beyond the normal scope of regular duties should be described below under column A and commented upon by the supervisor in column B. The employee can also use this space to comment on circumstances that may have affected any of the ratings noted above or for any other comments pertaining to the review.

Activities (A) (Employee)	**Comments (B) (Supervisor)**

Supervisor's comments and recommendation: If applicable, indicate performance areas where improvement is warranted and outline action plans to assist the employee in achieving a higher level of performance. Include specific activities and target dates for accomplishing these objectives. Also include any other comments, positive or negative, which you feel are important:
Supervisor's recommendations for special training courses for employee's development:

Performance review and career counselling performed by:
Supervisor's signature: ____________________
Name: ____________________
Date: ____________________

Employee's signature:
I have/have not discussed my career options. I have reviewed this evaluation and discussed the contents with my supervisor. My signature means that I have been advised of my performance and have been given the opportunity to make comments, but do not necessarily imply agreement with the evaluation or the contents.
Employee's signature: ____________________
Recorded name: ____________________
Date: ____________________

SUMMARY

Performance review is an ongoing process to document expected results, standards of performance, and evaluation of employees' performances. In a competitive world, organizations need to survive and grow through their non-substitutable human resources. Among others, it requires focussing on holistic performance evaluation through a structured review process. One-time annual review of performance is not the solution, as organizations need to track the information and make the review process continuous to enforce the performance control. It not only helps in correcting deviations from the planned goal achievement, but also facilitates in developing the employees who become capable in achieving business results. To make the performance review process effective, it is always desirable to make the review a two-way process, so that employees can share their valuable information that can help in eliminating future performance blocks. Also in the process, the organization can assess the employees' potentiality to enable them to assume the future challenges of the organization. Thus, the comprehensive performance review must focus on developing employees' capabilities to prepare them for both the present and future job roles, and deliver performance results. In this chapter, we have discussed all the important aspects of performance review, such as, definition and concept, aspects of employee development, its types, steps involved, benefits, and the process of counselling.

KEY WORDS

Probationary Review—Probationary review is conducted during the employee's probation period, which may vary from 6 months to 1 year, depending on the organizational practices. It is the usual practice in organizations to confirm employees in their present job, after they successfully complete their period of probation, which is assessed through such a probationary review.

Customer Focus—This is one of the important performance criteria. Employees' customer focus attribute is assessed through the measurement of their dedication to meet and even to exceed the expectations of customers, which may be both implicit and explicit. For employees, customers may be both internal and external. Employees with good customer focus attribute understand the customers' need in advance and enjoy a high degree of trust and respect from the customers.

Action Planning Phase—This is an important phase of performance counselling, when specific plans and actions for the development of employees are identified. The performance counsellor helps the employees to implement such action plans for effective results. Some counsellors develop the action plans to expose employees to a series of brainstorming sessions.

Counselling Interview—Counselling interview is a friendly, informal, and sincere two-way communication process. Although it is a formal process of performance review, an informal environment encourages subordinates to open up and they feel encouraged to discuss their appraisals and about themselves.

GENERAL REVIEW QUESTIONS

1. Discuss the concept of performance review. Is it a better term than performance appraisal? Give justification to your answer.
2. Explain how the performance review process can develop employees.
3. Consider the job of a marketing manager of a growing FMCG organization.

Identify major areas of responsibility and develop the appropriate rating scale to hypothetically rate your employee's performance.

4. Explain the rationality behind considering performance review as an ongoing process.
5. Short Notes:
   (a) Rehiring review
   (b) Problem solving ability
   (c) Performance counselling
   (d) Exploration phase

CRITICAL REVIEW QUESTION

6. Assume you are the CEO of a company that employs a huge number of industrial workers, who are below graduate level and who possess the technical job–specific skills. Your organization is highly technology driven and requires everyone to perform well, keeping pace with the machine cycle time. Any below-the-standard performer can create a total mess in the assembly line production system, as the job remains in each work station for a specific period of time. On the expiry of time schedule, the job reaches to the next workstation, even if it is not fully completed in the earlier workstation. In assembly-line production system, we cannot back track a job; as a result when the job travels through different workstations with incomplete workmanship, the end product fails to conform to the required quality and is rejected. As CEO, you are planning to develop a performance review system for your organization. Suggest which review process you deem fit and why?

FURTHER READING

Bhattacharyya, D.K. (2006), *Human Resource Management,* 2nd edition (New Delhi: Excel Books).

Bhattacharyya, D.K. (2007), *Human Resource Research Methods* (New Delhi: Oxford University Press).

Bhattacharyya, D.K. (2010), *Human Resource Development* (Mumbai: Himalaya Publications).

Campbell, D.J. and C. Lee (1988), 'Self-appraisal in Performance Evaluation: Development versus Evaluation', *Academy of Management Review,* 13: 302–14.

Cardy, R.L. (2003), *Performance Management: Concepts, Skills, and Exercises* (Armonk, NY: M.E. Sharpe, Inc).

Cawley, B.D., L.M. Keeping and P.E. Levy (1998), 'Participation in the Performance Appraisal Process and Employee Reactions: A Meta-analytic Review of Field Investigations', *Journal of Applied Psychology* 83: 615–33.

Gilliland, S.W. and J.C. Langdon (1998), 'Creating Performance Management Systems that Promote Perceptions of Fairness', in James W. Smither (ed), *Performance Appraisal: State of the Art in Practice* (San Francisco, CA: Jossey-Bass).

Grote, D. (1996), *The Complete Guide to Performance Appraisal* (New York, NY: American Management Association).

Hough, L.M., M.A. Keyes and M.D. Dunnette (1983), 'An Evaluation of Three "Alternative" Selection Procedures', *Personnel Psychology*, 36: 261–76.

Locke, E.A. and G.P. Latham (1990), *A Theory of Goal Setting and Task Performance* (Englewood Cliffs, NJ: Prentice-Hall).

Mohrman, A.M., Jr., S.M. Resnick-West and E.E. Lawler, III (1989), *Designing Performance Appraisal Systems: Aligning Appraisals and*

Organizational Realities (San Francisco, CA: Jossey-Bass).

Spencer, L. and S. Spencer (1994), *Competence at Work* (New York, NY: John Wiley).

Schippmann, J.S. (1999), *Strategic Job Modeling: Working at the Core of Integrated Human Resource Systems* (Mahwah, NJ: Lawrence Erlbaum Associates).

CASE STUDY

GLOMA's Performance Review System

Retention of employees has all along been a major problem for Indian pharmaceutical major GLOMA. GLOMA is now an Indian MNC having global business presence, specializing in generic and most popular OTC (over the counter—sold without prescription) medicines. Most of the formulations of GLOMA are patented and cannot be aped by the competitors unless alternative molecules are used. GLOMA's research and development team is highly dedicated and has been all along a prized possession for the competing pharmaceutical companies. Poaching of GLOMA's scientists is rare, unless the scientists themselves volunteer to leave. Mr R.K. Menon, a scientist of international name and fame, heads GLOMA's R&D Division. With a team of 150- strong scientists, Mr Menon is able to introduce new molecules every year to develop new formulations mostly in the generic segment. GLOMA's business strategy is to introduce new drugs for fighting against lifestyle deceases. Also systematically, GLOMA targets to eliminate competitors by introducing cost-effective drugs with high efficacy. Each product manager of GLOMA gets two new products to successfully position in the market, in addition to their existing one. The marketing team puts their concerted effort to target their competitors' weaknesses and demonstrates the potential problems to the physicians. Such unfreezing exercises are done through seminars, personal visits, and workshops in presence of the world-renowned scientist Mr Menon. With this, GLOMA is able to position their new products and consolidate their market share and grow.

For GLOMA, performance review is a continuous process and every time the CEO tracks the performance of core R&D scientists and the marketing team members. A competency-driven performance review system powered by the balanced score card accurately assesses GLOMA's individual and business level performances. The CEO continuously frames the strategies to achieve the results. Of late, he finds that every week scientists are resigning. Exit interviews could only document reasons for leaving as potential health hazards, family encumbrances, and so on. All are trivial and not sustainable, as GLOMA's research unit is world class and free from any danger of health hazard. Also, GLOMA's Employee Services division provides support to every GLOMA team member to the extent of solving problems, such as, children's education, doctors on call, transport facilities inside the estate, etc.

Digging further to the problem of attrition revealed that the real problem lies in GLOMA's performance review systems, which is unidirectional. A fatherly figure like Mr Menon feels that he is able to understand his people better and rates their performances accordingly. Scientists cannot contest Mr Menon, but grapevine information indicated that he often commits spillover error while rating his team members. This resulted to high attrition of those scientists who are presently moderate performers but potentially very good at delivering the results in subsequent performance cycles. Mr Menon is now literally left with a handful of blue-eyed performers. Achieving business goals with these performers is not possible for GLOMA, as it also plays with volume. In the current performance review, the CEO finds to his surprise that the research division could only achieve less than half of the performance targets.

As the Director-HR of GLOMA suggests, how you can resolve this crisis, introducing a new performance review system that can also ensure retention of scientists?

CHAPTER 5

Performance Management Systems

Learning Objectives

After reading this chapter, you will be able to understand:

- Definition, concept, and features of performance management system
- Importance, benefits, and steps of performance management system
- Importance and features of performance management system
- Process of building performance management system
- Dimensions of performance management systems
- Conceptual framework of performance management system
- Performance management system and organizational strategy
- Performance consulting
- Pillars of managing performance
- Performance management theatre
- Annual stock-taking of performance
- E-performance management

Marico's Performance Management

Marico is a leading Indian group in consumer products and services in the global FMCG market. Marico markets well-known brands such as Parachute, Saffola, Sweekar, Hair & Care, Nihar, Shanti, Mediker, Revive, Kaya, Sundari, Aromatic, Fiancee, and HairCode. Marico's brands and their extensions occupy leadership positions with significant market share in most categories—coconut oil, hair oils, post-wash hair care, anti-lice treatment, premium refined edible oils, niche fabric care, etc. Marico is present in the skin care services segment through Kaya Skin Clinics (48 in India and the Middle East), the Sundari range of Spa skin care products (in the USA and other countries), and also through a recently acquired nascent soap franchise (in India and Bangladesh). Products and services in hair care, skin care, and healthy foods. Marico is consistently consolidating its market share in the Indian FMCG market. With its prime brands like Parachute and Saffola, Marico could achieve a 20 per cent growth in its sales revenue. Today Marico has become a conglomerate. All this Marico could achieve because of its strong brand identity and its strategy to add value to existing products and services.

Achieving business results at Marico is strongly supported by its organization structure and performance management system. Marico's organizational structure is flat with only five levels of reporting between the Managing Director and an operator on the shop floor. They believe that a flat structure helps them in being more responsive to the environment while providing enriched roles to the members. The structure clearly defines roles and supporting relationships but is by no means rigid. Keeping in mind the fast and ever changing business environs, Marico's structure is dynamic and constantly evolving. Every management trainee at Marico enjoys the freedom to reach the top of the organization ladder through different options, depending on individual capacity. The human resource management system at Marico emphasizes on strategies to build a stable and high-talent organization. The innovations and the quest for excellence at Marico continue unabated. Even as the success stories continue, the focus from the consumer never shifts.

At Marico you cannot afford to be a non-performer. The organization has an enabling culture to deliver results!

INTRODUCTION

Performance management system (PMS) as a whole is a series of activities consisting of identification of critical performance dimensions, planning of performance, setting of performance goals and objectives, reviewing performance, sharing feedback, and finally developing the future performance through training. PMS, therefore, is a set of tools and techniques to improve the organizational performance. To sustain a competitive advantage, organizations need to recruit the best-fit and at the same time to focus on their continuous development so that they do not become redundant and obsolete in their skills and knowledge. To develop people, it is essential to focus on systematic knowledge and skill renewal through organizational training and development. However, this process must succeed the PMS, as PMS helps in identifying the training needs, based on the performance gaps.

A well-designed PMS ensures organizational sustainability aligning employees' compensation to their level of competency and contribution. PMS provides opportunities for concerted personal development and career growth, bringing all the employees under a single strategic umbrella. It provides equal opportunities to all cross-sections of employees of the organization to freely express themselves under structured conditions. To enable this, it is essential to develop a technology-intensive PMS. Such a system is instrumental in automating the entire range of performance management functions, including systematic appraisals, closing of skill gaps, and managing career and succession plans. Technology-enabled PMS is expected to provide following key benefits:

- Faster time-to-revenue with a powerful, engaged workforce, reducing employee turnover, rewarding star performers, and ensuring that every employee is working toward critical objectives.
- Focussed business agility to respond to competitive threats, duly aligning the workforce to business goals, identifying and closing skill gaps, and creating succession plans for critical roles.
- Reduced risk with simplified management, by reducing business disruptions, competitive threats, non-compliance, litigation, and lost business reputation.

PMS follows the following basic steps to effectively influence individual and team behaviour:

- Identification of behavioural goals
- Measurement of current behaviour

- Performing gap analysis
- Closing the gap
- Monitoring

For many organizations PMS is developed after identifying critical success factors (CSF), key performance indicators (KPI) and balanced scorecard (BSC). A large majority, however, focus on developing a BSC which for them serves as a PMS rather than a mere performance improvement tool.

In the context of the aforementioned organizations, we may define PMS as a balanced set of CSFs and a limited number of KPIs that help in measuring organizational performance. Inadequately designed performance measures, as observed by Neely et al. (1995) give rise to dysfunctional behaviour. Hence effective design of the performance measures through appropriate identification of KPIs is more important for the success of the PMS.

IMPORTANCE OF PMS

A system is a collection of parts (or sub-systems). All sub-systems are integrated into a system to achieve the overall goal of the organization. Organization is a system of people. Systems have inputs, processes, outputs, and outcomes, with continuous feedback among these various parts. Change in any sub-system brings change to the entire system. Within the ambit of such a definition of a system, the performance management process too qualifies as a system. Performance management sub-systems are integrated to accomplish the overall goal of the organization.

Performance management involves thinking through various facets of performance, identifying critical dimensions, planning, reviewing, and developing and enhancing performance and related competencies. It is simple, commonsensical and enjoyable. Therefore, performance management qualifies to be a system, as it is a set of techniques and procedures for improving organizational performance. To sustain competitive advantage, an organization not only requires recruiting the best people but also focusing on their continuous development through an effective PMS. While development of people is possible through ongoing training and development, and skill and knowledge renewal, it must succeed PMS, as PMS, inter alia, establishes the basis for identifying training and development needs.

PMS in organizations are not always very effective due to differences in approach and application. This is evident from various worldwide surveys conducted by Hughes and Watson Wyatt. Major flaws in PMS, as could be identified by these surveys are: lack of focus on performance improvement, ambiguous performance goals, poor feedback mechanism, and poor technology support, etc. All these are attributed to poorly designed PMSs. Often organizations dilute the sanctity of PMS by making it more personal.

FEATURES OF PMS

Performance management is the day-to-day management of the performance of an individual or a work-group, by both the immediate manager and the individual employees themselves. To achieve this, organizations make use of a structured framework with a set of conditions to manage the performance. As all these aspects are part of the system, i.e., sub-systems, performance management process qualifies to be a system. In a globally competitive economy, organizations need to gain competitive advantage by leveraging their non-substitutable resources, that is, the human resources. In view of this, the role of PMS assumes strategic importance. It must uphold its commitment to employee development and mutually agreed performance standards.

In line with Bevan and Thompson (1992), the main features of PMS can be outlined as follows:

Focus on Objective Setting

Objectives are the targets, which an organization sets for its employees. They appear in the form of an action statement which starts with a verb. Overall organizational objectives are decided at the strategic or corporate level. PMS helps percolate these organizational objectives to the employee level and translates them into individual targets.

Systems for Review of Objectives

Through the process of periodic performance review, PMS helps keep track of achievement of objectives. Such a review system largely depends on the type of PMS techniques used by an organization. It may be an age-old Management by Objective (MBO) system or a 360 degree PMS (multidimensional) or a more recent performance tracking technique like the BSC. Review of objectives helps in performance control and initiates steps to correct deviation in performance or to revise the targets.

Developing Personal Improvement Plans

Since PMS helps in individual performance monitoring, it ensures developing of personal improvement plans for the employees. A particular employee may lack in performance or he/she may exceed the given targets. In both the cases, it is important to design the personal improvement plan. While in the first case, it may be important to provide performance counselling, training, and development reinforcement, in the second case, the employee may be motivated further through a proper reward system.

Training and Development

As the focus of PMS is to manage and develop employee performance to sustain competitive advantage of the organization through proper alignment, it helps in identifying training and development needs. This further helps in developing need-based training and in measuring the return on investment (ROI).

Ensuring Formal Appraisal with Feedback

By introducing a formal appraisal system, PMS helps in giving performance feedback to employees. Both negative and positive feedback sensitize employees and help them to objectively analyse their shortfalls and positive aspects. While shortfalls can countered by reinforcement and setting the right direction, positive aspects can be used to leverage further employee development and growth by setting higher individual targets.

Compensation Review

Performance based pay is the prevailing concept. PMS used it in objective designing of compensation packages for employees, thus rewarding good performance and reducing the variable pay (performance linked) of non-performers. This optimizing of the cost of compensation helps the organization to remain competitive.

Developing Competence-based Organizational Capability

Competence based organizational capability helps in appropriate organizational change, keeping pace with competition. It also helps in human resource (HR) planning. PMS through qualitative and quantitative appraisal can assess the prevailing competency level of employees and thus helps in organizational capability review.

PROCESS OF BUILDING PMS

A PMS helps an organization to obtain and analyse relevant performance data in order to track the performance of employees both at the individual and at group level. Individual performances along with the overall performance of the organization help measure the results or the level of achievement of business goals. To do this, we have to first define the performance review process, which follows a combination of numeric and subjective rating approach. A good performance review process assesses employee performance along with the organizational performance. After effective design of the performance review process, it is desirable to decide on the review schedule which may be monthly, bi-monthly, quarterly, six-monthly, or annual. It is always desirable to complete the performance reviews within the pre-decided time schedule. Subsequently it is necessary to develop a system to gather reports and analyse the performance data. Most of the organizations make use of customized software for such purpose. Many software vendors develop their own software for performance review, which they call E-PMS. However, it is advisable to avoid use of generic E-PMS software, as often it may not be in accordance with the organizational needs. For example, effective performance reviews need to capture what is going on in the business, and with the changes in the business need to assess how the existing PMS of the organization needs to be altered or modified. A good performance review process also facilitates objective HR decisions and avoids litigation.

DIMENSIONS OF PMS

Performance is what is expected to be delivered by an individual or a set of individuals within a time frame. Such performance expectation can be stated in terms of results or effort, tasks, and quality, within specified conditions under which it is to be delivered. PMSs have many dimensions as follows:

- Output or result
- Input
- Time
- Focus
- Quality
- Cost

Output or Result Dimensions

Results and outputs are the visible and measurable dimension of performance. These give the status and summary of the finished and semi-finished products and services. They describe the results in terms of the measurable standard, for example, achieving 95 per cent of the standard output in a shop floor engaged in production of plastic moulded rifle butts. Some examples of results and outputs are the number of new customers, cost savings, production targets, sales targets, job accomplishments, meeting deadlines, etc.

Input Dimension

The input dimension consists of tasks and activities accomplished by the individual. Broadly this is concerned with the nature of activities to be undertaken, the time frame, the quality of inputs to be used, etc. Input dimensions of performance can be better managed when the envisaged inputs are correctly used, properly planned and implemented.

Time Dimension

This dimension of performance is defined in terms of time specific tasks, that is, tasks to be performed daily, weekly, monthly, yearly, etc. Here the time factor is important, as achieving the desired performance level within specified time frame is considered to be the target.

Focus Dimension

Focus dimension of performance is measured in terms of the performance focus, which could vary from employee to employee depending on the nature of job responsibilities. For example, an HR executive's performance focus may be defined in terms of reducing the rate of attrition, cost-effective design of compensation, developing employees' competence, etc. Similarly, for a marketing executive, this could be new market development, increasing the sales realization, etc. Thus depending on the nature of job, performance focus may vary.

CONCEPTUAL FRAMEWORK OF PMS

Ferreira and Otley (2005) have defined the conceptual model of PMS. Often we consider this as the generic model, although we have many other contributors. Three areas of this conceptual model are: the focus of PMS, the context of PMS, and the culture of PMS. Integrating the three we get the conceptual model of PMS.

The focus of PMS is to account for the performance of the organization. The accountability for a specific task or job accomplishment relies on the relationship between the supervisors and the employees. It is instrumental in bridging the gap between the PMS objective and the actual performance. Thus, the focus of PMS must ensure that the desired ends are achieved through the chosen means of action. This implies three things. First, the objectives that the organization and its individuals intend to achieve and the means to achieve the same should be clearly stated. Second, care must be taken to involve individuals and the organization in achieving those objectives or goals. Third, all implicit and explicit activities designed to achieve the objectives must be controlled through the PMS. PMS focus must explain the values and the action elements to achieve the objectives (Habermas, 1987; Power and Laughlin, 1996).

Ferreira and Otley (2005) relate the PMS with the context and culture of the organization. Its basic purpose is to account for the information implications within the PMS, degree of its coherence, and the degree of its adaptation to the changes in the organizations. Context indicates the location and nature of the entity (for us it is the organization) to which the PMS relates, while the culture is the beliefs and the norms of the entity and relates to its performance. As contextual and cultural aspects of the organization tend to change with the passage of time, PMS must take these into consideration and make necessary adjustments to cope with such changes.

The PMS conceptual model explains the interdependencies or the interconnectedness of the organization with its individuals, emphasizes on the contextual and cultural aspects of the organization, and gets influenced by the changes in the organization. Aspects of PMS design get moulded with contextual change, that is, the change in the organization. Similarly social and cultural processes also rationalize the PMS design and its conceptual model (Hasselbladh and Kallinikos, 2000).

PMS AND ORGANIZATIONAL STRATEGY

Strategy sets the direction and also defines the scope of an organization. While the direction helps the people working with the organization to channelize their efforts to achieve the common goals, scope limits the activities of the organization to focus such efforts. Both the direction and scope matched with resource allocation help the organization keep pace with the changing environment, and meeting the expectations of different stakeholders. Strategic human resource management (SHRM) is a competency-based approach 'that is tailored to the demands of the business strategy' (Miles and Snow 1984). Also it is the 'pattern of planned human resource activities intended to enable an organization to achieve its goals' (Wright and McMahan 1992).

PMS is one of the most important HR strategy factors. HR strategy factors largely encompass six areas: recruitment and selection, career development, performance appraisal, training and development, compensation designing, and HR planning. Career development and performance appraisal have direct linkage with PMS. While career development considers career mapping, succession planning and management development, and integrating career development with OD initiatives, performance appraisal designs appropriate tools and aligns such appraisal with training needs, promotion, transfer, and relocation.

PMS involves thinking through various facets of performance, identifying critical dimensions of performance, planning, reviewing and developing, and enhancing performance and related competencies.

Thus performance is what is expected to be delivered by an individual or a set of individuals within a time frame. What is expected to be delivered could be stated in terms of results or effort, tasks, and quality, with specification of conditions under which it is to be delivered.

Therefore, PMS reinforces strategic HR management principles as it helps an organization to achieve its strategic intent, that is, goals and objectives by ensuring and developing the desired set of competencies among people in the organization through various strategic interventions, as explained earlier.

ORGANIZATIONAL AND SOCIAL PERSPECTIVES OF PMS

Change is an inevitable part of any system, and as the organization is a system as a whole, it is also susceptible to change. With the globalization and the consequential increase in competition, organizations now derive their unique competitive advantage leveraging their human resources. PMS with a strategic focus make such human resources, as potential source of achieving the business goals. Managing the performance of the people is enforced by organizations through the management of differences among the people. Such differences among the individual employees of the organization in terms of skill, knowledge and competencies, are assessed using various tools such as Myers-Briggs Type Indicator, FIRO-B, and the DISC Behavioural Profile.

Managers also manage performance through appropriate questioning and listening skills. Employees by nature always prefer to have somebody who can indulge them to spell out their problems. They even prefer discussions on their perceived line of actions on the problems and to get the managers' suggestions. Therefore, in order to obtain the expected level of performance from employees, managers too need to show tolerance towards them and allow them to raise questions.

For organizations, effectiveness of PMS also depends on the managers' degree of freedom from bias and assumptions. Human behaviour, and so also the behaviour of managers, is prone to be culturally biased. This also exerts influence during performance evaluation by managers. Organizations, therefore, strategically manage their PMS with standard performance evaluation tools so that managers do not get any opportunity to use bias or hunches while evaluating employees. Standardized PMS enhances the quality of performance and also motivates people to perform better.

From the organizational perspective, PMS is holistic, hence apart from the performance deliverables, PMS focuses on employee development in order to get their agreement on performance standards. In Exhibit, 5.1 we illustrate a typical performance agreement of a hypothetical organization.

Managing the performance variation is also critical and requires special managerial skills. Employees vary in their performance, and proper understanding of such variation makes the process of managing the individual level performance much simpler. With the knowledge of performance variation, managers can customize their approach to performance management and thereby obtain better results.

PERFORMANCE CONSULTING

Performance consulting is a process in which a client and consultant partners to accomplish the strategic outcome of optimizing workplace performance in support of business goals.

-Jim and Dana Robinson (2008)

Exhibit 5.1 *Performance management systems map*

Performance Goals of an Organization/ Specific Business Unit/Work Group/Key Process	Individual Goals/Tasks	Targets and Measures
Contribute to new product development	Manage employees to involve them in new product involvement.	On time job execution Meeting of performance standards Filing of reports on time
	Execute assigned tasks and file reports.	On time job execution Meeting of performance standards Filing of reports on time
Achieve technical effectiveness	Contribute to the improvement of systems.	On time job execution Meeting of performance standards Filing of reports on time
Achieve operational effectiveness	Contribute to the task and administrative roles	On time job execution Meeting of performance standards Filing of reports on time

The terms performance consulting and high performance consulting are used interchangeably. It is a sub-discipline of consulting that focuses on understanding and developing a holistic strategy to positively change the performance. The holistic strategy of performance consulting, apart from performance improvement, also brings positive improvement in the performance introducing the changed measurement strategy, developing employees and also ensuring performance-based employee selection. The idea behind recruiting the right fit is to get the desired performance results, making the employees to work smart. The seminal work of Dana Gaines Robinson and James C. Robinson, used the term performance consulting, specifying the role of performance consultants to partner with the management to identify and achieve performance excellence. The role of performance consultants is just like 'keys and locks'. It means it cannot work unless it fits. Thus, the performance consulting process helps organizations to bring positive change in the work environment.

Performance consulting follows certain defined steps. Being data-driven, performance consulting facilitates people and their performance-related decisions. As a process, it requires the strategic performance-focused approach, aligning people with the organization. Therefore, performance consulting, as a process, focuses on business needs, performance needs, work environment, and capability needs. This has been illustrated in Figure 5.1. There are three types of performance consulting—organizational development, professional development, and personal coaching. Organizational development perspective helps to improve the overall effectiveness of the organization. Professional development emphasizes on the effectiveness of people, and coaching trains people to become more effective both at the personal level and at the level of the workplace.

ROLE OF PERFORMANCE CONSULTANTS

Performance consulting is the transfer of new skills and competencies acquired through on-the-job training, focusing on the performance needs of employees. The idea behind is to improve the overall performance. The responsibilities of performance consultants are illustrated as follows:

- To attain a balance between the needs of the organization and the employees.
- To create synergy and teamwork.
- To identify and solve the problems of the employees.
- To assess and measure the actual performance of the employees.

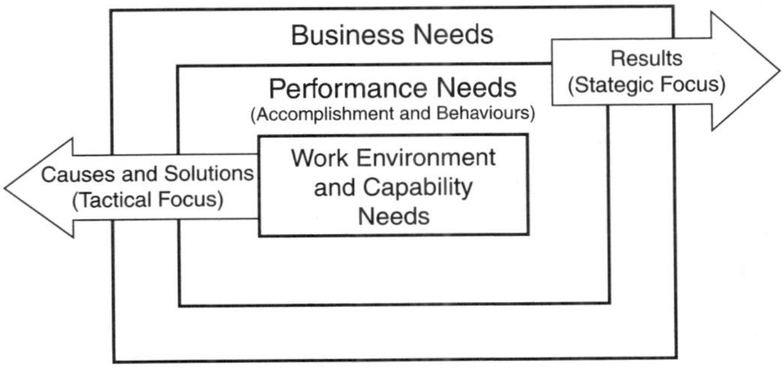

Figure 5.1 *PMS model*

- To identify and improve the internal and external factors affecting the performance of the employees.
- To motivate and support the employees.
- To review and give performance feedback to facilitate performance improvement.

From this list of responsibilities and functions, it is clear that performance consultants in fact become organization partners in facilitating goal achievement.

THE FOUR PILLARS OF PMS

Human resources is the only sustainable competitive advantage for any organization. Effective PMS through the process of HR integration, individually and also in groups, with the organization, ensures its appreciation. Proactive PMS, therefore, makes human resources more valuable, and with renewed knowledge and skill, people become more competent to perform better to perpetuate competitive advantage for the organization. Effective PMS, among others, also requires implementation of proper performance measurement systems, which can successfully track the individual and group level performances. According to Edward E. Lawler III, the four pillars of PMS focus on accomplishing the following:

- Define and agree on what performance the organization needs.
- Guide the development of individuals so that they can acquire the skills and knowledge needed to perform effectively.
- Motivate individuals to perform effectively.
- Provide data about the condition of the organization's human capital.

With these four pillars firmly in place, managers can successfully manage performance, ultimately influencing the company's bottom line and overall success.

Pillar One—Defining Performance: The foundation of PMS is to determine what has to be done and the process of doing the same. This is what we call the stage of 'defining the performance', that is, pillar one of PMS. Clear definition of performance helps employees to focus their efforts, feel motivated and achieve business results. PMS should explicitly identify the objectives and the ways of measuring the objectives.

Pillar Two—Guiding the Development of Individuals: The second pillar of PMS is to develop the knowledge and skills of employees, to enable them to perform better. At the outset this requires managers to identify the required competencies, its availability and lack or gap in employees, and ways of bridging such gaps through employee development. Without this exercise, it is not possible to assess employer's performance delivery.

When a CEO makes his own skill assessment

Michael Dell, founder of Dell Computers, performed his own skill assessment, asking his employees to evaluate him as an executive. Interpreting the results of this survey, Dell realized that he is viewed as impersonal and emotionally detached from the workforce. Dell met his top management team and committed that he would change. Accordingly, Dell continued to change and kept his commitment to give the message to his people that as CEO he also understands the need to meet the skill gap to perform better.

Pillar Three—Managing the Motivation: The third pillar of PMS is motivation. Employees perform only when they feel motivated. It requires direct linking of success to employee-valued rewards. Such rewards, either intrinsic or extrinsic, can motivate employees. Rewards should be adequate enough to make a difference in the minds of the employees.

Pillar Four—Providing Feedback: Effective PMS requires immediate feedback which helps employees understand their mistakes and initiate action to correct them thus avoiding major performance disaster. To perpetuate a continuous ongoing performance feedback process, many organizations make use of computerized or electronic PMS (E-PMS). The E-PMS can keep record of individuals' skill assessment and of all relevant information such as knowledge, competencies, performance goals, personal development requirements, etc. This E-PMS performance database becomes a useful source for employee feedback; it also allows managers to keep track of changes in employee performance over the years.

With these four pillars, PMS become effective in directing, motivating, and teaming up, and enhancing the performance of the organization.

PERFORMANCE MANAGEMENT THEATRE

Effective PMS maximizes organizational performance in core areas, success of which cascades to performance improvement at all the levels of organization. The concept of performance management theatre is based on the premise that communication is the key to any business transaction; therefore, communication plays an important role in employee performance. Thus, good performance precedes effective communication. Organizations need to improve both the internal and external communications to meet customer expectations. Communication performance is defined as performance management theatre. Performance management theatre follows certain stages:

- Auditing of the existing strengths and weaknesses of communication.
- Designing tailor-made communication style compatible with organizational requirements.
- Analysis of existing communication abilities of people using a scoring device, and tracking the changes required to meet customer expectations.
- Designing communication performance development programme.
- Ensuring that employees get trained on communication performance.
- Evaluate post-training employee communication performance against standard scoring.

The term performance management theatre is used, as theatre, per se, is enjoyable and informative, and when used as a tool for training and development, it becomes more effective. Theatrical art improves the communication abilities of people, which can have tremendous value addition to employees' performance delivery.

ANNUAL STOCK-TAKING OF PERFORMANCE

Annual stock-taking of performance is basically a performance audit function, which apart from usual employee evaluations, emphasizes on measuring the proper alignment of performance results with the organizational and employees' growth. For organization stock-taking of performance helps in achieving the goals by optimizing employee performance, duly identifying their strengths and weaknesses. For employees, on the other hand, it helps in providing guidance to perform the jobs and also help in defining the career path. Performance audit is a more holistic term, as it encompasses the examination, operation, and procedures of the management system to assess whether the organization is achieving economy, efficiency, and effectiveness in the employment of available resources.

Most of the organizations frame their own performance audit manual and conduct such audit through their in-house resource pool. For major organizational change and development decisions, however, at times, it may be necessary to hire external experts for decisional accuracy. Often we misconstrue performance audit as performance measurement, but they are different. Performance audit is more holistic than the performance measurement, as the latter is more activity focussed.

E-PERFORMANCE MANAGEMENT

E-performance management is the planning, implementation, and applifcation of information technology in managing the PMS. E-performance management is a part of e-HRM or HR information system (HRIS). Through IT enabled PMS, it is possible to integrate strategies, policies, and practices of the organization with the performance management process. E-performance management is the relational e-HRM function to support business processes. Relational e-HRM functions also facilitate training and recruitment functions of an organization. The other two e-HRM functions are operational and transformational. Operational e-HRM accounts for supporting administrative functions like the payroll, staff inventory, etc. Transformational e-HRM is concerned with strategic HR activities such as knowledge management, etc.

Throughout the world, many vendors provide e-HR solutions, of which e-performance management is a major area. Some vendors, however, specialize in e-performance management solutions. E-PMSs offer flexible, secure, intuitive, paperless, and customizable solutions to align employee goals, objectives, and actions with the overall business strategy of the organization.

Some of the important features of E-PMS are:

- Automates the time-consuming employee performance appraisal process.
- Accommodates any kind and combination of performance measures and KPIs and associates a value to each indicator according to organizational goals and needs.
- Defines performance standards.
- Defines performance indicators.
- Ensures distributed power to employees through empowerment and in the process fosters collaboration among departments.
- Customizes workflow to manage and execute jobs.
- Ensures confidentiality and data security of work process and documents.
- Provides real-time reports of performance evaluation, and other performance-related documents and processes.
- Provides flexible employee reviews to accommodate performance cycle.
- Facilitates performance-based HR decision-making.

E-PMS, therefore, manages the PMS, balancing intuition, innovation, and strategy to achieve excellence in the organization. Thus, E-PMS helps the organization in its growth and development.

PERFORMANCE PRISM

The term 'performance prism' indicates innovative performance measurement systems, like BSC, various business excellence models, six-sigma, stakeholders' value analysis, etc. The word prism implies a refracting transparent medium inclined to some angle. Therefore, performance prism is the measurement system that successfully tracks performance for effective organizational decisions. In our chapter on performance measurement, we have discussed about all the measurement systems, mentioned earlier.

SUMMARY

PMS is a set of techniques and procedures to improve organizational performance. To sustain competitive advantage, an organization not only requires recruiting the best people but also focusing on their continuous development through an effective PMS. While development of people is possible through ongoing training and development and skill and knowledge renewal, it must succeed PMS, as PMS, inter alia, establishes the basis for identifying training and development needs.

A well-designed PMS ensures organizational sustainability aligning employees' compensation to their level of competency and contribution. PMS provides opportunities for concerted personal development and career growth, bringing all the employees under a single strategic umbrella. It provides equal opportunities to all cross-sections of employees of the organization to freely express themselves under the structured conditions. But to do all these, it is essential to develop a technology-intensive PMS It is for this reason that organizations prefer a structured PMS. Such structured PMS can help in building productive and engaged workforce. Moreover, technology-intensive PMS solutions help in automating the entire performance management functions, including systematic appraisals, closing of skill gaps, and managing career and succession plans.

This chapter after defining the concept of PMS explains the benefits and steps, importance of PMS, importance of E-PMS, various dimensions of PMS, and its conceptual framework. Further, the chapter also explains certain terms of PMS, such as performance consulting, four pillars of performance, performance management theatre, annual stock-taking of performance, e-PMS, etc.

KEY WORDS

Time Dimension—This dimension of performance is defined in terms of time specific tasks, viz., daily, weekly, monthly, yearly, etc. Here the time factor is important, as achieving the desired performance level within the time frame is considered as the target.

Performance Management Theatre—The concept of performance management theatre is based on the premise that communication is the key to any business transactions, hence in employee' performance, communication plays the important role

Focus Dimension—Focus dimension of performance is measured in terms of the performance focus, which could be anything, like; HR, marketing, finance, etc. Depending on the organizational practices, performance focus may vary.

Annual Stock-taking of Performance—Annual stock-taking of performance is basically a performance audit function, which apart from usual employee evaluations emphasize on measuring the proper alignment of performance results with the organizational and employees' growth.

GENERAL REVIEW QUESTIONS

1. Define PMS. What are its main features?
2. How can we develop a PMS? How is PMS linked with organizational strategy?
3. Discuss PMS from organizational perspectives. How is it different from social perspectives?
4. Explain the concept of performance consulting. What important roles do the performance consultants play?
5. Explain the concept of performance pillars. How do performance pillars help in managing the performance?
6. Explain how the concept of performance theatre relates to PMS.
7. Short Notes
   (a) E-performance Management
   (b) Pay Review
   (c) Competence-based Capability
   (d) Quality Dimension of PMS

CRITICAL REVIEW QUESTION

8. Explain how different performance dimensions vary with respect to the nature of organization? Give your answer with respect to one FMCG organization and another service sector organization.

REFERENCES

Allen, K. (2004), *Max Weber: A Critical Introduction* (London: Pluto Press).

Bevan, S. and M. Thompson (1992), 'An Overview of Policy and Practice', in S. Bevan and M. Thompson (eds), *Performance Management in the UK: An Analysis of the Issue*, Part one (London: IPM (now IPD)).

Bhattacharyya, D.K. (2007), *Human Resource Research Methods* (New Delhi: Oxford University Press).

Bhattacharyya, D.K. (2009), *Compensation Management* (New Delhi: Oxford University Press).

Bhattacharyya, D.K. (2010), *Cross-cultural Management* (New Delhi: PHI Learning).

Collins, R. (1986), *Max Weber: A Skeleton Theory* (London: Sage).

Ferreira, A. and D. Otley (2005), 'The Design and Use of Management Control Systems: An Extended Framework for Analysis' (Discussion Paper, Lancaster University).

Habermas, J. (1987), *The Theory of Communicative Action Volume 2: The Critique of Functional Reason*, T. McCarthy (transl.) (London: Heinemann).

Hasslebladh, H. and J. Kallinikos (2000), 'The Project of Rationalization: A Critique and Reappraisal of Neo-Institutionalism in Organization Studies', *Organization Studies*, 21(4): 697–720.

Miles, R.H. and C.C. Snow (1984), 'Designing Strategic Human Resource Systems', *Organizational Dynamics*, 13(1): 36–52.

Neely, A.D., M.J. Gregory and K. Platts (1995), 'Performance Measurement System Design: A Literature Review and Research Agenda', *International Journal of Operations and Production Management*, 15(4): 80–116.

Power, M. and R. Laughlin (1996), 'Habermas, Law and Accounting', *Accounting, Organizations and Society*, 21(5): 441–65.

Sanz-valle, R., R. Sabater-Sanchez and A. Aragon-Sanchex (1999), 'Human Resource Management and Business Strategy Links: An Empirical Study', *International Journal of Human Resource Management*, 10(4): 655–71.

Townley, B., D.J. Cooper and L. Oakes (2003), 'Performance Measures and the Rationalization of Organizations', *Organization Studies*, 24(7): 1045–72

Weber, M. (1978), *Economy and Society* (Berkeley, CA: University of California Press).

Wright, P. and G. McMahan (1992), 'Theoretical Perspectives for Strategic Human Resource Management', *Journal of Management*, 18: 295–320.

CASE STUDY

Dabur—The Case of a People Integrated PMS

DABUR is a leading Indian conglomerate having interest in consumer goods, health care, personal care, and foods. With its presence in 1884 onwards, Dabur is now a leading Indian MNC having its presence in 50 countries of the world. Every product division of Dabur is under separate strategic business units, which are grouped under separate product lines. With its vision to dedicate to the health and well being of every household, Dabur always endeavours to provide innovative products to consumers, with professional management approach. Core values of Dabur are ownership, passion for winning, development of people, customer focus, teamwork, innovation, and integrity. With an e-learning programme, known as Employee Orientation on Web for Engagement and Reference (EMPOWER), Dabur today successfully develops its human resources to achieve business results in competition. Realizing the importance of human resources, Dabur focuses on effective PMS, which among others, focuses on nurturing a cohesive work environment, to make people feel the compelling need to perform. The culture is such that employees volunteer to perform. With such a performing work culture, Dabur is able to truly integrate their PMS with the strategies of the organization. True alignment of people with the organization, at Dabur takes place as presented in Figure 5.2

Even though the alignment process of people with the organization at Dabur takes place as per the illustrated model, Dabur adopts the following multi-pronged action plans to make their people truly good performers:

- Career development of employees.
- Career mapping and management development with OD initiatives.
- Delegation and de-centralization
- Identification of employee training needs to be done more frequently and followed more diligently
- Innovativeness and creativity of employees to be given more weightage and proper recognition, and suitably rewarded
- System of flexible rewards and choosing of incentives to be introduced

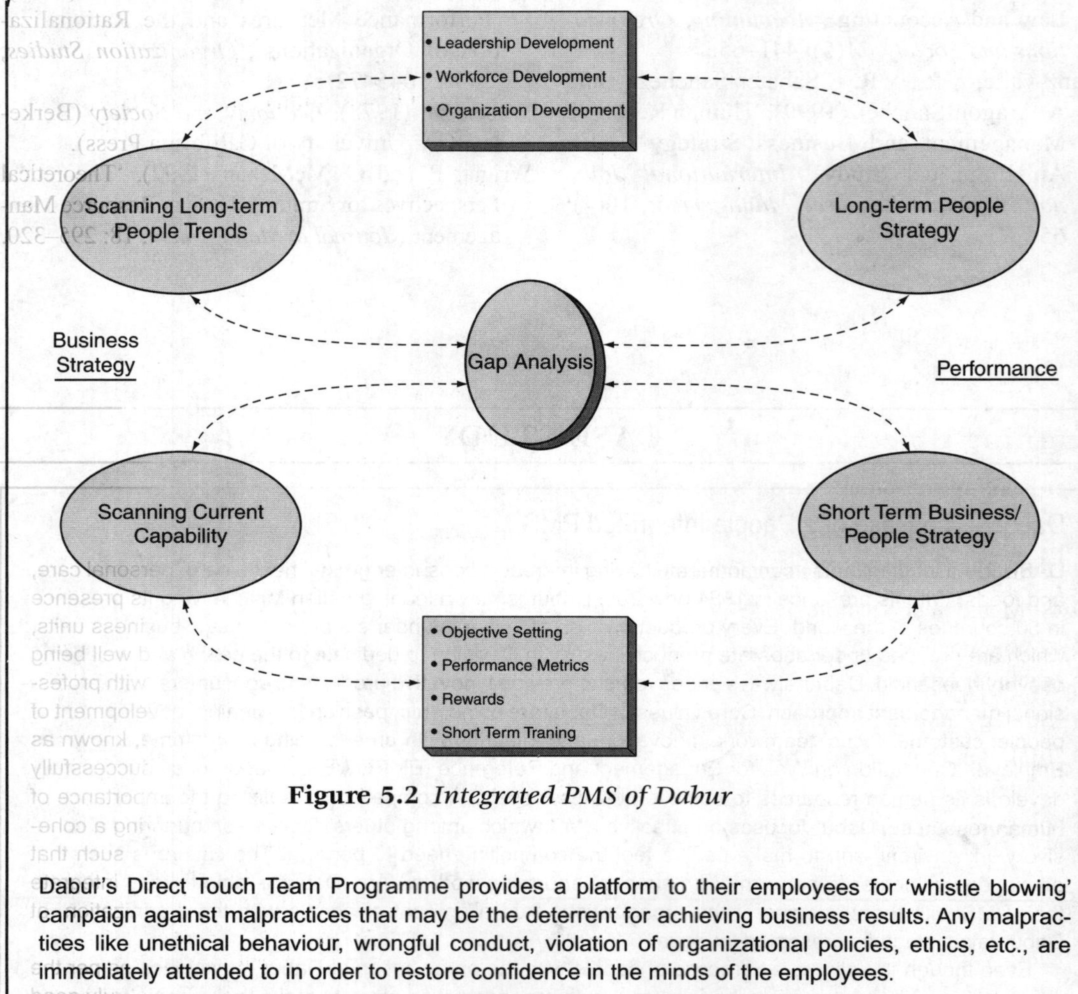

Figure 5.2 *Integrated PMS of Dabur*

Dabur's Direct Touch Team Programme provides a platform to their employees for 'whistle blowing' campaign against malpractices that may be the deterrent for achieving business results. Any malpractices like unethical behaviour, wrongful conduct, violation of organizational policies, ethics, etc., are immediately attended to in order to restore confidence in the minds of the employees.

Questions: Critically evaluate Dabur's approach to align people with the organization.

How can such alignment help Dabur become a good performing organization?

CHAPTER 6

Strategic Performance Management

Learning Objectives

After reading this chapter, you will be able to understand:

- Concept and definition of SPM
- Evolution of SPM and its characteristics
- SPM and generic strategies
- Components of strategic performance management process
- Strategy and performance management cycle
- Link between individual performance and strategy
- Performance and strategy
- Benefits of strategic performance management
- Advantages and disadvantages of strategic performance management
- Strategic performance management and the balanced scorecard
- Strategic performance management and metrics
- Strategic performance management and the environmental threats and risks

Achieving Excellence, Aligning Strategies with the Performance Management Systems

To survive in a competitive world with economic uncertainty and business upheavals, organizations worldwide now focus on achieving excellence, aligning their strategies with the performance management systems. It is now important for the organizations to adopt strategies to achieve their defined goals and objectives. A well-developed strategy map for any organization gives the sense of direction to all cross-sections of organizational members. Linking such strategies with the individual performance goals in the form of KPA (key performance areas) and KRA (key result areas) benefits the organization to reap the competitive advantage through the high performance level of organizational members.

Alignment of strategies with the people working in organizations could be best possible relating processes, systems, and relationships to the performance management systems (PMS) of the organizations. Such strategy aligned PMS facilitates organizations not only to transform the people cascading the strategic objectives; it can also facilitate effective utilization of corporate strategy, and in the process get more from the people. To do this effectively, it is important for the top management of the organizations to be committed and involved with the process, including understanding of organizational vision, mission, strategy, values, and life cycle. Using a balanced scorecard, organizations can pursue their strategy to get unique edge in a competitive market.

Before alignment of strategies with PMS, it is important to identify, analyse, and prioritize the core business processes and key customers. Effective analysis and definition of key customer requirements ensure shortlisting of critical business drivers and measures, which can then be cascaded to individual employees' goals and objectives (against the identified key drivers) and a well-drawn scorecard can provide a measurement tool, using which the company can identify the gaps between their plans and execution. Thus, effective balanced scorecard of any organization should align their strategy with their performance management systems, identifying their business process and definable customer requirements.

Human resource practices of the organizations are also aligned and integrated to business strategy to ensure congruence and synergy within the organization. This requires a systematic and holistic approach in ensuring that business strategy policies for managing human capital are all aligned with baseline targets to all workgroups, teams, and individuals. A strategy-linked incentive system for rewarding performance is used. Team-based rewards are instituted to avoid individual 'free-rider' problems. By doing so, people transformation can truly take place.

Personal scorecard measures and targets must be meaningful and directly related and attributable to each individual employee. Job competencies are integrated into personal scorecards, translating the same into non-financial goals and appropriate standards of behaviour. In the process, personal scorecards can also function as job descriptions and performance contracts.

Thus, strategy alignment and implementation, rather than strategy content, differentiates successful from unsuccessful organizations. Measurement is the key in transforming and maximizing employee performance and productivity.

INTRODUCTION

Performance management systems (PMS) and processes have now become more integrated, continuous, and strategic. Organizations today manage performance through the principle of mutual agreement, i.e., developing the performance goals, based on the business objectives through participative approach. Obviously, it helps in achieving the results, as people feel more committed to deliver. PMS processes further get reinforced with the integration of individual and organizational objectives. People in this process become more self-managed and autonomously focus on self-development to build their capabilities to achieve the results. This process, therefore, makes the traditional command and control redundant. Thus, PMS is essentially a strategic and integrated approach to deliver sustained success to organizations by improving the performance of the people developing the capabilities of teams and individual contributors.

Performance management is strategic as it is concerned with the broader issues facing the business, including its response to the changing environment. Without a strategic approach, in a competitive and ever-changing business environment, organizations cannot achieve its goals and objectives. Various empirical researches could establish that strategic performance management (SPM) could add value for the organizations. However, SPM can have both advantages and disadvantages. Advantages are higher result orientation, better strategic clarity, higher people quality, higher organizational quality, etc. Disadvantages are, however, badly aligned system, low information quality focus on control, too much focus on strategy, etc. Therefore, it can be empirically established that SPM gives more advantages than disadvantages. Thus, SPM is indeed beneficial for organizations.

Particularly in business turbulence, to encounter the problem of increasing number of competitors, changes in the regulatory environment, impact of technology, growing globalization, shifts in customers' behaviour and expectations, and low productivity, SPM can be a great advantage. So also in managing the organizational change, SPM is of great importance. Hoopes and Hale (1999) observed in managing organizational change, it is essential to get into the details of performance activities. Similarly, Martinez (1997), Wall (1998), and Brooks and Weatherston (2000) observed that SPM manages action to deal with the changes. It is for this reason, SPM is defined as a process to steer the organization systematically defining the mission, strategy, and objectives of the organization. Moreover, SPM as a process makes it possible for developing measurable critical success factors and key performance indicators to take corrective actions to keep the organization on track (Waal, 2007). The effectiveness of the process is defined as the achievement of financial as well as non-financial targets, the development of skills and competencies, and the improvement of customer care and process quality (Waal, 2007).

In organizations, SPM is used in numerous ways (Kaplan and Norton, 1996a; Chow et al., 1998; Zairi and Jarrar, 2000; Niven, 2002; Andersen et al., 2006). A tentative list of such usages of SPM can be listed as under:

- To perform health checks throughout the organization.
- To clarify and translate vision into operational strategy.
- To communicate and link strategic objectives and business measures.
- To enhance strategic feedback and learning to use performance levels.
- To conduct detailed operational planning of activities and processes.
- To establish an early warning system through monitoring of key indicators.
- To influence and alter employee behaviour to promote desired changes.

Various research studies indicate that companies who have implemented SPM perform better than companies that do not use SPM.

Strategic performance management practices can churn financial performance and success in organization. Strategic SPM guards the interest of various stakeholders, including the assurance of the interest of the shareholders, and thereby provides the sustainable strategic advantage to the organizations. Business systems and adaptability are the two key areas, which deserve attention to enable strategic SPM to deliver the results. To achieve this, it requires first understanding of the business systems of the organization and subsequently designs their performance management systems from the business perspectives. This is why organizations master the principle of coordination to become aligned, linked, and integrated. Huselid (1995) focused on the linkages between the human resource management systems, corporate strategy, and the performance of the organization. Becker and Huselid (2006) identified the key challenges facing strategic human resources management (SHRM) and discuss several new directions in both scholarship and practice. They argue for a clearer articulation of the link between HR and firm performance and the importance of integrating strategy implementation in this process. They also highlight the importance of a differentiated HR architecture within firms as well as across them.

From the above introductory discussions, therefore, it is clear that SPM can help managers to improve the performance management process in the organization. It facilitates pursuing of human resource strategies and in understanding whether or not the effective use of performance management system can really encourage the desirable work behavior.

DEFINITION

Strategic performance management, sometimes also referred to as corporate performance management or enterprise performance management, is a major focus for many organizations. The main goal of the SPM is to provide clear guidance and help organizations to get results. Particularly, SPM benefits those who already have a performance management strategy and who want to learn about current best practices to improve on it. In our introductory discussions, we have already defined SPM as a process to steer the organization through the systematic definition of mission, strategy, and objectives of the organization, and making these measurable through critical success factors and key performance indicators, in order to take corrective actions to keep the organization on track.

Performance management is strategic because of the following reasons:

- It is strategic—it is about broader issues and long-term goals.
- It is integrated—it links various aspects of the business, employee development, leadership, and coaching principles for both individuals and teams.
- It does focus on performance improvement—this includes both individual performance and team performance that is linked to and in alignment with corporate strategy.
- It embraces employee development—this helps create a culture of competence and accountability.
- It becomes a tool for behaviour modification—individuals are encouraged to behave according to core values and guiding principles, which leads to improve working relationships with each other.

Strategic performance management is the basis for success, especially during these most difficult economic times. It is because now organizations can only achieve success leveraging the potentiality of employees. SPM can make a difference between the success and failure of organizations.

EVOLUTION OF STRATEGIC PERFORMANCE MANAGEMENT

Strategic management, as a separate discipline, has emerged only in the 20th century. It is only at this stage, we have started looking at performance management from strategic viewpoint. Browsing through, it is possible to understand he linkage between the strategic, operational, and the individual level performance management. The chronological evolution of strategic performance management is documented in subsequent paragraphs.

During the 1920s, we used to focus on traditional performance measures, mainly relating it to financial ones. This is particularly tracked to the development of cost accounting during this period. With financial measures only, it was naturally not possible to track holistic performance at the individual, group, and organizational level. With the emergence of the concept of cooperation in 1946, pioneered by the management Guru Peter Drucker, based on his observations with General Motors (1943), the 'management by objective' as a performance management process had development. As we have already explained the concept of 'management by objective' in our introductory chapters, here we are not recapitulating the same. But we can say, with this the concept of strategic performance management matured. Management by objective (MBO) requires organizations to set the goals and objectives at the corporate level and cascade it down to the departmental/divisional goals and objectives and then to individual goals and objectives in the form of key result areas (KRA) or key performance areas (KPA). The entire process can be made participative as in world-renowned organizations like CHEVRON, Wal-Mart, McDonalds, etc.

During the 1950s and 1960s, the concept of strategic planning had emerged. Systematic and analytic framework of strategy formulation with the evidence from the corporate practices as in General Electric, etc. could help us to identify the performance measures with strategic focus. The period thereafter witnessed the extensive use of strategic perspective in managing the performance of the organization. With the advancement of computer integrated management practices, it was gradually possible to track non-financial measures of performance. The concept of critical success factors (CSF), pioneered by John F Rockart (1979) further accentuated the pace of strategic performance management. Today, professionally managed organizations try to integrate performance management into a cycle of planning and measurement stretching from the corporate, through business unit down to the individual level performance agreements and appraisals.

CHARACTERISTICS OF SPM

Some of the characteristic features of SPM are:

- It can ensure that employees get clarity and understand what is expected of them.
- It can improve the skills and ability to deliver on pre-determined expectations.
- It can gain support from management to develop their capacity to meet expectations through given feedback on their performance.
- It can embrace the opportunity to discuss and contribute to individual and team goals and objectives.
- It is also about ensuring that managers themselves are aware of the impact of their own behaviour on the people they lead.

Strategic performance management is about establishing a culture where individuals and groups take responsibility for the continuous improvement of business processes and of their own skills. It focuses on success, behaviour, and sharing expectations. Managers can utilize SPM as a tool to clarify what they expect individuals and teams to accomplish. Individuals and teams communicate effectively with management and with each other about their individual expectations and how they view strategic initiatives and their personal contributions.

Strategic performance management bridges the gap as it interrelates and improves the quality of relationships between managers and individuals, between managers and teams, between members of teams and the introduction of accountability. Expectations are clearly defined through a joint recognition of the requirements for success by both management and the employee. This is critical because today, less than half of all employees truly understand how their actions relate to the success of company initiatives. Most employees don't even know what's expected of them or how the company evaluates their personal contributions.

SPM is important because it plays a pivotal role in any organization's human resource framework. There are clear benefits from managing individual and team performance to achieve organizational objectives. Similarly, compensation in the form of pay, bonuses, stock options, and other benefits can be linked to the achievements of particular goals. A well-designed performance management process stimulates managers to develop high-quality strategic plans, set ambitious targets, and track performance. All these activities help in achieving strategic objectives and consequently sustained value creation.

SPM AND GENERIC STRATEGIES

Michel Porter's (1980) generic strategies are the most commonly identified syndromes in organizations. Organizations worldwide make use of these generic strategies even in managing their performance.

Porter (1980) proposed three generic strategies that can yield competitive advantage, namely cost leadership, product differentiation, and focus. To ensure long-term profitability, organizations need to embrace one of the generic strategies, rather than simultaneously following all. For example, cost leadership strategies require the organizations to lower costs and cost advantages through process innovations, learning curve benefits, economies of scale, product designs, optimizing the cycle time for production, reengineering, and even through backward integration. Videocon's acquisition of Thompson's colour picture tube manufacturing facilities provides cost optimization benefits to Videocon to manufacturing colour television sets. Product differentiation strategies on the other hand, help in customizing customers' needs. As it creates the niche, organizations can segregate them from other competitors, even when offering the same goods and services, with some value addition. It may even require the organizations to charge the premium price, but customers' may show their eagerness, obviously for new value addition. Product differentiation strategy, therefore, can be effectively implemented adding some unique or superior value. For example, Berger Paints have premier range of paints, for which they charge higher prices. Berger Paints could differentiate them from their arch competitors, Asian paints. However, effectiveness of differentiation strategies depends on the extent of customers' perceived differentiations, which may not just limit to quality, features, or support services. It may even extend to brand value and the image. The third generic strategy, i.e., focus is based on adopting a stand to withdraw from the same line of business, shifting their focus to some new line of business. Such a strategy becomes essential when the organization is unable to withstand the price competition. IBM, for example, has to withdraw from desktop business, facing price competition from HP-Compaq and Dell and start their new business line, i.e., the IT-enabled services (ITeS). According to Porter (1980), successful focus strategy depends upon an industry segment that is large enough to have good growth potential but is not of key importance to other major competitors. Market penetration or market development can be an important focus strategy. Also focus can be based on (1) differentiation that targets a specific segment of the market with unique needs that are not being met by others in the industry or (2) cost focused where the company has access to specialized production and operations equipment that can save costs in smaller production lots or runs.

Several research studies could address the relationship between generic strategy and performance. Some research observations conclude that pure or generic strategies of cost minimization or differentiation results in superior performance while some other studies could observe that combination strategies, i.e., low-cost and differentiation can make the bigger differences. Dess and Davis (1984) examined industrial products businesses and suggested that performance was achieved through the adoption of a single strategy. Hambrick (1983) investigated capital goods producers and industrial product manufacturers and found support for generic strategies. Ross (1999) also supported two distinct focus strategies including low-cost and differentiation—one aimed at distinct needs in terms of cost in a narrow target market and the other at distinct customization requirements in a narrow target market.

For achieving performance excellence, according to Parker and Helms (1992) mixed and reactive strategies and so also the focused generic strategies are usually adopted by the organizations. Various research studies conducted by Gupta 1995; Slocum, McGill, & Lei 1994 have documented how high performance level could be attained by the organizations with simultaneous focus on low cost and differentiation strategies. Such combination strategies, i.e., the simultaneous use of low cost and differentiation strategies can give higher returns on investment (Helms et al., 1997). Research work by Wright and Parsinia (1988) could establish the success of combined generic strategies in banking, retailing, distributing, and creative businesses. Hill (1988) also emphasized on the need for combination strategies for cost leadership and product differentiation for long-term sustainable competitive advantage.

PERFORMANCE AND STRATEGY LINKAGE

We have enough literature and research findings on strategy-performance relationships. Primarily, strategy research has its roots in industrial organization (IO) theory. Within Bain (1956) and Mason (1939), the IO framework of industry behaviour, organizational performance, or profitability is seen as a function of the industry structure. Industry characteristics rather than organization-based issues are found to determine firm performance (Barney, 1986). This structure-conduct-performance model from IO and economics has been used in industries with high concentrations and in similar firms (Seth and Thomas, 1994). Some studies, however, have not found a link between strategy and performance (McGee and Thomas, 1986, 1992). Others have found the link between strategy and performance lessened by situational variables including a focus on manufacturing and profitability (Davis & Schul, 1993; Zahra, 1993). To investigate the strategy and performance relationship, many researchers began utilizing approaches found to be generalizable across industries, specifically those proposed by Porter (1980, 1985, and 1987). Researches on strategy, therefore, reveals contradictory results on the link between singular generic strategy and performance. As Campbell-Hunt (2000) points out, the dominant paradigm of competitive strategy is now two decades old, but it has yet to prove its adequacy as a descriptive framework or progress its propositions about the performance consequences of different strategic designs. The type of reward practices used by the organization may influence the relationship between strategy and performance. This may help to explain some of the confusing and contradictory findings reported in prior strategy-performance studies. Thus, exploratory research on the relationship between strategy, rewards, and firm performance is clearly established through research.

Reward Practices

Linkage of organizational strategy, human resource (HR) practices, and performance could be found in several research studies (Balkin and Gomez-Mejia, 1987; Hambrick and Snow, 1989; Lawler, 1986; Ulrich and Lake, 1990; Waldman, 1994; Zingheim and Schuster, 2000, etc.) All these studies suggest that HR practices for an organization must be selected in conformity with the organizational strategy. This applies for the organizational reward system and practices also. Organizational reward systems should be so designed that it can motivate employee performance in line with its strategy and at the same time can attract and retain the talents, who can truly contribute to the achievement of strategic intents (Galbraith, 1973; Kilmann, 1989; Nadler and Tushman, 1988).

Further external and internal fit of organizational reward systems with the strategies can ultimately facilitate in organizational effectiveness. HR practices, per se, can be the unique source of competitive strategies (Becker and Gerhart, 1996). Gomez-Mejia and Balkin (1992), pioneers in compensation management practices also suggested the importance of strategy-aligned reward systems, discarding the conventional basis of compensation design, i.e., job analysis, job descriptions, etc. A strategy aligned reward systems can achieve higher levels of individual and organizational level performance. However, such assumptions are still in the theoretical domain for inadequate empirical exploration.

Firm Performance

Most of the research studies support the long-term benefits of strategic planning for the successful performance of an organization or business unit. Studies on organizational performance use a variety of success measures both financial and non-financial. Researchers employ financial measures such as profit, turnover, return on investment, return on capital employed, and inventory turnover. Non-financial measures include innovativeness and market standing. When performance is measured at a variety of levels (e.g., national, industry, company, and product), comparison of results is difficult.

Lusch and Laczniak (1989) define business performance as the total economic results of the activities undertaken by an organization. Walker and Ruekert (1987) found primary dimensions of business performance could be grouped into the three categories of effectiveness, efficiency, and adaptability. However, there is little agreement as to which measure is best. Thus, any comparison of business performance with only these three dimensions involves substantial trade-offs; good performance on one dimension often means sacrificing performance on another (Donaldson, 1984). Measures of firm performance, generally, include such bottom line, financial indicators as sales, profits, cash flow, return on equity, and growth. It is important to determine how a firm compares with its industry competitors when assessing firm performance (Dess and Robinson, 1984).

PURPOSE OF PERFORMANCE MANAGEMENT STRATEGY

Performance management strategy aims to provide the means through which better results can be obtained from the organization, teams, and individuals by understanding and managing performance within an agreed framework of planned goals, standards, and competence requirements. It involves the development of processes for establishing shared understanding about what is to be achieved, and an approach to managing and developing people in a way that will increase the probability that it will be achieved in the short- and long-term. Evaluating periodically, the human resource inside the organization can increase the motivation and commitment of employees and enable individuals to develop their abilities, increase their job satisfaction, and achieve their full potential to their own benefit and that of the organization as a whole. Unfortunately, not all organizations provide opportunities for personnel evaluation.

THE PROCESS OF PERFORMANCE MANAGEMENT STRATEGY

Performance management strategy has to focus on developing a continuous and flexible process that involves managers and those whom they manage acting as partners within a framework. This should set out how they can best work together to achieve the required results. It focuses on future performance planning and improvement rather than on retrospective performance appraisal. It provides the basis for regular and frequent dialogues between managers and individuals or teams about performance and development needs. Although, traditionally, performance management process applies mainly focus on individual performance and development issues, it can also be made applicable for teams (Armstrong, 2006).

Performance management measure outputs in the shape of delivered performance compared with expectations expressed as objectives. In this respect, it is concerned with targets, standards and performance measures, or indicators. But it also deals with inputs—the knowledge, skills, and competencies required to produce the expected results. It is by defining these input requirements and assessing the extent to which the expected levels of performance have been achieved by using skills and competencies effectively that developmental needs are identified. The process of performance management strategy, therefore, needs to focus on individual, team performance measurement, improvement, and future performance planning.

COMPONENTS OF STRATEGIC PERFORMANCE MANAGEMENT PROCESS

Strategic performance management is the configuration of mission, vision, objectives, and strategy of an organization which cascades to quantifiable critical success factors (CSF) and the key performance indicators (KPI) of an organization. For its quantitative attributes, it can help the organization to quickly tract the performance gaps, and, accordingly, initiate the corrective action. The process consists of various sub-processes, which inter alia encompasses performance planning, budgeting, performance target assignment, measurement, and compensation decisions. When these sub-processes are integrated, it leads to performance-driven employees' behaviours that contributes organizational excellence. Various components of SPM can be listed as under:

Strategy development: Strategy development process leads to framing of strategic objectives and the action plans. For performance management and its improvement, strategy development is done in measurable terms, duly identifying the critical success factors that lead to the achievement of competitive advantage. Critical success factors are identified from the core business and non-business issues that are considered as the major drivers to achieve strategic objectives of the organization. Organizations often dilute the strategy development process considering only the financial results, rather than emphasizing on the value creation process. Also, strategy development process sets the premises on narrow consideration of internal environment of organizations, rather than taking a holistic view on the real competitive advantage and the external environmental issues. This, therefore, dilutes the basic purpose of strategy development.

Budgeting and target setting: The process of target setting and the budgeting results in developing the actions plans, and, accordingly, allocate the resources so as to achieve the strategic intents of the organizations. This process also helps in setting the financial targets for the coming year. However, for obvious volatility of business, budgeting often becomes meaningless for less relevance in the changing environment. Often budgeting itself becomes a time-consuming cumbersome process for obvious involvement of people at different hierarchical levels.

Forecasting: At this stage, stock of detailed execution of activities are taken to assess whether the organization is on desired performance track, or require some corrective and so also the predictive actions. The forecasting process, therefore, helps in solving the real-time and so also the predicted performance problems in the organization.

Performance measurement: The process of performance measurement considers collection, consolidation, and distribution of performance data to compile the performance information. Such performance information then gets related to the critical success factors (CSFs) and/or the performance indicators (KPIs). Quantitative values of CSFs and KPIs may include both the financial and non-financial information, but may fail to track the behavioural attributes of the employees that might have led to the performance results. Hence performance measurement can fail to track the right corrective and preventive actions that may go into performance improvement (Wall, 2001).

Performance review: Unlike performance measurement, performance review process tracks the holistic performance results periodically, considering both the qualitative and quantitative aspects of performance. Being more elaborate and holistic, performance review process facilitate in taking the real-time corrective and preventive action to pull the performance level to the set targets. Rather than limiting the performance process impersonal, managers need to periodically conduct the performance review meetings to guide the employees.

Compensation design: Compensation policies of the organizations are aligned with the strategic and operational actions for dual objectives to optimize the cost of compensation and to motivate the good performers. Under performers also get the message that with scaling up of their performance they can earn more. The process, therefore, emphasizes on desired performance-related behaviour from the employees.

Thus it must be emphasized that strategic performance management is not about establishing a top-down, backward-looking form of appraising people. Neither is it just a method of generating information for pay decisions. Performance management is a strategic process because it is forward-looking and development oriented. It provides a framework in which managers can support their team members rather than dictate to them, and its impact on results will be much more significant if it is regarded as a transformational rather than as an appraisal process. To be successful in the long run, an organization strives for organizational fitness, which is defined as an organization's ability to adapt and survive in the ever-changing business environment.

Organizations that have implemented a performance management system, and are using it, perform both financially and non-financially better than organizations that are less performance management driven.

STRATEGY AND PERFORMANCE MANAGEMENT CYCLE

The cycle of performance management indicates the achievement of performance goals within a specific time frame. Such cycle includes right from performance planning, to developing the performance goals at the organizational level, division/department level, team/work group level, and individual level. Also it includes performance review systems, performance monitoring, and employee development to ultimately reach the performance goals. Corporate level strategy gives overall direction to divisional or departmental strategic plans and, in some cases, to organization-wide functional strategic plans, viz., the performance management systems. Strategic plans provide the organizational context within which the managers run their businesses. They do so by devolving responsibility for implementing strategy to business units. The business plans explain what each unit will do to implement it. Business plans cascade to form divisional business plans. Thus, a business unit may take directions from a number of strategic plans. For work-groups/team and employees' at their individual level, divisional strategic plan shows how they need to perform. For example, the marketing strategy may show the approach towards customers' retention and new business development. The operations strategy may explain the new or improved work processes and practices that can deliver the products and services, meeting customers' expectations. The human resource strategy develops approach toward attraction, motivation, retention and development of people to implement the strategic plans.

Performance management systems have traditionally been viewed as instruments for're-freezing' the organization or consolidating gains resulting from a change programme. Unfortunately, for obvious high rate of change, today's organization often cannot invest the time required for re-freezing. In such a turbulent business environment, often it is questioned, whether a performance management system can be implemented. However, experiences from global organizations indicate that successful introduction of performance management systems, making it an integral part of the change programme, can yield better results. Such results would be more evident when we design the system addressing the specific employees' and organizational needs.

In any organizational change programme powered by performance management systems, strategically organizations involve line managers. Line managers for their obvious proximity with the operations understand the importance of change within the deadlines, and accordingly are able to share the areas of priority in employees' performances.

The strategic approach to performance management cycle, therefore, requires organizations to develop a performance-oriented culture that enhances the capability of the line managers, support them, so that they can motivate people to willingly work to achieve the organizational goals. They do both with minimal control needed by management. This culture requires employees to commit to organizational objectives, achieve them and trust their organization to treat them fairly. An effective performance management system meets all these requirements.

Change management must be led from the top of an organization and this leadership cascaded down through every level of management. Individual line managers will have varying capabilities and inclinations to accept this role as leader. An effective performance management system both encourages and supports them as they do so. Both making them accountable for implementing the system and raising their expectations of what it can do encourages them. Accountability is achieved by a stipulation in their own performance agreement that they appraise their immediate subordinates before their own contract can be reviewed. Unfortunately, past experience has caused many managers to have low expectations of a performance management system. Unless they are made to value it as a useful management tool, they will not commit sufficient time and energy to it and it will quickly degenerate into an administrative encumbrance.

DIMENSIONS OF LINKAGE BETWEEN INDIVIDUAL PERFORMANCES AND STRATEGY

The link between business strategy and individual performance occurs in part through the organizational capability to create and embed people processes along a number of dimensions. These are vertical linkage (to create alignment with short-term business needs), horizontal linkage (to create cohesion), and temporal linkage (to transform to meet future needs). These clusters of people processes can be described and observed across all the businesses. The strength of the linkage between people processes and business strategy varies across the processes and across the businesses.

Vertical linkage expresses the most visible aspect, i.e., the linking of business goal to individual objective setting, to the measurement and rewarding of that business goal. The concept of horizontal linkage is more complex, as it establishes the links within and between the people processes. Because of its static nature, the need for temporal linkage occurs.

Strategic performance management is established through the vertical, horizontal and temporal linkages. However, operationally we find vertical linkage, as it establishes the link between the business goals, individual behaviour, and the ultimate individual team and organizational performance. Such vertical integration is achieved through the procedures, policies, and processes, and is widely acknowledged to be a crucial part of any strategic approach to the management of people (Schuler and Jackson, 1987; Tichy, Fombrun and Devanna, 1982; Truss and Gratton, 1994). It ensures the presence of an explicit complementary relationship between internal people policies and processes and the external product market or larger business strategy. It also creates and supports the individual behaviour and competencies that have the potential to be a source of competitive advantage (Wright et al. 1994). Linkage ensures a focus on what Jackson et al. (1989) have described as 'needed employee behaviour', that behaviour which is central to the delivery of the business strategy.

BENEFITS OF STRATEGIC PERFORMANCE MANAGEMENT

Strategic performance management requires organization's attention to focus on the strategic themes, drivers, and objectives. A model of operational performance management showing different facets of performance management is illustrated in Figure 6.1.

The model illustrates how strategic performance management links strategic planning and operational management. The strategy map and scorecard work within this approach to deliver the benefits.

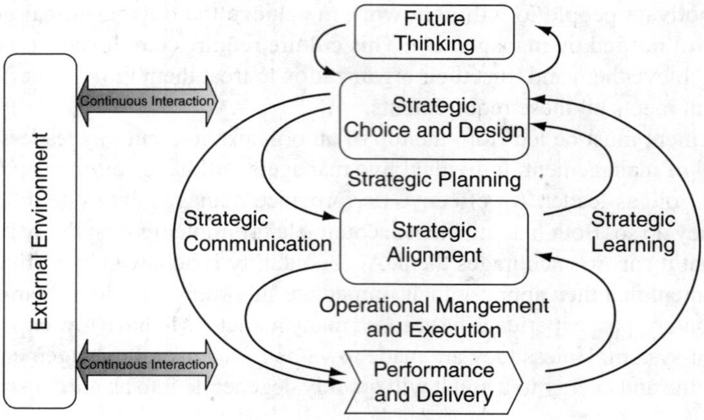

Figure 6.1 *Strategic management approach*

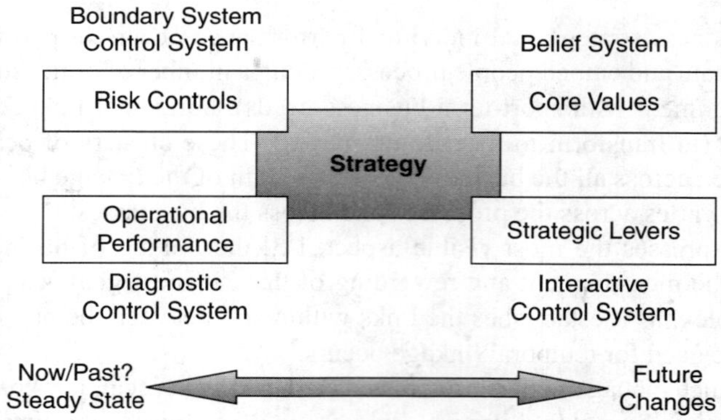

Figure 6.2 *Strategic performance management process*

However, when performance management becomes too focused on risks and control, it can only provide operational detail but cannot support the strategy. A properly designed and implemented balanced scorecard approach avoids these problems. It makes clear the directions for the organizations, articulation of the strategies with the details of objectives, measures, targets, projects, investments, and responsibilities. We can communicate it better, as strategic performance management process to deliver results by using Figure 6.2.

Focusing on the strategic issues requires creating of performance culture. Performance culture is a visible and explicit pattern of behaviour, action, and value, which facilitates in achieving the overall objectives of the organization. Further good performance culture encourages honest evaluation, feedback, and appraisal. It ensures informed decision-making both at the individual and at the collective level. With a self-regulating mechanism, good performance culture also ensures real-time response to the changing environment and circumstances. It is important to understand that frameworks, methodologies, and software do not create a performance culture. It can only play the facilitating role in enhancing the performance culture.

ADVANTAGES AND DISADVANTAGES OF SPM

SPM practices help the organization to derive many advantages. So also it leads to many disadvantages. Hence it is desirable for the organization to balance the advantages and the disadvantages to make best use of SPM. Some of the widely verifiable advantages of SPM are presented below:

- Increase in output.
- Increase in revenue.
- Increase in profit.
- Reduction in costs.

Such advantages improve the overall performance of the organization in the following ways:

- Closer collaboration and better knowledge sharing and information exchange between organizational units.
- Strengthened focus on what is important for the organization.
- Higher quality of performance information.
- Better strategic alignment of organizational units.
- Higher operational efficiency.
- Better understanding of organizational members of the strategy.
- Improvement in the decision-making process.
- Higher commitment of organizational members to the organization.
- More clarity of people about their contribution towards achievement of the results.
- Higher innovativeness.
- Better achievement of organizational goals.
- More pro-activity of organizational members.
- More clarity for organizational members about their roles and goals to be achieved.
- Higher quality of products and services.
- More effective management control.
- Higher employee satisfaction.
- Stronger process orientation.
- Strengthened reputation of the organization as a quality.
- Better strategic planning process.

DISADVANTAGES OF SPM

- It causes too much internal competition.
- There are too many performance indicators.
- The performance information is too aggregated.
- There is not enough strategic information in the system.
- The performance indicators are too subjective and, therefore, unreliable.

- There is too much historical information.
- Stronger accountability.
- Need for a broader set of measures of performance.
- Better facilitation of cross-functional understanding.
- Better goal setting.
- Formalization of the strategic planning process.
- Stronger individual accountability of employees.
- Stronger commitment of top management.
- Higher commitment to the strategy.
- Handling the increase in complexity of the organization.
- Better description of missions, strategies, and goals.
- Improve the performance of the organization.
- Obtain better understandings in knowledge and skills of people.
- Better control and with that a better 'obedience' of people.
- Tracking progress towards achievement of organizational goals.
- Aligning employee behaviour with strategic objectives.
- Better communicating of strategy to everyone in the organization.
- Aligning the organization to the strategy.
- Being able to measure people, projects, and strategies.
- Being able to measure performance at various organizational levels.
- Translating the strategy into operational terms.
- Need to make strategy everyone's job.
- Need to correlate measures and actions better.
- Linking rewards to performance.
- Enforcing and monitoring regulatory compliance.
- Requirement of a business opportunity.
- Expectation of the stock market.
- Requirement of governmental regulations.
- Decision support at top management level.
- Decision support at operational level.
- Providing a better picture of customer and product profitability.
- Making responsibility accounting possible.
- Identity possible needs for changes in strategy.
- Facilitate implementation of business strategy.
- Provide information for external reporting.
- Facilitate comparison with other, similar business units.

- Enhance quality of the organization.
- Determination of the bonus of management and/or staff.
- Monitor whether the business is creating value for shareholders.
- Facilitate a process orientation.

SPM AND THE BALANCED SCORECARD

The balanced scorecard is the most important SPM tool to realize the strategic intents. The scorecard is so designed that it can track the overall performance in key areas and processes, which aggregates to business results. Such key areas are divided into four perspectives, customer, internal-business processes, learning and growth, and financials. When individual, group or organizational level performance targets are translated into these four balanced scorecard perspectives, it gives more candid details of performance, and helps the organization to understand how every member contributes to strategic performance requirements. The balanced scorecard pioneered by Kaplan and Norton (1992) needs to be developed for the individual employees, groups, divisions, and departments and also for the overall organizations. The process involves, first deciding the overall scorecard for the organizations, and then cascade the same to the division, department, group, and individual levels. Integration of the performance results, ultimately, fits with the organization level scorecard. Assumptions of the balanced scorecard are that every employee of the organization, irrespective of their functional areas and hierarchical level, contribute to the four perspectives, and tracking such contribution helps to understand the performance results. Separately, we have discussed various perspectives of balanced scorecard in a different chapter.

SPM AND METRICS

We can't improve what we can't measure. Therefore metrics must be developed based on the priorities of the strategic plan, which provides the key business drivers and criteria for metrics, which the managers desire to watch. After developing the metrics, organizations need to develop the processes to collect relevant information for these metrics and reduce to numerical form for storage, display, and analysis. Decision-makers examine the outcomes of various measured processes and strategies and track the results to guide the company and provide feedback. Such metrics can directly exert impact on SPM as under:

- The value of metrics provides a factual basis for defining: the performance.
- Strategic feedback shows the present status of the organization from many perspectives for decision-makers.
- Diagnostic feedback guides improvements on a continuous basis.
- Track trends in performance over time.
- Feedback can be traced with the measurement methods.
- Quantitative inputs can be used for forecast methods and for decision support systems.

Again SPM as a process become more effective, when different metrics are used to understand how the performance results of the individual employees, groups, divisions, and departments contributed to realize the strategy of the organization. Well-designed metrics can not only track the performance results, it can also support the SPM process, as key performance indicators drawn in alignment with the organizational strategy, can be quantified and measured to facilitate objective decision- making. For SPM, we have different metrics. In a separate chapter on performance management research, we have explained such metrics for better understanding of its usages.

SPM FOR ENVIRONMENTAL THREATS AND RISKS

Responding to the change faster than the competitors is what we consider as the important competitive advantage for any organization. Environmental threats and risks for frequent change in the environment alter the way the organization works. Some organizations even lose their market leadership to their competitors. Effective SPM practices, can alter the adverse effects of environment on organization. It requires monitoring, understanding, and if necessary even preparing for the following:

- Industry Changes—new competitors, mergers and acquisitions, new suppliers, etc.
- Political Changes—change in government, legislation, taxation policies, etc.
- Economic Changes—inflation, interest rates, unemployment, stagnation, etc.
- Social Changes—population trends, community attitudes, cultural, etc.
- Technological Changes—breakthroughs, new products, enabling technologies, etc.

Thus SPM can, under the right conditions, be introduced during change. This, however, requires us to understand the role of SPM in the organizational change programmes, and so also the nature of the organization itself. Developing a vibrant performance culture becomes the important precursor for the success of SPM even in organizational change environment.

SUMMARY

Strategic performance management practices can churn financial performance and success in organization. Strategic SPM guards the interest of various stakeholders, including the assurance of the interest of the shareholders, and thereby provides the sustainable strategic advantage to the organizations. Business systems and adaptability are the two key areas, which deserve attention to enable strategic SPM to deliver the results. To achieve this, it requires first understanding of the business systems of the organization and subsequently designs their performance management systems from the business perspectives. This is why organizations master the principle of coordination to become aligned, linked, and integrated. Strategic performance management links strategic planning and operational management. The strategy map and scorecard work within this approach to deliver the benefits. To develop SPM in organizations, SMART objectives are used for proper horizontal alignment, so that people can work across the organization, sharing and integrating the objectives of the departments that interface with one another. Such horizontal alignment is important because employees must collaborate and rely on each other to achieve common goals.

In this chapter, we have discussed the basics of SPM, introducing its concept and definition, its evolution, characteristics, purposes, processes, linkage with generic strategies, its components, benefits, advantages and disadvantages, usages of balanced scorecard, and metrics.

KEY WORDS

Strategic Performance Management—It establishes a culture where individuals and groups take responsibility for the continuous improvement of business processes and of their own skills. It focuses on success, behaviour, and sharing of expectations.

Generic Strategies—Michel Porter's (1980) generic strategies are the most commonly identified syndromes in organizations. Organizations worldwide make use of these generic strategies even in managing their performance. Porter (1980) proposed three generic strategies that can yield competitive advantage, namely, cost leadership, product differentiation, and focus. To ensure long-term profitability, organizations need to embrace one of the generic strategies, rather than simultaneously following all.

Incentive Compensation—This process links strategic and operational actions for key value drivers, in a balanced way with compensation and benefits policies. The main business issue that drives organizations to improve the incentive compensation sub-process is that this process is not sufficiently aligned with the other sub-processes, therefore, it does not reward the right performance-driven behaviour of organizational members.

Performance Metrics—Performance metrics are developed based on the priorities of the strategic plan, which provides the key business drivers and criteria for metrics, which the managers desire to watch. After developing the metrics, organizations need to develop the processes to collect relevant information for these metrics and reduce to numerical form for storage, display, and analysis.

GENERAL REVIEW QUESTIONS

1. Explain the process of development of strategic performance management concept.
2. Discuss how strategic performance management relates to Porter's generic strategies.
3. Explain the purpose, process, and the components of strategic performance management.
4. Discuss how individual performance and strategy can be aligned.
5. What are the advantages and disadvantages of strategic performance management?
6. Explain how the balanced scorecard and metrics can strengthen the strategic performance management.
7. Short Notes
    (a) Performance Management Cycle
    (b) Environmental Threats and Risks
    (c) Vertical Linkage
    (d) Critical Success Factors
    (e) SMART Objectives

CRITICAL REVIEW QUESTION

8. Visit any technology-intensive Indian manufacturing organization and explain how this organization could successfully respond to their recent changes through strategic performance management practices. (Hint: Preferably choose some Indian car manufactures like Tata Motors, Maruti, Hyundai,etc.).

FURTHER READING

Andersen, B., B. Henriksen and W. Aarseth (2006), 'Holistic Performance Management: An Integrated Framework', *International Journal of Productivity and Performance Management*, 55(1): 61–78.

Armstrong, M. and A. Baron (1998), *Performance Management, the New Realities* (London: Institute of Personnel and Development).

Atkinson, A.A., R. Balakrishnan, P. Booth, J.M. Cote, T. Groot, T. Malmi, H. Roberts, E. Uliana and A. Wu (1997), 'New Directions in Management Accounting Research', *Journal of Management Accounting Research*, 9: 70–108.

Baraldi, S. and G. Monolo, (2004), 'Performance Measurement in Italian Hospitals: The Role of the Balanced Scorecard', in A. Neely, M. Kennerly, and A. Waters (eds), *Performance Measurement and Management: Public and Private* (Cranfield: Centre for Business Performance, Cranfield University), pp. 75–82.

Bhattacharyya, D.K. (2007), *Human Resource Research Methods* (New Delhi: Oxford University Press).

Bititci, U., K. Mendibil, S. Nudurupati, T. Turner and P. Garengo (2004), 'The Interplay between Performance Measurement, Organizational Culture and Management Styles', in A. Neely, M. Kennerly and A. Waters (eds), *Performance Measurement and Management: Public and Private* (Cranfield: Centre for Business Performance, Cranfield University), pp. 107–14.

Bourne, M., M. Franco and J. Wilkes (2003) 'Corporate Performance Management', *Measuring Business Excellence*, 7: 15–21.

Bourne, M., J. Mills, M. Wilcox, A. Neely and K. Platts (2000), 'Designing, Implementing and Updating Performance Measurement Systems', *International Journal of Operations & Production Management*, 20(7): 754–71.

Braam, G.J. and E.J. Nijssen (2004), 'Performance Effects of Using the Balanced Scorecard: A Note on the Dutch Experience', *Long Range Planning*, 37(4): 335–49.

Brooks, I. and J. Weatherston (2000), *The Business Environment: Challenges and Changes*, 2nd edition (New York, NY: Financial Times Management).

Brown, A. (2004), 'Implementing a System of Performance Management in England's Primary School', in A. Neely, M. Kennerly and A. Waters (eds), *Performance Measurement and Management: Public and Private* (Cranfield: Centre for Business Performance, Cranfield University), pp. 155–62.

Bryant, L., D.A. Jones and S.K. Widener (2004), 'Managing Value Creation within the Firm: An Examination of Multiple Performance Measurement', *Journal of Management Accounting Research*, 16: 107–31.

Chow, C.W., D. Ganulin, K. Haddad and J. Williamson (1998), 'The Balanced Scorecard: A Potent Tool for Energizing and Focusing Healthcare Organization Management', *Journal of Healthcare Management*, 43(3): 263–80.

Davis, S. and T. Albright (2002), 'Relationship between High Quality Implementation Procedures and Improved Financial Performance for New Performance Measurement Systems', *FSR Forum,* (September) 4: 22–31.

Davis, S. and T. Albright (2004), 'An Investigation of the Effect of Balanced Scorecard Implementation on Financial Performance', *Management Accounting Research*, 15(2): 135–53.

Dumond, E.J. (1994), 'Making Best Use of Performance-Measures and Information', *International Journal of Operations & Production Management*, 14(9): 16–32.

Epstein, M., P. Kumar and R. Westbrook (2000), 'The Drivers of Customer and Corporate Profitability: Modeling, Measuring, and Managing the Causal Relationships', *Advances in Management Accounting*, 9(1): 43–72.

Groves, G. and V. Valsamakis (1998), 'Supplier–Customer Relationships and Company Performance', *International Journal of Logistics Management*, 9(2): 51–64.

Haas, M. de and A. Kleingeld (1999), 'Multilevel Design of Performance Measurement Systems: Enhancing Strategic Dialogue throughout the Organization', *Management Accounting Research*, 10(3): 233–61.

Hair, J.F., R.E. Anderson, R.L. Tatham and W.C. Black (1998), *Multivariate Data Analysis* (Upper Saddle River, NJ: Prentice-Hall International).

Heras, M.A. (2004), 'Performance Measurement and Quality Systems: Results of Qualitative Research Carried Out in Companies that Had Won the Catalan Quality Award', in A. Neely, M. Kennerly, and A. Waters (eds), *Performance Measurement and Management: Public and Private* (Cranfield: Centre for Business Performance, Cranfield University), pp. 459–66.

Hoopes, L.L. and S.L. Hale (1999), 'Facing the Challenge of Change: Current Trends and Practices in the Property and Casualty Insurance Industry', *CPCU Journal*, 52(2): 90–105.

Hoque, Z. (2003), 'Total Quality Management and the Balanced Scorecard Approach: A Critical Analysis of Their Potential Relationships and Directions for Research', *Critical Perspectives on Accounting*, 14(5): 553–66.

Hoque, Z. and W. James (2000), 'Linking Balanced Scorecard Measures to Size and Market Factors: Impact on Organizational Performance', *Journal of Management Accounting Research*, 12(1): 1–18.

Hronec, S.M. (1993), *Vital Signs: Using Quality, Time, and Cost Performance Measurements to Chart Your Company's Future* (New York, NY: AMACOM).

IOMA, Business Intelligence at Work (2005), 'Two Studies Reveal How Firms Are Improving Their Budgeting and Planning. Performance Reporting: Majority of Companies Need to Fix Their Balanced Scorecards', *IOMA's Financial Analysis, Planning & Reporting 2005 Yearbook* (Newark, NJ: IOMA), pp. 4–5.

Kald, M. and F. Nilsson (2000), 'Performance Measurement at Nordic Companies', *European Management Journal*, 14(1): 113–27.

Kaplan, R.S. and D.P. Norton (1996a), 'Using the Balanced Scorecard as a Strategic Management System', *Harvard Business Review* (January/February): 75–85.

Kaplan, R.S. and D.P. Norton (1996b), *The Balanced Scorecard—Translating Strategy into Action* (Boston, MA: Harvard Business School Press).

Lawrie, G., I. Cobbold and K. Issa (2004), 'The Design of a Strategic Management System in an Industrial Private Sector Organization', in A. Neely, M. Kennerly and A. Waters (eds) *Performance Measurement and Management: Public and Private* (Cranfield: Centre for Business Performance, Cranfield University), pp. 579–86.

Lawson, R., W. Stratton and T. Hatch (2003), 'The Benefits of a Scorecard System', *CMA Management*, 77(4): 24–26.

Lawson, R., W. Stratton and T. Hatch (2004), 'Automating the Balanced Scorecard', *CMA Management*, 77(9): 39–43.

Lawson, R., W. Stratton and T. Hatch (2005), 'Achieving Strategy with Scorecarding', *Journal of Corporate Accounting and Finance*, 16(3): 63–68.

Lingle, J.H. and W.A. Schiemann (1996), 'From Balanced Scorecard to Strategic Gauges: Is Measurement Worth It?', *Management Review*, 5(3): 56–61.

Lingle, J.H. and W.A. Schiemann (1999), *Bullseye! Hitting Your Strategic Target through High Impact Measurement* (New York, NY: Free Press).

Lovell, B., Z. Radnor and J. Henderson (2002), 'A Pragmatic Assessment of the Balanced Scorecard: An Evaluation of a New Performance System for Use in a NHS Multi Agency Setting in the UK', *University of Bradford Working Paper Series*, 2(13): 339–46.

Lynch, R. and K. Cross (1990), 'Tailoring Performance Measures to Suit Your Business', *Journal of Accounting and EDP*, 6(1): 17–25.

Lynch, R. and K. Cross (1995), *Measure Up! Yardsticks for Continuous Improvement* (Cambridge: Basil Blackwell).

Malina, M.A. and F.H. Selto (2001), 'Communicating and Controlling Strategy: An Empirical Study of the Effectiveness of the Balanced Scorecard', *Journal of Management Accounting Research*, 13: 47–90.

Marr, B. and A. Neely (2003), *Balanced Scorecard Software Report* (Stamford, CT: Gartner, Inc. and Cranfield School of Management).

Marr, B., G. Schiuma and A. Neely (2004), 'The Dynamics of Value Creation: Mapping Your Intellectual Performance Drivers', *Journal of Intellectual Capital*, 5(2): 312–25.

Martinez, M.M. (1997), '3 Strategies for Successful Business Partners', *HR Magazine*, 42: 1–4.

Mooraj, S., D. Oyon and D. Hostettler (1999), 'The Balanced Scorecard: A Necessary Good or an Unnecessary Evil?', *European Management Journal*, 17: 481–91.

Neely, A. and R. Austin (2000), 'Measuring Operations Performance: Past, Present and Future', in A. Neely (ed), *Performance Measurement: Past, Present and Future* (Centre for Business Performance, Cranfield School of Management, Cranfield University), pp. 419–26.

Neely, A. and M. Bourne (2000), 'Why Measurement Initiatives Fail', *Measuring Business Excellence*, 4(4): 3–6.

Neely, A., M. Kennerley and V. Martinez (2004), 'Does the Balanced Scorecard Work: An Empirical Investigation', in A. Neely, M. Kennerly and A. Waters (eds), *Performance Measurement and Management: Public and Private* (Cranfield: Centre for Business Performance, Cranfield University), pp. 763–70.

Niven, P.R. (2002), *Balanced Scorecard: Step-by-Step Maximizing Performance and Maintaining Results* (New York, NY: Wiley & Sons).

Norreklit, H. (2000), 'The Balanced on the Balanced Scorecard: A Critical Analysis of Some of the Assumptions', *Management Accounting Research*, 11(1): 65–88.

Papalexandris, A., G. Ioannou and G.P. Prastacos (2004), 'Implementing the Balanced Scorecard in Greece: A Software Firm's Experience', *Long Range Planning*, 37(4): 347–62.

Porter, M. (1985), *Competitive Advantage: Creating and Sustaining* (New York, NY: Free Press).

Rheem, H. (1996), 'Performance Management Programs', *Harvard Business Review*, 74(5): 8–10.

Rigby, D. (2001), 'Management Tools and Techniques: A Survey', *California Management Review*, 43(2): 139–60.

Robinson, S.P. (2004), 'The Adoption of the Balanced Scorecard: Performance Measurement Motives, Measures and Impact', in A. Neely (ed), *Performance Measurement: Past, Present and Future* (Centre for Business Performance, Cranfield School of Management, Cranfield University), pp. 883–90.

Rockart, J.F. and C. Bullen (1981), 'Premier on Critical Success Factors' (Massachusetts, MA: Centre for Information Centre Research, Sloan School of Management, Massachusetts Institute of Technology).

Said, A.A., H.R. HassabElnaby and B. Wier (2003), 'An Empirical Investigation of the Performance Consequences of Nonfinancial Measures', *Journal of Management Accounting Research*, 15: 193–223.

Scheipers, G., A. Ameels and W. Bruggeman (2004), 'The Cascading Process for Multi-Level Balanced Scorecard Design: The Case of a Belgian Wastewater Management Company', in A. Neely (ed), *Performance Measurement: Past, Present and Future* (Centre for Business Performance, Cranfield School of Management, Cranfield University), pp. 1209–16.

Self, J. (2004), 'Metrics and Management: Applying the Results of the Balanced Scorecard', *Performance Measurement and Metrics*, 5(3): 101–5.

Shulver, M. and N. Antarkar (2001), 'The Balanced Scorecard as a Communication Protocol for Managing across Intra-Organizational Borders' (Proceedings of the 12th Annual Conference of the Production and Operations Management Society, Orlando, FL).

Silk, S. (1998), 'Automating the Balanced Scorecard', *Management Accounting*, 79(11): 38–44.

Sim, K.L. and H.C. Koh (2001), 'Balanced Scorecard: A Rising Trend in Strategic Performance

Measurement', *Measuring Business Excellence*, 5(2): 18–28.

Speckbacher, G., J. Bischof and T. Pfeiffer (2003), 'A Descriptive Analysis on the Implementation of Balanced Scorecards in German Speaking Countries', *Management Accounting Research*, 14: 361–87.

Tapinos, E., R.G. Dyson and M. Meadows (2005), 'The Impact of Performance Measurement in Strategic Planning', *International Journal of Productivity and Performance Management*, 54(5/6): 370–84.

Waal, A.A. de (2002), 'The Role of Behavioural Factors in the Successful Implementation and Use of Performance Management Systems' (PhD dissertation, Vrije Universiteit Amsterdam).

Waal, A.A. de (2007), *Strategic Performance Management: A Managerial and Behavioural Approach* (London: Palgrave MacMillan).

Wall, S. van der (1998), 'The Talent Solution: Aligning Strategy and People To Achieve Extraordinary Results', *HR Magazine*, 43(8): 136.

Williams, M.S. (2001), 'Is Intellectual Capital Performance and Disclosure Practices Related?', *Journal of Intellectual Capital*, 2(3): 192–203.

Zairi, M. and Y. Jarrar (2000), 'Becoming World Class through a Culture of Measurement', in A. Neely (ed), *Performance Measurement: Past, Present and Future* (Centre for Business Performance, Cranfield School of Management, Cranfield University), pp. 688–94.

CASE STUDY

Balanced Scorecard for Strategic Performance Management at Universal Bank

Bank Universal of Indonesia faced the unique crisis of organizational transformation after the Asian currency crisis of 1997. At this point of time, most important management tools used in managing the performance was the balanced scorecard. With the good corporate governance and alignment within the organization, the performance measurement initiative of the bank reached to momentum. Customer service, operational efficiency, and pro-active HRD practices were the three focus areas in the balanced scorecard adopted by the Indonesian banks to overcome the crisis.

Bank Universal was established in the year 1990, merging three small banks. Initially, it focused on corporate banking and later on expanded to retail banking, primarily in Jakarta and other major cities of Indonesia. With 2200 employees and an asset size of $1.2 billion, the bank virtually collapsed during the crisis of 1997. With the scientific performance management systems (using Balanced Scorecard) and sustained HR initiatives, the bank ultimately could survive the crisis and is at present achieving double digit return on equity. From a business point of view, the bank strategically focuses on sector-specific financing like automotive sector (mainly refinancing the suppliers, dealers, and the end users of product of the automobile industry), coal mining (supply chain side), traders, plywood supply chains, etc. Focusing on niche retail banking, the bank has achieved expertise. Another reason to be sector specific is to avoid mistakes in financing the large companies, who became the major defaulter and major contributor to high NPAs of the bank during the period of crisis.

Introduction of balanced scorecard helped the bank to balance their focus on its process, customer service, learning and growth, and finance. For banks without efficient process, quality of people who serve the customers, it is not possible to get good return on investment. With initial implementation of the balanced scorecard at the corporate level, the bank took this to the branch operation level and then cascaded it to the individual employee level. In four stages, the bank could implement the balanced scorecard, across the organization;with three strategic themes like handling of past problems (related to loan portfolios), embracing a new business model (to enhance profitability), and adopting a new market strategy to develop the good banking image.

After implementation of the balanced scorecard the bank could observe that people can appreciate each other. The marketing people can appreciate the service people and the service people can appreciate the operational and process people, who in turn can appreciate the human resource people. All could collectively contribute to the performance of Bank Universal. Effective coordination and communication throughout the organization improved the performance and the bottom line.

Bank Universal's Web site at http://www.bankuniversal.co.id.

Read this case carefully and relate it to any India organization, clearly segmenting individual areas of activities and operations, particularly after the global meltdown. Explore the possibility of introducing balanced scorecard. Also indicate how it can augment the business results of your selected organization.

CHAPTER 7

Competency-based Performance Management Systems

Learning Objectives

After reading this chapter, you will be able to understand:

- Definition and concepts of competency
- Managerial skills and competencies
- Skill inventories
- Multi-skilling
- Skills for the new millennium
- Developing competencies for effective performance management
- Types of competencies
- Characteristics of competencies
- Competencies identification and assessment process
- Competency mapping
- Steps of a competency identification process
- Steps to introduce competency-based systems
- Developing competency models
- Examples of HR competencies
- Competency-based performance management systems
- Elements of performance-based competencies
- Competency dictionary

L&T Infotech—Competency-based PMS

Larsen & Toubro Infotech Limited (L&T Infotech) is a 100 per cent subsidiary of the technology-driven engineering and construction major, Larsen & Toubro Limited. The company offers comprehensive, end-to-end software solutions and services. Leveraging the legacy of the parent company, L&T Infotech, a PCMM Level 5 company, could successfully introduce the competency-based human resource management system. Successful mapping of job competencies could help the company to align all major HR decisions like recruitment, training, job rotation, succession plans, and promotions on the documented competency maps. Competency-based HR interventions could put the company on the highest performance track. As a matter of strategic HR practices, the company made compulsory job rotation for every employee. Such job rotation programmes need not always be within the job family, it may even be cross-functional. To achieve excellence, the company used the expertize of PeopleSoft in competency mapping. Systematically, the company reviews the job competencies to assess the gap, if any. As a matter of practice, the company undertakes a minimum of two appraisals in a year. Another distinctive approach followed by the company is a systematic review of competencies after every project execution. Competency development of employees, therefore, is an ongoing supportive initiative, in which employees of the organization volunteer.

INTRODUCTION

Organizational business practices are not getting distorted only for business discontinuities like deregulation, globalization, technological convergence, the Internet, etc. In a globally competitive market landscape, today customers compete for value for their money. For organizations, therefore, 'customers' are the ultimate source of competence. It is the customers who dictate their terms, and organizations need to respond to such needs of the customers leveraging their core competencies. Organizational core competencies translate into core products and services, which create a niche in competition. Core competencies are the collective learning in the organization, especially the capacity to coordinate diverse production skills and integrate streams of technologies. First, companies must identify core competencies, which provide potential access to a wide variety of markets, make a contribution to the customer benefits of the product, and are difficult for competitors to imitate. Next, companies must reorganize to learn from alliances and focus on internal development. Hence, organizations today realize that in order to harness the boom time, competence of its human resources should exceed the expectations of its customers consistently. Human capital is the ultimate weapon for achieving competitive advantage. Successful organizations worldwide could achieve market leadership, systematically identifying, developing, rewarding, and aligning people competencies with their unique differentiating organizational capabilities.

The concept of competency was pioneered by McClelland (1973). McClelland identified different competency variables, which can help in predicting the job performance. The basic premise of McClelland's contention is that individual performance is not just the function of intelligence, knowledge, and skill, rather it is the competencies. Competencies in addition to the knowledge, skill, and abilities (KSA), also consider the behavioural aspects. Job performance becomes more effective when employees with the right competencies perform the job. Thus, McClelland's competency concept considers both the KSA and the behavioural inputs for successful performance. Competency mapping is the process of identification of competencies that contribute to successful job performance. Organizations do competency mapping following the work breakdown structure (WBS) concept, which breaks the job into different elements and then relate such job elements into the required nature of activities along with the requirements of competencies. Once this is done, performance measurement is done against such competency maps to understand the competency gaps. Identified competency gaps are then improved through various employee development initiatives. These apart, competency mapping can be done through assessment centres, introducing the multi-rating systems, use of psychometric tools, simulation exercises, interviews, role-plays, group discussions, etc.

MANAGERIAL SKILLS AND COMPETENCIES

Skills of the managers have now become important factors to address the global competitiveness at organizational and also at the national level. Obviously, imparting skills through training and development is yet not recognized as an important initiative at organizational level both for the problem of quantification of benefits, and in organizational beliefs that training can hardly help people to develop their skill. Skill is defined as a coordinated series of actions that serve to attain some goal or accomplish a particular task. Operationally, skills are defined widely as overt responses and controlled stimulation. Overt responses may be verbal, motor, or perceptual. Verbal response typically stresses on speaking (which requires memorization of words); motor responses stress on movements of limbs and body; and perceptual responses stress on understanding of sensory response. Controlled stimulation on the other hand, are energy inputs to the workers, which we express in units of frequency, length, time, and weight. Technological change and skill requirements have been made a subject of investigation in enormous studies across the world. There is a general consensus that technological change alters the job but the observations differ in its nature and form. Technological changes, per se, require broader variety of skills and higher average skills from the workers. From another viewpoint technology is instrumental in fractionating and de-skilling of jobs. Redesigning of jobs subsequent to technological change separates the planning and the concept of job in its totality from the execution aspect of work. De-skilling and skill downgrading also occurs due to differential growth of higher versus low skill occupations and industries. These phenomena are especially evident in India. From the 1981 census reports onward, we find a major occupational shift of workers from primary sector to secondary sector and from secondary sector to tertiary sector. Simultaneous structural change in occupational pattern is also evident, as the number of blue-collar workers has been drastically reduced while the number of white-collar workers has significantly increased. Another school of thought argues that de-skilling is a secondary consequence of de-industrialization, which again is prompted by the technological change.

Thus, transformations in skill due to technological change occur along two tracks: (i) compositional shift, i.e., structural change in occupational pattern due to creation or elimination of jobs of a given skill level and the distribution of persons to job in sectoral economy and (ii) changes in work content (the technical nature of work and the role relations surrounding work performance).

Internationally, the careers of the future will require greater education (more in the form of institutionalized knowledge) at the job entry level and will also demand for continuing education to keep pace with technological dynamism. Greater level of technological literary, even for lower skill and low paying occupations will be in demand in future.

Thus, in the era of technological change and globalization, through skill change or upgradation, organization can also achieve effectiveness and excellence.

From the above perspective, we can categorize skill either as generic or technical, entry level or advanced. Conventionally, skill can be defined as that knowledge or those attributes which are deemed vital to organizational success.

There are four general types of skills as under:

- Technical—which relates to specific concepts, methods, and tools specific to an organization.
- Supervisory—which enables one to effectively supervise others.
- Interpersonal—which enables people to communicate and interact effectively.
- General business—lines of business and support infrastructure.

Technical skills are observable, demonstrable, and testable. The other skill types are softer, more subjective, and difficult to quantify.

Any organization going for skill renewal or skill-change exercise needs to undertake the following tasks:

- Profile the skills required for jobs.
- Assess the skill levels acquired by individuals.
- Conduct a gap analysis between required and acquired skill.

Training should ideally occur before the skill is needed so that daily work can be reinforced through training.

SKILL INVENTORIES

A skill inventory is a device for pin-pointing information about individuals and their suitability for different jobs. Skills inventories include the name of the employee and a listing (or inventory) of job-related skills, training, and/or experience which could prove useful in a future assignment. The purpose of skill inventories is to provide the organization with quick, accurate information on all employees in order that management can choose the best-qualified person for promotion or transfer. For example, a skill inventory may consist of the following information: age, address, health, education, willingness to travel, experience in the past and present jobs, and foreign languages spoken. If an overseas assignment requires the speaking ability of people in a particular foreign language, a well-documented skill inventory can quickly identify availability of those employees from the database of the organization and select the suitable candidate for the job. Thus, maintaining a skill inventory is essential for achieving organizational effectiveness and excellence, even in a changed situation.

MULTI-SKILLING

For effective employee performance, multi-skilling of people is very important. Multi-skilling is defined as the process to train employees in a variety of skills, even crossing the traditional trade-specific or craft-specific skill sets. Thus to develop multi-skills, employees require additional training to enable them to perform more jobs within the same job family or to do the entire jobs from a holistic point of view. Multi-skilling is often misconstrued to succeed downsizing. But downsizing occurs for skill obsolescence, among other reasons, while multi-skilling is for holistic development of human potentialities to effectively address to the requirements of changing production process (more flexible and customized), organizational systems (decentralized control), and state-of-the-art technology (numeric control, computer numeric control, direct numeric control, etc.). Multi-skilling facilitates intra-occupational and inter-occupational job mobility and thereby reinforces organizational effectiveness and excellence.

SKILLS FOR THE NEW MILLENNIUM

In the changed global business scenario, organizations need to develop the following skills in all cross-sections of employees to sustain in competition and to achieve excellence.

Partnership and collaboration skills: In the new millennium, managers across all levels need to understand the importance of strategic associations. It is such a critical skill set that without mastering it, managers would not be able to identify partnership and collaboration opportunities, understand the structure of working relationships with the partners or collaborators, negotiate the terms, and close such deals. Both at the national and international level, organizations are forging strategic alliance to strengthen their market position. Even in terms of domain of market, two companies can have alliance of no-competition. For example, in India, IBM and PWC do not compete for the same product-mix in the same market. Similarly, to reduce the rate of attrition, IT companies have made no-poaching agreement with each other. Partnership and collaboration skills require managers to continuously scan the environment and identify such opportunities to achieve the strategic objectives.

Quick decision-making skill: Developing skills for quick decision-making is also very important. Delaying response time to change will lead to the loss of market opportunities. Hence managers need to master the art of quick decision-making, developing their capability to understand the change scenarios. Managers need to understand; monitoring day-to-day operations is one aspect and making a strategic move in the changed situation through quick decision-making is another aspect. In a situation of global meltdown and market volatility, many organizations to ensure quick decision-making or response pre-conceive the scenarios and structure the strategies, so that in a given scenario, they can quickly take the desired decision. However, such decisions even though not always error free can benefit the organization as an early mover. With the decisional flexibility, organizations can quickly reverse or change the decision, adjusting with the situation. For example, IBM prefers to operate in rented accommodations to smoothen their exit root, while many organizations prefer to add brick and mortars to expand their business. This is an era of lean management, which requires organizations to operate in an environment of flexibility. A quick decision-making ability of managers supports all such requirements.

Skill to attract and retain the talent: Only with strategic and innovative rewards or compensation design, attraction and retention of talent may not be always possible. In a knowledge economy, people prefer to stick around the job, which gives them opportunity to learn and grow, helps to align their self-goals with the organizational goals, provides them the right platform to incubate and nurture their creativity, and enables them to translate their creative ideas into action through innovative product or process design. Thus, retention and attraction of talents would be best possible through nurturing of a compelling workplace culture, which among others, provides opportunities to learn, grow, and innovate. To build such an environment in the workplace, managers need to acquire the right skill, so that as a coach and mentor to employees, they can help in the attraction and retention of talents.

Skill to predict the future: The rate of change in the new millennium being very fast, among others, managers must also acquire skills to predict the future. Through different sources, managers develop their insights to successfully predict the future in different time horizon. They can validate such insights through networking, sharing diverse assumptions with each other, etc. To effectively predict the future, many managers identify in advance certain trigger points and relate the same with different scenarios to predict the future.

Skill to integrate technology with business: Managers in the new millennium must also gain skill and familiarity with the new technology, to understand how such technology integrates with the business process. For example, without understanding how ERP (enterprise resource planning) modules facilitate in decision-making, managers won't be able to succeed in the new millennium.

Skill to balance the stakeholders' needs: For any organization, stakeholders are diverse, and their interests often conflict. Effective managers must have the requisite skill to balance such multiple and diverse stakeholders' needs through stakeholder analysis.

DEVELOPING COMPETENCIES FOR EFFECTIVE PERFORMANCE MANAGEMENT

Successful managers in the new millennium need to balance the demands of multiple and diverse stakeholders such as members of their own team, colleagues from other units in the company, external partners, customers, shareholders and convince them about the companies' core competencies. Without this, companies are likely to lose their focus, and the resultant poor performance. Working in the e-economy is challenging, managing there is even more so. HR as well as top managers must identify the right characteristics required for recruiting in the new economy. Apart from the regular requirements, organization needs to keep an eye for soft skills, which are essential for success in the disruptive new economy.

Competencies are important in human resource and knowledge management approaches. Boyatzis (1982) and Spencer and Spencer (1993) define competencies as the capacities that exist within a person and which predict superior performance. They are usually seen to encompass a personified knowledge, skills, attitudes, and behaviours which predict competent performance in a certain job. Lucia and Lepsinger (1999) differentiate competencies as aptitudes, personal characteristics, skills and knowledge from the actual behaviours that people need to perform at the workplace. The distinction between competencies as underlying human qualities on the one hand and observable performance outcomes on the other has a long tradition in psychology. This distinction greatly influenced traditional approaches of skills or competency management. Especially when it was first introduced as a human resource management approach, for example by Spencer and Spencer (1993), Boyatzis (1982), and Lawler and Ledford (1992), a certain combination of individual skills was seen as the determinant of competent job behaviour. Knowledge management approaches, on the other hand, usually focus more on employees of technical or professional knowledge, for example, when predicting whether an expert will successfully solve a given problem, or effectively complete a given project assignment. However, they share the same basic assumption with HR approaches that is to predict future performance from some personal characteristics.

Within the above theoretical framework, therefore, we can say, a prerequisite for improved performance both at the individual and at organizational level, is development of competencies. Competency development first requires identification of competencies, and mapping the same for different jobs in accordance with the changing expectations of the customers, and then listing the gaps, if any, in the existing level of competencies of employees' and finally focusing on various competency development exercises, like training and development, etc. to close the gaps. Competency-based performance management, therefore, requires evaluation of performance results in accordance with the required set of competencies, which even goes beyond the bottom line results.

TYPES OF COMPETENCIES

Daniel Katz (1955) has classified competencies into the following areas:

- Technical or Functional Competencies—These are the knowledge, attitude, and skills-related to technical or functional expertize required to perform a role.
- Managerial Competencies—These are the knowledge, attitude, and skills required to plan, organize, mobilize, and utilize resources.
- Human Competencies—These are the knowledge, attitude, and skills required to motivate, utilize, and develop human resources.
- Conceptual Competencies—These are the knowledge, attitude, and skills to visualize the invisible, i.e., the thinking at abstract levels and use of the thinking to plan future business.

But competencies are not mere knowledge, skills, and abilities (KSAs) and should ideally include values, motives and traits, and self-concept. Surface knowledge and skill competencies are easy to develop and training is the most cost-effective way to develop them. Core motive and trait competencies at the base

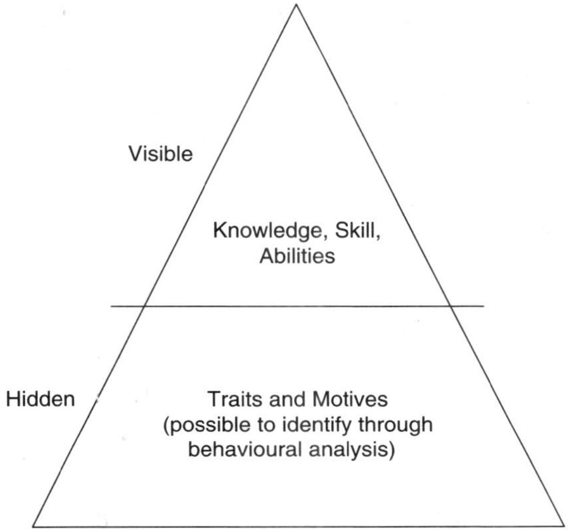

Figure 7.1 *Personality iceberg*

of the personality iceberg are more difficult to assess and develop. In many organizations, we still focus on hiring based on surface knowledge and skill competencies, but ideally the converse would be a better option where the focus should be on recruiting based on core motives and competencies, and teach the knowledge and skills required to do specific jobs.

Research conducted in 1999–2000 by three leading performance management companies world-wide indicate that companies using competencty-based performance management programmes returned 20–30 per cent more to shareholders than companies using traditional methods like job descriptions, salary grades, etc.

COMPETENCY CHARACTERISTICS

Based on the organizational experiences, we can identify the following characteristics of competencies:

- Motives—The things a person consistently thinks about or wants and that which causes action. Motives 'drive, direct, or select' behaviour towards certain actions or goals.
- Traits—-Physical characteristics and consistent responses to situation or information.
- Self-concept—A person's attitudes, values, or self-image.
- Knowledge—Information a person has in specific content areas.
- Skill—The ability to perform a certain physical or mental task.

As explained earlier, knowledge and skill competencies tend to be visible and relatively 'on the surface' characteristics of people. Self-concept, trait, and motive competencies are more hidden, 'deeper' and central to personality.

Surface knowledge and skill competencies are relatively easy to develop; training is the most effective way to secure these employee abilities. Core motive and trait competencies are more difficult to assess and develop; it is most cost-effective to select these characteristics.

COMPETENCY IDENTIFICATION AND ASSESSMENT PROCESS

To diagnose competencies, organizations adopt several approaches. A manual top-down-driven approach is described in Wolfe and Grosch (1990). It starts out on the organizational level where core competencies of an organizational unit are distinguished from competencies of individual employees. In order to ensure that employee competencies are managed in line with the future needs of the organization, the skills management initiative starts by looking at future developments of the market and the needs of the customer and from these goes on to define the core competencies of the organizational unit.

At this stage the required competencies are identified and defined both for the individual job and for the job family. The competency requirements are identified in terms of required technical skills and knowledge, management skills, and social and personal skills (Faix et al. 1991). All these are understood from the critical success factors (CSF) of job requirements and, accordingly, competency models developed (Lucia and Lepsinger, 1999). After the process of identification and the definition of competencies, assessment of existing competencies is made for individual employees. Competency assessment process is so designed that it gets integrated with the performance evaluation process, and also facilitates self-assessment by the employees themselves. Organizations using the software support can make the competency assessment and renewal process on-line and transparent. The idea behind is to make the employees aware where they stand vis-à-vis their competency requirements. The competency integrated performance appraisal process also helps in strategic decision-making of the organizations, as organizations can make future plans and programmes leveraging their employees' capabilities. The uniformity in the skill profiles and competency requirements helps the organizations to initiate the need-based competency development to renew the organizations.

Yet from other perspectives, based on organizational practices, we can list the methods of competency identification through the process of competency mapping. Competency mapping is a process of identifying key competencies for a company or institution and the jobs and functions within it. Competency mapping is important and is an essential exercise. Every well-managed organization should have well-defined roles and list of competencies required for performing each role effectively. Such a list should be used for recruitment, performance management, promotions, placement, and training needs identification. The most effective method of doing competency mapping is through behavioural event interview (BEI) techniques, conducted through a `competency requirement questionnaire. However, any competency mapping exercise first starts with the job analysis that requires employees to describe what they are doing, and what skills, attitudes, and abilities they need to have to perform it well. There would be a situation to request them to list down the attributes needed to make it up to the next level, thus making it behavioural as well as skill-based. Secondly, having discovered the similarities in the questionnaire, a competency-based job description is crafted and presented to the HR department for their agreement and additions, if any. Thirdly, having agreed on the job requirements and the skills and attitudes needed to progress within it and become more productive one starts mapping the capability of the employees to the benchmarks. There are several index points within the responsibility level. An almost (but not quite) arbitrary level of attainment is noted against each benchmark indicating the areas where the assessee is in terms of his/her personal development and achievement. These provide a fairly good picture of the employee to see whether he (or she) needs to perform better or to move up a notch on the scale. Once the employee 'tops' every indicator at his/her level, he/she moves on to the next and begins there at the bottom—in short, he/she gets promoted.

This reasonably simple though initially (the first year only) tedious method helps everybody to know what the real state of preparedness of an organization is to handle new business (or its old one) because it has a clear picture of every incumbent in the organization. It helps in determining the training and development needs and, importantly, it helps to encourage the best and develop the rest. A win–win situation for everyone!

The process of competency mapping makes use of different frameworks/models. Some of these commonly known frameworks/models are job competence assessment model (JCAM), single job competency model, one-size-fits-all model, multiple job models, role set-based competency model (RSBCM), etc.

Irrespective of the models, all competency mapping approaches generally use a combination of:

- Interviews
- Work studies
- Group work
- Task forces
- Questionnaire
- Use of job descriptions, performance appraisal formats, etc.

Competency mapping is always done in the defined job context following a set of approaches, like:

- Workforce skills analysis
- Job analysis
- Supply and demand analysis
- Gap analysis
- Situation analysis

Skill Analysis helps to describe skills required to carry out a function. However, this is a dynamic approach, as it also considers nature of work changes in an organization.

Job Analysis focuses on tasks, responsibilities, knowledge, and skill requirements, which are required for successful job performance.

Both the workforce skills analysis and job analysis are done from inputs collected from survey (through questionnaire responses), interviews with managers and employees, and benchmarking information with successful organizations. For technology-intensive and machine-enabled jobs, skill set requirements and cycle-time for jobs (as printed in the literatures) also contribute as critical input information for such jobs.

Supply Analysis is done considering workforce demographics (in terms of occupations, grades, structure, race, origin, gender, age, service experience, education, training, health status, retirement time, and similar other information), trends, and present workforce competencies. This, therefore, helps to understand the existing workforce status.

Demand Analysis on the other hand helps to identify workforce of the future in line with the vision, mission, objectives, goals, and strategies of an organization. Critical inputs from demand analysis contribute to development of competency model for workforce of the future.

With the above input reinforcers, organization undertakes gap analysis to understand the differences between the workforce of today and the workforce of the future. After such identification of differences, organizations need to plan to address those.

Addressing such gaps is done through solution analysis, taking into account both ongoing and unplanned changes in the workforce. Solution analysis also weighs different options to get the work

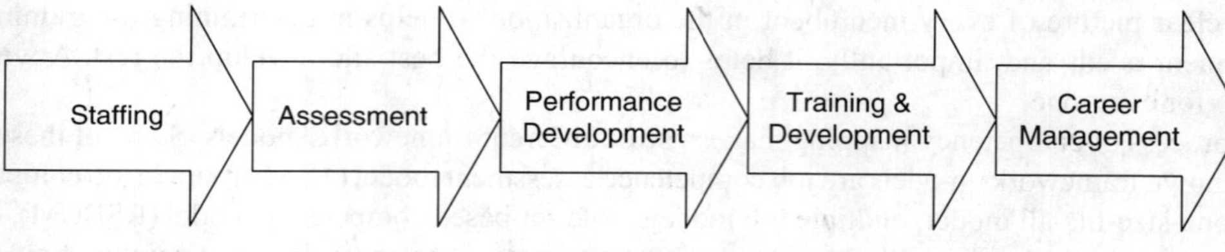

Figure 7.2 *Competency mapping process*

done, either considering institutional or contractual employment. New recruitment, restructuring, training and re-training, redeployment and rightsizing, all are done, in the light of new competency model, in this phase.

After suitable competency mapping, the next course of action for an organization, however, is to decide whether to downsize/right size or to go for training, re-training, and redeployment.

Competency mapping, therefore, has now become essential for every organization to achieve excellence, gain competitive advantage, and renew them through proper restructuring. Only focus on skill and continuous skill development is not the answer for gaining competitive advantage for today's organization. It is essential to leverage the human potential in respect of competency mapping to understand both the existing set of competencies and the gap if any. The process of mapping is illustrated in Figure 7.2.

STEPS OF A COMPETENCY IDENTIFICATION PROCESS

Based on the above discussions, we can list the steps of competency identification as under:

- Examining the purpose and setting of competency modelling.
- Selecting a position and a group of employees.
- Selecting the set of performance outcomes.
- Performing competency elicitations.
- Obtaining individual competence-performance structures.
- Obtaining organizational competence-performance structures.
- Validating the results.

STEPS TO INTRODUCE COMPETENCY-BASED SYSTEM

Before going in for a competency-based system, it is advisable that one should study the organizational needs and its acceptance by all. This is very critical because competencies are contextual and can change from time to time. One should never attempt to copy the competencies from other organizations however similar the role may seem to be. We may look amongst many others, the following critical factors before venturing into competency mapping:

Vision and Mission of the Organization: This is very important and any system designed should be in alignment with this.

Hierarchical Levels: You may need to look at the hierarchical levels of the organization since competencies differ from one level to another.

Role: You may need to split the roles to design competencies, which differ based on this.

Organizational Life Cycle: Try to analyse which part of the life cycle your organization is currently at. For example, the holistic life cycle model defines five stages like birth, growth, midlife, maturity, and decline.

Culture: Organizational cultural diagnosis is critical and will give valuable inputs into the realm of the value systems within an organization. This in turn can be helpful in getting the management's attention for driving the initiative.

ADVANTAGES OF A COMPETENCY-BASED APPROACH

Recruitment and Selection: Knowing the requisite competencies for a particular role helps the interviewers in assessing the candidates better and maintains consistency in case of multiple interviews.

Performance/Potential Assessment: This would help map the current set of competencies of an individual with the expected set of competencies required for him to perform his next role in a new position or in a higher rank.

Compensation Management: Competencies can help in developing job families and linking it to job worth can allow a better compensation management.

Training: This can help in identifying the training needs of an individual/role and help design and evaluate it better.

DEVELOPING COMPETENCY MODELS

The key to gaining competitive advantages is the ability of the workforce of an organization to maximize the advantages of state-of-the-art technology, superior products, and steady source of capital to enter into the marketplace. A company's technological tools are only as useful as its employer's ability to employ them; they are perceived in terms of how effectively the benefits are communicated (McLagan, 1989).

Competency models are specific to jobs and so also specific to the persons or the job owners. Critical success factors for the job and so also the person who does the job widely varies. The reason is attributable to behavioural dynamics. Job-related behaviour varies with the jobs and so the person. For example, one male sales executive and another female sales executive doing the same jobs in the same organization may have a different set of competency requirements, the reason being the person-specific attributes and characteristics. The potentiality of a person in terms of aptitude, reasons, and inclination to acquire a particular set of competencies are different. Therefore, for the same job, there may be two different competency models. For protocol-bound operation-level jobs, however, competency models may be the same. Therefore, while developing the competency models, all these aspects deserve attention. Well-developed competency models help organizations to identify the essential knowledge, skills, and attributes needed for successful performance. Also the models integrate the job with the organizational and human resource management strategies. It becomes ultimately the basis for recruitment, compensation design, training and development, performance appraisal, and so also succession planning.

Thus, competency model accounts for both the innate and acquired aspects. The typical pyramidal structure of the model documents all the skills and knowledge that are possible to develop, and at the same time all the innate behavioural attributes that are embodied with the job.

EXAMPLES OF HR COMPETENCIES

Business Partner—Competencies include:

- Knows mission
- Understands business process and how to change to improve efficiency and effectiveness
- Understands clients and organizational culture
- Understands public service environment
- Understands team behaviour
- Communicates well
- Possesses the ability to be innovative and create a risk-taking environment
- Applies organizational development principles
- Knows business system thinking
- Possesses good analytical skills including the ability to think strategically and creatively
- Possesses the ability to build trust relationships
- Links HR to the organization's mission and service outcome

Change Agent—Competencies include:

- Understands business process and how to change to improve efficiency and effectiveness
- Understands clients and organizational culture
- Understands public service environment
- Understands team behaviour
- Communicates well
- Assesses and balances competing values
- Knows business system thinking
- Applies information technology to human resource management
- Possesses good analytical skills including the ability to think strategically and creatively
- Designs and implements change process
- Uses consultation and negotiation skills including dispute resolution
- Possesses the ability to build trust relationships
- Possesses marketing and representational skills
- Uses consensus and coalition building skills
- Demonstrates customer service orientation

Leadership—Competencies include:

- Understands team behaviour
- Communicates well
- Assesses and balances competing values
- Possesses good analytical skills including the ability to think strategically and creatively

- Uses consultation and negotiation skills including dispute resolution
- Uses consensus and coalition building skills
- Understands values and promotes diversity
- Practices and promotes integrity and ethical behaviour

COMPETENCY-BASED PERFORMANCE MANAGEMENT SYSTEMS

David Martone (2003) defined a competency-based performance-management system as a documented and well-structured model that considers the skills and behaviours for successful performance in the present and so also the future job roles. By making it transparent, it helps employees to understand the job expectations from their organizations. Also it becomes the competency-based performance-management system and becomes the framework to align employees' job performance with the organizational goals.

Achieving goals both for the individual employees and for the organizations are the key drivers for achieving organizational success. A competency-based approach to performance management requires the organization at the outset to define the organizational short-term and long-term goals and then identify the skills and behaviour requirements. Such expectations are then weighed in terms of available skills and behaviours, and gaps, if any, are then addressed through competency development programmes. A competency gap helps employees to understand where they stand vis-à-vis the competency requirements. With a self-introspection, employees can hone their own competencies and can complement with others in the organization, and accordingly both at their individual and collective level they deliver the performance results for the organizations. A number of organizations build competency-based programmes to develop the employees' capabilities, so that they can meet the expectations level of the organizations.

Operationally, all employees are expected to have certain core competencies and behaviours, based on their skills and area of expertise. However, individual differences do not always make such competencies uniformly available in all employees. It is for this reason that organizations need to make good the competency gap for enabling employees to deliver results. However, developing competencies and meeting the competency gap may not be always possible. Particularly in Indian organizations, skill transition, either due to technological change or process changes, may not be always possible, for knowledge specificity. Lack of skill interchangeability makes it difficult for skill renewal and so also competency development. In such cases, however, organizations feel constrained to develop the performance goals, keeping pace with the available competencies of employees. A glaring example is the 135 years old East India Pharmaceuticals, a company which exists without any product diversification, mainly for their captive market share in government run hospitals. But this is not good, as in a competitive world, today's organizations cannot survive without their renewal, a precursor for which is the competency development.

Competency-based performance management approach also helps the organization to develop the performance criteria for all the cross-section of employees. This process then becomes the basis for the employees to understand what competencies need to be mastered for their self-learning and career advancement. With a competency-based performance-management system in place, organizations can successfully manage the talent pool, do succession planning, and develop the bench strength for the future. Additionally, it will create a basis for recognition and reward, merit increases, and promotions.

ESSENTIAL ELEMENTS OF PERFORMANCE-BASED COMPETENCY

Following are the key elements that should be considered in designing and implementing a competency-based performance-management system.

Establish Competencies: Employers need to specify the set of competencies that they expect their employees to possess. It is pertinent to mention that for the same job profile, competency requirements may vary. However, there may be some commonality also. From organizational perspectives, we can broadly classify competencies into two types—cultural and organizational. Cultural competencies may encompass integrity, professionalism, accountability, quality, results focus, and profitability. These are basically the traits that represent the culture of an organization. Organizations need to select three to five cultural competencies, depending on the culture of the organization, define those duly listing the expected behaviours and actions of employees, which is instrumental for achieving the desired performance results. Like-wise, organizations need to select the organizational competencies like specific skills instrumental to perform the job or the task assigned to the employees. Such competencies may be categorized as customer service, business development, technical competency, interpersonal relational competency, etc. Both the cultural and organizational competencies are essential to achieve desired performance results.

Set Goals and Performance Expectations: After establishing the competencies and meeting the competency gap, if any, of employees, organizations select goals not exceeding five for the employees, keeping pace with the nature of work they need to perform and that helps organizations to achieve the results. Some of the behavioural criteria for some competencies are illustrated in Table 7.1.

Competency-based performance systems, apart from achieving the organizational goals and meeting the performance expectations also extend support to the process of recruitment and selection. Matching with the competency maps, managers can pre-decide the requirements of skills, experience, and behavioural pattern in a prospective employee, and accordingly recruit them. Some of the generic set of individual competencies that can enhance the performance is listed in Table 7.2.

Table 7.1 *Behavioural criteria for some competencies*

Set of competencies	Behavioural criteria
Integrity	Honours commitments Honest and complies with business ethics Inspires people and becomes a model to them
Quality conscious	Ensures control Focuses on continuous improvement Emphasizes on customer satisfaction Delivers quality services
Cultured	Communicates effectively Focuses on continuous improvement High morale High standards of personal conduct and work Believes in developing the subordinates Supports employee development programmes Complies with organizational policies

It is important to note that the list of generic competencies is not exhaustive. Depending on the nature of organizations, the requirement of generic competencies may vary. These competencies can be reviewed, developing specific questions.

Let us hypothetically discuss some generic competencies and attributes that individuals are usually expected to possess for the said set of competencies in Table 7.3.

Table 7.2 *List of generic competencies*

Analytic	Proactive	Attention to details
Can handle change	Ability to coach	Understands commercial applications
Effectively communicate	Cost-conscious	Innovative
Customer centric	Ability to take decision	Believes in delegation
Dependable	Value diversity	Can motivate people
High emotional intelligence	Empathetic	Can empower
Gives and receives feedback	Ability to give leadership	Has listening ability
Can perceive and judge	Has patience	Ability to plan and organize
Can manage stress	Can solve problems	Quality conscious
Result oriented	Safety conscious	Believes in self-development
Ability to be strategic	Takes initiative and responsibility	Believes in teamwork
Makes effective application of technology	Ability to apply technology	Can manage time
Effective in written communication		

Table 7.3 *Generic competencies and attributes*

Generic competencies	Set of attributes
Strategic/customer focus	Anticipation/proactive thinking Commercial awareness Customer focus Decision-making ability Leadership ability Perception/judgement Results focus Strategizing ability Time management
Process/improvement focus	Analytical ability Change-handling ability Creativity/innovation Delegation Persistence/perseverance Problem-solving ability Quality focus Technology application Written communication

People/empowerment focus	Coaching ability Communication Drive/motivation Emotional intelligence Empathizing ability Empowerment ability Feedback (giving and receiving) Listening Self-development
Risk/value creation focus	Attention to detail Cost-consciousness Dependability Diversity focus Planning and organizing Safety focus Stress management Taking initiative/responsibility Teamwork ability

COMPETENCY DICTIONARY

For obvious popularity of competency mapping and developing the set of desired competencies in employees, and for achieving the performance goals of the organizations, many organizations now prefer to develop the job descriptions based on the competencies. A structured approach to competency definition for any specific set of competencies requires the development of a competency dictionary. Competency dictionary becomes a valuable guide for the organizations, for future references, like recruitment and selection, training and development, setting of performance standards, etc. It brings order to the system of interpretation of competency sets, behavioural and skill requirements, etc. This also helps in strategic decision-making, goal setting, etc. Therefore, every organization after suitable competency mapping develops the competency dictionary.

Some of the generic competencies in organizations are leadership, management, decision-making, communication, proficiencies, etc. Here we are illustrating a competency dictionary for leadership and decision-making for a hypothetical organization.

Generic competencies and its definition	Specific attributes of generic competencies
Leadership—It is a valued competency which is not just restricted for top level managers, but for all cross-sections of employees. People with high leadership competency can get the job done and ensure achievement of organizational results.	Coaching Empowerment Power of influencing others Teamwork Vision
Decision-making—This is another generic competency and the ability of people to make the right decisions can benefit the organization in achieving the results.	Analytic Decisive Innovative Judgemental Not risk averse

SUMMARY

Skills, multi-skilling, and competency are the major issues concerning performance management. The problem of skill obsolescence is now a global phenomenon. At organization level, skill renewal initiative is seriously lacking, as they are now more comfortable to opt for downsizing or rightsizing through redundancies. In India also, despite creation of the National Renewal Fund (NRF), organizations prefer to spend NRF money (which are available on soft interest terms) more on voluntary retirement schemes (VRS) than skill renewal and redeployment of existing workers. There exists a gross misconception that skills for the Indian workers cannot be renewed for their obvious trade-specific and industry-specific bent. Moreover, existing workmen are by and large in their high age bracket. This misconception further accentuated due to the problem of quantification of benefits of skill development and change or renewal training. However, we have now more developed tools for such quantification and at least some empirical evidence to counter such apprehension. A well-structured competency mapping with systematic HRD intervention can successfully renew the skill and contribute to competitive advantage. Skill renewal, among others, can avert manpower redundancies. It has now a strategic dimension for long-term profitability and growth of an organization.

The competency-based performance management systems can work in any type of organization—large or small, and for-profit or not-for-profit organizations. One can literally feel the difference in organizations where such a programme has been implemented: employees are enthusiastic, focused, energized, and clear about what they are working on and how their efforts contribute to the overall goals of the organization. With a little planning and vision to develop and implement such a process we can observe the differences in energy levels and contribution of employees and the corresponding improvement in business results.

KEY WORDS

Skill Inventories—A skill inventory is a device for pin-pointing information about individuals and their suitability for different jobs. Skill inventories include the name of the employee and a listing (or inventory) of job-related skills, training, and/or experience which could prove useful in a future assignment. The purpose of skill inventories is to provide the organization with quick, accurate information on all employees in order that management can choose the best-qualified person for promotion or transfer.

Supply Analysis—is done considering workforce demographics (in terms of occupations, grades, structure, race, origin, gender, age, service experience, education, training, health status, retirement time and similar other information), trends, and present workforce competencies. This, therefore, helps to understand the existing workforce status.

Technical or Functional Competencies—These are the knowledge, attitude, and skills related to technical or functional expertise required to perform a role.

Multi-skilling—For effective employee performance, multi-skilling of people is very important. Multi-skilling is defined as the process to train employees in a variety of skills, even crossing the traditional trade-specific or craft-specific skill sets. Thus to develop multi-skills, employees require additional training to enable them to perform more jobs within the same job family or to do the entire jobs from a holistic point of view. Multi-skilling is often misconstrued to succeed downsizing.

'Competence' and 'Competency'—'Competence' means a skill and the standard of performance reached while 'competency' refers to the behaviour by which it is achieved. In other words, one describes what people can do while the other focuses on how they do it. Competences refer to the range of skills, which are satisfactorily performed, while competencies refer to the behaviour adopted in competent performance.

Motives—The things a person consistently thinks about or wants and that which causes action. Motives 'drive, direct, or select' behaviour towards certain actions or goals.

GENERAL REVIEW QUESTIONS

1. Explain the concept of competency. How does competency development help in effective performance management of an organization?
2. What is a skill inventory? How does skill-inventory help in competency mapping in an organization?
3. Discuss the process of competency identification in an organization.
4. What are the important steps involved in introducing the competency-based performance management system in an organization?
5. Develop a competency map for a marketing manager of a new generation software company, clearly showing the weight distribution to different competency areas.
6. What are the important sources of competency information? How do you relate such sources for competency development?
7. Explain the concept of competency dictionary. How does it help in effective performance management systems in an organization?
8. Short Notes
   (a) Generic Competencies
   (b) Behavioural Criteria
   (c) PCMM
   (d) Competency Mapping
   (e) Supply Analysis

CRITICAL REVIEW QUESTION

9. You have been retained by a multi-national static metre manufacturer operating in India. Static metres are used by the electricity boards to take the reading and bill the customers. Quality conformance requirements for static metres are very high, with a maximum of ±1 per cent tolerance limit. The company requires a competency-based performance management system. Develop your line of actions.

REFERENCES

Bhattacharyya, D.K. (2006), *Human Resource Management*, 2nd edition (New Delhi: Excel Books).

Bhattacharyya, D.K. (2007), *Human Resource Research Methods* (New Delhi: Oxford University Press).

Bhattacharyya, D.K. (2010), *Organizational Change and Development* (New Delhi: Oxford University Press).

Boyatzis, R.E (1982), *The Competent Manager: A Model for Effective Performance* (New York, NY: John Wiley & Sons).

Faix, W.G., C. Buchwald and R. Wetzler (1991), *Skill-Management: Qualifikations planung fur Unternehmen und Mitarbeiter* (Wiesbaden: Gabler).

Green, P.C. (1999), *Building Robust Competencies: Linking Human Resource Systems to Organizational Strategies* (San Francisco, CA: Jossey-Bass).

Hogg, B. (1989), 'The AMA Competency Programme', in Lee, Geoff and David Beard (eds), *Development Centre Relating the Potential of Your Employees through Assessment and Development* (London: The Tata McGraw Hill Training Series).

Katz, R. (1955), 'Skills of an Effective Administrator', *Harvard Business Review*, 33: 33–42

Lawler, E., G. Ledford (1992), 'A Skill-Based Approach to Human Resource Management', *European Management Journal*, 10(4): 383–91.

Lucia, A.D. and R. Lepsinger (1999), *Competency Models: Pinpointing Critical Success Factors in Organizations* (San Francisco, CA: Jossey-Bass).

Martone, David (2003), 'A Guide to Developing a Competency-Based Performance Management System', *Employment Relations Today*, 30(3): 23–32.

McClelland, D.C. (1973), 'Testing for Competence Rather than Intelligence', *American Psychologist*, 28(1): 1–14.

McLagan, P.A. (1989), *Models for HRD Practice* (Alexandria, VA: American Society for Training and Development).

Parry, S.B. (1996), 'The Quest for Competencies', *Training*, July, 48–56.

Spencer, L.M. and S.M. Spencer (1993), *Competence at Work: Models for Superior Performance* (New York, NY: John Wiley & Sons).

Wolfe, R.M. and J.W. Grosch (1990), 'Personality Correlates of Confidence in One's Decisions', *Journal of Personality*, 58: 515–34.

CASE STUDY

Swadeshi Textile—Overcoming the Crisis Through Competency Renewal

Swadeshi Textile, a typical textile manufacturing organization, which had shown convincing growth rate for successive years, now faces the problem of market saturation. The company had grown over a number of years as a major player in its sector. It had a strong customer base and enjoyed effective relationships built on a strong technical foundation for its products. But, as with many such organizations, it faced an uncertain future as its main market had matured and was probably already beyond saturation point. Over and above, technical developments in competing products are now threatening the original way the product ranges of the company were built.

In ownership pattern, the company was typically a family managed one, and with recent IPOs (initial public offerings), it became a public limited company, with majority stake, however, still within the family. Mostly from the forest products, the company produces the viscose staple fibre, the core raw material for the textile industry. Sourcing of forest products for various environmental issues has now become difficult for the company. They even face resistance from the local people, while they harvest the forest products from their captive forests. Ultimately the company was forced to import the pulps from other South-East Asian countries, which resulted in huge production cost over-run, reducing their profit margin to a marginal level. The company then took the decision to increase the sale price of their products. It was their belief that with the kind of brand image that they enjoy, it would be possible for them to captivate their loyal customers even with the increased price. The result, however, was the other way round. Most of the textile manufacturers shifted their sourcing to imported synthetic pulp. With the latest technology, they are now able to reduce the chemical hazards of synthetic pulp. Mixing synthetic pulp with the viscose staple fibre, and by reducing the chemical hazards of synthetic, they are now able to produce the fabrics, known as anti-crease cotton. In tropical countries like India, the product was an immediate success. Gradually, the company entered into question mark category.

To overcome the impasse, the company then decided to move to the latest technology for blending of imported synthetic pulp with the locally sourced viscose staple fibre to offer the ready-made solution to their captive customers at a very competitive rate. But such decisions of the company were late, as most of their customers shifted to their competing organization or went for backward integration to produce the fibre on their own. It was at this stage that the company had to draw their strategy for survival. To achieve the strategic intent, the company reviewed their core competency and how it cascades to the individual level competencies of their people. To their utter surprise, they could identify huge competency gaps in their production and marketing functions. With the prevailing labour laws and standards and the replacement of existing employees, managing the redundancies was not possible. The company then left with the only option to renew the competencies of the existing people and make them competent enough to perform the phase of transition. Extensive competency-based training was imparted both for the marketing and production people. In addition, the company also undertook organizational development programmes, which together make their people competent enough to perform in changed circumstances. Competency-based training and organizational development initiatives were reinforced by introducing the mentor–mentee relations and a series of motivational programmes. With the renewed competency, handholding by their superiors, and the series of motivational programmes, the company could ultimately regain their position within a short span of time.

Question: Encyclopedia Britannica, a legacy-bound and more than 200-year-old organization, had to go for distress sale to the present owners, for their inability to switch over from printed version of Encyclopedia to electronic version, primarily for Microsoft's Encarta. From web-materials, collect the details and suggest how competency development could have helped Encyclopedia Britannica to turn around, avoiding the distress sale.

CHAPTER 8

Performance-based Compensation

Learning Objectives

After reading this chapter, you will be able to understand:

- Concept of performance-based compensation
- Compensation design through job evaluations
- Various incentive schemes
- Performance-based compensation design
- Benefits of performance-based compensation
- Performance-related pay
- Compensation broadbanding using PMS
- Compensation design through skill-based programmes
- Obstacles to the introduction of skill-based pay
- Application of skill-based pay
- Competency-based pay
- Obstacles to the introduction of performance-related pay
- Performance guide charts
- Performance-based executive compensation
- Calibration of executive compensation to performance
- Performance measurement in executive incentive programmes

Align Individual Performance with the Team Performance

High rate of attrition has all along been a problem for the multinational private sector bank, having business presence in India. The CEO of the Indian outfit could identify the reasons for such attrition as the poor performance measurement systems. The prevailing performance measurement systems emphasize too much on the quantitative aspects, ignoring the qualitative aspects of employees' performance. Each employee gets their business target in the form of his or her key result areas (KRAs). A sizeable amount of variable compensation is aligned with the target achievement. The CEO of the company feels high rate of attrition is attributable to stretched quantitative targets, which not even the 50 per cent of the employees could achieve. This resulted in substantial losing of their compensation part. It was at this stage that the CEO of the company asked the HR department to come out with a new performance-driven compensation plan that can increase the level of motivation for the employees, and at the same time can contain the high rate of attrition. The HR department of the company could come out with the new performance-driven compensation plan, which among others emphasized on the alignment of individual and team performance with the variable pay, introduction of Scanlon plan for computing the incentive pay, which can tap the ingenuity of the employees to improve production, etc. The results in both the cases were outstanding, and the rate of attrition of employees gradually decreased.

INTRODUCTION

Performance means the degree or extent with which an employee applies his skill, knowledge, and efforts to a job assigned to him/her and the result of that application. Performance appraisal means analysis, review, or evaluation of performance or behaviour analysis of an employee. It may be formal or informal, oral or documented, open or confidential. However, in organizations we find formal appraisal systems in documented form. It is, therefore, a formal process to evaluate the performance of the employees in terms of achieving organizational objectives.

The term 'compensation', as a substitute word for 'wages' and 'salaries', is of recent origin. Literatures on wages and salaries are enormous and consider the issues, more from the legal perspectives. Wages as a cost factor has now become very significant, hence strategic management of wages, for organizations, is now very important. Compensation, therefore, is viewed as strategic management of wages and salaries. In India, particularly, we have very scanty literature on compensation, although it has now become imperative for organizations to balance the cost of compensation and employee motivation (for retention) to survive in a competitive world. Employee compensation is a better term than employee benefits or wages and salaries. What the employee provides the employer is labour service, usually called work. This labour service consists of many different kinds of employee behaviour, for example, showing up regularly and on time, carrying out tasks dependably, cooperating with others, making useful suggestions, etc. So pay or compensation represents an exchange between the employee and the organization. Each gives something in return for something else. In the past, the compensation issue was more confidential and governed by individual employer's preference and choices. However, in today's competitive world, compensation issues are more transparent and every employee can make an informed choice to join an organization based on the compensation packages. Thus, trading off compensation cost optimization and employee retention have now become most important priorities for today's organizations. Introducing performance-based compensation can benefit the organization. Performance-based compensation not only validates the compensation design, but also helps in optimizing the cost of compensation.

For all important decisions concerning people, like transfer and promotion, remuneration, reward, training and development, so also for long-term manpower planning and organization development, performance appraisal is necessary. A well-documented performance appraisal system helps in understanding the attributes and behaviours of employees. It is also necessary for motivation, communication, strengthening superior–subordinate relationship, target-fixing (key performance areas/key result areas), workforce planning, and for improving the overall performance of the organization. One of the important functions of performance management systems is to design suitable reward systems, relating rewards to employees' performance. Other human resource management-related performance-based decisions also to a great extent influence the compensation decision, viz., a promotional decision based on employees' performance, etc.

DEFINITIONS

Operationally, we can hardly make any differences between the term compensation and wages. Both are intended to price the efforts of the employees. However, the word compensation is used more holistically, to acknowledge the strategic importance of wages. Theoretically, the word compensation means something, such as money, given or received as payment for damages. However, in HR literature, we consider the term from broader perspective, i.e., strategic use of wages paid to employees. Even some organization prefers to use the term rewards instead of wages or compensation. In HR, we do not consider reward just to acknowledge good performance, rather we consider it as strategic design of compensation, so that when employees get it at end of the month, they feel they are not just getting their wages, but being rewarded.

A compensation or wage structure in a given case takes into account the industrial adjudication and considerations of right and wrong, fairness and unfairness. Because of the social conscience and the welfare policy of the state, collective bargaining is now the most dynamic form of negotiation for deciding the wage structure in a particular organization. Hence wage issues no longer remain a pure mathematical problem. However, in the new economy, we are now employing more and more knowledge workers, for whom compensation design largely depends on the performance level.

VARIOUS CONCEPTS OF COMPENSATION

Wages is any monetary compensation paid to an employee for the services he/she renders. Primarily, wages in any form provide financial support for the labour, or it is a price paid for the labour. In organizations, wages are divided into two broad categories: base wages and other benefits or allowances. Benefits or allowances are essentially made available to prevent the erosion of wage income in real terms. The basic salary is the real wages and the basic salary with allowances represents money wages. Some of the allowances, however, are statutory in nature. Good organizations, however, voluntarily pay more allowances over and above the statutory requirements. Although we make the distinction between the terms wages and allowances; in India various Acts related to labour administration, defined the term wages differently. The only commonality in the definitions of wages provided by different Acts is that in all the cases definition of wages includes also the dearness allowances. The Workmen's Compensation Act, 1923, Section 2 (m), defines wages considering the 'wages for leave period, holiday pay, overtime pay, bonus, attendance bonus, and good conduct bonus'. The Payment of Wages Act, 1936 section 2 (VI) considers wages as 'any award of settlement and production bonus, if paid, constitutes wages'.

The legal connotations, therefore, do not consider alignment of wages or compensation with the performance of employees.

Traditional theory of wages emphasize on its determination based on the market forces, i.e., the demand and supply. The theory of negotiated wages on one hand, considers the basis of wage determination through the collective bargaining process. On the other hand, performance-based wages or compensation emphasize on determination of wages based on employees' performance. From the economic perspectives, we find 'marginal productivity theory', subscribes to wage determination based on the estimate of value that will probably be produced by the workers. At least in this case, we find certain trace of wage determination is somewhat related to the performance level of employees. Performance-based compensation design emphasizes on the individual work, i.e., the value of the individual employees' performance to the organization.

DETERMINING COMPENSATION THROUGH JOB EVALUATION

Before the introduction of performance management systems in organizations, job evaluation was the only option, based on which compensation design used to be done. Job evaluation helps us to understand the individual worth, and it is widely used. It is the process of determining the worth of one job in relation to that of another without regard to the personalities. It analyses and assesses the content of jobs, to place them in some standard rank order. The end-result is used as the basis for a fair and logical remuneration system.

A properly devised job evaluation scheme provides management with definite, systematic and reliable data for working out wage and salary scales. Thus, logical wage negotiation reduces wage grievances and dissatisfaction with wage differentials and ensures fair treatment for each employee. It also provides a logical basis for promotion.

INCENTIVE SCHEMES

Incentives are paid to the workmen over and above the normal wages to reward their good performance. In places, where piece-rate system of wages exist, payment of incentives is relatively simple as for manufacturing additional units than the standard one, workers can be paid extra wages, which they are supposed to get for each additional unit. This incentive scheme is known as straight piece-rate scheme. In time-rate system, however, such incentives are computed following standard hour systems. To illustrate, let us assume a given volume of job is given to a worker for standard 8 hours work. If the worker is able to complete the job within 6 hours, then for the hours saved, i.e., 2 hours, he/she should be given the incentives duly upgrading his hourly wage rate apportioning his 8 hours rate for 6 hours. Let us assume 8 hours are needed as standard time for completing a job and the rate per hour is Re.1. If the worker finishes the work in 6 hours, he will also get Rs. 8, which upgrades his hourly wage rate then from Re. 1 to Rs. 1.33p. Yet in another way we can look into the nature of incentive schemes from the organizational practices.

For designing performance-based compensation, it is imperative to understand the theoretical contexts of various incentives. As the list is long, here we are listing those incentive schemes, which are common for organization.

Barth System—Under this system, there is no minimum guaranteed wage. The formula (considering hourly wage rate of Re. 1) is as follows:

Wage = Std. time 8 hrs × time-taken (6 hrs) × hourly rate Re. 1 = Rs. 7 (approx.)

Bedaux System—This system is also called 'units' or 'points' system. It has a guaranteed basic rate like the Halsey and Rowan Systems. Under this system each minute of Standard Time is expressed in terms of units or points after a detailed time study. The guaranteed basic wage is paid unto 60 points per hour scored by the worker. Points earned above 60 are paid at 75–100 per cent of the basic wage rate (the standard daily rate for the job which is always higher than the minimum guaranteed wage).

Taylorian System—In this scheme, there are two piece-rates: one lower and one higher plus a bonus paid as a percentage of the time rate. Obviously such a system would automatically discourage low production and would be installed where the average performance is well below expectations.

Merrick Differential Piece Rate System—Under this system there are three piece rates:

- Up to, say, 83 per cent of the standard output—a piece-rate + 10 per cent of time rate as bonus.
- Above 83 per cent and up to 100 per cent of standard output—same piece rate + 20 per cent of time rate.
- Above 100 per cent of standard output—same piece rate but no bonus.

Gantt Task System—This has three stages of payment:

- Below the standard performance, only the minimum guaranteed wage is to be paid.
- At the standard performance, this wage + 20 per cent of the time rate will be paid as bonus.
- When the standard is exceeded, higher piece-rate is paid but there is no bonus.

The main objective of this scheme is to raise the performance up to the standard level which is the task set before the workers.

The Emerson Empiric System—Under this system, standard time is established for each job. The efficiency of the worker is determined by dividing the time taken into the standard time. Up to 67 per cent efficiency the worker is paid at this time rate and from this point to 100 per cent, a bonus of 1 per cent is paid for every additional 1 per cent output. At 100 per cent efficiency, a bonus of 20 per cent is paid.

Accelerating Premium System—This provides for a guaranteed minimum wage for output below the standard. For low and average increase in output above the standard small increments in earnings are allowed. Increasingly, large earnings are conceded for the above average output, the increment being different for each 1 per cent increase in output.

Scanlon Plan—The Scanlon plan was designed to involve the workers in making suggestions for reducing the cost of operation and improving the working methods and sharing in the gains of increased productivity. The Rucker plan is similar to the Scanlon plan, the only difference being that in the latter the incentive earnings are calculated on the basis of the 'value added' by the manufacturing process. The Kaiser plan is also like these—a gains-sharing scheme. While the Rucker plan excludes all the supply and material costs, the Kaiser plan excludes all costs over which the workers have no control.

Halsey Premium Plan—It guarantees a fixed time wage to slow workers and, at the same time, offers extra pay to efficient workers. Extra pay in the form of bonus is given based on the amount of time saved by the worker, which is calculated @ 33-1/2 per cent of the time saved. Thus the cost of labour is reduced because of the percentage premium system.

Rowan Premium Plan—Under this plan, the time saved is expressed as a percentage of the time allowed, and the hourly rate of pay is increased by that percentage of the time allowed, and the hourly rate of pay is increased by that percentage so that total earnings of the worker are the total number of hours multiplied by the increased hourly wages.

While determining performance-based compensation, it is imperative to consider various incentive schemes, and select the appropriate one, keeping pace with the specific nature of work.

PERFORMANCE-RELATED COMPENSATION DESIGN

Employees are the backbone of any organization. Organizational growth and sustainability highly depend on the quality of performance of the employees. Performance management system, therefore, must objectively link the individual level performance of employees with the overall performance of the organizations. Wages or compensation is the most important vehicle of performance management. Most of the organizations, therefore, embrace the system of performance-linked compensation for its obvious strategic dimension. It facilitates compensation cost optimization, as non-performers do not required to be paid like the performers. Even with higher payment of compensation to performers, organizations can optimize the compensation cost, as the variables, i.e., the part of compensation payable on performance, need not be paid to the non-performers. Moreover, performance-linked compensation system motivates good performing employees and increases the retention of talents.

The chapter at the outset discussed the performance management basics, delineating it from the traditional precepts, and then discussed how performance-based compensation design can benefit the organizations.

Performance appraisal systems in any organization formally analyses, reviews, and evaluates performance of an employee in achieving the organization's mandated objectives. Like any other function, performance appraisal is also an important human resource management activity. Performance management, on the other hand, is an integrated process. It sets objectives, appraises employees, translates objectives into individual key performance areas (KPA), helps in compensation design, and in the process, benefits the organization to achieve its business goals and objectives. We call it a development tool, as it facilitates performance improvement, career development, and training. Thus performance management involves thinking through various facets of performance, identifying critical dimensions of performance, planning, reviewing, and developing and enhancing performance and related competencies. It is an ongoing communication process that involves both the managers and the employees:

- To identify and describe essential job functions and relating them to the mission and goals of the organization.
- To develop realistic and appropriate performance standards.
- To give and receive feedback about performance.
- To write and communicate constructive performance appraisals.
- To plan education and development opportunities to sustain improvement or build on employees' work performance.

Performance appraisals are bundles of tools used to evaluate the effectiveness or otherwise of a performance management system.

To sustain competitive advantage, organizations are not only required to recruit the best fit and systematically train and develop them, but also monitor the performance of employees and focus on performance improvement through various HR interventions. Globally, it is now well established through a series of empirical research that performance management is the most important area of an organization and perhaps has started getting supreme priority now.

BENEFITS OF PERFORMANCE-BASED COMPENSATION

From compensation management point of view, performance management systems help in achieving following critical goals:

- It helps in recognizing the efforts and contributions of employees objectively and thereby facilitates in effective job pricing, both through cost optimization and rewarding of talented performers.
- It facilitates in suitable compensation design, rewarding employees based on the performance linkage.
- It supports employee motivation (which leads to increased performance), helping employees to receive their performance feedback, understanding their strengths and weaknesses. Employees can develop themselves through self-introspection and thereby feel intrinsically motivated. So also performance-based pay helps in getting extrinsically motivated. Both the motivational constructs lead to improved performance.
- It facilitates employees to develop their core faculty of goal achievement.
- It retains good performers, through competitive compensation design, offering increased flexibility to earn more, based on performance level.
- It attracts good performers from competing organization.

Introduction of performance-related pay in many organizations is difficult, as it directly conflicts with the structured pay systems. In many organizations, it is also observed that the violation of principle of seniority-based compensation leads to the stagnation of many senior level employees, who get demotivated for stagnation in their pay scales. Such de-motivation lowers their level of performance and many such employees gradually leave the organization. Steel Authority of India (SAIL) lost many of their senior level employees when they launched their voluntary retirement scheme (VRS), for not getting the seniority protection in pay scales. The same thing happened in case of the State Bank of India. In both the cases, the private steel plants and the private sector banks got immensely benefitted for ready-to-use manpower.

Another crude operational issue is designing incentives, aligning with the performance, without specifying any minimum performance requirement. It means every one become eligible for the incentives, as individual contributions is not factored in designing the compensation. While 100 per cent factoring of individual performance is not desirable (as it culminates conflicts), total ignorance of it is also not desirable. Performance-linked compensation in such cases provide for incentives for results that exceed the stated goals, combining individual, departmental, and organizational goals.

In order to reap the strategic benefits of pay for performance, many organizations limit the increase in the pay only to bare statutory minimum, while increasing the amount of salary for those who are good performers. In both the cases, compensation decisions are based on realistic assessment of performance. Thus in such cases, organizations do away with the traditional cost of living and seniority precepts for compensation design. However, such practices have both advantages and disadvantages. Advantages are it rewards the merit, improves the teamwork, provides job satisfaction, and finally achieves the desired results. Disadvantages are difficulty to institutionalize the systems and monitor it, difficulty in identifying appropriate performance evaluation tools, and dilution of loyalty of employees (as it ignores the seniority factor).

PERFORMANCE-RELATED PAY

The term performance-related pay (PRP) encompasses several company wide schemes, like employee participation and share ownership schemes, etc. and general linkage with the compensation which the employees get. PRP schemes are designed and administered based on a view of what the businesses needs are. It often fails to deliver because it is not aligned closely to business strategy. Secondly, performance-driven compensation can support constant change and performance improvement, but they can't deliver these by itself contrary to popular belief. Third, line managers can muddle the process, unless they get the help.

Despite such difficulties in implementing PRP, organizations adopt this. We have listed some of the important areas, which deserve attention from the organizations, while they implement PRP.

Competition and Cost Control: Performance-related pay enhances corporate performance in a competitive environment. When we link performance and pay together, we also expect employees to behave accordingly. For example, when organizations compete with customer satisfaction, we expect employees to focus on this aspect, ensuring quality of goods and services.

Individualization: Collective relationships in a workplace are a common organizational pursuit to achieve teamwork. PRP is essentially driven by an individualization agenda. We can de-collectivize the workplace and the employer relationship by individualizing things, particularly through the reward mechanisms. Also we can use PRP in teamwork, i.e., in social partnership. The problem emerges; when organizations go for merit only pay increases, i.e., the extreme form of compensation individualization. Hence, effective PRP requires organizations to balance both the individualization and the collectivization.

Mismatch with the Strategy: Organizations adopt various strategies, depending on their business priorities. A common cost minimization strategy requires different range of behaviours. Although there exist possibilities or co-existence of different compensation programmes for different functions and divisions in the same organization, time dimensions may conflict with each other. Short-term focus, individual effort, and so on need to be supported by a compensation policy, which is different from long-term focus. Hence, effectively organization has to select PRP, keeping pace with the strategies.

Monitoring and Evaluation: This is really important and organizations often lack in this. It is not enough to just introduce PRP systems; it is also important to understand how PRP actually benefits the organization. Tracking changes after introduction of PRP through an effective monitoring and evaluation system can do this.

Culture: PRP often runs into conflict with the organizational culture. Organizations, which support diversity and pursue principles of equity, may not find it easy to implement, as PRP makes differentiation in pay packages on merit criteria. Many organizations give priority on quantitative achievement of results. However, some functions may demand high quality of performance. Quality cascades customers' satisfaction. Again organizations' compensation culture may assign maximum weights on the fixed component, reducing variables to a bare minimum. Incentives and other variables also may be at a fixed proportion, depending on hierarchical levels, independent of functional domains. Hence designing PRP compatible with organizational culture may again be difficult.

Use of PRP as an Instrument of Management Control: Many organizations wrongly use PRP as an instrument of management control, pay-roll control, or performance control. But this is not the right approach. In true sense, an effective PRP can help in empowering employees. But using PRP as a control mechanism defeats such pursuit. Again in teamwork systems, linkage between the basic pay and team contribution hardly exists. We have many interesting team performance bonuses and gain sharing schemes. Thus organizations must use PRP for strategic benefits and not as a tool for control mechanism.

Problems in Monitoring the PRP

PRP clarifies employees what they are expected to do in their jobs. Organizations embracing PRP should always try to set jointly clear targets and goals, which are stretching, challenging, and achievable. However, it is also important to make it monitorable. PRP initiatives of organizations often go wrong because they are too complicated and line managers don't know how to operate them. Often in organizations line managers are not communicated properly. Line managers fail to make any connection between the PRP and the things they need to manage, i.e., their business priorities. Thus to facilitate effective monitoring, organizations need to train the line managers so that they can understand its basics and job correlation. In many organizations, it becomes a perennial trade union issue also. Once it is understood properly, it can be monitored effectively.

Selection of Appropriate Performance Appraisal Tools

PRP initiatives can also fail due to wrong selection of appraisal tools. Many organizations assign overweight to such factors, on which employees hardly have any control. Some of the policies of the organizations may limit the extent of customer services. But such deficiencies may have some adverse effects on customer satisfaction, onus of which, organizations may wrongly assign to the individual employee, which PRP systems even stretch to link with the customers' feedback.

Perceptual Differences Between the Managers and the Employees

Employees often perceive senior managers' compensation is disproportionately higher, hence PRP in reality deprives them from their genuine pie, and while benefits the senior managerial employees, as their contributions are more traceable. To obviate such apprehensions, it is essential to communicate to the employees the mechanism of PRP design, so that they can also trace their contribution and matching compensation.

LACK OF PARTICIPATION OF EMPLOYEES IN DESIGNING PRP

In most organizations, PRP is designed by the top brass of the management and then imposed on down the level. Since PRP system alters the existing compensation structure, participation and involvement of all cross-sections of employees, line managers, trade union leaders, etc. can truly help. Organizations can not only get new inputs from all these people, they also feel consulted, and hence they cooperate in implementation.

Often organizations emphasize on improved performance through financial rewards alone, but this again is not always right, as we also have other types of rewards. Financial incentives are necessary but not sufficient to motivate and improve performance. Hence, we must have a stronger link between reward strategy and business strategy.

We can design PRP either based on individual performance criteria like piece rate wages or collective performance pay schemes like profit sharing. The empirical literature shows that generally profit sharing arrangement have smaller productivity effects than piece rate schemes. Also empirically, it was established that PRP increases productivity of any organization substantially.

COMPENSATION BROADBANDING USING PMS RESULTS

Systems of broadbanding in compensation design; helps to replace the multiple pay grades and ranges, and operationally make the compensation administration process much simpler. In organizations with multiple pay grades, employees reach the compensation progression through time scale (seniority based) or performance-based promotion or upgradation. The system requires close administration of compensation programme, raising the human resource overhead costs. With broadbanding, however, pay grades and job titles being less, the process becomes easier, as pay bands can be directly linked with the performance of individual employees. Broad banding is not just easy to administer, it also optimizes the cost of compensation as the employees with less performance, even when work in the same position, may get less compensation than their peers working in the same level and job. In typical seniority-based compensation design structure, it is, however, difficult to implement for obvious resistance from the employees. Many organizations still subscribe to the principle of equity in their compensation programme.

COMPENSATION DESIGN THROUGH SKILL-BASED PROGRAMMES

Organizations that pursue skill-based compensation programmes reward their employees on attainment of additional knowledge and skills. The underlying philosophy behind this is that on acquiring higher qualifications and skills, knowledge of the employees enhances and, accordingly, it exerts positive impact on their performance. Some organizations, therefore, motivate their employees to acquire higher knowledge and skill with additional increments or pay rise, as such investment reflects through incremental performance results. With the increased knowledge and skills, employees can also improve their competencies. To introduce skill-based compensation, at the outset, it is necessary to document the skill requirements for various job components at different job levels, and make it transparent to employees. With strong career planning and career development programmes, employees can autonomously understand which skill enhancement programme(s) can help them to get a pay rise. The system can be better institutionalized when organizations extend training support to the employees to acquire the new skill. This is also a process of multi-skilling. Employees gradually become competent to perform in different cross-sections of jobs. Many organizations have institutionalized the system by recognizing some qualifications like CAIIB qualification in banks, PhD for college teachers, etc. However, skill-based pay systems can generate competition among employees. Nevertheless, it ultimately benefits the organization to accomplish its performance goals.

MAJOR OBSTACLES TO THE INTRODUCTION OF SKILL-BASED PAY

Although skill-based pay provides multiple benefits, to introduce it, organizations encounter serious problems. Some of the major obstacles to introduce the skill-based pay can be listed as under:

Defining skill sets—It is difficult to document the skill sets of a job. Even though organizations can at the outset document skill sets for a well-defined job, it becomes quickly obsolete. Jobs are getting restructured every now and then with the changing technology and new product designs, rendering redundancy of earlier documented skills. Another problem encountered by the organization is to narrow down skill sets, jobs being highly interrelated. We, therefore, cannot identify job-specific competency differences.

Pricing skill sets—This is another major obstacle in introducing skill-based pay. Effective pricing of skill sets is seemingly difficult for the organizations. Often we benchmark with the market pricing, but many organizations may require some unique skill sets for their typical nature of job. In such cases, price rationalization becomes difficult, as we have to depend on the subjective assessment. Some of the skill price rationalization criteria could be competitive value of skill, amount and degree of effort required acquiring the skills, amount and degree of effort required to implement the learned skills in tasks and jobs, etc.

Validation of skills—This is also difficult to validate some skill sets. For some jobs, we can use job trial or performance tests to validate the skills and competencies of employees, but for many others, we have to depend on our hunches and subjective assessment. Hence, to achieve success in implementation of skill-based pay, it is necessary to introduce a credible skill validation process.

Skill re-certification tests—For some skill sets, it is necessary to ensure that concerned employees are able to sustain their skill, through a periodic skill re-certification programme.

Skill obsolescence—Technology changes render change of necessary skill sets. This makes earlier learned skills obsolete, requiring organizations to renew the existing skills through sustained training and development initiatives.

High cost of training—To introduce skill-based pay, organizations need to focus on employees' learning of new activities. Any training and learning initiatives enhance downtime, apart from usual cost of training. Often the benefits accrue fail to recoup the expenses, resulting in failure of organizational initiatives. Such possible threat outweighs the benefit of skill-based pay.

Increased payroll costs—Often, skill-based pay increases the overall payroll costs. This, however, depends on the nature of the job. If the jobs are simple, employees can quickly learn the skill sets required to perform the job and accordingly can maximize their earnings stepping up production, even when organizations may require curtailing the same. This problem would be more acute for those organizations whose production planning is market dependent. It would be difficult for such organizations to practice lean management or lean manufacturing.

Regulatory bottlenecks—Skill-based pay programmes, among others, require organizations to increase the variables, which put the pay at risk. Thus, reduced fixed or basic pay at less than statutory minimum wages may lead to legal complications for average or below average performers, who fail to earn the variables for their inability to acquire new skill sets.

APPLICATION OF SKILL-BASED PAY

Despite having major obstacles to introduce skill-based pay, many organizations can make best use of it for all cross-sections of employees, including managerial levels. To successfully apply, organizations need to design it with technological considerations, so that identified skills do not get quickly redundant. Identified skill elements should be relevant and accepted both by the employees and the management; it should be consistent and implemented with integrity. A participative task force should be formed to look into various aspects, right from development to implementation of skill-based pay. The task force considers all the issues pointed out in the list of obstacles and then determine the relative value of skills. The task force implements the skill-based pay in a phased manner.

COMPETENCY-BASED PAY

Theoretically, in today's organizations we are more used to the term competency rather than skill. Competency is more holistic, as it aggregates knowledge, skill, and abilities of employees, and even integrates with the behavioural requirements. Instead of paying for the position and the job title, competency-based pay emphasizes on the job accomplishments, much wider than job efficiency (outcome of skill only). Competency-based pays directly measure knowledge and skills in terms of criticality involved, amount of depth in the job content, and the skills breadth.

OBSTACLES IN INTRODUCING PERFORMANCE-RELATED PAY

A major goal of any compensation programme is to motivate employees to deliver their best. Resurgence of merit pays, though not new as technique, mainly focuses on employee performance. Hence, in other words, the traditional merit pay can be termed as performance-linked pay. However, at the outset, it is important to remember that performance-linked pay or compensation is not the absolute criterion for compensation design; it can only be said as one of the criterion. We have discussed all through this book, the various dimensions of compensation determination.

Relating compensation directly to performance is not so easy. In fact, in some types of organizations it may not even be desirable. Both the management and the employees need to agree to relate compensation to performance.

PERFORMANCE GUIDE CHARTS

Organizations develop performance guide charts to introduce performance-linked pay programmes. Such charts are prepared after performance evaluation and tentatively cover degree of performance, i.e., the performance rating, recommended rate of increase in different quarters (where organizations introduce quarterly review of performance), etc.

Notice here that employees have been ranked with a 5-point scale. Each employee's present performance ranking has been mapped using this scale and the recommended quarterly raise in the compensation has been indicated. Also note that employees do not get any raise, when they fail to meet the expectations. A tentative performance guide chart is presented in Table 8.1 below.

USE OF PERFORMANCE CRITERIA FOR DESIGNING EXECUTIVE COMPENSATION

Use of performance criteria to design executive compensation, account for measurable performance targets, behaviour, job requirements, and experience of the executives, job role, peer compensation, market considerations, and the size of the organization. Table 8.2 clearly explains the same.

These criteria are then studied in the context of the time span and the nature of measurement. Time span may be long- or short-term compensation. The nature of measurement, on the other hand, accounts for profitability vs. market-based measures, qualitative vs. quantitative measures, etc. (Gomez-Mejia & Balkin, 1998).

CALIBRATION OF EXECUTIVE COMPENSATION TO PERFORMANCE

The concept of calibrating pay to performance is the 'market value measure'. On the 'X' axis we could include shareholder value, revenue growth, or other suitable metrics of business performance. The key

Table 8.1 *Performance guide charts*

Name of the Employees	Performance Rating	First Quarter	Second Quarter	Third Quarter	Fourth Quarter
Mr A	Outstanding (1)	15%	13%	11%	9%
Mr B	Exceeds Expectations (2)	13%	11%	9%	No increase
Mr C	Meets Expectations (3)	11%	9%	No increase	No increase
Mr D	Meets minimum expectations (4)	Token raise to boost the morale	No Increase	No Increase	No Increase
Mr E	Does not meet expectations (5)	No increase	No increase	No Increase	No Increase

Table 8.2 *Measurement of performance criteria*

Criteria	Parameters
Performance targets	Key result areas (KRA), key performance areas (KPA), key sales objectives (KSO), or even some protocol-bound performance specification
Behaviour	Performance impact
Job requirements	Quality of actions in terms of job requirements, or fulfilment of a prescribed role
Experience of the executives	Experience, talent, and skills
Job role	Hierarchy and the role requirements
Peer compensation	Pay differences between the executives
Market considerations	Benchmarked compensation information
Size of the organization	Large, medium, or small
Nature of the organization	Public limited, closely held, family business

to the model is ensuring that the measures being selected are pertinent, so that the right set of behaviours are being encouraged. To simply say that a particular executive is a high performer may not only be a sweeping generalization, it may also be in reference to measures that are not currently important to the organization. A pay calibration model is illustrated in Figure 8.1.

PERFORMANCE MEASUREMENT IN EXECUTIVE INCENTIVE PROGRAMMES

In most of the organizations, executives are rewarded independent of company performance. Such practices, in fact, built the argument that executives get rich at the expense of shareholders. Because of such negative perception, linking executive compensation to organizational performance, shareholders' value creation has become extremely important. Effective performance measures ensure that executive compensation is commensurate with performance. Regardless of the industry, there are certain criteria that incentive performance measures should ideally meet. They should be:

- Aligned with shareholders' interests
- Definable
- Measurable

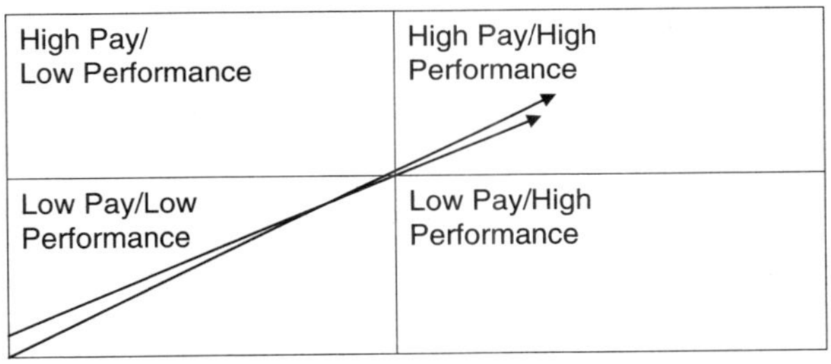

Figure 8.1 *Pay calibration*

- Controllable
- Easily communicated and understood

Assessing potential performance objectives against these criteria can help to ensure the appropriateness of the measure or measures ultimately used.

As an indication of how certain measurement categories stack up, Table 8.3 briefly evaluates shareholder return-based measures and company-specific measures against the criteria above. Total shareholder return (TSR) has become a popular performance measurement criterion, particularly for stock options plan. Some organizations, however, emphasize on other internal financial performance criteria like ROE, EPS, and EVA.

Against the above criteria, there is merit for both shareholder return-based measures and company-specific measures.

The important point from Table 8.3 is that in some cases company-specific measures may be more appropriate than shareholder return measures, particularly in circumstances where executives have very little influence over the market valuation of their companies. A thorough process, as laid out in the next section, can ensure that the most effective and appropriate measures are used.

To choose an effective method, organizations need to consider various external and internal considerations to identify the correct performance measures over time.

Some of the external inputs for performance measures could be:

- Market practices for short-, medium-, and long-term incentives.
- Identify external value drivers to understand the state of the economy.
- Understand the relevance of any financial ratios that are generally attributable to industry situation.

Similarly, internal inputs for performance measures are:

- Understand the internal value drivers.
- Focus on key strategic objectives.
- Link the executive behaviour and its relation with the business performance.

Both the internal and external value drivers significantly influence executive incentive payment decision in any organization.

Table 8.3 *Shareholder return versus company-specific measures*

Criteria	Shareholder return-based measures (TSR, share price growth)	Company-specific financial measures (ROE, EPS, etc.)
Degree of alignment	Directly aligned.	Indirectly aligned. More emphasis on long-term value creation.
Definable	Yes.	Typically definable. More concerned with the financial reporting.
Measurable	Easily measured.	Easily measured and can be communicated periodically.
Controllable	Somewhat.	More controllable.
Ease in communication	When properly designed.	When properly designed.

SUMMARY

The purpose of performance-based pay is to reward employees for factors other than the value of the job. This chapter discussed the methods of designing performance-based pay, going beyond the traditional paradigm of compensation design, which considers cost of living, and other statutory wage provisions. However, the chapter also focused on the possible dangers of designing compensation, solely on performance criteria, as often it may ignore other vital issues of people management aspects. It may not be always possible or even desirable to introduce performance-related pay in organizations. Many organizations embrace the system for their cost control, rather to derive the strategic benefits like employee motivation and retention. Hence, introduction of performance-related pay requires the organizations to understand the basics of performance management systems and its relations to other facets of human resource management issues. The chapter also discussed many other performance evaluation tools, but its selection highly depends on the nature of organization and its activities. Developing a performance standard for all types of job may be difficult, despite having advanced mechanisms like balanced score cards, competency-based assessment, etc. Thus, though it is effective, it requires adequate pre-work and feasibility study before introduction.

KEY WORDS

Minimum Wages—Wages, which are need-based and statutorily decided both by the central and the state government. Payment of minimum wages is obligatory for the organization.

Job Evaluation—Process of measuring the relative worth of a job to decide the wage rate.

Fair Wages—It is the wage, which is above the minimum wage but below the living wage. Thus the lower limit of the fair wage is the minimum wage and the upper limit is set by the 'capacity of the industry to pay'.

Performance Management Systems—System of integrating individual employee performance with the organizational performance.

Living Wages—Wage rate which not only provide the bare essentials of food, clothing, and shelter but a measure of frugal comfort, including education for his children, protection against ill-health, requirements of essential social needs and a measure of insurance against the more important misfortunes, including old age.

KRA—Key Result Areas to indicate the performance target of individual employees of an organization, aligning with the business goals.

ESOP—Employee stock options, offered as incentives by the organization to ensure increased level of motivation and retention of employees.

Assessment Centres—One of the modern methods of performance appraisal. This method tests candidates in a social situation by a number of assessors, using a variety of criteria. This method is useful in measuring interpersonal skills, organizing and planning ability, creativity, resistance to stress, work motivation, decision-making power, etc.

GENERAL REVIEW QUESTIONS

1. Explain the concept of performance-based employee compensation design. What are its significances.
2. Explain how compensation broadbanding is done using performance management systems.
3. Explain the concept of skill and competency-based compensation designs. What are its important obstacles?
4. Explain the concept of performance-based executive compensation design. What are its important components?
5. Discuss how calibration of executive compensation to performance management systems is practiced in organizations.
6. What is performance guide charts? How does it help in compensation design?
7. Short Notes

   Broad Band Pay
   Compensation Benchmarking
   Employee Rewards
   ESOPs

CRITICAL REVIEW QUESTION

8. A particular organization, engaged in the business of life-style drugs, already offers best of the industry salary rate to its employees. Due to increase in the inter-industry job mobility, the company has already started losing talented employees. Initially, the company did not give any attention to this issue, as they get skilled manpower from their relatively small competitors, for obvious competitive compensation package. However, their talent flight has now become so acute, the company now decided to go for introducing performance-based compensation system. You have been retained by the company to suggest them the line of action. Give your viewpoints.

REFERENCES

Arthur, J.B. (1994), 'Effects of Human Resource Systems on Manufacturing Performance and Turnover', *Academy of Management Journal*, 37: 670–87.

Bardwick, Judith M. (1991), *Danger in the Comfort Zone* (New York, NY: American Management Association).

Becker, B. and B. Gerhart (1996), 'The Impact of Human Resource Management on Organizational Performance: Progress and Prospects', *Academy of Management Journal*, 39(4): 779–801.

Bhattacharyya, D.K. (2009), *Compensation Management* (New Delhi: Oxford University Press).

Bhattacharyya, D.K. (2007), *Human Resource Research Methods* (New Delhi: Oxford University Press).

Bhattacharyya, D.K. (2006), *Human Resource Management*, 2nd edition (New Delhi: Excel Books).

Blake, R., J. Mouton (1964), *The Managerial Grid: The Key to Leadership Excellence* (Houston: Gulf Publishing Co).

Boselie, P. (2002), 'Human Resource Management, Work Systems and Performance: A Theoretical-Empirical Approach' (Thela Thesis, Tinbergen Institute Research Series 274, Amsterdam).

Dasgupta, A.K. (1976), *A Theory of Wage Policy* (New Delhi: Oxford University Press).

Evans, W.A. (1970), 'Pay for Performance: Fact or Fable', *Personnel Journal*, 49(9): 726–29.

Guest, D.E. (1997), 'Human Resource Management and Performance: A Review and Research

Agenda', *The International Journal of Human Resource Management*, 8(3).

Gomez-Mejia and B. Balkin (1998), 'Effectiveness of Individual and Aggregate Compensation Strategies', *Industrial Relations*, 28(3): 432–45.

Huselid, M.A. and N.L. Rau (1997), 'The Determinants of High Performance Work Systems: Cross Sectional and Longitudinal Analyses' (paper presented at the Academy of Management Annual Meetings, Human Resources Management Division).

Pfeffer, J. (1994), *Competitive Advantage through People* (Boston, MA: Harvard Business School Press).

Subramanian, K.N. (1987), *Wages in India* (New Delhi: Tata McGraw Hill).

Verma, P. (1987), *Labour Economics and Industrial Relations* (New Delhi: Tata McGraw Hill).

CASE STUDY

Performance-related Pay for Auto India

Performance-related compensation schemes are commonly used by organizations to reward improved productivity through increased salary or benefits. Often this scheme is misconstrued as indirect management control systems. Auto India, a leading manufacturer of automobile spares, recently adopted a bonus scheme, with the basic intention to reap the benefits of increased productivity. This significantly called for alteration of existing compensation systems, making employees more accountable or responsible for results.

Some of the high achievers of the company, in the succeeding months of new bonus scheme, could significantly increase their compensation level, while a large number of employees, on the contrary, faced significant reduction in their compensation package. The company, before introduction of a new bonus scheme, explained to all its stakeholders the genesis and operational nitty-gritties. Individually, all the line managers were trained to understand how it works and helps in achieving the business goals. The company is 100 per cent unionized with representation from two major registered and recognized unions. One of the union leaders collected payroll information for 6 successive months after the introduction of the new bonus schemes; its analysis indicated actual compensation costs have decreased over the period. Both the union leaders jointly issued a notice to the management, explaining their understanding of the systems, an extract of which is reproduced below:

Performance-related pay is defined as a variety of systems linking pay to performance. It is based on the assumptions that the organizations are able to measure individuals, team/unit, and organizational outputs, as all these contribute to organizational performance. Also it should be administered in such a way that organizations can capitalize the expected value from the employees who are recipients of performance-related pay. Any performance-related pay initiatives should match with the organizational performance budgeting, duly considering the economic constraints of the organization. Thus, performance-related pay should attempt a trade-off between various options, taking into account the background and culture of the organizations.

While designing new performance-related pay schemes, organizations should ensure its acceptability to all cross-sections of employees. In the heart of the systems we have the right fit performance appraisal tools. It should balance the individual and team performance, bring changes in the human resource management practices, understand the impact on employees' motivation, develop a culture of mutual trust, and leverage the organizational change. Organizations, after introduction, should also ensure its periodic evaluation to understand its success or otherwise.

We feel that our organization has failed to account for all these issues, leading employees to survive in uncertainty and suffer from extreme financial hardships. Hence, we oppose the newly introduced performance-related pay and appeal before the management to revert to the old compensation system, which follows more the principles of equity, respect seniority, and also assigns some weights on seniority without harming the collective interests of the employees.

While explaining the genesis of the new bonus scheme, the company did make it clear to both the unions that the company wants to reward high achievers and differentiate them from others who fail to achieve. This will enable the company to relate the compensation to market rates and at the same time to motivate those who deliver their best.

Question: As a compensation expert, critically analyse the case and suggest, where the company went wrong to introduce the performance-related pay?

CHAPTER 9

Performance-based Career Planning, Career Development, and Succession Plans

Learning Objectives

After reading this chapter, you will be able to understand:

- Understand the interrelation between career planning, career development, and succession planning with the performance management function of an organization
- Understand the process of career planning
- Understand how career development initiatives extend support to career planning activities of an organization
- Understand the importance and significance of succession planning
- Understand how internal supply of manpower can be strengthened by an organization through career planning, career development, and succession planning

Career Development Through Performance Management

Effective human performance at all levels in an organization is instrumental for its growth. Self-development and career development through work is now being viewed more importantly, more particularly for the new generation of workers. There always exist gross incongruences between an individual's own concept of career progression and an organization's own career progression path, barring a few whose goals are always integrated with the organization's goals thereby creating an enabling organization. Modern performance management systems encompass career planning, career development, and succession planning.

With the technological obsolescence, organizations, on the one hand, are witnessing manpower redundancy and, on the other hand, the problem of talent retention. To address both the issues, career planning and development programmes can play a most crucial role. To increase the retention of talented manpower, organizations make balanced use of intrinsic and extrinsic motivational reinforcers. Thus to avoid the manpower redundancy for obvious skill and knowledge obsolescence consequent to technological change, organizations emphasize on career planning and development. Systematic renewal of knowledge and skill obsolescence of employees through career planning and development helps the organization to sustain their competitive strength, realize their strategy, and achieve their intended goals and objectives. Without career planning and career development, organizations cannot even retain people, who may be otherwise satisfied with motivational cues. Career planning and development programmes also support the succession plans, to man future vacancy at higher levels. Many organizations, as a matter of policy, prefer to man senior positions grooming people from within. Hence, it is always desirable to develop successors within the organizations for future key positions. Increased job mobility now reduces the employment span of good performers in organizations. Internationally, it is observed that the top performers by and large go for job shift within less than 3 years time. This again substantiates the need for career planning and development activities in alignment with the performance management systems, as performance results are the most important determinants for such programmes.

INTRODUCTION

Effective performance management system encompasses career planning, career development, and succession planning. The terms 'career planning' and 'career development' are used interchangeably in most organizations. It is also correct that, but for their subtle difference in definitional context, their process remains the same. We have, however, considered both the concepts more holistically, excepting some discussions on their meaning.

Similarly, discussion on succession planning remains incomplete without relating the same to management development and organizational development as succession planning immediately succeeds it. Moreover, the success of one is dependent on the success of the other.

All the above decisions, i.e., career planning, career development, and succession planning highly depend on performance management systems prevalent in organizations. Based on performance results, organizations can chalk out action plans for talent development and talent retention.

DEFINITIONS AND CONCEPTS

Career is a sequence of attitudes and behaviour associated with the series of work-related activities over a person's lifetime. We can also define career as a succession of related jobs, arranged in hierarchical orders, through which a person moves in an organization. Although we perceive career from an individual employee's perspective, it can also be organization centred. Thus, career is often defined separately as external career and internal career. External career refers to the objective categories used by society and organizations to describe the progression of steps through a given occupation, while internal career refers to the set of steps or stages which make up the individual's own concept of career progression within an occupation. For such two different approaches, in organizational context, career can be identified as an integrated pace of vertical and lateral movement in an individual's career. Such integrated approaches are intended to minimize diversity of hopes and expectations of employees matching individually perceived careers with organization-centred careers.

IMPORTANT ELEMENTS OF CAREER

Analysing the definitional context, it is, therefore, clear that career has the following important elements:

- It is a properly sequenced job-related activity. Such job-related activities vis-à-vis experience include role experiences at different hierarchical levels of an individual, which lead to an increasing level of responsibilities, status, power, achievements, and rewards.

- It may be individual-centric or organization-centric. Individual-centric (internal) career is an individually perceived sequence of career progression within an occupation. For example, in the medical profession, we have clearly defined stages of education—internship, residency, hospital affiliation, or private practice. Similarly, in college teaching, we have stages like lecturership, readership, and professorship. In industrial occupation, those who get entry in the Indian administrative and allied services also have such clearly defined stages of career. For example, in Indian ordnance factories, Class-I officers start at assistant works manager level and gradually rise to the level of works manager, deputy general manager, additional general manager, general manager, and so on. These being clearly defined stages of career, an individual before joining such services can very well perceive his sequence of career progression. But such clearly defined stages of career progression are not made available for all occupations or job titles both in public and private sectors. In such cases, individuals nurture their own perceived stages of career progression.
- It is better defined as an integrated pace of lateral movement in an occupation of an individual over his employment span. Individual-centric career being not an objective or at times even realistic description of career steps in a given occupation, it often goes against the hopes and expectations of employees as organizations may have a different perceived career plan for the employees. Integrated approach, therefore, minimizes such dissonance and ensures a mutually acceptable and satisfying career progression.

MEANING AND OVERVIEW OF CAREER DEVELOPMENT

Career development essentially means the process of increasing an employee's potential for advancement and career change. In other words, it is a process of planning the series of possible jobs which an individual may hold in the organization over time and developing strategies designed to provide necessary job skills as the opportunity arises. Therefore, career development relates to the readiness for progression through a series of positions during an individual's career. Career development may be differentiated from career planning and career management. Career development is a systematic process of guiding the movement of human resources of an enterprise through different hierarchical positions, whereas career planning is a process of establishing career objectives for an employee (or by the person himself) and developing planned strategies to achieve them including activities which help in making choices with respect to occupations, organization's job assignments, and self-development measures. Career management, on the other hand, relates to specific human resource management activities, such as recruitment, selection, placement, and appraisal to facilitate career development.

IMPORTANCE OF CAREER DEVELOPMENT

Every organization needs to provide career development opportunities to its employees. Indian organizations at present are facing major restructuring problems to keep pace with the economic restructuring programme of the country. Market globalization, technology upgradation, import liberalization, de-licensing, increased competition together have now prompted Indian organizations to restructure their production vis-à-vis the organization. Redeploying the manpower, through proper training, in restructured jobs is one of the important priorities for the organization, particularly for those who are at the lower level. But employees with matching skill and knowledge now find them in better bargaining position for increased job mobility. Most of the foreign and multinational companies are now winning away the employees with matching skill and knowledge from Indian organizations with better offer of pay and career. Therefore, poor career development programme may affect an organization at least in two ways:

- High employee turnover, particularly those in their beginning of the career.
- Decreasing employment involvement.

Recruitment expenses, training expenses, and reduced performance during orientation (loss of output, increased wastages, etc.) together add to the cost of employee turnover. Decreased employee involvement also affects functional efficiency and productivity of the employees. Other important reasons for career development can be listed as follows:

- The changing environment is now making jobs more complex. Suitable career development programmes enable employees to be better prepared for future positions in the organization. It also gives the opportunity to identify prospective managers from within. Manning vacancies from within is cost efficient and at the same time the system motivates employees.
- Suitable career development programmes will enable the organization to receive maximum contribution from employees. Since this helps employees to enhance their skills for higher positions, both under-utilization of employees' potential work energy and their under-employment can be avoided.
- Career development makes employees more adaptable to changing requirements of the organizations. Requirements of the organization may either change due to new technology [computer numerically controlled technology (CNC), numerically controlled technology (NC), direct numerically controlled technology (DNC), and flexible manufacturing system (FMS)], or new management philosophy and style (like, Just-in-time manufacturing, Total Quality Management, etc.).
- It provides an objective basis to describe the steps of progression in a given organization and, therefore, minimizes unfair promotion practices of employees reducing the change of 'promotion by discretion'. Thus suitable career development programme avoids employees' resentment on promotion issues, which has now become a major causal factor of industrial disputes in India.
- Most of the organizations are now also manned by women and other minority classes of employees. Career development programme ensures equitable opportunity for career progression of these classes of employees also. Thus it meets the requirements of equal employment opportunities for all.
- Career development programmes give opportunities to employees to acquire more skills, obtain desired jobs, share increased responsibility, enjoy scope of job mobility, and derive increased job satisfaction.

SIGNIFICANCE AND ADVANTAGES OF CAREER DEVELOPMENT

The significance and advantages of career development both from organizations' and employees' viewpoints can be summed up as follows:

- It reduces employee turnover by providing increased promotional avenues.
- It improves employees' morale and motivation.
- It enables organizations to man promotional vacancies internally, thereby reducing the cost of managerial recruitment.

- It ensures better utilization of employees' skills and provides increased work satisfaction to employees.
- It makes employees adaptable to the changing requirement of the organization.
- It reduces industrial disputes related to promotional matters and thereby provides opportunity to the organization to sustain harmonious industrial relations.
- Employees' loyalty and commitment to the organization can be substantially increased and thereby organizations can enjoy the privilege of increased employee productivity.
- Career development programmes being an objective description of career progression, ensure equitable promotional decisions even for women and minorities in an organization.

PURPOSES AND OBJECTIVES OF CAREER DEVELOPMENT

The purposes and objectives of career development programme, therefore, can be listed as follows:

- To attract and retain effective persons in an organization.
- To utilize human resources optimally.
- To improve morale and motivation level of employees.
- To reduce employee turnover.
- To practice a balanced 'promotion from within' policy.
- To make employees adaptable to changes.
- To increase employees' loyalty and commitment to the organizations.
- To maintain harmonious industrial relations.
- To inculcate equitable employment practices providing equal career progression opportunities to women and minorities.

TYPES OF CAREER DEVELOPMENT PROGRAMMES

In an organization, there are different types of development programmes to enrich different skills of human resource. These include organization development, employee development, management development, and career development. Organizational development programmes are planned and managed from the top, so as to bring about planned organizational changes and for increasing the organizational effectiveness. Management development is concerned with upgrading the manager's skills, knowledge, and ability of the employees to enable them to accomplish additional process of guiding the movement of human resources through different hierarchical levels.

Whatever may be the differences, career development is interrelated with other human resource development functions.

DIFFERENCE BETWEEN CAREER DEVELOPMENT AND CAREER PLANNING

Career planning process evaluates one's abilities and interests, considering alternative career opportunities, establishing career goals, and planning practical development activities. Thus, from an individual's point of view, it helps in making choices with respect to occupation, organization, job assignment, and self-development measures. However, organizational career planning is different from individual career planning, as organizational career plan is a map of sequence of jobs for an employee within the organization itself, whereas individual career planning is a map of sequence of jobs of the individual concerned without regard to the organization. Career development process, on the other hand, aims to increase an employee's potential for advancement and career change by providing necessary job skills.

Career planning, personnel skills inventories, career information systems, and career counselling are different career planning activities in an organization. Thus, information of jobs to decide the skills needed through effective system of job analysis and job descriptions are required. Suitable performance appraisal system to monitor performance, clear career goals of employees, effective human resource planning system, and designated career paths and job families enable career-planning process to move logically and scientifically. In addition, career planning process being concerned with the individual employees, an effective information system is necessary to make all these data available to the employees concerned from time to time. Career development process, on the other hand, calls for assisting employees in assessing their own internal career needs, developing and publishing available career opportunities in the organization, and finally aligning employee needs and abilities with career opportunities.

However, there cannot be an effective career development without career planning in the organization. Therefore, career development is an integral part of career planning process as career planning provides opportunity for assessing occupational and career choice of an employee, his performance appraisal, and devising a suitable development programme for him. Conventionally in any given organization, career planning process primarily deals with employees at lower hierarchy, whereas career development entails objective description of career progression path for all levels of employees.

DIFFERENCE WITH MANPOWER PLANNING

Often career planning is considered synonymous with the manpower planning. Manpower planning, among other things, provides higher management the data on the inventory of skills and potentials available in the organization, based on which, expansion, technology upgradation, etc., are undertaken by the organization. Inventory of manpower resources, manpower needs in terms of number, types, skills, levels and time, possible changes in functions and activities with the passage of time, desired behavioural or attitudinal changes required meeting the manpower needs, training opportunities, resources, and training time, etc., are the basic information required for manpower planning.

However, manpower planning also encompasses career development process as the latter provides the basis of manpower planning by planning the series of possible jobs which an employee may hold in the organization over time.

DIFFERENCE WITH SUCCESSION PLANNING

Succession planning involves identification of likely vacancies for higher level executives and locating likely successors to man such vacancies. Career development on the other hand covers employees at all levels including executives in an organization. Succession planning in reality, therefore, is management development initiatives for the executives. Career development programme normally considers likely career progression in a given occupation, while succession planning chart is a 'runner up chart' for higher generalist positions like general manager, managing director, etc., who may be groomed up from different specialist positions like marketing, production, personnel, finance, etc.

DIFFERENT STAGES OR CYCLES OF CAREER DEVELOPMENT PROCESS

In order to design suitable career development programme, it is necessary to understand the different career stages or development cycles of an individual employee. Actual stages differ from individual to individual for obvious difference in perceived internal career. However, career development cycle or stages, keeping in view the general requirements of people at different hierarchical stages, may be grouped under the following four categories:

Exploratory Stage

This stage starts when a new employee joins the organization. When an employee with his qualification and knowledge joins an organization, and finds himself in an apparent mis-match condition which cannot be set right even with induction programmes of the organization, it takes quite some time for him after thorough training to become adaptable with the organization and more particularly with his job assignment.

Therefore, it is essential for the organization to sustain the behavioural as well as operational deficiencies to help him to develop in the course of time. The best solution at this stage is to allow the new entrant to perform some specific job and to confer freedom in functioning. This will help the new entrant to gradually develop to the requirements of the organization. Some companies even allow the new entrant to undergo a compulsory job rotation for reasonable time period. The purpose of such job rotation is to allow the employee to select his preferred job from a wide range of available jobs in the organization. However, for obvious functional specialties and different educational requirements, such scheme is not quite successful in Indian organizations.

Establishment Stage

After a new entrant chooses his career from different given alternatives (where such options are available), he needs to be provided with regular feedback on his performance. Such performance feedback enables the new employee to understand effectiveness of his performance and at the same time he can also initiate required corrective action to make good of his functional deficiencies. Performance appraisal and its feedback have also motivational values as the new employee enjoy a sense of accomplishment when he gets feedback on his assignment from management and specifically when he understands that his promotional decision has been taken based on his performance. A successful career development process at establishment stage, therefore, is important to retain employees in the organization and at the same time to develop a sense of loyalty and commitment to the organizations.

Maintenance Stage

This is a mid-career stage for employees, who strive hard to retain their established name and fame. Therefore, at this stage employees need to put their continuous efforts for self-development. For an organization, career development process at this stage, therefore, calls for renewing and updating the skills of employees particularly in the context of changing environment to help employees to overcome their mid-career crisis. In many organizations, absence of career development programme makes employees in this stage of their career to opt for job switch. Therefore, this stage is crucial and unless the organization adopts suitable career development programme, it may face high employee turnover, who are in their mid-age group.

Stage of Decline

Employees at this stage are being prepared for retirement, get scared from possible threat of reduced role of responsibilities in the organization. Such complexity is behaviourally associated with the old age of the employee which, unless set right through suitable career development programmes, may even render such employees inefficient or mis-fit for the organization. Career development process at this stage, therefore, should aim at helping the employees to get mentally prepared for retirement rituals, particularly to prepare them to accept a reduced role and responsibilities, so that they can find themselves accommodative with family and society in later part of their life.

ISSUES IN CAREER DEVELOPMENT PROCESS

Edgar H. Schein (1969) suggested the following issues to be considered at different stages or cycles of career development process.

Exploratory Stage

At this stage an organization should

- Ensure the availability of accurate information about the organization and the various occupations existing in the organization to the new employee.
- Create opportunities to enable new employees to get acquainted with the organizational careers through job rotation, internship, visit to different units, seminars, etc.
- Sponsor educational and training programmes for ensuring supply of potential talent in future.

Establishment Stage

At this stage an organization should ensure

- Identification of the best possible talent for the organization.
- Conveyance of correct and positive image of the organization to the employee.
- Maximum learning and favourable attitudes of the employees towards the organization.
- Assigning challenging jobs to employees to enable them to test their abilities and skills.
- Providing adequate feedback on performance of employees to enable them to assess their strengths and weaknesses.
- Designing of development plan, identification of development needs, deciding next career steps, etc.

Maintenance Stage

This being a mid-career stage, the organization should provide

- A continuing process of performance appraisals, feedback, career counselling, long-range career planning to ensure proper deployment of the employees and also to enable them to feel challenged, motivated, and committed to the organization.
- Strategies to motivate plateaued employees, so that they can be productively utilized even without promotion.

- Adequate opportunities for transition from specialist cadres to generalist positions at higher echelons of the organization.
- Adequate career-paths to enable employees to accommodate their personal and family needs, especially during critical phases of their life or family cycle.
- Help employees to adjust to their changing role as their career shifts from active (operational) positions to advisory positions.
- Help employees to prepare for retirement.

Decline Stage

This being a stage of separation, the organization should try to

- Manage retirement without destroying the employees' sense of self-worth.
- Invent new and creative part-time roles for retired employees who can use their knowledge, experience, and wisdom.

At every stage of the career, employees also make an effort to develop their own information sources. They analyse the feedbacks on their performance, seek opportunities for development, study the career-paths available to them and provide organization details of their perceived needs, goals, and ambitions. Thus career is as much the responsibility of the individual employee as it is the responsibility of the organization.

CAREER ANCHORS

Career anchor is a syndrome of talents, motives, and values, which gives stability and direction to a person's career. Such talents, motives, and values give shape to certain attributes, which an individual derives from his/her early experiences and which help him to conceptualize his/her own perceived career. This perceived career anchor, therefore, often goes against organizational career plans and thus, employees develop a sense of dissonance or incongruity about their career plans. Many organizations, therefore, try to identify perceived career anchor for their employees to develop matching career development programmes. Many empirical studies have so far been carried out to identify the perceived career-anchor of different type of employees. Edgar H. Schein, summing up the findings of empirical study on management graduates, identified five such career anchors for employees.

Managerial Competence

This competence is a fundamental characteristic for those who prefer to rise to the top. Such employees were found to have the following three areas of competence:

Interpersonal Competence: They have the ability and desire to handle a variety of interpersonal and group situations. They exhibit leadership skills, resolve group conflict, and also feel at ease to tackle unfavourable situations to their advantage.

Analytic Competence: This competence helps such employees to identify problems, analyse the same, and develop situations to resolve the problems. Analytical skill being an important prerequisite for the success of managers, such competence naturally makes such employees befitting for managerial positions.

Emotional Competence: Employees bestowed with such competence can bear high levels of responsibility and even can afford to remain cool in difficult situations, which makes them competent to exert leadership powers without much of a problem. Such competence develops empathetic skills in employees which develop a matured decision-making power even in situations of crisis.

All these competence together develop a matured personality in employees making them suitable for managerial positions in an organization.

Technical/Functional Competence

Persons with such competence prefer to remain in technically satisfying jobs than rising to the higher managerial level. Such technically satisfying jobs may be either engineering, systems analysis, or even different functional areas of management like finance, personnel, marketing, etc. In manufacturing units, some executives always prefer to remain in shop-floor as they derive satisfaction from such jobs rather than general managerial jobs at higher echelon of management. These types of people are committed to the profession and consider their work as primarily important rather than the benefits and/or future prospectus.

Security and Stability

Employees who are anchored in this competence will always get motivated for a career which ensures job security and/or long range stability in the form of good retirement programmes. This type of people get motivated only when they are ensured a stabilized career situation which may not even at times be fitting to their level of knowledge and skills and even they may subordinate some personal needs (for example, acceptance of less pay and amenities) to satisfy their perceived security. Effecting transfer and promotion for this type of employees is quite difficult. Most of the employees under such category may be identified in government and public sector undertakings.

Creativity and Challenge

People with such syndrome are very small in numbers. They always venture for starting their own business to become an entrepreneur more for creating something new to have their own identity than for making money. Such type of people when employed in an organization always want to be functionally autonomous to exercise their own special talents and they have craving for independence. Such type of employees being anchored for creativity and developing something new, they should always be given challenging work assignments and scope for their identification through innovative product design.

Freedom and Autonomy

There are some people in the organization who always like to work at their own pace. Organizational constraints like fixed working hours, lack of variety of work, defined working conditions, etc., prevent them from becoming functionally autonomous and independent. Such people, due to absence of freedom or independence in their organization, often leave the job to start their own consultancy and freelancing. Teachers, professors, advertising professionals like artists and copy-writers, management consultants, etc. fall under this category.

Other Anchors

The complexity of behavioural parameters has of late identified some other career anchors which we find is very much related to different occupations. A separate class of people may have a strong craving for identity. Those who are in military organization get such identity as their occupational title, which they use as prefix to their names, like, Major, Col, Brig., etc. Such identification is so visible that they get special uniform matching their levels in the organization. Affiliate needs and interpersonal talents to work for a cause is yet another anchor which we find in some persons. The search for power, influence, control, and job variety are examples for other career anchors which people try to achieve in their occupational roles. Knowledge of this career anchors are essential for any organization to plan for career development. Each employee who nurtures specific career anchors (internal motives and values), should make it explicit to the organization so as to find matching occupational role without much of behavioural dissonance. Such matching process, therefore, is the principal task of planning for career development.

CAREER DEVELOPMENT AND EMPLOYEE EMPOWERMENT

Employee empowerment is defined as an extension of employee participation vis-à-vis involvement. Such definition of empowerment is more explicit when we review the contribution of Judith Bardwick (1991), who states that empowerment means giving everyone, instead of just people with certain positions or certain job titles, the legitimate right to make judgements, form conclusions, reach decisions, and then act.

Some career development process ensures promotion of employees from one career path to another. It gradually makes them independent functionaries at later career stages. Such system, therefore, often makes managers uneasy to open up the organizational planning process to individual employees. On the contrary, it will also develop a sense of misgivings as they may not really believe that the organization is truly opening up its planning process to them.

ISSUES INVOLVED

The following issues need to be considered to empower employees through successful career development process.

- Commitment of the top management to ensure that organizational career planning process will adequately consider individual career planning (which are internally perceived by the employees).
- People need to be infused with a sense of confidence to enable them to work to their true potential.
- Basic information like mission of the organization, its objectives and plans, career opportunities, etc. need to be communicated to the people.
- Available career planning resources in the organization should also to be communicated to the employees from time to time.
- The organization should help employees to make them competent to sort out data, formulate goals, and overcome obstacles to realize the goals.
- Employees also need to be communicated about the status of their present position, organizational expectations, and their level of performance.
- Individual managers should support their employees in career planning.

- The organization should be responsible to the individual career plans adopting an integrated career development process, which accommodates both individual needs and organizational needs.

It is, therefore, amply clear that career development process can be successfully utilized as an empowerment tool by any organization if the above issues are duly taken care of.

INDIAN SCENARIO

In India, most of the organization seriously lack in scientific career development scheme for employees working at various levels. For absence of such objective schemes, career development as promotional decisions often suffer from managerial discretion causing employee unrest and unfavourable industrial relations situation. In some organization career development for employees at higher echelon are all along existing, making such occupation group entitle for career development on regular basis. Such organizations even do not have effective career development schemes for employees down the level where such decision, as mentioned above, are exerted by managerial discretion. This difference in career development approach, therefore, demotivates employees and, even at times, stands against successful empowerment from which an organization can otherwise reap motivational benefits and increased functional effectiveness and productivity.

CAREER PLANNING AND CAREER DEVELOPMENT PROCESS

The dynamics and complexities of career development process have been made amply clear through earlier discussions. It is clear that career development process cannot be undertaken in isolation. Some issues are to be taken care of by the organization itself, while some others are concern the individual employees. Thus an improved career planning process is the joint responsibility of both the organization and the employee. Internal career needs (of individual employee), therefore, need to be integrated with the external career opportunities (of the organization). Unfortunately, organizations do not interact with the employees to understand their perceived career needs, instead they depend on guesswork to assume the needs, motives, and anchors and move them around on discretion. Such practices, therefore, lead to employees' dissonance. Thus, for having good and improved career development process, it is necessary both for the organization and the employees to understand each other's needs and opportunities.

INTEGRATION OF CAREER DEVELOPMENT PROCESS WITH CAREER STAGE AND FAMILY ISSUES

Since career development process is a continuous one and encompasses the entire employment so also the life span of an individual. It should also examine how the work, reward system, etc. can be integrated with the personal and family issues of the employees at different career stages. Most of the organizations experience mobility or job switch of executives at their maintenance or mid-career stage. This is because most employees at this stage experience structural changes or life plateauing for absence of adequate career paths, which can accommodate their personal and family needs.

At this career stage, promotion and outstation transfers of employees often invite problems, unless such decisions of the organization are favourable to the employee's family. Moreover, at this career stage, employees prefer to have an advisory role. All these aspects, therefore, deserve adequate attention of the organization, while it works out a career development plan for employees who are at their mid-career.

DEVELOPING CAREER PATHS COMPATIBLE WITH CHANGING NEEDS

Career development process should be made compatible to the changing needs of the employees in their life cycle. This calls for creating flexible opportunity structures and career paths to enable employees to identify them with such role positions at different stages of their life-cycle. New employees should have adequate opportunities to gain on-the-job knowledge and experience, so also to undergo training and education programmes for enriching job skills. The organization, therefore, needs to identify suitable role positions for such employees, who are at their beginning of career stage. Similarly, organizations should have adequate provision for renewals and updation of knowledge and skills for old employees, particularly in the context of changing environment, so that they should not lose their self-worth. For such employees, this is also to be followed by active pre-retirement planning and counselling so as to enable them to accommodate nicely with their family and society.

Improved career development process should also appreciate changing social values with respect to work, life, and leisure. Work, per se, is differently perceived by different people. For some, it is a source of self-fulfillment, creative pursuit, future growth and development, rising to the higher corporate ladder, etc. Different employees are at different places in the Maslow's Hierarchical Needs ladder. Hence, different yardsticks should be employed for each employee depending upon his/her perception of values.

Education and occupational mis-match need not always be for reasons of non-availability of matching jobs but for reasons which may be for perceived values of the individual. Many educated persons may opt for low profile artistic or craftsmanship jobs purely to derive creative satisfaction. Similarly, there are people who give more priorities for such work which do not demand much of their time and effort. These people give more importance to their leisure time activities (hobbies, drama, music, etc.) to seek self-satisfaction.

Career development process, therefore, should consider these aspects, or otherwise, the whole exercise will suffer from the problem of employee dissonance.

STEPS OF CAREER PLANNING PROCESS

Career planning process involves different activities or steps in an organization. Such steps are listed below.

Preparing Personnel Skills Inventories

The first step is to prepare personnel skills inventories. Such skills inventory is an information system which contains data on employees' skills and career goals. In addition, there are required data banks, which provide the following information:

- The organization structure and the persons manning different positions in the organization, their age, education, experience, training and career goals, status, and duties and responsibilities.
- The performance record and ratings, interpersonal abilities of the employees.
- Their preferred location, desires, and constraints.

- Whether the present strength is short or surplus to the requirements. If it is short, the extent of shortage at different levels and the organizational resources available to make good such shortages in future. If it is surplus, the measures available to redeploy them through proper restructuring.
- Future requirement of manpower for expansion or diversification of the company or for natural wastages like death, disability, retirement, discharge and dismissal, resignation, etc.

In most of the organizations, such information are computerized and periodically reviewed and updated. After preparation of personnel skill inventories and additional data, it is necessary to develop career paths for employees.

Developing Career Paths

Career paths are logical mapping out of jobs, which represent a potential progression tract that an employee may follow over time. Such mapping of job progressions is done in the form of career ladders clubbing together similar lines of occupations in job families. Job families are groups of homogenous jobs, i.e., jobs with similar characteristics. An illustrative model of career paths for marketing jobs is presented in Figure 9.1, which shows a simple job ladder.

While Figure 9.1 shows the career progress track in a marketing department, Figure 9.2 illustrates the model of career paths for a production department. However, in all cases, career paths are not so simple. For example, in manufacturing jobs for having multiple feeder posts at the lower level, career paths are more complex than the earlier one. For successful mapping out of career paths, at the outset, it is essential to identify the job families. After such identification, requisite skills for all the positions along with these paths need to be determined. This helps in developing such skills in employees where these are deficient and selecting the person with such skills for the different positions in the

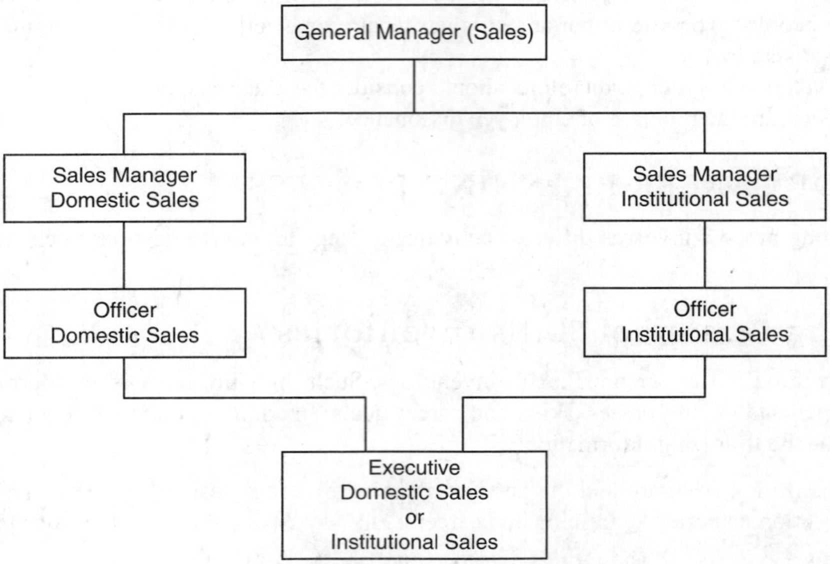

Figure 9.1 *Career paths for marketing jobs*

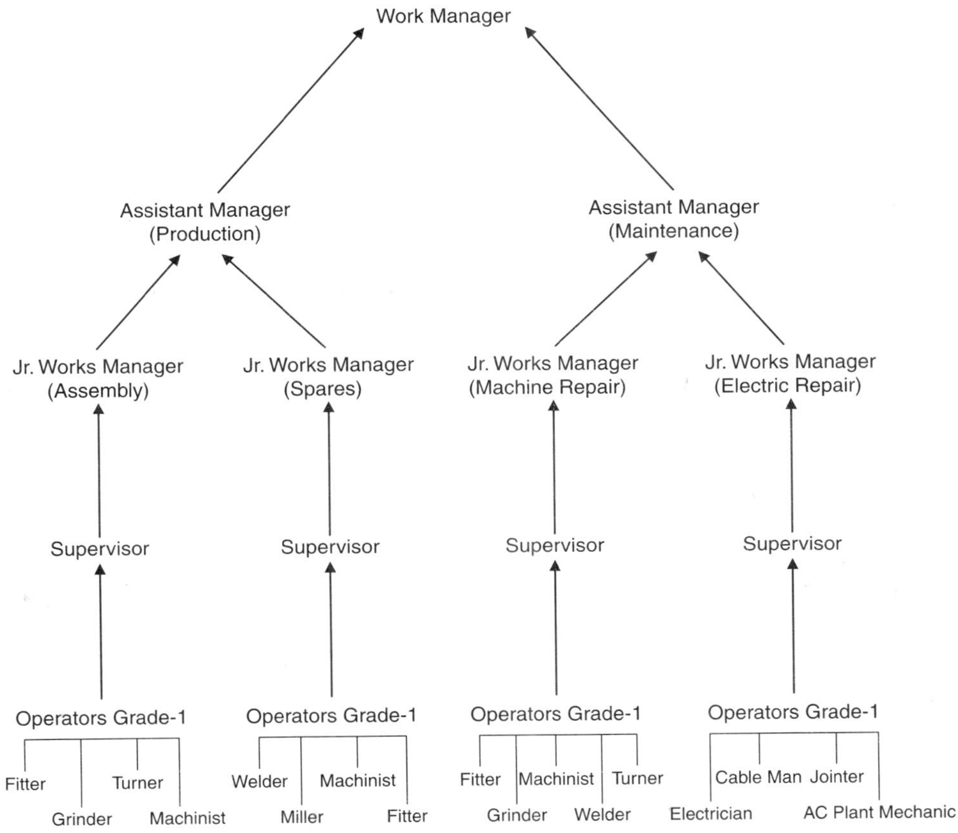

Figure 9.2 *Career paths for production department*

organization. However, the most distinguishing feature of career paths is that it need not always be linear or straight. Similarly, it also does not always indicate upward movement in the organization's hierarchy. Some organizations often re-designate employees at the lower level only to prepare them for future promotion. For example, highly skilled workmen may be re-designated as master craftsmen in a manufacturing organization without any effect on their pay packets only to elevate them gradually to supervisory positions later. Thus, lateral movement within the levels is also a distinguishing feature of career paths.

Put the Right Man at the Right Place

The third step in career planning process is to identify suitable employees who have the ability, potential, and willingness to take up higher responsibilities and rise to the organizational ladder. For this, most of the organizations have performance appraisal and merit-rating systems. This system enables organizations to compare the performance measures of different individuals in terms of job requirements and help in identifying training requirements, selecting for promotions, providing financial rewards, etc.

Impart Training

Subsequent steps in career planning process are the framing and implementation of training programmes. Training programmes are so designed, that it can meet the skill and knowledge gap, as could be identified through the performance appraisal process. Those organizations which witness the crisis of regular renewal to cope with the changing environment need to emphasize more on career planning, else they may face the crisis of manpower obsolescence. Most Indian organizations today impart training to their employees on quality circles (small group activities), value engineering technique, total quality management principles, ISO: 9000, etc. Most Indian organizations today impart training to their employees on quality circles (small group activities), value engineering technique, total quality management principles, ISO:9000, etc.

Review and Counsel

In addition to the above, career planning process is also concerned with developing suitable promotion and transfer policies, periodic review of career development plans, and career counselling. Career counselling provides guidance to the employees on occupational training, education, and career goals.

Succession Planning

Growth and survival of the organization are the responsibilities of the top management. To fulfill such responsibilities each organization needs to plan management succession. Succession planning is done in different time frames to ensure the availability of right managerial personnel at the right time in right positions for continuing organizational vitality and strength. Most of the organizations plan for immediate requirements matching with their budgets and business plans. This short-sightedness leads them to an alarming situation, when they find shortage of managerial manpower to man different positions in the organization, resulting in organizational collapse. To avoid this, good organizations try to make succession planning in three different time frames, i.e., immediate (within 1 year), intermediate (1 to 5 years) and long-range (beyond 5 years). Prevailing managerial attitude, i.e., a potential threat from successor, which may not sustain the desire of the managers to cling to their chairs, also stands against the success of the succession planning.

Steps of Succession Planning

The first step is to prepare and develop a management staffing plan for all anticipated needs in different time frames. For important positions at the top managerial level, such planning should be done even for shorter duration, keeping in view the potential threat from eventual natural wastages (death, disability, premature retirement, etc.) and so also from job switch and change (which has now increased many times for obviously enhanced scope of job mobility.) Other effects of external factors like, economic factors, overall manpower factors should also be considered while making such plan. Each organization has to review their business plans. Effects of such plans on managerial needs also need to be studied.

The second step is staffing and development. Staffing is concerned with recruitment, selection, and placement. Selection and placement may be either done from outside or from within the organization through promotion and transfer. Development of managerial personnel are done through training, job rotation, creating 'Assistant-to' positions, projects and boards assignments, performance appraisal, counselling, and guidance. In many organizations, management adopts what they call grooming process for filling up important managerial positions. A manager is 'groomed' by giving temporary assignments, attaching him/her with the higher officer or sometimes designating the potential promote as 'officer on special duty'.

The third step is to ensure congenial organizational environment to retain the desired managerial personnel. Unless this is done, the whole exercise of developing a successor may have to be repeated.

The fourth step is to develop a good performance appraisal system to get feedback on managerial performance and to review their progress and shortfalls.

The final step in the succession planning is the preparation of management resource inventory. Such inventory contains details of personal data, performance records, skills, potential, career goals, and career paths of managerial personnel. To make the succession planning process effective, it is important to strengthen it through management development programmes. It is a scientific training process for managers and executives to enrich their knowledge and skills, so as to make them competent to manage their organizations effectively. Unlike general purpose training, management development programmes aim at developing conceptual and human skills of managers and executives through organized and systematic procedure. Apart from training, management development programmes in organizations also make extensive use of job rotation, creation of assistant-to-position, assignment of identified successors to various boards and projects, etc. Finally, organizations also undertake the strategy of organizational development to bring about planned changes from the top for developing the future managers.

PMS CAREER PLANNING, CAREER DEVELOPMENT, AND SUCCESSFUL PLANNING

We have already discussed about intrinsic motivation of managerial level employees and also to ensure their retention. Organizations globally are now making use of career planning, career development, and succession planning. This is particularly important for managerial level employees. Many organizations have their own structured career plans or career progression path. Employees depending on their level of performance rise through the career ladders. However, today's business volatility has increased the pace of job mobility, particularly for those who are excellent performers. Effective performance management systems can track such excellent performers and can further nurture their talent using various human resource development programmes. Career development is in fact facilitating the employees to rise through the ladders, acquiring higher skills, and knowledge. Through succession plans, organization can identify the successors for future managerial positions, and accordingly can develop them through various human resource development initiatives. In all these cases, performance management systems play the most crucial role, as it systematically tracks the potentiality of people and accordingly can develop them so that organizations can sustain competitiveness with the best possible human resources.

SUMMARY

Career planning and development is a holistic approach for objective description of career progression path for all levels of employees in an organization. Even though the two concepts are used with different connotation in some organizations, like career planning for non-executive level and career development for executive and managerial levels, for our purpose, we have considered both the terms more in general, rather than specific. Since availability of internal manpower for manning present and future vacancies is extremely important for an organization to address to either planned strategic move or uncertainties, without career planning and development, performance management systems becomes meaningless and shortsighted if it only focuses on operational issues.

Retention of the key performers is an important strategic issue for organizations. Retention is best ensured for those organizations that have a well transparent career planning and development initiative. Similarly for internal manning of managerial vacancies, organizations should also have appropriate succession planning, or else this may jeopardize organizational plans. Succession planning succeeds management development and organizational development. Performance management systems in organizations reinforce career planning, career development, and succession planning.

KEY WORDS

Career Planning—A charted career progression path for various categories of employees in an organization.

Career Cycle—Career development stages of an employee, more related to age group and promotional levels.

Career Development—Process of creating opportunities for employees to rise through the career progression path.

Career Anchors—Career anchor is a syndrome of talents, motives, and values, which gives stability and direction to a person's career.

Succession Planning—Process of identifying potential successors among employees for future managerial positions.

Employee Empowerment— Process of involving employees in the decision-making and other activities of an organization.

Career Plateauing—Blocking of career progression path of an employees, either due to individual employee's incompetence or due to skill or knowledge mismatch with the organizational requirements.

Career Paths—Career paths are logical mapping out of jobs, which represent a potential progression tract that an employee may follow over time.

GENERAL REVIEW QUESTIONS

1. What is career development? Why is it important for an organization? Does it differ from career planning?
2. Do you think career planning should be individual centric or organization centric? Briefly discuss the career planning programme of an organization you know.
3. What are the factors you consider important for successful career planning?
4. Discuss the important steps in career planning process?
5. Define succession planning. Enumerate the steps involved in succession planning.
6. Discuss why it is important for performance management systems of an organization to track the career planning, developing, and succession planning?
7. Performance aligned career plans create a win-win situation both for the individual employees and for the organizations. Do you agree with this statement?
8. Short Notes

   (a) Career plateauing
   (b) Career ladders
   (c) Job families
   (d) Skill inventories
   (e) OD intervention
   (f) Succession plans

CRITICAL REVIEW QUESTION

7. A knowledge `intensive research and development organizations, engaged in contract research in pharmaceuticals, retained your services to draw a performance aligned career development systems for their scientist. Suggest how you will go ahead with the job?

FURTHER READING

Bardwick, Judith M. (1991), *Danger in the Comfort Zone* (New York, NY: American Management Association).

Ball, Kirstie (2000), 'Interface Value' *People Management*, January 6, pp. 40–42.

Bhattacharyya, D.K. (1988), 'Impact of Technology on Human Resource Management', *Personnel Today*, January–March.

Bhattacharyya, D.K. (1993), 'Promotion from Within—A Positive Motivational Reinforce for White Collar Employees' (a study on commercial banking organizations in India, Ph.D. thesis, University of Calcutta).

Bhattacharyya, D.K., (1994), 'Employees Leasing and Labour Market Flexibility—An Empirical Study of Its Problems in Selected Manufacturing Units', *Indian Journal of Labour Economics*, 37(4): 549–55.

Bhattacharyya, D.K. (1995a), 'Employees Empowerment—A Study of Selected Banking Organization in India', in HRD Repositioning (National HRD Network, Conference Volume), pp. 33–48.

Bhattacharyya, D.K. (1995b), 'Corporate Body Builder—The Emerging Role of HRD Professionals—A Prescriptive Model for Success', *Indian Journal for Training and Development* (New Delhi), April–June.

Bhattacharyya, D.K. (1995c), Manpower Obsolescence (a study in Indian ordnance factories, international Congress on economic transition with human face, Indian Industrial Relations Association, New Delhi, 3–6 September).

Bhattacharyya, D.K. (1995d), *Career Planning and Development* (Kolkata: IIMS).

Bhattacharyya, D.K. (2000) 'Competency Mapping and Manpower Redundancy—A Macro Level Study of Indian Organizations', *Management and Accounting Research*, October–December, 4(2): 97–105.

Bhattacharyya, D.K. (2001a), 'Impact of Labour Earnings on Productivity', *Management and Change* (New Delhi), January–July.

Bhattacharyya, D.K. (2001), 'Managing Manpower Redundancy—A Strategic Human Resource Manager Approach for Rightsizing Employees', in *Contemporary Trends on Human Resource Management* (Kolkata: SAS Consultants), pp. 5–13.

Bhattacharyya, D.K. (2006), *Human Resource Management*, 2nd edition (New Delhi: Excel Books).

Carl, C. Hoffmann, P. Kathleen, Hoffmann and Emily, D., Eason (1992), 'Complexities of the "Simple" Report Request', *HR Magazine*, November, pp. 49–57.

Carnegie Mellon University, Software Engineering Institute (1995), The Capability Maturity Model (Addison Wesley Longman, Inc.).

Dreyfuss, J. (1988), 'Catching the Computer Wave,' *Fortune*, 26 September, pp. 77–82.

Drucker, P.F. (1989), *The New Realities* (New York, NY: Harper & Row), p. 175.

Eric, G. Flamholtz (1974), *Human Resource Accounting* (California, CA: Dicken Son Publications Co., Inc.).

Ellen, Enst, Kossek, Willard Young, Debra C., Gash and Nichol Victor (1994), 'Waiting for Innovation in the Human Resource Department—Godot Implements a Human Resource Information System', *Human Resource Management*, 33(1): 135–59.

Fombrum, C., M.T. Noel and A.D. Marry, (1984), *Strategic Human Resource Management* (New York, NY: John Wiley).

Falicia, Nathan (1987), 'Analysing Employers' Costs for Wages, Salaries and Benefits', *Monthly Labour Review*, October pp. 3–10.

Hal, Glatzer (1995), 'HR Systems Get Reengineering', *HR Magazine*, July, pp. 44–47.

John Edwards, Chris Leck, Ray Loveridge, Roger Lumley, John Morgan, and Mick Silver (1983), *Manpower Planning* (New York, NY: John Wiley & Sons.

John, Bramham (1994), *Human Resource Planning* (Hyderabad: University Press (India) Limited).

Martin, Godfrey (ed.) (1997), *Skill Development for International Competitiveness* (Cheltenham: Edward Elgar Publishing Company).

Michael, J. Kavanagh, Hal, G. and Scott I. Tannenbaum (1990), *Human Resource Information Systems: Development and Application* (Boston, MA: PWS-Kent Publishing Company).

Paul, Miller (ed.) (1992), 'Integrating Strategy and Human Resource Management in Brian Towers', in *The Handbook of Human Resource Management* (Cambridge, MA: Blackwell Publishers).

Robert, E. Sibson (1992), *Strategic Planning for Human Resources Management* (New York, NY: American Management Association).

Schein, E.H. (1969), *Process Consultation: Its Role in Organizational Development* (Reading, MA: Addison-Wesley).

Steven, A. Larson (1993), 'Selecting a New Payroll/HRIS', *Management Accountant*, October, pp. 28–31.

Walker A.J. (1980), 'A Brief History of the Computer in Personnel', *Personnel Journal*, 16: 33–36.

William P. Antony, (1991), *Strategic Human Resource Management* (Hinsdale, Illinois: Dryden Press).

William, E. Berry (1994), 'The Human Resource Information System', *Management Accountant*, January, pp. 56–57.

CASE STUDY

Sun Microsystems—Career Development Opportunities

In a rapidly changing work environment, talent retention is a great challenge for any organization. Without retention of talent organization cannot sustain in competition. Creating career development opportunities for the employees, companies can achieve success in talent retention. By aligning career development with the individual employees self-development, organizations can get better results in talent retention.

Sun Microsystems, the arch competitor of Microsoft, right from their beginning (formed in 1982) faced a major crisis of recruitment and retention of talents. The young entrepreneurs of Sun, right from their beginning promoted the culture of innovation. Innovate and create the future; this is what Sun till now subscribes to. Today Sun boasts to possess the most talent workforce of 30,000 and operate from 55 countries with $10 billion revenue. With its global headquarters in Palo Alto, California, the company is a global leader in enterprise network computing, with its products ranging from Java, workstations, and servers to other software services, with almost $10 billion in revenues.

The company follows the product-based divisional structure. Even though the product divisions function independently, they are well aligned. Each product division gets the support from the corporate resources group in human resources (HR), finance, legal, and IT services. At Sun, HR always emphasize on value addition, keeping pace with the change. Three C philosophy of Sun's HR is competitive workforce, competitive organization, and competitive workplace. To realize three C, Sun's HR promote the culture of career development, financial opportunity, work variety, and commitment to people. Career development programme at Sun gets the highest priority, as the company works in a fast-changing environment, and employees always need to learn new knowledge and acquire new skill to rise through the career ladder. Every employee of Sun knows their defined career paths; the company plays the role of catalyst with their 'figure it out' career development programmes. Sun believes in career; employees must feel self-reliant.

With a free agency model of employment relationship, Sun believes career development is the employees' responsibility; organization can only play the role of catalyst, i.e., providing support and growth opportunities. The career services programme of Sun through several career action centre counselors support employees' career development. For Sun, career development is a long-term commitment. Sun's approach to career development started in 1991 with a built-in philosophy that career is employees' primary ownership; organizations can only extend support.

With continuous career development support, the company today benefits all cross-sections of employees. Career action centre's prime responsibility is to help employees to explore their career opportunities, develop their attitude to rise through the career ladders, and support the employees to realize their career aspirations.

Question: Study the career development systems in Sun and critically comment when the system is worthwhile in today's scenario of competition?

Adapted from: http://www.elsdon.com/case.htm.

CHAPTER 10

Team Performance Management

Learning Objectives

After reading this chapter, you will be able to understand:

- Definitions and concepts of a team
- Principles of team performance management
- Methodology of team performance management
- Types of teams
- Approaches to change team behaviours
- Work wheel and team performance
- Measuring team performance
- Managing team performance
- Different stages of teamwork
- Team building exercises

Developing Team for Effective Performance

Developing team performance culture for one of the public sector banks in India was a major problem. Besieged with high NPAs and reducing corporate clients have adversely affected the bank's profitability, and even in some of their product-mix, they have badly underperformed over the years. It was at this stage, the bank had to initiate major restructuring of the work processes, and teamwork was one of their priority areas. At the initiate stage of implementation, the major problem was to make the employees buy the idea of teamwork, as the work systems are based on individually assigned job description, and every employee is responsible for his/her part of job. Any financial loss for decisional errors makes the employees personally liable, and they need to make good such loss. This resulted in many bank officials losing their pension, gratuity, and some had even to go for premature withdrawal from their provident fund account to make the payments. Teamwork makes them collectively liable, but results are much better.

Realizing such infeasibility in institutionalizing the teamwork culture, the bank thought of restructuring their work processes and introduced the incentive scheme for incremental business results. All cross-sections of employees were taken through rigorous teamwork sessions and they were made to believe that they are working to achieve a common goal. Through simulated exercises and business games, they were convinced how a collaborative teamwork can significantly enhance their performance levels. For the specific nature of banking services, the bank went for developing cross-functional teams. Every employee of the bank, irrespective of their nature and level of activities, was exposed through the entire banking operations. The relationship managers and executives were given the role of manning the counters for customer services, the customer service people were taken through the field marketing duties. This process could make them understand each others roles and gradually they started working together, forgetting their functional boundaries. The entire process worked well and within a year of its implementation, the bank started getting better results. Team leaders were chosen by rotation, irrespective of their hierarchical level. They were given the freedom and autonomy to decide their targets, form the team norms in line with Tuckman's (1965) stages of team formation, i.e., forming, storming, norming, performing, and adjourning.

Successful implementation of teamwork in the bank not only increased the performance level of employees but also increased their earnings in the form of incentives and reduced the decisional errors.

INTRODUCTION

Organizational performance depends on factors like strategy, structure, technology, type of people employed, and management style. Among all these, however, people factor or the behaviour of individual employees is most crucial. It is the people who make their contribution to achieve the expected level of performance at the individual, group and at the organizational level. Various researchers on team performance like Burns and Stalker (1966), Morgan (1993), Weber (1964) could relate the employees' performance to the structure of the organizations. Herzberg (1968), McClelland (1988), Maslow (1943), Roethlisberger and Dickson (1964), and Taylor (1947), however, focused on what motivates the individual worker. However, the arguments on organizational down-sizing or right-sizing emphasize on the empowerment of workers (Conjer, 1993; Moss-Kanter, 1993; Drucker, 1988; and Tjosvold, 1991). Interdependence between individuals emphasizes on the work of the group (Smith et al. 1994) and the work of the team. Brown (1995) emphasizes on the trend in pointing out the rapid growth in group-based rewards as opposed to individualistic-based reward schemes. Likert's (1961) linking pin theory sees its expression in these ideas that everyone is part of one or more teams, whether production or service oriented or part of the management.

Team performance enhances the organizational performance, as all the team members pursue the common organizational goal, and their collective efforts give the benefit of synergy. Successful team performance is attributable to positive teamwork and attitude of the team members. Team members when work in a team pursue two roles, i.e., their individual functional roles and their roles as team members. A marketing manager, when working with a team, is required to work in marketing areas in terms of the assigned job descriptions. But the role of this marketing manager becomes common to that team optimizing inventory and materials holding costs, just-in-time inventory planning, lean management practices, etc. when working as a team member in inventory control and materials management team. Similarly, operations managers of the said team in addition to the functional role of managing the operations need to ensure flow of materials on time to continue the production or operations, etc. The success of team performance depends on how effectively the team members behave and interact with each other, to what extent they are convinced about the need for achieving the common goals, and finally the presence of teamwork culture in the organization. In team performance management, the concept of team role (Belbin 1981, 1993; Davis et al. 1992; Margerison and McCann, 1990; Spencer and Pruss, 1992; and Woodcock 1989) requires the employee to perform his/her functional role. The concept of team player (Parker, 1990), on the other hand, requires them to work in one or more team roles. For example, an innovative team member can share new ideas with the team, gather important information, and effectively coordinate with other team members' jobs.

Personality characteristics can also determine the team roles (Margerison and McCann, 1990; Parker, 1990), so also the behaviour and the attitudes of the people. Variation in the behaviours and attitudes of the person in terms of the occupation could be observed by Belbin (1981, 1993). His study also authenticates that team performance is knowledge dependent. Knowledgeable team members can successfully play their respective team roles and, accordingly, achieve higher performance. Cohen and Ledford's (1994) study could establish the mechanism to measure the team performance using the objective data.

DEFINITION AND CONCEPTS

Teamwork trends are increasing visible in today's organizations. To gain better performance results, organizations are shifting from individual work systems to teamwork, and teams have now become the main building block (Guzzo and Shea, 1992; Kozlowski and Bell, 2003) to achieve performance excellence. However, this teamwork culture often goes against the pay for performance plan, which is more individual centred (Prendergast, 1999). Such paradoxical situation, i.e., organizing work on teamwork and pay for performance (individual rewards) often defeat the culture of teamwork in organizations.

A team represents a small group of people with a common purpose or goal. Each member of the team plays the interdependent roles with their complimentary skills. A team may consist of both the members with homogenous skills and work experiences or members with diversity of skills and work experiences. The second one is known as cross-functional teams, and is more evident in today's organizations. Effective teamwork is an important prerequisite for effective performance management. Performance management, per se, centres on individual performance to the best of their abilities. Any employee individually achieves the performance goals or results meeting or exceeding the performance requirements. Team performance management, however, on the other hand requires organization to develop a shared understanding for the team members, to collectively achieve the business results for the company.

Effective team performance management makes the team members focused on their job responsibilities and job performance, and produces better results in consistence with the organizational requirements. Also effective team performance management enables the team members to develop better performance in their future tasks or job roles.

Performance management for teams is different from team building (and it is also different to performance management for individuals). There are many different definitions of 'team building', but in most of the cases, it refers to an activity that helps develop the team in some way or the other. It can include a wide range of activities like

- Outdoor activities.
- On-site or off-site workshops.
- Having lunch together.
- Sharing an email list or bulletin board.
- Meeting in the coffee lounge during work breaks.

All these activities are introduced with the belief that members of the team will improve the way the group operates. However, its impact on collective performance is more intuitive rather than the actual. It is only for this reason that team performance management is important. Team performance management is focused directly on the achievement of the team's key business objectives. It bridges the gap between the team building 'enablers' and business performance results. It establishes a direct connection between collective behaviours and team performance.

PRINCIPLES OF TEAM PERFORMANCE MANAGEMENT

Team performance management is predicated on the following three principles:

Team behaviours are different from individual behaviours
It is not important for us to understand what an individual does in a team, rather it is important to know what team does collectively. The differences between the individual's behaviour in a team, and the collective behaviours of a team, depend on factors like the environment they work in, or the team processes they use for communicating, deciding, rewarding, etc.

The behaviours that make a team successful vary
The behaviours of successful teams vary from team to team and from time to time. For example, a successful R&D team behaviours may vary with the behavioural pattern of a successful marketing team.

Team behaviours can be changed using a team performance management process
The performance management process used in a team may be either similar or different than the performance management processes for individuals. Again depending on the peculiarity of a team behavioural goals and profiles of team members may vary.

Organizations usually follow the methodology for team performance management activities in the following ways:

- Establishing the behavioural goals aligning with team performance. This can be done using a team profile questionnaire to track what behaviours can make the team successful.
- Establishing the desired behavioural requirements using the management team roles indicator.
- Comparing the target and current behaviours using a behavioural gap analysis.
- Take action to close the gap, enforcing the behavioural requirements for the success of team.

Therefore, the difference between traditional team building and team performance management is that while the former engages in activities in the belief that they will indirectly lead to improvements in team performance (which in reality may or may not happen), the latter identifies the team behaviours that lead to direct business success, and then change the process to elicit the desired behaviours.

In a team performance management system usually organizations make use of two types of measures—external and internal. External measures give us the performance results, while the internal measures give us the internal behaviour.

External measures quantify the team results that involve assessment of the performance of the team, the output and the contribution to business success. Some of the examples are:

- Sales revenue achieved (sales team).
- Reduction in man-days loss achieved (HR team).
- Reduction in rejection rate achieved (operations team).

Internal measures quantify the team behaviours, which involve quantification of team behaviours, involving the assessment of the means used to achieve the end results. Such measures speak about how the team goes about its business? Therefore, internal measures need not only include the individual activities, rather the activities that can be undertaken by the team or a sub-set of team collectively.

Examples of these collective behaviours might be:

- The number of timely cross-selling opportunities passed between sales people (sales team).
- The number of successful collective bargaining made in a period (HR team).
- The time spent in fixing a maintenance problem (operations team).

It is important to reach to a consensus about the team standards and the measurement criteria right at the beginning of the team performance management process. In a relatively stable nature of teamwork, team standards need not be periodically revised. However, with the organizational restructuring and change in the technology and business processes, team standards are expected to change.

Types of Teams

Depending on the specific requirements of the organizations, the following types of teams are formed for achieving excellence in performance management:

Organizational teams—a 'top management team', bound together because it contributes to overall objectives.

Work teams—self-contained and permanent, delivering output. They focus on achievement of common purpose and are a function of common purpose and are a function of individuals working well.

Project teams—brought together to complete a task. Once the task is complete, they disband.

Ad hoc teams—set up to deal with a problem. They are short-lived and operate as a task force.

Approaches to Change Team Behaviours

A systematic process for changing team behaviours in a way that leads directly to increased performance and business benefits, follow certain principles as under:

Identification of behavioural goals: This includes compiling opinion from the team, customers, management, staff, peers, and others to list what behaviours will lead to team success.

Measurement of current behaviours: This involves assessment of the current behaviours of the team for making direct comparisons.

Undertake a gap analysis: Identify the gaps between target and the current behaviours.

Close the gap: Adopt suitable training interventions and team actions to change the behaviour of the team.

Monitor: Monitor the team intervention programmes and take corrective actions, wherever required.

In any organization, performance management systems must focus on giving opportunities to the employees to perform their best. The system must facilitate employees to deliver even exceeding the performance targets, and support free flow of communication between the employees and the leaders. Leaders must also ensure and even nurture the development of employees through skill and knowledge renewal.

Team performance management now determines the success of any organization. Effective management of team, in addition to the incremental benefit to performance results, ensures workers' motivation. Motivated workers volunteer to take higher performance targets and achieve the best quality level.

Despite all these benefits of teamwork, managing the team performance is a great challenge for today's organizations. For example, giving too much negative feedback at quick successions, ultimately defeats the purpose, as demotivated and demoralized employees start underperforming. The first requirement for successful team management is to facilitate the team members to understand the team's roles and the roles of each team member. The second prerequisite is to ensure total transparency through ongoing communication. Team members need to be informed about what they are expected to achieve. Managers and leaders must immediately intervene to resolve any conflict and misunderstanding in the team.

Successful team management requires systematic training, constant monitoring of teamwork, and motivation. Similar changes in the work environment or culture, emphasis on time management, etc. can get better results from the team.

Team building is the most commonly used technique for organizational change and development. Team building emphasizes on binding people together to achieve common goals of the organization and, in the process, develop the shared vision to provide a common direction to all. In very simplistic terms, a team consists of a group of people to work together to accomplish some common goals. In that context, a team has two common aspects: the task aspect and the people or relationship aspect. Task aspect defines the task or the job to be done or carried out, including its sub-sets. . People or relationship aspects focus on interaction and working together. It includes communication, mutual responses, leadership, conflict management, etc. In another way, we can define the task aspects are those which cover the content aspects, while people or relationships aspects focus on the process aspects of teamworking. Teams focus primarily on the following issues:

- Intra-team task focus, i.e., the content aspect.
- Intra-team people focus, i.e., the process aspect.
- Inter-team task focus within the organization.
- Inter-team people focus within the organization.

For organizational change and development team building helps as it eliminates many harmful interpersonal relational problems, and, ultimately, strengthen the problem solving abilities of the people, leveraging the benefit of synergy.

WORK WHEEL AND TEAM PERFORMANCE

Using the work wheel model of team performance, pioneered by the Margerison and McCann (1995), we can understand the key work elements that focus in explaining why it is that some work teams work effectively and achieve their objectives while others fail. The research has supported an understanding of team performance in terms of nine team performance factors, summarized as the types of work wheel, shown in Figure 10.1.

Effective teams continually demonstrate a focus on all nine performance factors. The eight factors arranged around the spokes of the Wheel are known as the teamwork functions and show relative statistical independence. The ninth activity, linking, is placed in the centre of the wheel as it is a characteristic shared with the eight work functions. For example, inspecting work must be done in a 'linking' way if it is to be shared with all the other functions. The importance of each work function to teamwork is described in more detail below:

Advising

Advising work is concerned with giving and gathering information. It involves finding out what others are doing in the organizational area of work and ensuring that the organization follows the best

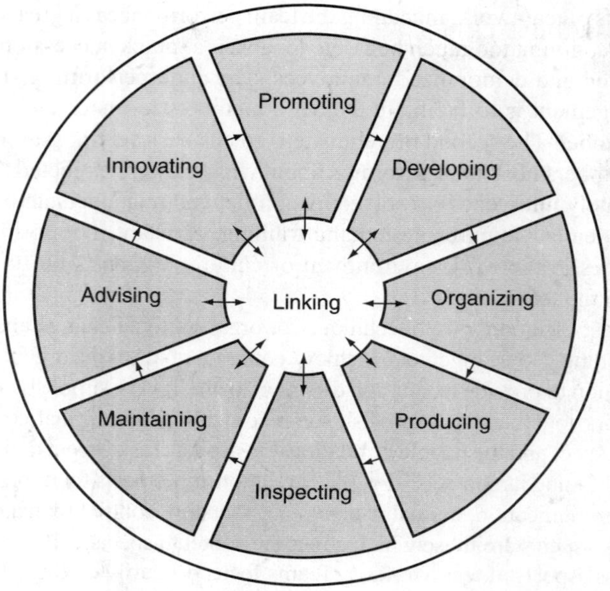

Figure 10.1 *Margerison–McCann types of work wheel*

practices. For effective advising, organization generates information from articles, reports, or books, or by meeting and talking with people. It means ensuring that we have all the information available for the team to make the best decisions and deliver results.

Innovating

Innovating is a key aspect of teamwork and involves challenging the way things are currently being done. Globally, technology is changing very fast, and among others it also changes the way we perform our tasks. Through innovation we need to update our process of doing work. For every work team, innovation is very important. It not only ensures a better way of doing work, but also enables organizations to achieve cost competitiveness, quality, and overall excellence.

Promoting

Only innovation cannot make an effective team. It requires efforts from the team members to mobilize reasons in terms of people, money, and equipment. This is what we call promotion of innovative ideas in the organizations. Resources to implement new ideas need to be obtained by the team persuading or exerting influence on the top management of the organization. Similar efforts need to be given to promote the innovative products and services to the customers. Thus, without the capability to promote new ideas or innovation, teams cannot achieve excellence.

Developing

Developing indicates the activities involved in moulding and shaping the ideas to meet the needs of the customers or the end-users. It involves listening to the needs of the customers and incorporating those in organizational plans. Also in the process of developing, the team considers the resource constraints of the organization.

Organizing

The process of organizing emphasizes on getting into action to make things happen. Team organizing requires clearly spelling out to team members what they need to do and why. Also it guides the team members in the process of doing their jobs, establishing clears goals and action plans within the time and budget constraints.

Producing

At this stage of the work wheel, team members concentrate on producing the results on a regular basis to the level of high standards to achieve both the effectiveness and the efficiency. Thus, it is a stage of producing continuous output.

Inspecting

Simultaneous with the task of producing, team members need to ensure regular quality audits of their products and services. The purpose is to deliver error-free products and services to the customers to get their enhanced level of satisfaction. The process of inspecting also monitors the financial, safety, security, and legal aspects of teamwork.

Maintaining

Maintaining is the process of upholding standards to ensure effective teamwork. The team can fail when the team processes are not regularly checked and maintained. Maintaining ensures upholding quality standards along with regular reviews of team effectiveness.

Linking

The linking process pulls the team members together and thereby stand the differences between a work group and a team. Proper linking makes a team effective and efficient. The linking process encompasses tasks, people, and the leadership.

Therefore, the work wheel model suggests that the work functions adjacent to each other are similar, rather than those which are non-adjacent. To illustrate, the work of promoting requires skill sets which are different from the work of inspecting. Also, the model suggests that all teamwork can be classified into some key areas. This apart, the work wheel complies with the generally accepted criteria, i.e., generalizability, comprehensiveness, prudence, etc.

MEASURING TEAM PERFORMANCE

It is important to systematically measure a team's performance through an objective review process to understand the degree of effectiveness of teamwork. While it is important to measure the short-term outputs, it is equally important to measure the long-term perspectives in terms of assessing the degree of creativity of team members, ability to effectively promote the team for long-term sustainability, etc. Such measurement need not always be objective. Most of the organizations make use of a questionnaire and, using the multi-rater assessment, assess the team performance in all the nine team performance factors mentioned in the work wheel. We have many standard questionnaires available to measure team performance. The most popular among them is the team performance profile questionnaire (TPPQ), which has 54 items. However, this questionnaire fits well with the work wheel model. By profiling the team performance, organizations can therefore gain in terms of:

- Team performance assessment with a common and shared understanding of the critical factors that are instrumental for high performance.
- Team effectiveness improvement through team development ensuring that team members focus on critical areas for achieving success.

Therefore, the work wheel model enables organizations to perform ongoing teamwork assessment and, at the same time, ensures ongoing team development to constantly improve team performance.

MANAGING TEAM PERFORMANCE

Management of team performance, at the outset, requires developing a common language to facilitate shared understanding. Shared understanding provides an opportunity to team members to develop suitable action plans for improving team performance. A tentative approach adopted by the organization to manage team performance within the ambit of the work wheel model is to adopt an informal approach in questioning the team members on certain aspects explained below:

- Nature of information required.
- What could be the best way of doing the job?
- What type of stakeholders need to be influenced by the team?
- Does the teamwork conform to stakeholders' expectations?
- In what way can the team be organized?
- Are the team members aware in clear terms of the outputs and outcomes of the products/services?
- What are the areas that require verification to understand that the team is working in right perspectives?
- Does the organization adopt best standards and procedures for effective teamwork?
- What is the degree of internal and external linkage of team efforts?

Based on the consolidation of responses received against the aforementioned questionnaire, it is possible for the organization to identify where the team performs well and where it lags. To team members also it provides an objective basis to understand what they are doing. Also it facilitates comparison of different views of team members and others to strengthen the team focus on the team vision and mission. Thus, the major thrust in managing team performance lies in developing a common language for shared understanding of team members to facilitate them to focus on critical success factors for achieving team results in terms of output and outcome. Also, in the process, organizations can measure the gaps to develop suitable action plans to fix it and to improve team performance.

DIFFERENT STAGES OF TEAMWORK

Tuckman (1965) presented the four stages model of teamwork. Like the work wheel model, this model is also widely used by organizations to form the work teams and also to measure their degree of progress. Figure 10.2 describes the model of the four stages of teamwork.

Forming
↓
Storming
↓
Norming
↓
Performing

Figure 10.2 *Tuckman's stages of teamwork model*

After the formation of the team, it goes through the storming stage to set the ground rules and norms. After this stage, the team starts performing. The entire cycle right from the formation of team to team performance earlier (in the 1980s) used to take six-months time. However, with today's complexity of business, this cycle time for some organizations even got reduced to six days, or even less than that. Using the work wheel model we can more reliably measure and manage team performance, both in quantitative and qualitative terms. With the feedback information from team members and outsiders, we can correctly diagnose the problems and initiate suitable action plans to successfully manage team performance. Similarly, Tuckman's model also reinforces the process of successful management of team performance.

Models such as the types of work wheel provide a reliable and valid way of measuring and managing team performance by generating qualitative and quantitative feedback data both from team members and outsiders. Organizations can diagnose and even predict the problems much before they happen. Using Tuckman's model, often for unscrupulous team members, actual problems may remain unidentified, as some of them deliberately avoid discussions, which can eventually bring out the real issues during the stage of storming, and hence deciding the rules and norms at the stage of norming becomes incomplete and the team remains non-performing at the final stages of norming. For these reasons, organizations prefer simultaneous use of work wheel and Tuckman's model to effectively manage the team.

This problem was experienced by the author of this book while forming a cross-functional marketing team for a start-up hotel. Stiff competition among hotels often requires them to go for price war to attract and retain customers. In the present case, all possible avenues to price control in the hotel were explored and management was literally left with no alternative to sustain in price competition. In his role as a consultant, the author formed a cross-functional marketing team with the following members:

Marketing manager
Chef
Stewarts
Room service man
Door man
Front desk people
Room disposal crew
Procurement section people

The members were asked to brainstorm with a single point agenda, i.e., how to save on food cost without deteriorating quality. All employees in the discussions shared their views and, ultimately, could not come out with any solution, excepting the room disposal crew who pointed out that almost 40 per cent of the food items served in rooms get wasted. Further investigation revealed that food consumption rate has been fixed almost 10 years before which is no longer sustainable in the present food consumption rate of hotel customers. To start with, the hotel was asked to reduce the food quantity by 10 per cent to study whether there is any complaint from the customers. Subsequently, it was reduced up to 30 per cent without any substantial complaints from the customers. Gradually, this was embedded with the food service norms, which could help the hotel to reduce the cost and achieve good performance results.

In this case, mere brainstorming approach could help identify the hotel performance problems using a cross-functional team approach.

TEAM BUILDING EXERCISES

At an organizational level, various team building exercises are used that focus more on T-group, role playing exercises, constitution of specific task analysis, etc. T-group or sensitivity training is a learning approach. Here, a small unstructured group of people learn from their own interactions their issues pertaining to their interpersonal relations. With 10–12 participants, the T-group meets with a facilitator without any specific agenda. For T-group, the agenda evolves during the course of discussion. The purpose is to understand their interpersonal relations and how it is perceived by other members. The group evolves like a learning laboratory, as knowledge is acquired in the process of experiencing (each other), reflecting, hypothesizing, experimenting, and conceptualizing. Essentially, the T-group helps in two different ways as follows:

- Understanding about self and achieving personal growth (more interpersonal focus).
- Understanding group dynamics and relationship between members.

Objectives of T-group

The primary objective of the T-group is to enhance understanding about oneself, gaining insight into one's own behaviour, and analysing its impact on others. One can understand how one's behaviour integrates or gels with others. This apart, other objectives of the T-group in the context of performance management issues can be enumerated as under:

- To enhance the understanding and awareness of group and inter-group processes.
- To facilitate and inhibit group effectiveness.
- To create greater awareness of self-behavioural processes.
- To increase diagnostic skills in inter-personal and inter-group situations.
- To help in discovering one's dominant potential, transforming the learning into action.

Laboratory experimentation helps in developing new behaviours, which in the process benefits organizations to bring the desired change, developing the capabilities of people to perform.

Benefits of T-group Training

In performance management, T-group benefits individuals, groups, and the organization as a whole. Individual level benefits are spontaneous perception of behaviour with reduced levels of stress, which releases the potentiality of mental and physical health, and decreases defensive behaviour. Perceptual clarity makes people more realistic and achievement oriented. It enhances self-esteem, develops the capability of people to explore options, and enhances the power of decision-making. At an individual level, people also feel motivated for obvious strengthening of their internal locus of control.

Group or inter-personal level benefits are developing insights to understand others. With enhanced self-esteem, people can comfortably communicate with each other and can become more supportive and productive in relationships. With the increase of mutual trust and respect, we can subdue our aggression and develop better relationships, which pave the way for effective teamwork. Collaborative behaviour increases our inter-dependence and facilitates both individual and organizational growth through improved inter-personal relations.

Organizational level benefits of T-group training are increase in openness, trust, and inter-dependence, which together culminate to a conducive work environment to maximize the potential from all. With the recharged or reinforced capabilities of people, organizations can successfully manage future challenges.

ROLE ANALYSIS

Role analysis clarifies and prioritizes role expectations, both from the role senders' and the role occupiers' perspectives. A role is defined as the pattern of behaviour expected from a particular job position in the organizational hierarchy. A specific job position confers a job role, and the person who occupies such a job position is the role occupier. A job position is conferred by the organization maintaining a specific hierarchy. A particular role occupier works under some immediate boss, who becomes the role sender. Role senders expect some specific performance and desired behaviour from role occupiers. Some of the role expectations are task, job, work, and position. Task roles are the basic job element, job role is the component of work; work role is the expected performance standards, while positional role is the hierarchical level as per the structure of the organization, which clarifies to others and so also to oneself. People in general understand their role and the tasks expected of them.

From the above perspectives, therefore, role can be differentiated from job description. The major point of distinction is while job description is static and impersonal, role is dynamic and personal. Role occupier's personal qualities, growth, perceptions, motivations, ambitions, values, etc. are some of the major determinants of his/her role. Hence, despite being in the same job role, role deliverables vary from person to person.

Performance management through role analysis is important, as it helps in establishing clarity in terms of expected level of performance and behavioural inputs in the changed circumstances. The idea behind this is that in changed circumstances, organizations need to adjust the job role. Through role analysis, such changed expectations can be measured and communicated to the role occupiers to deliver in the changed circumstances.

Some of the important areas of role analysis are:

- Detailed understanding of the coverage in terms of the function and level.
- Setting up of a core task force to carry out the role analysis.
- Selection of persons for specific task forces.
- Understanding the role sender and the changing role expectations for preparation of key performance areas (KPAs) for the role occupier.
- Identification of required set of competencies for the specific job role.
- Identification of performance gaps through competency mapping and developing plans for closing the performance gaps.

With all the aforementioned perspectives, role analysis is carried out either by engaging the consultants or through in-house resource persons, or a combination of both. Accordingly, the core task force is given the task to perform the analysis and suggest the changes in the role expectations keeping in view the required level of organizational change and development. All these need to be done within the budgetary constraints in a given time frame. Simultaneously with the role analysis, systems, procedures, work instructions, etc. are developed or updated and, wherever necessary, powers are delegated.

SUMMARY

The performance of the team is an important variable in the performance of the organization as a whole. Team performance is the ability and behaviour of the team members, evident from the roles that the team members play. Team roles could either be functional or based on the personality characteristics of the team members. Most organizations make use of Belbin's approach of team profiling, and accordingly predict which team is high performing or which team is likely to have relatively lesser rate of success. Organizing the work around teams is now a global phenomenon, as collectively people deliver more. Team performance management has now become so important that even team-based compensation plans have been adopted by many organizations to make people work effectively in a team. Team performance management is different from team building (and it is also different to performance management for individuals). Team building means undertaking a series of activities to build a team. Team performance management, on the other hand, directly relates to the achievement of the team's key business objectives. It directly establishes the connection between the collective behaviours and team performance. In this chapter, we have discussed the process of team performance management and have also reviewed some team building techniques.

KEY WORDS

T-group—T-group or sensitivity training is an experiential learning approach. Here a small unstructured group of people learn from their own interactions their issues pertaining to their inter-personal relations. With 10–12 participants, the T-group meets with a facilitator without any specific agenda. For T-group, the agenda evolves in course of discussion. The purpose is to understand their inter-personal relations, and how it is perceived by each other.

Linking—Linking process pulls team members together, and thereby makes the differences between a work group and a team. Proper linking makes a team effective and efficient. The linking process encompasses tasks, people, and leadership.

Work Wheel Model—Using the work wheel model of team performance, pioneered by Margerison and McCann (1995), we can understand the key work elements that focus in explaining why it is that some work teams work effectively and achieve their objectives while others fail. The research has supported an understanding of team performance in terms of nine team performance factors,

Work Teams—These teams are self-contained and permanent, delivering output. They focus on achievement of common purpose and are a function of common purpose and of individuals working well.

GENERAL REVIEW QUESTIONS

1. Explain the concepts of team. Discuss how teamwork helps in making the performance management process effective in organizations?
2. What are the important principles of team performance management?
3. What methodology do organizations follow for effective team performance management?
4. Explain in what way teamwork can change the behaviours of team members.
5. Explain the concept of work wheel model. How does it help in measuring team performance management in an organization?
6. In the light of Tuckman's model, explain various stages of teamwork, and critically comment on the nature of differences of Tuckman's model with the work wheel model.
7. What type of team building exercises is more suitable for a knowledge-intensive IT organization? Give justification to your answer.
8. Short Notes
   (a) Team Building
   (b) Project Teams
   (c) Innovating
   (d) Linking
   (e) Role Analysis

CRITICAL REVIEW QUESTION

9. Suomoto Enterprises, a large conglomerate having presence in FMCG, Pharma, and Textile segments would like to retain your services to develop the culture of teamwork and subsequently to practice the team-based performance management. Develop your action plans with justification.

REFERENCES

Belbin, R.M. (1981), *Management Team: Why They Succeed or Fail* (London: Heinemann).

Belbin, R.M. (1993), *Team Roles at Work* (Oxford: Buccerworth-Heinemann).

Bhattacharyya, D.K. (2009), *Organizational Behaviour—Concepts and Applications* (New Delhi: Oxford University Press).

Bhattacharyya, D.K. (2010), *Cross Cultural Management—Text and Cases* (New Delhi: PHI Learning).

Brown, D.I. (1995), 'Team-Based Reward Plans', *Team Performance Management*, 1: 23–31.

Burns, T. and G.M. Stalker (1966), *The Management of Innovation* (London: Tavistock).

Cohen, S.G. and G.E. Ledford, Jr (1994), 'The Effectiveness of Self-Managing Teams: A Quasi-Experiment', *Human Relations*, 47: 13–43.

Conjer, J.A. (1993), 'Leadership: The Art of Empowering Others', in J.R. Gordon (ed), *A Diagnostic Approach to Organizational Behavior* (Boston, MA: Allyn & Bacon), pp. 420–28.

Davis, J., P. Millburn, T. Murphy and M. Woodhouse (1992), *Successful Team Building: How to Create Teams that Really Work* (London: Kogan Page).

Drucker, P.F. (1988), 'The Coming of the New Organization', *Harvard Business Review* (January–February), pp. 45–53.

Dulewicz, V. (1995), 'A Validation of Belbin's Team Roles from 16PF and OPQ Using Bosses' Ratings of Competence', *Journal of Occupational and Organizational Psychology*, 68: 1–18.

Goleman, D. (1998), *Working with Emotional Intelligence* (New York, NY: Bantam Books).

Guzzo, R.A. and G.P. Shea (1992), 'Group Performance and Intergroup Relations in Organizations', in M.D. Dunnette and L.M. Hough (eds), *Handbook of Industrial and Organizational Psychology*, 3: 269–313.

Herzberg, F.W. (1968), 'One More Time: How Do You Motivate Employees?', *Harvard Business Review*, 46: 53–62.

Kozlowski, S.W.J. and B.S. Bell (2003), 'Workgroups and Teams in Organizations', in W.C. Borman, D.R. Ilgen, and R.J. Klimoski (eds), *Handbook of Psychology: Industrial and Organizational Psychology*, 12: 333–75 (London: Wiley).

Likert, R. (1961), *New Patterns of Management* (New York, NY: McGraw-Hill).

McClelland, D.C. (1988), *Human Motivation* (Cambridge, MA: Cambridge University Press).

Margerison, C. and D. McCann (1990), *Team Management* (London: W.H. Allen).

Maslow, A.H. (1943), 'A Theory of Human Motivation', *Psychological Review*, 50: 370–96.

Morgan, G. (1993), *Imaginization: The Art of Creative Management* (London: Sage).

Moss-Kanter, E. (1993), 'Power Failure in Management Circuits', in D.S. Pugh (ed), *Organization Theory: Selected Readings* (London: Penguin).

Parker, G.M. (1990), *Team Players and Teamwork: The New Competitive Business Strategy* (Oxford: Jossey-Bass).

Parkinson, R. (1995), 'A Silk Purse Out of a Sow's Ear', *Organizations and People*, 2: 22–25.

Prendergast, C. (1999), 'The Provision of Incentives in Firms', *Journal of Economic Literature*, 37: 7–63.

Prince, G. (1989), 'Recognising Genuine Teamwork', *Supervisory Management*, (April), 25–31.

Roethlisberger, F.J. and W.J. Dickson (1964), *Management and the Worker* (New York, NY: Wiley).

Smith, P.B., M.F. Peterson and J. Misumi (1994), 'Event Management and Work Team Effectiveness in Japan, Britain and the USA', *Journal of Occupational and Organization Psychology*, 67(4): 33–43.

Spencer, J. and A. Pruss (1992), *Managing Your Team* (London: Piatkus).

Taylor, F.W. (1947), *Scientific Management* (New York, NY: Harper & Row).

Tjosvold, D. (1991), *Team Organization: An Enduring Competitive Advantage* (Chichester: Wiley).

Tuckman, B.W. (1965), 'Development Sequence in Small Groups', *Psychological Bulletin*, 63(6).

Weber, M. (1964), *The Theory of Social and Economic Organizations* (New York, NY: Collier Macmiltan).

Woodcock, M. (1989), *Team Development Manual*, 2nd edition (Brookfield, VT: Gower).

CASE STUDY – 1

Transforming Through Teamwork—Case of DSP, Durgapur

Organizational effectiveness depends not only on the talent available in the organization but also on the quality of leadership available at its disposal. An organization's success depends on the ability of its leaders to align individual goals to the business goals and objectives and to bring the best out of all the members of the team through resolution of conflict and proper team building. The essence of team building is promoting the culture of group dynamics. Group dynamics promotes interactions between people, where at least one person takes the lead in conversation to offer his or her thoughts and opinions freely. In a teamwork culture, it is essential for the organization to promote group dynamics, so that people can largely be involved in managing their discussions, which pertain to achieving the organizational goals.

A successful transformation of attitude of employees is the prerequisite for the success of team-based performance management systems. The positive attitude of employees cascades to the effective group dynamics and ultimately enhances the decision-making capability of people and their competency.

Realizing this, Durgapur Steel Plant (DSP), a public sector steel manufacturing unit of the Steel Authority of India Limited (SAIL), promoted the culture of teamwork. The integrated steel plant, one of the largest industrial complexes in the state of West Bengal, spread over an area of 6.5 sq km, employs a workforce of about 16,000 people. The plant has the rated capacity to produce 2.1 MT of hot metal, 1.9 MT of crude steel, and 1.6 MT of saleable steel.

With tremendous setback in their performance in successive years, DSP had huge accumulated loss for years together. The problem mounted during the first phase of economic globalization and deregulation with prince decontrol mechanism, announced by the Government of India. From a literal captive market privilege, suddenly SAIL units, including DSP, witnessed a sea change in market dynamics which, among others, required the company to quickly respond to the change thereby transforming the entire organization including the attitude of the employees. To promote group dynamics, SAIL, at the outset, emphasized on developing a shared vision, urging all its plants to quickly endorse their employees to nurture this and reflect it in their day-to-day work.

Let us have a close look at SAIL's vision:

> 'To be a respected as a world class corporation and as a leader in Indian business in quality, productivity, profitability, and customer satisfaction'.

The guiding principle on which the vision statement is based is:

- We build lasting relationships with customers based on trust and mutual benefit.
- We uphold highest ethical standards in the conduct of our business.
- We create and nurture a culture that supports flexibility, learning, and is proactive to change.
- We chart a challenging career for employees with opportunities for advancement and rewards.
- We value the opportunity and responsibility to make a meaningful difference in people's lives.

DSP's organizational objectives are based on the vision and reflect the organizational intents in its journey towards excellence. Every employee of DSP was given the extensive message of change in the market scenario and was systematically provided with the information on detailed stage-by-stage change initiatives taken at the corporate level, to facilitate the understanding of organizational preparedness to compete in the environment. Rigorous in-house training to all employees gave them a positive outlook to the need for change. *KIZEN* with five S, total quality management (TQM), quality circles, etc. reinforced their change initiatives, which, among others, also helped in transforming the attitude of the employees.

Among all SAIL units, DSP today proclaims to be the most successful one in reaping the advantage of transformation through attitudinal change and group dynamics. The year 2007–08 spells out the results as under:

Four figure profit in 2007–08 for the first time in its history. The plant achieved a profit before tax of Rs 1,009 crore—62 per cent more than the previous year's growth of Rs 624 crore. The plant achieved the highest ever sales turnover of Rs 5,275 crore—23 per cent higher over the previous year's figure of Rs 4,288 crore. Durgapur Steel Plant, according to the officials, had concluded the 2007–08 fiscal with 'all time best' performance in all the major areas of production like hot metal, crude steel, and saleable steel.

Question: Among the public sector companies we have many such examples of successful teamwork. Visit the Web sites of ONGC, SAIL, and Durgapur Steel Plant and make a comparison between them.

CASE STUDY—2

Transforming Organization Through Teamwork

Any major organizational change involves three distinct conditions: the future state, where leadership wants the organization to get to; the present state, where it currently is; and the transition state, where the conditions and activities must be moved through to reach the future. The process usually starts with a need or desire for a new future state, so initiative for self-managing teams usually comes from one of these three sources:

- A major shift in the external environment which forces the organization to find faster, cheaper, and better quality ways of meeting customer needs.
- A change in technology or a new factory which provides opportunities for breaking with the past.
- A senior manager or executive team will introduce the concept, having discovered it elsewhere (Hirschorn 1984).

The first two sources provide a valuable excuse for unfreezing the organization and can lead to a rapid introduction of new working methods. By their nature, however, they are reactive, involving the organization in having to catch up. The third approach may well be the most difficult because it is proactive, particularly so if there is no clear commercial imperative.

Whatever the source or change imperative, the greater the clarity with which an organization can describe its future and current states, the more successfully will transition be managed.

However, describing the desired future for self-managing teams is complex because it typically goes beyond the prevailing management or work paradigms and requires the creation and sharing of some kind of vision for how the organization will operate.

Leadership capability also has to keep this vision open and powerful to avoid obstacles, which have to be overcome if this is to be achieved, actually destroying it.

For all organizations going for a drastic change, this is always a worry, particularly in post-acquisition phase. For an Indian MNC (consumer electronics major), this was also a major concern after they took over two age-old plants of legacy-bound multi-national organizations in Kolkata. To give space to the employees, who were in general reluctant to the merger with the Indian MNC, the company adopted a multi-pronged approach to transform the work culture. Being legacy bound, workers of the old MNC had the feeling that they are privileged class employees than other run-of-the-mill organizations in India; hence, Indian organizations taking over them is always detrimental to their interest and general welfare. A couple of erstwhile old MNC employees had left the job opting for voluntary retirement. Some adopted a 'wait and watch' strategy and joined almost six months after acquisition. Around one-third of the employees only joined the new entity right from the beginning.

The old MNC at the time of takeover was on the verge of bankruptcy running at a huge loss, costs were beyond control, finished inventory were accumulating, while inventory for the raw materials and spares hit a dangerously low level, taking the company to a state of shamble and shock.

To save the organization from the downward spiral, the new entity decided to transform slowly, fearing that employees may otherwise make the transformation process futile. First, they made a thorough assessment of their organization. It included a critical review of areas where they could retain expertise, competence, and competitiveness as well as areas where they were disadvantaged.

The CEO of the Indian MNC, being associated with the organization over a long period, earned the confidence of the president and the chairman, who gave him literally a blank chit to transform and grow.

The expertise of dealing with the layoffs, handling diverse opinions, and making balanced judgements helped the CEO to wing the approval of employees regarding certain decisions and finding the best possible solution as quickly as possible under pressure.

The leadership qualities of the CEO and other senior officials also helped them to smooth the decision-making process. They reached out to their 1000 employees to assuage their confusion created by the political parties and trade unions that the Indian company is incapable to turnaround and would just grab the assets of the acquired MNC. They infused confidence and credibility through telephonic conversations and massive one-to-one meetings during the initial phase of work culture transformation. They kept employees abreast of the time-to-time progress to endorse their support for the change and to motivate them to get involved in transforming the organization. With innovative operational styles to scale new heights, the new entity could turn around within 1 year of their takeover.

Teamwork was the most important essence of their work culture transformation. A multi-disciplinary team which is forward thinking, focused on innovation, and which values diversity, integrating technology, economic and social developments, and interacting with the changing business environments and markets of consumer electronics took the organizations to a new level of efficiency, unparalleled in the Indian market. Using the team as incubator in the change process and promoting innovation capabilities with the support of their research teams helped the company to tap the latent talents of erring employees who themselves promoted the culture of knowledge management and could come out with the new market-friendly low price models of colour TV sets. While operational imperatives to continue with the production deadline were all along their priority, they never subdued their initiative to promote creativity through extensive communication. Aligning the organizational architecture with the social (working environment) and the market architecture, through teamwork, amidst the crisis of non-cooperation and hostility in fact helped the company to transform the work culture in post-acquisition phase within a time-bound schedule. Management promoted close relationships with internal customers, making it compulsory for all senior executives to spend 80 per cent of their time to communicate with the people during the initial phase of their transition.

Question: Study the case above and make a comparison between the earlier case and the present one in teamwork approach.

CHAPTER 11

Performance Measurements Through Balanced and HR Scorecards

Learning Objectives

After reading this chapter, you will be able to understand:

- Definition and concepts of balanced scorecard
- Different perspectives of the balanced scorecard
- Benefits of the balanced scorecard
- Concepts of HR scorecard
- Approach to HR scorecard
- Process of developing HR scorecard
- Benefits of HR scorecard
- Need for implementation of the balanced HR scorecard

Managing Crisis with a Scorecard-based Performance Management System

Bank Universal was established in the year 1990, merging three small banks. Initially it focused on corporate banking and later on expanded to retail banking, primarily in Jakarta and other major cities of Indonesia. With 2200 employees and an asset size of $1.2 billion, the bank virtually collapsed during the Asian currency crisis of 1997. With the scientific performance management systems (using balanced scorecard) and sustained HR initiatives, the bank ultimately could survive the crisis and is at present achieving double-digit returns on equity. From a business point of view, the bank strategically focuses on sector-specific financing like the automotive sector (mainly refinancing the suppliers, dealers, and the end users of product of the automobile industry), coal mining (supply chain side), traders, plywood supply chains, etc. Focusing on niche retail banking, the bank has achieved expertise. Another reason to be sector specific is to avoid mistakes in financing the large companies, which became the major defaulters and major contributors to high NPAs of the bank during the period of crisis. Introduction of balanced scorecard helped the bank to balance their focus on its process, customer service, learning, and growth and finance. Banks that do not have efficient processes and good quality service do not get good return on investment. With initial implementation of the balanced scorecard at the corporate level, the bank took this to the branch operation level and then cascaded it to the individual employee level. In four stages, the bank could implement the balanced scorecard across the organization, with three strategic themes like handling of past problems (related to loan portfolios), embracing a new business model (to enhance profitability), and adopting a new market strategy to develop the good banking image.

After implementation of the balanced scorecard, the bank could observe that people can appreciate each other. The marketing people can appreciate the service people and the service people can, in turn, appreciate the operational and process people who, in turn, can appreciate the human resource people. All could collectively contribute to the performance of Bank Universal. Effective coordination and communication throughout the organization improved the performance and the bottom line.

INTRODUCTION

Conventional performance measurement cannot accurately provide a comprehensive view about an organization. The balanced scorecard approaches, linking the core financial goals of the organizations with the other drivers that are a determinant of overall success of the organization, ensure a better and comprehensive view about the organization. The balanced scorecard translates the organization's mission and strategy into some quantified key performance indicators (KPIs). Such KPIs provide the framework for measuring the performance through a well-designed balanced scorecard. KPIs are the base elements of work that correlate with the strategic goals of the organization, and obviously on achieving the KPIs, organizations can achieve its performance goals.

The basic contention of the balanced scorecard is that financial measures as a stand-alone indicator cannot provide the total performance information about the organization. Rather by integrating the financial measures with other important perspectives, i.e., customer, internal business processes, and learning and growth, through a better combination effect, organizations can drive more successfully the performance, including the financial performance. How such perspectives relate to one another can be understood through KPI metrics. For example, financial perspectives are strengthened by the customer perspective, as customers buy the products and services of the organization, and customers' buying determine the financial success. Better internal process supports the customer perspective, as it reinforces customers' satisfaction. Similarly, the learning perspective reinforces the internal process, which cascades to better customer satisfaction. Therefore, all the four perspectives of the balanced scorecard help the organization for a conceptual mapping of KPIs, which ultimately provide the balanced measurements of the performance of the organization as a whole.

In line with Kaplan and Norton, therefore, we can argue that the balanced scorecard for performance measurement is in reality a mixture of financial and non-financial measures that ultimately leads effective assessment of organizational performance. A combination of the balanced scorecard metrics also provides the opportunity to the organization to compare and benchmark products and services against the competitors.

In a competitive business environment, it is important for an organization to align its business activities to strategy, resource allocation budgeting, and reporting. More importantly, human resource (HR) management functions need to be managed strategically. Managing performance of employees is one of the most crucial HR functions. The balanced scorecard in its true sense facilitates the strategic alignment of HR functions Today, the scope of the balanced scorecard has even been extended to balanced HR scorecard. As among all performance measurement tools, the balanced scorecard and the balanced HR scorecard are the most crucial ones. In this chapter, we have discussed these two aspects separately. The other performance measurement tools, however, have been discussed in a separate chapter.

DEFINITION AND CONCEPTS

The balanced scorecard is a strategic management approach developed by Kaplan and Norton (1992). The balanced scorecard clearly prescribes what an organization should measure to balance its financial perspectives. In its true sense, the balanced scorecard can be better referred to as a management system rather than only a measurement tool to track the degree of balance in the financial results of an organization.

Through balanced scorecards, organizations can realize their vision and strategies, translating those into action plans. In the process of translating the activities into the balanced scorecard, organizations can develop the strategic framework and achieve the performance goals. Also the scorecard can set the direction to achieve the performance goals. Kaplan and Norton described that the balanced scorecard while retaining the traditional financial measures, also helps the organization to measure the potentiality to create future value, accounting for the contributions in four perspectives, i.e., customers, finance, internal business process, and learning and growth.

DIFFERENT PERSPECTIVES OF BALANCED SCORECARD

After understanding the four perspectives, organizations need to develop metrics based on the analysis and data collection.

- The learning and growth perspective.
- The business process perspective.
- The customer perspective.
- The financial perspective.

The Learning and Growth Perspective

This perspective requires organizations to emphasize on employee training and development for their continuous development. Enhanced knowledge and skill of employees can bring positive change in their performance, and so also benefit the organization to achieve competitive strength. In volatile market conditions, and so also in the era of rapid technological change, systematic renewal of knowledge and skill of employees through training and development is very important. For this reason, every cross-section of employees of the organizations need to focus on self-development and also facilitate the development of their peers and subordinates. This is why the development role of managers is now recognized and given importance. Standard metrics are developed to measure employees' performance. Although for knowledge-intensive organizations this perspective is very important, Kaplan and Norton emprise its need in every organization. They consider learning to be more important than training. Learning requires in-house mentors and tutors, free flow of communication, and employees' access to their seniors when they face any problem in doing their jobs. Learning is also facilitated by the use of technological tools, which Baldrige attributes to 'high-performance work systems'. Through learning, employees can grow and self-improve. Growth is a more holistic term than development. While development is momentary, growth is permanent. With development, an employee can achieve one-time performance results, while with learning reinforced growth employees can recurrently deliver better performance results.

The Business Process Perspective

Kaplan and Norton, two proponents of the balanced scorecard, suggest employees' performance focus on internal business processes. Knowledge of internal business process perspective enables employees to understand the way that the business is conducted in the organization, the extent of conformance of products and services to customers' needs, the mission of the organization, the process of strategic management, etc. Theoretically, in organizations we see two types of business processes: the mission centric and the support oriented. Employees' performance can be traced to the internal business processes through developed metrics. An employee achieves performance excellence when he/she contributes to positive changes in the internal business processes, which cascades to increased level of future performance.

The Customer Perspective

When organizations are customer centric and are able to satisfy the customers, success can be achieved at much ease. No organization survives with dissatisfied customers. Inputs from all cross-sections of employees add to customers' satisfaction. In other words, every employee adds value to the customers, irrespective of their nature of work. A dissatisfied customer shifts to other suppliers and their dissatisfaction also influences the other prospective customers of the organization. This culminates in business failure. For all these reasons, employees must perform to meet the customers' demand and make the customers satisfied. Thus, to measure employees' performance from customers' perspective, it is essential for the organization to develop various metrics analysing the customers' data.

The Financial Perspective

As has already been stated, Kaplan and Norton did not make the need for financial results redundant. Finance and so also the financial results should continue to receive organizational priority. In fact, without discarding the need to focus on finance, they had also incorporated the need for future value addition potentiality of the organizations. Some of the important financial metrics like employees' capability to assess the risk, capability to justify cost benefit, etc. are the most critical performance indicators for this perspective. Again, like in other perspectives, every cross-section of employee must also perform to meet the financial perspective.

Thus, balanced scorecard translates strategy into action. The concept takes the cues from the organizational vision and strategies and then develops key performance indicators in all the four perspectives. Each performance indicator is measured in terms of certain well-designed metrics against which the performance of an employee is compared. Operationally, balanced scorecard can be organization, jobs, and individual employee specific. Most organizations, based on the identified critical success factors (CSF), prepare a generic balanced scorecard, and then assign weights to each performance factor, depending on the nature of the job and the level of the employees. With the support of information technology, however, balanced scorecards can nowadays even be cascaded to individual level employees and can facilitate scientific performance appraisal. It is now the most scientific and effective strategic planning and implementation tool.

To create a balanced scorecard, organizations at the outset identify the vision, aligning their values and philosophies. Then, through mission, organizations concretize this vision. Mission clarifies the purpose of the organization. Objectives are then set within the ambit of mission, which then cascade to specific strategies and action plans. Such specific action plans become the key performance indicators (KPI), which become the ultimate performance goals for the organization. KPIs are translated into measurable performance scorecards encompassing all the perspectives.

BENEFITS OF THE BALANCED SCORECARD

Some of the benefits of the balanced scorecard can be listed as under:

- It aligns key performance indicators with the overall strategy of the organization, and in the process facilitates effective measurement of realized strategy vis-à-vis the performance goals of the organization.
- Balanced scorecard makes available the holistic picture of business results; therefore, it can also be used as organizational health index.
- It enforces a positive work culture in the organization, as in the process of its development all cross-sections of employees need to get involved, communicate with each other, understand the business imperatives and the strategies of the organization, irrespective of the nature of their activities and hierarchical levels.
- It makes available the strategic feedback and in the process provides the accurate and precision level inputs for future decision-making.
- It reduces the time for information search, as befitting information can be made readily available.
- It makes the performance management process scientific.
- It makes the performance assessment process transparent.
- Employees can self-assess their performance and understand how their contributions fit with the overall strategies of the organizations.
- Management can take the corrective actions on a real-time basis to make good the performance gaps.

All the above benefits, therefore, motivate an organization to introduce the balanced scorecard to realize the strategic intents.

HR SCORECARD

HR scorecard helps in measuring the efficiency and productivity of the HR department. It considers all the quantifiable areas of the HR department, and accordingly grades the HR department. Quantifiable variables of the HR department that can measure its efficiency and effectiveness depend on the choice and selection of the respective organizations. It is impractical to assume that a standard HR scorecard could be a panacea for all. Obvious reasons for variation can be attributed to goals and purposes of the organizations. Some of the commonalities in HR scorecard are:

- Scorecard that measures performance of employees to realize the goals of the organizations.
- Scorecard that optimizes HR costs and helps in tracking the return on investment on people.
- Scorecard that helps in aligning HR functions with the business of the organizations.
- Scorecard that helps in aligning HR functions with the strategies and policies of the organizations.
- Scorecard that helps in adopting appropriate HR practices, i.e., the quality HR practices.
- Scorecard that ensures attracting and retaining the right HR professionals.

All these elements present in the HR scorecard, and the possibility of its quantification, by and large helps an organization to truly understand how the potentiality of human resources are harnessed for the best and efficient results of the organizations.

Effective HR scorecard enhances the focus of the HR department to deliver quality, duly identifying the weak areas and initiating the appropriate action. Also using the metrics, it is possible to appraise the performance of individual employees and so also the performance of the organization. Because of its transparency, people at all levels of the organizations can also track their contributions to the organizations and enforce self-control to improve and deliver the best. Hence from the employees' point of view, it is also motivating.

Some of the common areas where HR metrics can be developed using an effective HR Scorecard are:

- Employee recruitment.
- Training and development of employees.
- Workforce management.
- Evaluation of employee performance.
- Promotions and transfer of employees.
- Redundancy.
- Employee relations.
- Organization of data.
- Total rewards.
- Career development.
- Competency mapping.
- Time management.
- Performance appraisal.

With all these elements present in HR scorecard, and possibility of its quantification, by and large helps an organization to truly understand how the potentiality of human resources are harnessed for the best and efficient results of the organizations.

The HR Scorecard Approach

Once integrated, the HR scorecard aligns support functions with the business strategy illustrating:

- The strategic impact of HR services and projects and enabling HR to demonstrate its value through more than short-term financial outcomes.
- Adopting the HR scorecard as a strategic management.
- System ensures that HR views all of its activities in terms of their contribution to the organization's goals.
- By developing a strategic programme for measuring and managing human capital, HR executives have the opportunity to spearhead the development of better strategic management.

Process of Developing the HR Scorecard

If structured properly, adopting the HR scorecard would allow the HR organization to take the initiative, instead of being reactive to the demands of the enterprise. A comprehensive approach that creates strategic alignment between HR and the enterprise at all levels including strategy, resource allocation, budgeting, and reporting is absolutely essential.

Developing the HR scorecard as a new management process provides the foundation to make HR a true strategic partner and enable the enterprise to realize the full value of its human capital.

The first step in establishing HR as a strategy-focused organization requires the development of a HR scorecard that can be linked to enterprise strategy and achieve perfect organizational alignment. Successful project execution requires an HR scorecard, which is a management system project that demonstrates a high level of user friendliness. All scorecard users should be able to manage scorecards unaided by IT specialists or power users. Training must be straightforward to accelerate adoption, and information must be accessible without a tedious navigation process.

The HR scorecard development process will entail the completion of several processes using the following methodology:

Development of a Solid Strategy: Development of a solid strategy that is aligned with the enterprise strategy is a keystone to success. Without a solid strategy, success is unobtainable. However, without execution, a solid strategy is meaningless.

Strategy Mapping: Development of a strategy map, including selection of performance measures, establishes targets and objectives, identifies initiatives and ownership to deliver the strategy.

Establish Measures for Each Objective: After translating strategy into objectives, managers and employees must know if and when objectives are being achieved. Therefore, each objective is given at least one measurement that is included in the key performance indicators.

Cascading of Scorecard: Keeping in mind operational, management and front line employees do the actual work that makes strategies happen. Organizations must develop scorecards at every level so that each person can see how his or her specific responsibilities align and contribute to the higher level goals.

Scorecard Implementation: Finalize scorecard designs and develop an implementation plan.

Post Implementation: After the scorecards are deployed, managers need to periodically re-examine their existing core processes to ensure they are linked to the corporate strategy.

HR Scorecard at Tata Engineering

HR scorecard at Tata Engineering is used as a tool for simultaneously aligning all four perspectives to achieve business objectives. It brings about a greater harmony of the business perspectives at functional and divisional levels. Hence, each and every perspective should be evaluated on the returns generated. It is integrated with the Tata Business Excellence Model (TBEM) to nurture the environment of high performance and organization-wide learning and sharing. It serves as the guiding force for HR support functions.

The company addresses HR's role on four perspectives as under:

Financial: To improve the return on human capital.

Customer: To develop human resources to meet the expectations of internal and external customer.

Internal Processes: To align HR with the business goals meeting the stakeholders' expectations.

Learning and Growth: To build HR capability to deliver results.

For all HR activities, quantifiable and objective measures are identified and, accordingly, performance targets are assigned at the individual and team levels. Further, to facilitate the process, a strategic action plan is drawn up to provide the sense of direction to the employees to achieve their performance goals.

Benefits of the HR Scorecard

Some of the benefits of the HR scorecard can be enumerated as under:

- Formulate HR strategy that is aligned with the overall corporate strategy.
- Clarify the vision/mission of the organization.
- Create a consensus and ownership of the strategy in the management team.
- Improve communication of the strategy across the enterprise.
- Prioritize HR initiatives by linking activities to business goals.
- Help support functions identify and communicate their unique strategies.
- Create a framework for initiative prioritization and budgeting.
- Align measurement with business goal achievement.
- Measure HR's strategic contribution in concrete and clearly understood terms.
- Provide real-time graphical display of key performance indicators.

NEED FOR IMPLEMENTATION OF BALANCED SCORECARD AND BALANCED HR SCORECARD

Research conducted by the Harvard Business School demonstrates that overall only 1 out of every 10 companies that formulate strategy can effectively implement it. Many factors make it difficult to implement strategy today. The pace of change continues to accelerate, technology changes frequently, and the workforce is more diverse and mobile than ever before. While the business world continues to evolve, management systems cannot keep the pace of change. The majority of measurement and management systems are designed to meet the needs of a stable, incrementally changing world, which cannot meet the needs and expectations of the dynamic economy. Various researches could confirm that a balanced scorecard approach has now emerged as the most effective way of managing and executing dynamic strategy of the organization. Subsequent development of the balanced HR scorecard could further reinforce this. Obviously for such reasons, it has now become imperative for organizations globally to implement these scorecards with a holistic focus on financial perspectives, which necessitates integrating the other three perspectives with finance, and then cascade all these to specific performance elements in terms of KPIs.

For doing these, organizations need to understand the specific performance elements that can be delineated to the four perspectives. It requires thorough understanding of the process and individual functional elements. For example, to successfully develop the balanced HR scorecard, organizations need to understand the HR competencies. Here we have illustrated some of the core HR competencies that can form the part of KPIs for the HR functions.

HR Competencies

1. Business Partner—Competencies Include:

Knows mission

Understands business process and how to change to improve efficiency and effectiveness

Understands clients and organizational culture
Understands work environment
Understands team behaviour
Communicates well
Can be innovative and create a risk-taking environment
Applies organizational development principles
Knows business system thinking
Possesses good analytical skills including the ability to think strategically and creatively
Possesses the ability to build trust relationships
Links HR to the organization's mission and service outcome

2. Change Agent—Competencies Include:

Understands business process and how to change to improve efficiency and effectiveness
Understands clients and organizational culture
Understands work environment
Knowledge of team behaviour
Good communication power
Ability to balance the competing values
Knows business system thinking
Applies information technology to human resource management
Possesses good analytical skills including the ability to think strategically and creatively
Designs and implements change process
Uses consultation and negotiation skills including dispute resolution
Possesses the ability to build trust relationships
Possesses marketing and representational skills
Uses consensus and coalition-building skills
Demonstrates customer service orientation

3. Leadership—Competencies Include:

Knowledge of team behaviour
Good communication power
Ability to balance the competing values
Power of strong analytic, strategic, and creative thinking
Ability to influence people to reach to consensus
Value diversity
Promote and practice integrity and ethical behavour

Effective development of the balanced HR scorecard requires thorough understanding of the HR deliverables in terms of performance drivers and performance enablers. Performance drivers are the core HR KPIs, while the enablers reinforce the performance drivers. For example, training and development is the good enabler that can drive the employees' performance through competency development. With a balanced HR scorecard, organizations can truly transform HR as a strategic partner, aligning HR with all the levels of organizational activities. Subsequent measurement of HR's performance, using the scorecard, can also facilitate the organization to understand the degree of HR's contribution in achieving the performance goals of the organization as a whole.

SUMMARY

The balanced scorecard is a powerful tool for measuring organizational performance from the strategic and holistic perspectives. A narrow focus on relating organizational performance only on the financial outcomes today no longer holds good. With the balanced scorecard, it is possible for the organization to successfully assess the important processes and set the performance criteria for the employees at the individual and team level in specific and quantitative terms. Also, the balanced scorecard can be integrated with the overall organizational performance goals. Like the balanced scorecard, the HR balanced scorecard helps HR professionals manage their strategic responsibilities more effectively. To integrate HR into a business performance measurement system, it is important to understand, at the outset, the important HR deliverables and how it relates to organizational strategy implementation plans.

KEY WORDS

Strategy Mapping—Development of a strategy map, including selection of performance measures, establishes targets and objectives, and identifies initiatives and ownership to deliver the strategy.

Cascading of Scorecard—Keeping in mind operational, management and front line employees do the actual work that makes strategies happen. Organizations must develop scorecards at every level so that each person can see how his or her specific responsibilities align and contribute to the higher level goals.

Learning and Growth Perspective—This perspective includes employee training and corporate cultural attitudes related to both individual and corporate self-improvement. In a knowledge-worker organization, *people*—the only repository of knowledge—are the main resource. In the current climate of rapid technological change, it is becoming necessary for knowledge workers to be in a continuous learning mode.

HR Enablers—HR enablers strengthen the HR drivers, so that HR drivers can achieve the performance goals. For example, training and development function is an important HR enabler to drive the employees' productivity.

GENERAL REVIEW QUESTIONS

1. What is a balanced scorecard (BSC)? What are its different perspectives?
2. Explain how a BSC can be related to the vision and mission of an organization?
3. What are the various benefits of a BSC?
4. Explain the term 'HR competencies' and detail areas of such competencies, which can subsequently be the basis of developing HR KPIs.
5. Explain HR scorecard. How can this be developed? What are the key benefits?
6. How can HR be a strategically important function?
7. Short Notes
   (a) KPIs
   (b) Learning perspectives
   (c) Leadership competencies
   (d) HR deliverables

CRITICAL REVIEW QUESTION

8. A very well-known software development organization after obtaining P-CMM level 5 certification wishes to introduce balanced scorecard for effective performance measurement of software developers. Suggest how the organization can do so.

REFERENCES

Arthur, J.B. (1994), 'Effects of Human Resource Systems on Manufacturing Performance and Turnover', *Academy of Management Journal*, 37: 670–87.

Becker, B. and B. Gerhart (1996), 'The Impact of Human Resource Management on Organizational Performance: Progress and Prospects', *Academy of Management Journal*, 39(4): 779–801.

Bhattacharyya, D.K. (2006), *Human Resource Management*, 2nd edition (New Delhi: Excel Books).

Bhattacharyya, D.K. (2007), *Human Resource Research Methods* (New Delhi: Oxford University Press).

Boselie, P. (2002), 'Human Resource Management, Work Systems and Performance: A Theoretical-Empirical Approach' (Thela Thesis, Tinbergen Institute Research Series 274, Amsterdam).

Evans, W.A. (1970), 'Pay for Performance: Fact or Fable', *Personnel Journal*, September, pp. 726–29.

Guest, D.E. (1997), 'Human Resource Management and Performance: A Review and Research Agenda', *The International Journal of Human Resource Management*, 8(3).

Huselid, M.A. and N.L. Rau (1997), 'The Determinants of High Performance Work Systems: Cross sectional and Longitudinal Analyses' (paper presented at the Academy of Management Annual Meetings, Human Resources Management Division).

Kaplan, R.S. and D.P. Norton (1992), 'The Balanced Scorecard Measures that Drive Performance', *Harvard Business Review*, January–February, pp. 80–91.

Marr, Bernard (2006), *Strategic Performance Management* (Oxford: Butterworth-Heinemann).

Marr, Bernard (2009), *Managing and Delivering Performance: How Government, Public Sector and Not-for-Profit Organizations Can Measure and Manage What Really Matters* (Oxford: Butterworth-Heinemann).

Marr, Bernard (2010), *The Intelligent Company: Five Steps to Success with Evidence-Based Management* (Oxford: Wiley).

Pfeffer, J. (1994), *Competitive Advantage through People* (Boston, MA: Harvard Business School Press).

CASE STUDY

Murugappa Group—Where Excellence Is Achieved Through Performance Management Systems

In India, we have very limited number of business houses having more than 100 years of existence. Headquartered in Chennai, the Rs 13,617crore ($3.03 billion as on 31 March 2010) Murugappa Group is one of India's leading diversified business houses. The group started its journey in the year 1900, and since then it has had a growing with thriving presence in engineering, abrasives, finance, general insurance, cycles, sugar, farm inputs, fertilizers, plantations, bio-products, and nutraceuticals. Presently, the group has 29 companies spread across 23 states in India, with 32,000 employees in its payroll. Though having predominant presence in India, the group truly reaped the benefits of globalization with strategic alliance and partnering with global organizations like Mitsui Sumitomo, Foskor, Cargill and Groupe Chimique Tunisien, etc. Meticulously, the group could embed the philosophy of win–win in business and, accordingly, created a work culture of professionalism, which among others ensures empowerment. 'Be modest and be humble' are the two core values, which the group enshrines on all cross-sections of employees to follow.

For Murugappa, HR function is everybody's responsibility. Every manager needs to be an HR manager, and only then can he/she gain the support of the people. The group, like others, faces HR challenges, but with a common thread of values, the group is able to manage the HR function without any major hassles of industrial relations. Continuous focus on leadership development, employee retention, and quality HR practices are some of the thrust areas of the HR departments of the group. For its excellence in HR practices, the group has been accredited with SA8000 certification. This certification is awarded to recognize the efforts of the company for successful implementation of HRMS (human resource management systems). Along with quality HR practices, the group has also embraced knowledge management practices to strengthen the practices of quality HR through employee development.

Performance measurement systems in the company is primarily 360-degree, which is a standard open evaluation system based on balanced scorecard. Performance evaluation is done both on-line and off-line. Through performance evaluation training needs are identified, and the company extends a minimum of 8 man-days training support for every executive. In reality, the group's performance management practices are holistic in nature, primarily to make positive and proactive impact on the minds of organizational members. To respect everybody's contribution toward the organization, performance management process is differentiated across the hierarchy. While for executives and managerial employees, the focus is more on overall business results and competencies, for entry level people, the focus is more on tasks. For entry level people, individual contribution and for executives and managerial employees' team performance are given more importance. Also at the same, the group emphasizes on alignment of the business processes with the performance management systems, using three dimensions: context, commitment, and capability. For Murugappa, context is set by their performance culture embracing the strategy, structure, and systems or processes. In this way, the company creates the culture of employee engagement, where everybody feels part of the organization and contributes their best for achieving the business results.

Question: Study the Web site information of Murugappa Group and elaborate how the group could achieve excellence in their performance for pro-active HR practices.

CHAPTER 12

Performance Management and Mentoring

Learning Objectives

After reading this chapter, you will be able to understand:

- Definitions and concepts of performance mentoring
- Characteristics of mentoring
- Mentoring and coaching
- Benefits of mentoring
- Types of mentoring
- Foundations of a mentoring programme
- Ethical guidelines for effective mentoring
- Culture of mentoring
- Executive mentoring

Mentoring for Effective Performance

Lew Platt, the former CEO of Hewlett-Packard (HP), believed that mentoring is like educating our children. It is both a business and social imperative. HP has a large number of K-12 level manpower, and hence to make them to deliver results, HP emphasizes on continuous mentoring. Platt observed that all the young faces of today are the faces of the workforce and customers of tomorrow. Hence, like a teacher in a class, we must perform the role of a mentor for handholding of youngsters. In organizations, we require business mentors who sincerely invest in others' growth, capable to exert positive influence, so that the mentees feel at ease to learn and grow. It requires inculcating a culture of mentoring. Mentoring culture continuously develops the mentoring capacity, competence, and so also the capability of the organization as a whole. Some of the important hallmarks of a mentoring culture are accountability, alignment, communication, values, and visibility. HP practices successful mentoring culture, and in the process, today they are widely visible in the global IT industry. With the HR vision of achieving organizational excellence through development of people.

ONGC in India also emphasizes on extensive mentoring programme. ONGC's polices are employee-friendly and encourage workers' participation in management. The process is facilitated by informative, consultative, associative, and administrative forum that encourages participation and foster innovative culture. Also such practices, including the mentoring programme, could facilitate in building a positive work environment to propel excellence in ONGC's performance.

INTRODUCTION

Mentoring is defined as those activities, conducted by a mentor to help another person to successfully perform the assigned job and also to develop, so that the person, who is being helped, can rise through the ladder. The person who helps is known as the mentor and the person who receives the help is known as the mentee. Every organization that aspires to align their human resources to grow emphasizes on mentoring, as such emphasis can benefit the organization, making people competent to perform. Usually, in organizations, mentors are chosen from those who understand the job better and who are capable of guiding the new recruits to gradually adapt themselves to jobs and make them learn and develop. Mentoring process is done using different approaches like coaching, training, discussion, counseling, etc. According to Fred Nickolas (2002), a mentor requires to follow the patterned behaviour or process. During the mentoring process, the mentor often needs to be informal, to inculcate a sense of confidence in the minds of the people, so that they can volunteer to learn and develop. The Merriam-Webster Dictionary defines a mentor as 'a trusted counselor or guide'. From this perspective, it is often said that the mentor needs to be an individual who is older in age and senior in organizational hierarchy.

DEFINITIONS AND CONCEPTS

The term 'mentor' originated in Greek mythology. However, in organizations it was first institutionalized with the seminal work of Kram (1985). Since then, several pioneering research works on mentoring, popularized mentoring in organizations. According to Burke and McKeen (1989), Hunt and Michael (1983), Zey (1988), and Scandura (1992), mentoring is an essential component of an effective training and development process within organizations. It is defined as a relationship through which employees of the organizations are exposed to practical knowledge, guidance, support, and feedback from more experienced employees within a given setting (Haney, 1997). To upgrade skills and so also to enhance the satisfaction of employees, in the era of competition and market uncertainty, mentoring is now considered as one of the most powerful tools to enhance employees' development and performance. Also to make employees compatible with the organizational culture, mentoring is considered as the most useful means (Jossie, 1997; Gunn, 1995). In today's workplace, employees need to be multi-skilled and powered with a wide range of cognitive, interpersonal, and technical skills. The basic premise of mentoring is to emphasize on the situational or experiential learning (Kerka, 1997). Employees of the organizations attach meaning to the work constructs. Hence, they need guidance to learn contextually in relations with others. Good mentors facilitate learning to help employees to understand the ways and means of problem solving (Kaye and Jacobson, 1996). In the process, protégés internalize the process and construct their understanding.

Mentoring offers primarily two types of benefits: vocational and psychosocial . Vocational benefits are achieved in terms of acquisition of specific skills, viz., apprenticeship (Haney, 1997). Psychosocial benefits are those which assist the employees to socialize, improve their interpersonal skills, and allow them for collaborative critical thinking, planning, reflection, and feedback (Galbraith and Cohen, 1995). It enhances employees' collegiality (House, 1981).

Kram (1983) suggested four phases of mentoring relationship process: initiation, cultivation, separation, and termination. Creating a positive mentoring relationship is the prerequisite for the success of any mentoring programme. Once the relationship is developed, a mentor can influence the mentee for positive behavioural changes, and with this support the mentee can increase the level of performance. Therefore, the mentoring programme can systematically develop the knowledge, skill, and the leadership ability of every cross-section of employees of the organization (Murray, 1991).

Mentoring programmes can be both formal and informal. Which type of mentoring programme is suitable for the mentees or protégés can be mutually decided by the mentors and protégés (Chao, Walz, and Gardner, 1993; Noe, 1988). Also for effective results in mentoring programme, it is desirable to give the protégés the freedom to select the mentor (Scandura and Siegel, 1995). The success of mentoring over training and other forms of employee orientation programmes is now well recognized, and most of the organizations now extend support for such programmes.

The protégé's perception of the value of the experience is strongly influenced by the actual or perceived similarities between himself and the mentor (Ensher and Murphy, 1997). When a protégé sees himself as having something in common with his mentor, a bond or trust develops more easily. A foundation of trust permits the protégé to try out new ideas and roles with minimal risk (Kaye and Jacobson, 1996). The mentor's beliefs about the relationship also influence its effectiveness. When a mentor has a laissez-faire orientation or sees the relationship as a contingency connected to rewards, the mentoring relationship is less effective than when the mentor sees himself as facilitating a personal transformational process for the protégé.

Among others, mentoring does help in maturing an organization by increasing the retention, developing new leaders, creating a high performance culture, and so also providing career growth for the employees.

Thus, we can call mentoring a form of training, learning, and development, and so also a means to reinforce personal development of employees. However, it is our assumption that mentoring can only be done by those who are the best. But any organization that aspires to institutionalize mentoring needs to involve all cross-sections of employees in the process of mentoring; hence, it can't just be limited to the people who are the best and top in the hierarchy.

CHARACTERISTICS OF MENTORING

In the context of the aforementioned discussions, we can outline the characteristics of mentoring as under:

- It supports holistic employee development.
- It helps employees to manage their career and at the same time to improve their skills.
- It provides an opportunity to employees to discuss their personal issues and truly learn the job for better performance.
- It helps in reaching both the organizational and individual goals.

MENTORING AND COACHING

Mentoring and coaching are often construed as synonymous. But this is not always true. Coaching is a process of developing skills and knowledge of people to improve their job performance. Hence, coaching primarily focuses on achieving the goals of the organization. In that respect, coaching is more specific to facilitate achievement of employees' goals so that organizational goals are achieved—it is narrow in approach. Often organizations that expect their employees to deliver results even with stretched goals limit their focus on coaching.

On the contrary, mentoring is more holistic. It facilitates employees' total development, builds relationships, and even inculcates confidence in employees which autonomously compels to take higher responsibilities and deliver the best results. In our country, the Gurukul system of learning was more a mentoring approach, as Gurus used to empower learners (mentees) focussing on holistic development.

An institutionalized form of the Gurukul system is the guild system in organizations, and from here the apprenticeship concept had emerged.

Based on these definitions, most coaches and mentors agree that a good coach can also be a mentor and a good mentor can also be a coach, befitting the situation and the relationship. In considering the best fit, therefore, the two approaches should be regarded as synergistic and complementary rather than mutually exclusive.

To successfully implement mentoring and coaching programmes in organizations across all the functional levels, at the outset, commitment from the top management is essential. With top management support, results are miraculous. In the true sense, mentoring being a sustained effort for performance improvement, often organizations may not be able to extend the support for resource constraint. In such cases, coaching is considered as the better alternative. Results from the coaching programmes are immediate. This is why most of the organizations prefer coaching over mentoring, particularly when they feel the challenge of immediate change and growth. Through effective coaching, organizations can quickly build the employees' capabilities and empower them for autonomous problem-solving and decision-making. Companies that commit to coaching and mentoring gain in terms of increased employees' loyalty, participation, and commitment to improve the performance both at the individual and at the organizational levels.

Coaching empowers employees and makes them understand their potential. It also helps them to achieve their potential. For obvious one-to-one interaction, the coach and the coachee can collaborate with each other to set their performance goals, keeping pace with the needs of the organization. For obvious personal level interaction both can understand when to stretch goals and what supports are needed to realize the stretched goals. Coaching helps in developing goals and so also the steps involved in realizing such goals in measurable and manageable terms. As coaching need not be on an ongoing basis, it can adopt a bundle of approaches like personalized learning, on the job study and feedback, telephones, e-mails, etc. Characteristically, coaching and mentoring may be considered as the same. But they are different in many respects. The purpose of coaching is to motivate and empower employees, while mentoring essentially focuses on skill development and transfer, orientation about the company's policies and culture, new technology adoption, sharing of technical expertise, etc. We can list the difference between coaching and mentoring in line with Alred et al. (1998) in Table 12.1.

Table 12.1 *Differences between coaching and mentoring*

Mentoring	Coaching
It ensures long-lasting relationship.	In this case, relationship is relatively for a shorter duration.
It can also be informal and can take place at any point of time and anywhere, depending on the needs of the mentee.	It is more formal and structured.
The process considers the mentee from a broader perspective.	It focuses on specific issues or specific areas of development of the individual.
Mentor during the process of mentoring shares his/her own experience.	Coach shares his knowledge, specific to the occupational role.
Here the focus is on career and personal development.	Here the focus is on development/issues at work.
Revolves more around developing the mentee professionally.	Revolves more around specific development areas/issues.

Benefits of Mentoring

Mentoring benefits the organization in many ways. Some of these benefits are listed below:

- It exerts positive impact on recruitment and retention.
- It is very effective for succession planning.
- It makes organizations adaptable to change.
- It increases productivity through better engagement and job satisfaction.

Also mentoring benefits the mentored person in several ways, as under:

- By facilitating development of mentored person in terms of knowledge, technical skills, and behavioural improvements.
- By better management of career goals.
- By developing wider network of influence.
- By increasing the confidence and self-awareness which helps in building performance and contribution.

Mentoring also benefits the organization as a whole, more particularly the line managers and the HR as both of them benefit through better employee focus and engagement.

Types of Mentoring

Mentoring can take several forms, and depending on the specific requirements of the mentee, specific types of mentoring are chosen by the organization. Some of the widely used mentoring forms are explained below:

One-to-one Mentoring: This consists of usually one but sometimes more than one mentee to each mentor, with each mentoring relationship existing independently.

Group Mentoring (or mentoring circles): This typically consists of a group of several mentees and mentors, with the ratio of one mentor for every two to three mentees, but no individual mentor being allocated to a mentee.

The advantages of group mentoring are:

- Efficient use of mentors, with a higher ratio of mentees to mentors.
- The mentees in the group can build a rapport and integrate with colleagues.
- The mentees can receive multiple sources of feedback.

However, group mentoring has several disadvantages:

- Some people do not work well in a group environment.
- There may be concerns about confidentiality.
- The mentee has less or possibly no one-on-one contact with a mentor.
- Group mentoring has to be more structured than one-to-one mentoring as scheduling is necessary in order to accommodate everyone.

Remote Mentoring: Some organizations are geographically dispersed. For example, several software engineers and project managers may be located in different countries for an India-based software developer. In such cases, it may not be feasible to conduct on-site mentoring programme. Mentors here need to conduct the programme via e-mail, teleconferencing, or through telephone. This is also known as e-mentoring.

FOUNDATIONS OF A MENTORING PROGRAMME

To develop the human resources, organizations use the mentoring programme as a tool. Through interactive formal and informal mentoring, mentors make the mentees understand their job and achieve excellence in doing the jobs. Mentees also get the privilege of questioning and exploring the criticality of jobs, whenever there may be the need. To conduct an effective mentoring programme, organizations need to comply with the following assumptions:

- Must enforce deliberate learning: Mentors should promote intentional learning, making use of several methods like instruction, coaching, sharing of experiences, modelling and advising, with the focus on building the capacity of the mentees.
- Must share both the failures and successes: Sharing of such experiences of the mentor helps the mentee to understand the dynamics of experiences and, accordingly, they can also count on their practices with appropriate selection of right or wrong.
- Mentors need to tell their stories: Telling to the mentees personal scenarios, anecdotes, and case examples develop better insight for the mentees.
- Mentoring should be ongoing.
- Mentoring needs to be a joint venture between the mentor and the mentee.
- Mentoring must provide a sense of purpose to evoke responses from the mentees.

ETHICAL GUIDELINES FOR AN EFFECTIVE MENTORING PROGRAMME

To ensure that the mentoring programme of the organizations yields results, it is necessary to follow certain ethical guidelines. Such ethical approaches may vary from organizations to organizations. Even then, we can follow certain generic ethical guidelines:

- Ensure discussion between the mentor and the mentee. Such discussions may be continuous, may be conducted at length, so that the relations between the mentor and the mentee strengthens.
- Both the mentor and the mentee should respect each other's time.
- The mentoring process should facilitate in achieving the mentees' goals, and not the goals of the mentors.
- Mentors must be sensitive to diversity and cultural issues while mentoring.
- With the above ethical protocol, it is expected apart from the ethical compliance, organizations can also achieve the desired results.

CULTURE OF MENTORING

Mentoring culture can be defined as certain beliefs and norms that are instrumental in shaping the process of mentoring in organizations. With a positive mentoring culture, organizations can achieve excellence in business. Mentoring culture primarily focuses on nurturing a positive environment of mentoring within the organization, facilitating multiple mentoring opportunities, and building a supportive environment to facilitate individual and organizational growth.

Some of the important constituents of mentoring culture are:

Accountability: To make people accountable, it is necessary to inculcate shared intention, sense of responsibility, and ownership. All these make people committed for action and consistent in practice. Also a sense of accountability makes people involved in goal setting, clarifying of expectations, defining of roles and responsibilities, monitoring of progress and measuring results, collection of feedback, and formulation of action plans for achieving goals.

Alignment: This culture of mentoring focusses on the consistency in mentoring practices, keeping pace with the culture of the organization. Cultural-fit between the mentoring and the makes the process of mentoring more successful. Also it promotes shared understanding on the organizational values, practices, missions, and goals.

Communication: The culture of communication by increasing the mutual trusts and relationships, achieve excellence and positive results in mentoring. Communication also creates value, promotes learning, and strengthens mentoring within the organization.

Value and Visibility: For developing a sound culture of mentoring, mentors also make effective use of storytelling, role modelling, rewarding, recognition, celebrating, etc. Such activities create proposition and also sustain the inculcated value and visibility. Mentees can also successfully emulate the best practices.

Demand: The mentoring culture in organizations need to be developed in a way so that people autonomously demand mentoring support. Employees perceive mentoring as a way to strengthen and develop them.

Multiple Mentoring Relationships: Sound culture of mentoring also ensures role reversal for the mentees, i.e., mentors become mentees and mentees become mentors. Such multiple mentoring relationships facilitate reflective conversation and add value to the process of mentoring.

Making Use of Multiple Mentoring Opportunities: This combination approach also firmly reinforces the culture of mentoring. For example, many organizations combine group and one-on-one mentoring to reinforce the process of learning.

Education and Training: For improving the culture of mentoring, some organizations often emphasize on strategically integrating the training and development function with the process of mentoring. This type of integration facilitates the exchange the best practices and promotes peer learning.

All these cultural constructs of mentoring facilitate in augmenting learning, maximizing time and effort, and better utilization of resources. Mentored people feel more aligned with the organization and, ultimately, they create value for the entire organization.

Mentoring at IBM

Mentoring at IBM is one of the critical employee development initiatives. IBM ensures clarity of mentoring goals and objectives, access to mentoring relationships across different functional and expertise areas, and employee input into the matching process. At IBM, traditional mentoring programmes are strengthened by web-based experiential learning, through which even employees are exposed to cross-functional aspects to develop them holistically. Mentoring relationships at IBM support the strategic objectives, and also build trust establishing cross-country connections across the IBM people. For its global presence, IBM's mentoring programme emphasizes virtual learning on just-in-time basis. This is what IBM calls speed mentoring. Speed mentoring at IBM emphasizes on virtual group mentoring to solve specific problems and to share information having relevance for IBM.

EXECUTIVE MENTORING

Conventionally in organizations, mentoring programmes are used for operation-level workers to make them understand the technology-enabled process of manufacturing. However, today's complexity of business also requires systematic executive mentoring. Executive mentoring is reinforced by the management development and education programmes in organizations. Executive mentoring, by stimulating the individual growth of the executives, builds their capabilities and enables them to deliver the business performance. It benefits the executives and, indirectly, also benefits the organization in the following ways:

- It builds a solid personal foundation and inculcates strong confidence in executives.
- It develops executives' personal vision and uncovers their value priorities.
- It enables executives to think strategically and inspires people down the line with a shared vision, mission, and values.
- It facilitates in determining appropriate goals, strategies, tactics, and action plans.
- It enhances their management and leadership skills.
- It identifies their personal winning strategies.
- It helps executives to overcome their unhealthy habits, which are counterproductive for performance.
- It helps executives to change themselves positively and, accordingly, they can demonstrate high commitment for achieving the performance results for the organizations.

SUMMARY

Performance mentoring in organization is used primarily to develop leadership and build the capabilities of the employees so that organizations can sustain and grow. Through mentoring, senior or more experienced persons of the organization guide and help the junior level employees for their career and personal development. In a mentoring process, the mentor helps the mentee to successfully perform the assigned job and also to develop, so that the person who is being helped can rise through the ladder. Organizations emphasize on mentoring to make people competent to perform.

A mentor is a person chosen from the organization, among those who understand the job better and who are capable of guiding the new recruits to gradually adapt to their jobs and make them learn and develop. The mentoring process involves different processes, like coaching, training, discussion, counseling, etc. To upgrade skills and so also to enhance the satisfaction of employees, in the era of competition and market uncertainty, mentoring is now considered as one of the most powerful tools to enhance employees' development and performance. Also, to make employees compatible with the organizational culture, mentoring is considered as the most useful means. In essence, mentoring develops the skills of self-leadership, understanding of the reality, and, more particularly, the emerging situations in a competitive market scenario.

KEY WORDS

Protégé—Protégé is the mentee, i.e., one who gets mentored. When a protégé sees himself as having something in common with the mentor, a bond or trust develops more easily. A foundation of trust permits the protégé to try out new ideas and roles with minimal risk.

Value and Visibility—For developing a sound culture of mentoring, mentors make effective use of storytelling, role modelling, rewarding, recognition, celebrating, etc. Such activities create proposition and also sustain the inculcated value and visibility. Mentees can also successfully emulate the best practices.

Alignment—This culture of mentoring focuses on the consistency in mentoring practices, keeping pace with the culture of the organization. Cultural-fit between the mentoring and the makes the process of mentoring more successful. Also it promotes shared understanding on the organizational values, practices, missions, and goals.

Remote Mentoring—If the mentor and mentee do not work in the same location, the mentoring may have to be done over the phone or via e-mail and/or some other method of electronic communication—also known as e-mentoring—e.g. instant messaging or social networking.

GENERAL REVIEW QUESTIONS

1. Discuss the concept of performance mentoring. What are its important characteristics?
2. Explain how mentoring and coaching can influence employees' performance. In what way does mentoring differ from coaching?
3. What are the important benefits of mentoring? How can such benefits improve employees' performance in organizations?
4. Discuss the areas of priority for an organization to introduce a mentoring programme.
5. What are the important cultural constructs of effective mentoring? How can organizations meet such requirements?
6. Short Notes
   (a) One-to-one mentoring
   (b) Multiple mentoring relationships
   (c) Executive mentoring
   (d) Psychosocial benefits of mentoring

CRITICAL REVIEW QUESTION

7. Some of the major Indian organizations like NTPC, ONGC, Infosys, TCS, Tata Iron and Steel, etc. make extensive use of mentoring. Visit their Web sites, and based on Web site information give an outline of mentoring practices in Indian organizations.

REFERENCES

Bhattacharyya, D.K. (2010), *Human Resource Development* (Mumbai: Himalaya Publishing).

Bhattacharyya, D.K. (2009), *Compensation Management* (New Delhi: Oxford University Press).

Burke, R.J. and C.A. McKeen (1989), 'Developing Formal Mentoring Programs in Organizations', *Business Quarterly*, 53(3): 76–99.

Chao, Georgia, Pat Walz and Philip Gardner (1992), 'Formal and Informal Mentorships: A Comparison on Mentoring Functions and Contrast with No Mentored Counterparts', *Personnel Psychology*, 45: 619–36.

Ensher, E.A. and S.E. Murphy (1997), 'Effects of Race, Gender, Perceived Similarity, and Contact on Mentor Relationships', *Journal of Vocational Behavior*, 50: 460–81.

Galbraith, M.W. and N.H. Cohen (1995), *Mentoring: New Strategies and Challenges* (San Francisco, CA: Jossey-Bass).

Gunn, E. (1995), 'Mentoring: The Democratic Version', *Training*, 32(8): 64–67.

Haney, A. (1997), 'The Role of Mentorship in the Workplace', in M.C. Taylor (ed.), *Workplace Education* (Toronto, ON: Culture Concepts), pp. 211–28.

House, J.S. (1981), *Work, Stress, and Social Support* (Reading, MA: Addison–Wesley).

Hunt, D.M. and C. Michael (1983), 'Mentorship: A Career Training and Development Tool', *Academy of Management Review*, 8(3): 475–85.

Jossi, F. (1987), 'Mentoring in Changing Times', *Training and Development*, 51(8): 50–54.

Kaye, B. and B. Jacobson (1996), 'Reframing Mentoring', *Training and Development*, 50(8): 44–47.

Kerka, S. (1997), 'Constructivism', *Workplace Learning and Vocational Education, ERIC Digest No.* 181 (Columbus, OH: ERIC Clearinghouse on Adult, Career, and Vocational Education).

Kram, Kathy (1985), *Mentoring at Work* (Glenview, IL: Scott, Foresman & Co.).

Karm, K.E. (1983). 'Phases of the Mentor Relationship', *Academy of Management Journal*, pp. 608–25.

Murray, M. (1991), *Beyond the Myths and Magic of Mentoring: How to Facilitate an Effective Mentoring Program* (San Francisco, CA: Jossey-Bass).

Noe, R.A. (1988), 'An Investigation of the Determinants of Successful Assigned Mentoring Relationships', *Personnel Psychology*, 41: 457–78.

Scandura, Terri (1992), 'Mentorship and Career Mobility: An Empirical Investigation', *Journal of Organizational Behavior*, 13: 169–74.

Scandura, T. A. (1998), 'Dysfunctional mentoring relationships and outcomes', *Journal of Management*, 24(3), pp. 449–467.

Zey, M. (1988), 'A Mentor for All Reasons', *Personnel Journal*, 67(1): 46–51.

CASE STUDY

McDonald's—The Destination to Career Growth and Performance

McDonald's develop their performance objectives and, initially, explain the performance objectives to the employees. The process is done by the senior management, who then explain to the rank and file the overall objectives of the organizations for the coming year, and then make them understand how their contribution at the department and at the individual level would help the company in achieving the same. Such traceability of individual performance to the overall objectives of the organization make people feel responsible to deliver their best. The company essentially believes in teamwork. Hence, individual team member's understanding of their performance objectives and its cascading effect to the team and the organization as a whole, when further spelt out by the managers in measurable terms, automatically develops their self-esteem as they gain a sense of ownership. At this stage of performance goal setting, managers also emphasize on mutual agreement. The compelling culture of performance makes every member of the organization volunteer to achieve the results. Every employee of McDonald's gets the opportunity to choose in which skill areas they need more inputs, and accordingly they can choose their learning and so also the option top renew their skills. Employees' development is also facilitated by systematic mentoring programmes. Mentors help the mentees to acquire new skill sets on job and gradually become a good performer. The primary focus of the mentoring programme of McDonald's is to make people gradually adapt to the culture of increased performance and sense of responsibility, and even volunteer to develop their juniors. At McDonald's, people are enthusiastic about performance, want to learn new skills, and are even eager to take up new responsibilities and more complex work.

The compelling culture of performance has now made McDonald's the ultimate destination for young job seekers.

The global fast-food giant attributes its success to employee development and career paths. Globally, many managers of McDonald's started their careers with their restaurants. The company's performance development system is so designed that it drives consistent performance improvement of employees, and so also their development and growth. The system includes individual performance and development plans, employee reviews, and roundtables for performance calibration and talent review. The founder of McDonald's, Ray Kroc, believed that good performers need to be always taken care of.

The company's name is so deep-rooted in the minds of the people that they get application from a large number of prospective candidates. Employer branding for McDonald's is so strong that a series of research studies indicated that parents largely believe that their children must work at McDonald's. Parents believe that by working with McDonald's, they could see positive changes in the minds of their children, such as improved communication skills and increased confidence. On the other hand, McDonald's could also observe high levels of satisfaction and commitment among their young employees.

Question: From the above case study explain how McDonald's has been so successful in branding itself as the most favourite destination for young job seekers.

CHAPTER 13

Performance Measurement

Learning Objectives

After reading this chapter, you will be able to understand:

- Definition and concepts of performance measurements
- Measuring of performance
- Selection of performance measurement criteria
- Integrated performance measurement systems
- Statistical methods of performance measures
- Performance measures through ranking and rating
- Scales for evaluation of performance measures
- Performance matrix and models
- General and specific performance measures
- Key performance indicators
- Performance measures through productivity indices

Linking Organizational Strategies to Individual Level Performance Goals

By aligning strategies with performance management systems, organizations achieve excellent performance results. Organizations adopt strategies to achieve their defined goals and objectives. A well-developed strategy map for any organization gives the sense of direction to all cross-section of organizational members. Linking such strategies with the individual performance goals in the form of key performance areas(KPA) and key result areas (KRA), benefit the organization to reap the benefits of competitive advantage through the high performance level of organizational members.

Alignment of strategies with people working in organizations could be best possible by relating processes to the performance management systems (PMS) of the organizations. Such strategy aligned PMS facilitate organizations not only to transform the people cascading the strategic objectives but it can also facilitate effective utilization of corporate strategy, and in the process get more from those people. To do this effectively, it is important for the top management of the organization to be committed and involved with the process, including understanding of organizational vision, mission, strategy, values, and life-cycle. By using a balanced scorecard, organizations can pursue their strategy to get a unique edge in a competitive market.

Before alignment of strategies with PMS, it is important to identify, analyse, and prioritize core business processes and key customers. Effective analysis and definition of key customer requirements ensure short listing of critical business drivers and measures, which can then be cascaded to individual employees' goals and objectives (against the identified key drivers), which can be called as the key performance indicators (KPIs). Like KPIs, human resource practices of the organizations are also aligned and integrated to business strategy to ensure congruence and synergy within the organization. This is a holistic approach to align the organizational strategies with the performance goals at the individual, group, department, division, and organizational level. It can also facilitate introduction of performance linked compensation design and set the behavioural standards at the individual level.

INTRODUCTION

Measuring is the act of assigning numbers to properties or characteristics. We measure to quantify a situation, to regulate, or to understand things we see. We measure with gauges and instruments or simply by counting things. Managing performance is highly dependent on well-designed PMS, which provides a clear link between strategy and human behaviour. Performance of the organization is completely dependent on the performances of its processes. In fact, in any organization, its performance is equal to the sum of the performance of its processes. Processes are the sequence of cross-functional activities performed by people and machines, which combine valuable resources to convert inputs into outputs. ISO 9000 documents define a process as a 'Set of interrelated or interacting activities, which transforms inputs into outputs'. These activities require allocation of resources such as people and materials. It is processes, which provide the link between organizational level goals and the work performed by employees. Processes can be measured effectively. Measurements may be applied to many aspects and attributes of processes and the critical few are time, quality, cost (financial), and scale.

Performance measures can help us understand and improve performance. It is exciting to measure, to benchmark, and to stretch to do better. It is important that performance measures be as direct as possible. Some of the important cardinal principles of performance measurements are as follows:

- Measure performance parameters as directly as possible viz., to improve employees' attendance measure attendance. Similarly to improve cycle times, measure cycle times.
- Perform both enumerative as well as analytical studies. Enumerative studies are those that show how things are but cannot put any value in predicting. A census is an enumerative study. Analytical studies are those that study the process and show what that process is capable of doing in the future unless something changes that process.

Dr. Walter Shewhart (1931), a pioneer in statistical process control, said a process consists of equipment, methods, materials, and people blended to produce output in a given environment. Hence to improve performance, better process measurement techniques are most important. Statistical process control helps to quickly detect the occurrence of assignable cause or process shifts so that investigation into the process and corrective action there upon can be taken before any non-conforming units are manufactured. Assignable causes are those, which may occur due to improperly adjusted machines, operators' errors, and defective raw materials or other inputs. These cause some variability in the quality characteristics. A process that is operating under assignable causes over and above change causes is said to be out of control.

That measurement of process is an integral part of performance management system, is evident from Figure 13.1.

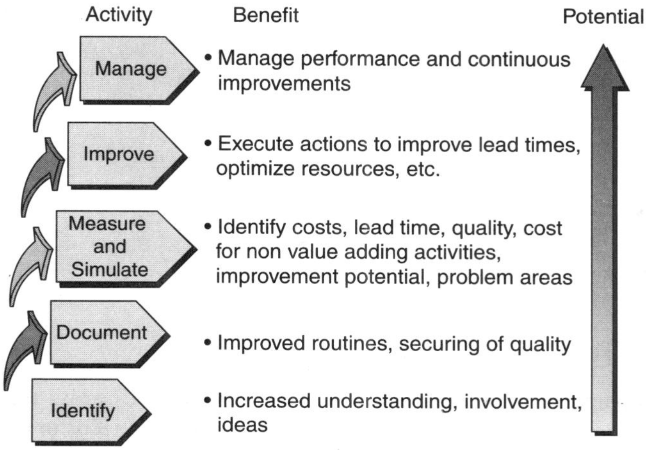

Figure 13.1 *Measurement process of PMS*

MEASURING PERFORMANCE

Many types of methods can be used for performance measurement. Any performance measure focus on three aspects, i.e., inputs (management, strategies, and resources), outputs (products produced and services rendered), and outcomes (impact). We can further analyse inputs at more precise level in terms of throughputs, i.e., timeliness and reach of the resources. Which method fits the organizational requirement has to be assessed by the human resource (HR) managers. Here, however, we have discussed the general features and pros and cons of various methods for appreciation. Various measurement techniques are listed below:

1. Qualitative or quantitative measurement.
2. Observation or subjective response.
3. Methods for collecting information.
4. Naturalistic observation of 'behaviour stream'—what's happening where, when, and at what frequency.
5. Structured observations.
6. Questionnaires.
7. Interviews.
8. Simulation.
9. Performance trials.
10. Fitting trials.
11. Observing traces of behaviour, etc.

    (a) Evaluative criteria.
    (b) Frequency of problems.
    (c) Completion of tasks.
    (d) Productivity.

(e) Elapsed time.
(f) Rate of performance.
(g) Accident rate.
(h) Energy utilization.
(i) Accuracy.
(j) Complaints.
(k) Frequency of complaints.
(l) Independence.

Measurement Quality

Just measuring performance is not enough! As major HR and various cross-functional decisions are taken based on the performance measurement, quality of measurement needs to be ensured. The following terms are intertwined with the measurement quality:

- Reliability—measurement technique does what it is supposed to do.
- Sensitivity—technique is able to capture differences in performance.
- Validity—applies to all the cases of concern.
- Power—categorical, ordinal, interval.

Comparing results and methods ensure reliability, which may be inter rater and intra rater. If the measurement is reliable then by default stability is ensured. Sensitivity is the test in different settings and users. Validity avoids sampling bias and replicates the same results.

Selection of Performance Measurement Criteria

Most commonly used performance measurement criteria are:

- Production counts.
- Personnel data.
- Judgmental methods.
- Work samples methods.

Production counts measure what a worker produces on the job. The worker with the higher production count is assumed to be the better worker. However, for many jobs, it may not be feasible to measure performance in terms of production counts. This is more applicable for managerial jobs. Moreover there is some possible dangers in production count method. It might change the behaviour of the worker. They may get pre-disposed to achieve higher results at the cost of job related stress, which in turn may be detrimental to decrease overall job performance. It may also create '*The Hawthorne Effect*', i.e., deliberate change of behaviour to create favourable impression. More important is that production counts by default may not be attributable to workers' performance. There may be other factors which influence workers' performance. In such cases product count as a performance measurement tool may utterly defeat the purpose. For all these problems, production count should not be used as a stand-alone method for performance measurement.

Another popular way to objectively measure job performance of employees is to use information from the personnel data. What could be the type of information that needs to be couched from personnel data largely depends on the raters' way of interpreting good performance. It is necessary to develop a personnel index based on the identified performance criteria and then match the information to measure the performance based on the employee's data. The biggest problem in this case is attributable to raters' failure to understand the criteria and too much leniency on some narrow parameters like absenteeism, etc.

Absenteeism as performance measurement criteria is often used by many organizations and based on the respective employees' absenteeism data, performance rating is done. The biggest problem is to define absenteeism by the rater. How it is defined may greatly affect the job performance. Secondly, absenteeism may not be normally distributed and hence as a work performance variable, it may create difficulty. Finally, measures of absence are largely unrelated—on a year-to-year basis and hence such data has low reliability.

Apart from these, work samples as measures of job performance are also extensively used by many organizations. This approach requires measurement of specific tasks associated with the specific job title. Thus it considers developing of a job performance construct based on two factors, i.e., performance of specific individual tasks (which forms part of workers' job description) and behaviours which facilitate the effective job performance for the said tasks. As this requires detailed analysis of job and relates it with specific tasks involved, it requires strenuous testing, which may not be liked by the organizations.

Integrated Performance Measurement Systems

The process of combining different attributes of the organization within a hierarchical structure is called an integrated performance measurement framework (PMF). PMF establishes direct link between the top-level measures (such as shareholder value added (SVA)) and the action plans of the entire organization. These collectively add up to the achievement of the established goals. Performance measurement criteria are different for various levels. Strategic measures capture the value of stakeholder's investment benchmarking with other competitors. Tactical measures are key performance indicators, which collectively capture the overall performance of the enterprise and act as predictors of future success. Operational measures or in-process and output measures are used for monitoring, control, and improvement of the basic work processes of the enterprise. This we have illustrated while explaining the performance matrix.

STATISTICAL METHODS OF PERFORMANCE MEASURES

Statistical methods can help us in performance measures, if we broadly adopt the process approach as advocated by Dr. Walter Shewhart (1931). Two main aspects of statistical methods deal with statistical distributions and statistical control.

At the outset, HR managers should understand statistical concepts on variation, including statistical distributions and statistical control. HR managers should also understand special causes, common causes, and control charting. In addition, they should clearly understand the concept of manipulation with a process.

Workers perform the operations in the system. Variation study demonstrates how workers in a given process are capable of performing. . This natural pattern of variation shows, what the process is capable of doing to improve the work performance. If the process is in control, then performance of workers would be in its natural capability, or else performance will be less than the expected levels or standards.

Use of Control Charts for Measuring Performance Variation

To measure the variation in performance, we can make use of statistical methods by developing control charts. The control chart is a tool for on-line process control, widely used for the detection of assignable causes of variation. It is a graphical display of a sample quality measure versus sample number (or time). The chart shows a centre line that represents the average value of the quality characteristic, corresponding to the in-control state. Two other parallel horizontal lines, called the upper control limit (UCL) and the lower control limit (LCL) are also shown on the chart. Control charts compute control limits and values that fall outside the control limits (outside the UCL and LCL) are considered as signals of special causes and must be investigated. Good performance measures are also assessed using statistical methods like run charts. When the results are plotted, values are observed in relation to the centre (median) line.

In any process, proper checks through control charts are exercised at strategic points. In the case of measurable quality characteristics a pair of control charts—one for X bars to control the average level of the process and the other for R to control dispersion are used. Many quality characteristics are not measured on a numerical scale. In these cases, we may judge each unit of product as either conforming or non-conforming on the basis of whether or not it possesses certain attributes, or we may count the number of non-conformities (defects) appearing on a unit of product. Control charts for number of defects or defectives are used in such situations. As long as the points plot within the control limits, the process is assumed to be in control and no action is necessary. However, a point that plots outside the control limits is interpreted as evidence that the process is out of control and investigative and corrective action is required to find and eliminate the assignable cause or causes responsible for this behaviour.

Control Charts for Measuring Performance Attributes

Similarly for measuring attributes, attribute control charts like p, np, u, c, are also used. The Proportion Defective Chart (p-chart) is used to control the proportion of defective product in samples taken from a process. This chart is also referred to as the fraction non-conforming or fraction defective chart. P-chart or fraction defective chart is defined as the ratio of the number of defective items in a population to the total number of items in that population. The sample fraction defective (p) is defined as the ratio of the number of defective units (d) in the sample to the sample size 'n' , i.e., $p = d/n$, where 'n' is a sub-group size. If LCL is negative, it is taken as zero.

The Number Defective Chart (np-chart) is an alternative chart that may be substituted for the p-chart. The underlying distribution for the np-chart is the binomial. In the case of the np-chart, the sample size must be constant. Rather than calculating the proportion of defective items in a sample for plotting on a p-chart, the np-chart allows the actual number of defective units to be plotted directly. This eliminates the need for one calculation (p) thereby decreasing the probability of an error. The np-chart also is somewhat easier for production operators to understand.

C-chart or control charts for non-conformities is used to control the average number of defects per inspection unit in samples of fixed size. The inspection unit may be one item or multiple items. The underlying distribution for the c-chart is the Poisson. A defective (or non-conforming) unit is a unit of product that does not satisfy one or more of the specifications. Each specific point at which a specification is not satisfied, results in a defect or non-conformity. In this case, each sub-group consists of a single unit and 'c' would be number of defects observed in one unit. It should be remembered that each inspection unit must always represent an identical 'area of opportunity' for the occurrence of defects.

U-charts (sometimes referred to as 'rate' charts) deal with event counts when the area of opportunity is not constant during each period. The steps to follow for constructing a u-chart are the same as a c-chart, except that the control limits are computed for each individual quarter because the number of standard units varies.

All these control charts, one way or the other help us to measure the performance standards in quantitative terms. Figure 13.2 illustrates these concepts in a detailed manner.

Apart from these, histograms (for spread of data), Pareto graph (80/20 rule, i.e., 80 per cent improvement in performance can reasonably be expected by eliminating 20 per cent of the causes of unacceptable quality or performance), process capability study, etc., are also very effective for quantitative performance measurement.

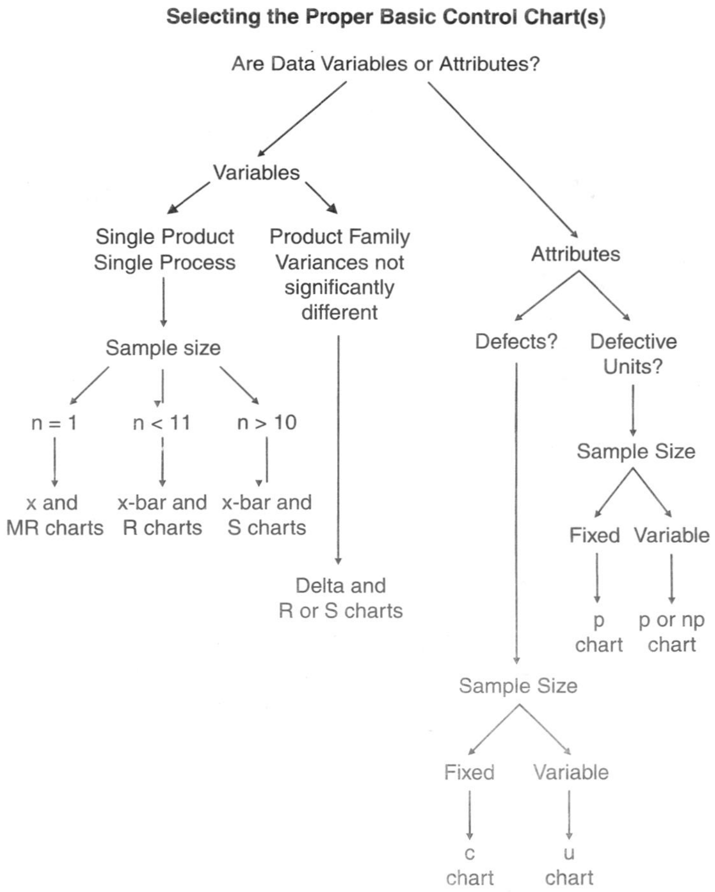

Figure 13.2 *Control charts*

A histogram is a graphic display of resource utilization and it is shown using coloured vertical bars to indicate over-utilization and under-utilization of resources over a period of time. Pareto principles are based on 'a vital few trivial many'. This is because of inter-dependence and inter-relationship in motive strengths. HR managers can make extensive use of both histograms and Pareto graph in other HR research areas also.

Process capability is a statistical measure of the inherent process variability for a given characteristic. The process capability index is the value of tolerance specified for the characteristic, divided by the process capability. Process capability indices include the widely used C_{pk} and C_p. A process capability index can only be calculated from data collected while the process is in control. Hence when performance variability is within control, we can develop a capability index measuring process capability as $\bar{P}$—the average proportion defective produced by the process when it is operating in control. Therefore, if a $\bar{P} = 0.0016$ it indicates that on average 99.84 per cent of the product produced by this process when it is operating in control is acceptable, while 0.16 per cent are defective.

PERFORMANCE MEASURES THROUGH RANKING AND RATING

Performance measurement through rating and ranking system is again another important area of consideration. Rating systems measure worker's performance compared to some set standard. The rating is done listing desired objectives, skills or traits alongside a scale, which may be 1–5, 'poor to excellent' type. For making the ranking process simple, we normally make use of easy-to-read type of scale, keeping in view the basic scale construction norms, as detailed earlier. This, however, significantly depends on the judgment of the rater. Commonly we find use of subjective rating or observer rating scales. Subjective rating scales are psychophysical and it measures response to environment quantitatively. It is basically designed on ergonomic principles and developed through a process of empirical testing. Because of ordinal measurement of response, reliability, and validity such type of scales can be tested. Observer rating scales are used in real time for establishing a scoring algorithm for overall activity. This scale requires task analysis to break down task into components and assign scoring algorithms for each task component. To ascertain the degree of fit, one must obtain both an outside evaluation (observer rating) and a subjective evaluation (subjective rating). Different types of scales which are used for performance rating are as follows:

Graphic Rating Scales: This is the single most common way of evaluating worker performance. Here the manager or the rater can directly judge quality of performance of employees on a specific response scale. Response scales may be:

- *Continuous Scales:* Which computes score measuring the distance from one end of the scale.
- *Verbally Anchored Scales:* Here some discrete categories are anchored on either end of the scale with the range of abilities. The nature of verbal anchor scales varies with the specificity of the verbal anchors.
- *Numeric Scales:* In this scale, verbal anchors with a numerical range within each category are shown.

Graphic scales are simple to use and allow for computation of scores to compare workers' overall job performance. However, problems with graphic rating scales are enormous. If such problems are not taken care of, the whole purpose of performance rating may be defeated. For not defining precisely the anchors, such scale may sometimes be ambiguous. Raters may use the scale in different ways, which may raise the problem of validity (when two workers are rated by different raters). However, such problems now-a-days are eliminated significantly by using various behaviour-based scales, which help us to assess specific work related behaviours. Some of the behaviour-based scales are discussed below.

Several alternate measurement methods and systems have been developed over the years including management-by-objectives (MBO), behaviourally anchored rating scales (BARS), the mixed-standard scale (MSS), quantitatively measurable performance criteria, and the use of multiple raters or 360-degree feedback.

Management-by-Objectives (MBO)

Performance management systems utilizing MBO strategies requires managers to set mutually agreed upon, observable, and measurable objectives and goals for the employees and their bosses. 'Each level of the organization sets goals that complement those set at the next highest level. In many cases, individual monetary rewards (bonuses, merit increases, etc.) are tied to MBO goals' (Wright, 1994). One criticism of the MBO strategy is that employees tend to focus on attaining their objectives to the detriment of their other, non-measured responsibilities. Edwards, Borman, and Sproull characterize (1985) MBO 'as one of the greatest management illusions. The technique simply increases pressure on the individual and is self-defeating'.

Behaviourally Anchored Rating Scales (BARS)

Behaviourally anchored rating scales are 'descriptions provided on appraisal forms and surveys which describe a precise level of performance'. These are designed to reduce the rating errors of conventional scales. The scale includes number of performance dimensions like leadership, teamwork, communication, initiative, adaptability, etc. BARS were developed with the hope of improving rater accuracy by providing job-related behavioural anchors and altering the format of rating scales. BARS anchor each rating interval with descriptions of a behavioural incident. BARS eliminate the confusion and common error caused by open-ended rating scales (i.e., what is the difference between satisfactory and good?). Another advantage provided by BARS is that they focus the appraisal on behaviour rather than personality characteristics (Brown, 1985). Unfortunately, while behavioural anchors offer specificity in setting performance levels, research has indicated that BARS offer no performance measurement superiority over conventional systems. They are also time consuming and difficult to develop, especially if there are many dissimilar job slots. To develop BARS for just one job, that job must be separately and carefully analyzed and performance levels must be described in detail for several of the job's areas (Edwards et al., 1985).

BARS are similar to graphic rating scales, but uses specific behaviours to anchor the scale. The development of BARS requires extensive input from supervisors in order to determine which behaviours are task relevant and assess some important aspect of job performance. The care taken in developing BARS helps to reduce across supervisor variability.

The Mixed-Standard Scale (MSS)

Mixed-standard scale is considered 'superior to BARS in reducing halo and leniency errors. MSS disguises dimensions and ordinal relationships among items so that the rater cannot detect an order of merit in the items. In MSS, all items are presented in random order and raters must respond without knowing whether a low, medium, or high rating for a particular item has a positive, neutral, or negative correlation to performance. Raters are required to choose one of the following three responses for each item: the ratee's performance is lower (or poorer) than the item description (-); the ratee's performance fits the item description (0); or the ratee's performance is higher (better) than the item description (+). This format provides for error counts that can be used to identify rater errors, systematic rating tendencies, and ambiguous dimensions, thereby providing the opportunity for rater feedback. MSS can be used with multiple raters. Despite its advantages, many raters experience frustration with this system, and it has little industry support' (Edwards and Sproull, 1983).

Mixed-standard scale (MSS): Good, average, and poor performance is assessed with respect to specific job related behaviours. A number of different items are used to assess each performance dimension. For example, an MSS for police officers might measure the dimensions of judgement, relations with others, and job knowledge. The advantages of MSS are they refer to concrete observable behaviour, and they require relatively simple judgements on the part of the supervisor.

Behavioural Observation Scales (BOS)

Behavioural observation scales was developed by Latham and Wexley (1977) who believed that both graphic rating scales and BARS require supervisors to make vague judgements. The BOS is a list of 'critical' behaviours which the supervisor has to rate in terms of frequency. Items indicate either desirable or undesirable aspects of work performance:

Worker never needs her or his work to be double-checked ________

Worker misses workdays ________

RANKING SYSTEMS

Ranking systems take a markedly different approach by comparing employees against one another and then assign a rank order. This is similar to grading system in the classroom. Here we do not apply a set standard to all employees and the best performer can determine where everyone else will fit in. This system promotes healthy competition among employees and when reinforced by an effective incentive programme, it even develops a cascading effect on productivity enhancement. There are various types of ranking, which is primarily decided based on the organizational need and nature of data.

- **Forced Distribution:** It divides the workforce into three categories: high performance, average performance, and low performance. This distribution is known as forced, as only a small percentage of workers can receive high or low rankings. The forced distribution helps to solve the problem of supervisors who like to rate the vast majority of workers at the highest level.
- **Full Ranking:** Here instead of sorting workers into general categories, we do a complete rank ordering of all employees, so that no two workers are at the same level of job performance.

Paired Comparison Method: This method of ranking orders workers by comparing each worker to every other worker, thus forcing the rater to make relative judgments. However, operational difficulty may be experienced in case we have more employees.

Which type of ranking method is more suitable in a given situation will depend on number of factors. For example, degree of efforts, which HR managers may like to put for ranking and the intended usage of ranking results, are two primary factors to decide suitability of a ranking method. Forced distribution may be extremely necessary in cases where decisions like lay-off, etc., need to be taken.

Comparing Job Performance Rating Systems

We really do not have any consensus on effectiveness of a job rating system. Despite its numerous flaws, graphic-rating scales are still considered effective. Perhaps for this reason, psychological thought process of the individuals while filling out the rating forms has now become more important than the type of rating system. Many organizations use only a single measure of job performance. In such cases, it becomes difficult to find converging or diverging evidence to authenticate judgmental ratings. This is why using inter-rater reliability to estimate validity is considered more appropriate for measuring job performance. However, if we are able to define job performance very precisely, performance measures are likely to become more accurate. HR managers need to take guard against possible rating errors like halo, leniency, and range distortion. Halo errors stem from the general impression of the rater about the person being rated. Leniency errors may either result in rating all very high or very low. Range restriction errors fail to make fine distinctions between the performances of employees doing similar nature of job. Apart from these, at times there may be memory distortions of the rater, in cases when a rater requires to rate a large number of employees. To guard against all these problems, Schmidt et al. (1979) have suggested quantifying the value of job performance, using standard deviation as a measure. This method assesses the difference, in money terms, between the value of an average worker and the value of an exceptional worker.

Multiple Raters/360-degree Feedback

Multiple-rater and 360-degree feedback instruments are better performance assessment alternatives to eliminate errors in performance measurement. Multiple-rater feedback is different from 360-degree feedback. 360-degree feedback collects and analyse inputs from the employees' immediate boss, peers, direct reports, suppliers, and customers (if applicable). Some organizations also do collect self-rating inputs from the employee concerned. Multiple-rater feedback on the other hand consists of more than one rater, usually four or more. It is not necessary for the multiple raters to collect inputs from all sources, like what we do in 360-degree feedback. Numerous research studies like Pollack and Pollack (1996) have proved that multiple assessment tools are more reliable and valid for performance measurement.

Scales for Evaluation of Performance Measures

Here we will discuss some of the practical means of performance research using rating and ranking system. While technical details of various validated scales have been discussed in general chapters, here scale constructions and measurement tools are more need based for correct evaluation of performance. Some of these are discussed below:

Results-based Scale: For this scale, we need to develop a statement on the critical result, which helps us to get the expected output and then administer on the selected employees whose performance evaluation is done. Using a yes or no type of statements, where 'no' indicates 1 and 'yes' indicates 5, we calculate the average of critical results (CRs) and then compare the ratings on a 5-point scale.

Measurability Scale: For this scale, result or measure(s) are objectively quantified in terms of cost, quality, and timeliness using a 5-point scale, where 1 indicates 'not at all' and 5 indicates 'to a very great extent'. Performance rating is done based on the score assigned for each such identified measures.

Monitoring Scale: This scale is used to track the work to ensure that it is actually accomplished. For example, in case of any critical results data it is important for the rater to authenticate the source of the data, to understand whether it is just a sample or it need to be collected, who will collect the data, and who will receive it. Here again a 5-point scale, starting from 'not at all' to 'to a very great extent' is used.

Feedback Scale: This 5-point scale measures performance feedback on the critical result areas to assess an employee.

Exceeds Expectations Scale: The 'exceeds expectations' criterion assesses on a 5-point scale, whether employee's performance meets the expectation measure. This scale helps us to understand whether more efforts or skill are required on the part of employees to achieve a high performance score. This helps in better quantification of degree of efforts.

Linked with Goals Scale: This scale evaluates the extent to which the result is valued by the organization. It compares the critical results and measures performance against organizational goals.

PERFORMANCE MATRIX AND MODELS

Developing a performance matrix and emulating examples of world class performance excellence models help HR researchers to scientifically list the action plans for improving the performance management system of an organization.

Thomas F. Gilbert (2003) based on his research, contributed immensely in this area. Performance matrix is a construct of performance system which sequentially illustrates decisions to be taken for improving performance management systems in an organization. A simple model of performance matrix deals with three levels—policy, strategy, and tactics. Some authors also call it performance-engineering model (PEM). Like three levels, this simplified performance matrix or PEM has three stages, i.e., stage A, stage B, and stage C. Stage A considers identification of accomplishments, decision on important requirements together with decision on unit of measurement, and finally developing standards. In stage B, we consider measurement of opportunity, by identifying critical performance improvement plans, measuring, and analysing it. In stage C we analyse methods of accomplishment using environmental methods, people programmes, and management action.

Based on the above inputs, in line with Gilbert (2003), a sample performance matrix or performance engineering model can be drawn as in Table 13.1. This is an excellent guide for managers to keep a track of which decisions they must make and also in what sequence. Some other examples of performance matrix for the whole organization can be drawn after excellence models of EFQM, Malcolm Baldrige, and Shingo.

Shingo Prize Model

The Shingo Prize Model lists criteria, practices, techniques, and processes which can be incorporated by an organization to achieve world class level of quality, cost, delivery, and business results. Such suggested practices and techniques may not be applicable for every organization. It has to be strategically incorporated, keeping pace with organizational specific needs. In fact, it is a replication of Toyota Production System, by a well-known Japanese industrial engineer, Dr. Shigeo Shingo. The model is known as Shingo Prize Model, because this prize was established in 1988 to promote awareness of lean

Table 13.1 *Performance matrix*

Stages / Levels	A Accomplishment Models	B Measures of Opportunity	C Methods of Improvement
I Policy (Institutional Systems)	*Organization models:* Cultural goal of the organization Major missions Requirements and units Exemplary standards	*Stakes analysis:* Performance analysis Potential for improving performance (PIP) Stakes Critical roles	*Programmes and policies:* Environmental programmes (data/tools/incentives) People programmes (knowledge, selection, recruiting) Management programme (organization, resources, standards)
II Strategy (Job Systems)	*Job models:* Mission of job Major responsibilities Requirements and units Exemplary standards	*Job assessment:* Performance measures Potential for improving performance (PIP) Critical responsibilities	*Job strategies:* Data systems Training designs Incentive schedules Human factors Selection systems Recruitment systems
III Tactics (Task Systems)	*Task models:* Responsibilities of tasks Major duties Requirements and units Exemplary standards	*Task analysis:* Performance measure or observations Potential for improving performance (PIP) Specific deficiencies Cost of programmes	*Tactical instruments:* Feedback Guidance Training Reinforcement

(Based on the model of Praxis Corporation, 1979)

Notes: Exemplary performance is the worth of the historically best instance of the performance. PIP is a conceptual tool, which gives us the basis for comparing potential opportunities to improve performance. Comparing two worthy indices expresses it, i.e., exemplary (which is the standard) and exemplary worth index. Suppose we want to measure PIP for the outbound caller in a call center. An average outbound caller makes 40 effective calls in a day and each call ensures business worth Rs. 80, while the total cost per day for the company is Rs. 2,000. The exemplary index is indicated as W_{av}, which is (40 x 80)/2000 = 1.6. Suppose an exceptional outbound caller makes 80 successful calls in a day (with all other data remaining the same). In that case the exemplary worth index is indicated as W_{ex} = (80 x 80)/2000 = 3.2. In this case we can compute the PIP of the average outbound caller as W_{ex}/W_{av}, i.e., 3.2/1.6 = 2.

manufacturing concepts and world-class philosophy of business performance. Adoption of this model in performance management practices enables an organization to focus on improvements of core manufacturing and business process to achieve world-class business performance. As per this model, there are two prime enablers which influence the core operations of business. These enablers are leadership and empowerment. Through these enablers organizations exert influence on the core manufacturing and non-manufacturing operations. The model assigns weightage to each parameter and measures the same with the required systems and practices of the model. In core manufacturing, the model emphasizes on the following areas:

- Manufacturing vision and strategy.
- Innovation in market service and produce.
- Partnering with supervisors, customers, and environmental practices.
- World-class manufacturing operations and process.
- Non-manufacturing support function, etc.

Likewise, the model also examines the non-manufacturing support functions that go into the core manufacturing process.

As per the model, when the organization activates core manufacturing and non-manufacturing functions, it can achieve improvement in quality, cost and productivity, diversity and service, and all these cascade to overall improvement in the customer satisfaction and profitability of the organization.

EFQM Model

The European Foundation for Quality Management (EFQM) business excellence model is yet another example of world class performance management model. This model is a nine-box business excellence model, intended to help an organization to conduct self-assessment in measuring their performance results in terms of financial, customer satisfaction, people satisfaction, and impact on society. Leadership, policy and strategy, people management, resources, and process management act as enablers to improve performance results. EFQM model is relatively simple to follow as the prime driver for organizational improvement in this case is assumed as leadership. This leadership activates those enablers that ensures performance results likepeople, policy, strategy, and partnership, to get improvement in people results, customers results, society results, and ultimately the key performance results.

Malcolm Baldrige Criteria for World-class Performance

ISO 9000 based documentation of quality management systems of an organization can be extended to Baldrige criteria for performance excellence framework. Thus, this model enables an organization to integrate their quality management system with their performance management system. Based on ISO 9001, this framework is explained as under:

- Strategic planning process.
- Customer focused operating system.
- Operating system.
- Teamwork structure and guidelines.
- Administration of compensation and recognition systems.
- Advanced quality-planning process for bringing new products to market.

The business management system (BMS) or performance excellence framework, using Baldrige criteria requires the same documentation like quality documentation system of ISO 9000, excepting some practices, which are additionally provided. Such additional practices in Baldrige criteria are as follows:

- Strategic planning process.
- Customer focused operating system.
- Operating system.
- Teamwork structure and guidelines.
- Administration of compensation and recognition systems.
- Advanced quality-planning process for bringing new products to market.

The existing corrective and preventive action system (ISO 9000), by default, evolves into a continuous improvement system.

GENERAL PERFORMANCE MEASURES

Apart from job or function specific performance measurement, we have some general performance measures as follows:

Quality addresses how well the employee or work unit performed the work and/or the accuracy or effectiveness of the final product. Quality refers to accuracy, appearance, usefulness, or effectiveness. Quality measures can include error rates (such as the number or percentage of errors allowable per unit of work) and customer satisfaction rates (determined through a customer survey).

Quantity addresses how much work the employee or work unit produced. Quantity measures are expressed as a number of products produced or services provided, or as a general result to achieve.

Timeliness addresses how quickly, when, or by what date the employee or work unit produced the work. Organizations need to make sure to include timeliness measures when applicable; otherwise, it is implied that the element must *always* be done and there is no margin for error.

Cost-effectiveness addresses cost savings to the organization. Organizations must develop measures that address cost-effectiveness on specific resource levels (money, personnel, or time) that can be documented. Cost-effectiveness measures may include such aspects of performance as maintaining or reducing unit costs, reducing the time it takes to produce or provide a product or service, or reducing waste.

DEVELOPING SPECIFIC MEASURES

To develop specific measures, organizations after determining the general performance measures, indicated above, determine the process of measuring the quantity, quality, timeliness, and/or cost-effectiveness for each of the element. After determining the performance measures, organizations document the factors to be appraised, and accordingly assign the performance measurement responsibility to the respective managers or executives.

DECIDING THE PERFORMANCE STANDARDS

Performance standards are the performance thresholds, either decided by top management or decided mutually. Performance standards spell out the performance requirements or the expectations from the employees about what they are expected to achieve. For every critical performance element, organizations establish the thresholds and communicate the same to employees, to enable them to understand what they need to deliver to ensure successful performance. Along with the documented performance standards, it is necessary to design the appropriate scale to measure the performance levels of employees. Anything at or above the threshold is considered most successful. Anything below is considered to be unacceptable.

ANNUAL STOCK-TAKING OF PERFORMANCE

Annual stock-taking of performance is basically a performance audit function which apart from usual employee evaluations emphasize on measuring the proper alignment of performance results with the organizations' and employees' growth. For organization, stock-taking of performance helps in achieving the goals by optimizing staff performance, duly identifying the strengths and weaknesses. For employees, on the other hand it helps in providing guidance to perform their jobs and also help in defining their career path.

PERFORMANCE METRICS

Apart from evaluating employees' performance using the ranking scale, organizations can measure the performance against some standard performance metrics. By combining performance metrics and performance narratives (tracked through scales), organizations can get better results. Performance metrics, also known as key performance indicators (KPIs) need to be organization specific and also at times unique for typical functions or jobs.

Key Performance Indicators (KPI)

Developing KPIs as performance measurement tools, at the outset requires the organizations first to understand its directions and strategic goals. Thereafter, it is also important to understand the system of internal operations, activities involved in it, and how non-performance of such activities affects the strategic goals achievement. KPI defines the factors of influence, monitoring of which is possible by measuring the performance level of individual employees, groups, and the organizations as a whole. Therefore, KPI can be better defined as the effectiveness measurement indicators that help in achieving the strategic goals of any organization. KPI is effective for performance measurement as it presents the performance values.

Once KPIs are finalized, for its measurement, organizations make use of balanced scorecard, and arrange such KPIs in four perspectives, i.e., financial, customer, innovation and learning, and internal business process. All the KPIs become a part of one or the other perspectives. For example, KPIs for financial perspectives may consider the cost indices, return on investment, net-worth, liquidity, solvency ratio, cash flow, etc. Similarly, KPIs on customer perspectives include customer satisfaction and marketing actions' efficiency in terms of new customers acquired, number of customer complaints, customer attrition, etc. For innovation and learning, KPIs consider the number of new idea generated, number of new products developed, employees' acquisition of new skill and knowledge, etc. Finally, for internal business process, KPIs measure the degree of effectiveness of existing operational and administrative activities in terms of measurement of administrative expenses as percentage of total revenues, cycle time from order to delivery, lead time for procurement of materials, etc.

It is, however, important to understand that KPIs cannot be universal, even though the perspectives of the balanced scorecard are generic, i.e., applicable for every organization, irrespective of their nature of activities. Therefore, KPIs are organization specific and every organization needs to develop the same. Some of the areas that need consideration while developing the KPIs are as follows:

- Nature of business.
- Organization development direction for business.
- Organizations' structure.
- Features of organizational interfaces with the internal and external environment.
- Expectations of the organizations from the implementation of balanced scorecard, etc.

Cause and Effect Relation Between KPIs: While developing KPIs it is important to first establish the cause and effect relationship between KPIs and performance. Such relationships could be either clear or unclear. Clear cause–effect relationships are those which are computable, and which facilitate the organization to calculate the KPIs' values. Unclear (hidden) indicators present cause–effect relationships between KPIs, which belong to different categories or subcategories. While building the conceptual KPI map, it is important to limit the same to a manageable number of 15–20 numbers, for a specific management level. For employees down the managerial level, however, it must be even less. Unnecessary and more KPIs can muddle the purpose by providing conflicting information. Hence organizations need to be extra careful while framing KPIs.

Also cause–effect relationship between KPIs needs to be considered, as it forms the structure of the systems, and so also helps in balancing the scorecards. Determination of such relationships can be performed using the following steps:

- Evidence of logical interrelation between indicators.
- Evidence of functional relations between indicators and the possibility of its attribution to mathematical formulas.
- Evidence of attributing correlation between the indicators in terms of correlation coefficient.

Finally, creation and formation of KPIs map requires balancing of scorecards. This is done based on relatively stable relationship between the KPI values and strategic intents of the organization. Although KPIs need to be revisited on continuous basis to understand its efficacy, relatively stable relationship between the strategy and KPIs value is important, or else organizations may not be in a position to correctly gauge its activity dynamics.

After the KPIs are finalized based on the above procedures, the next course of action is cascading the KPIs, i.e., the process of distribution of authorities and responsibilities for indicators down the level, among the managers, and other members of the organizations, who pursue the organizational goals and objectives.

The cause and effect relationship between indicators cannot always be presented by any mathematical formulas. For example, achievement of desired performance value in the research and development function (part of learning and development perspective) of any organization may not be directly attributable to impurity segregation process of an iron foundry (part of internal process). However, it certainly creates the strategic bases to achieve the results in improving the internal process. Before using the molten iron in casting, impurities need to be segregated to ensure quality. Such segregation is done by dropping the molten iron either manually or using the remote controlled machines. In the process of dropping, impure properties get segregated.

Classification of Indicators for Management According to Their Importance: While developing the model of KPI, organizations need to consider the types of KPIs depending on its degree of importance. KPIs can be either strategic or standard.

Strategic KPIs are linked directly with the organizational strategy. Achievement of target values of such KPIs cause significant changes in the organization as a whole. Achieving such KPIs involve a complex set of activities, and managers need to take the required initiatives and systematically monitor across different hierarchical levels to achieve the intended target values. Organizations by achieving the target values of strategic KPIs can substantially gain competitive advantages.

On the other hand standard type of KPIs is linked neither to strategic nor to operational management. These are in-built with the performance management systems, and achievement of its target values helps us to measure the present state of business in the organization. For example, 'exceeds expectation' level of customer satisfaction cannot be a target value, but its achievement certainly strengthens the achievement of results from customer perspectives.

However, it is important to understand that choosing standard or strategic indicators depend on respective organizational strategies. Therefore, what is strategic for one organization may be standard for another.

Implementation of KPIs: After developing the KPIs, it is necessary to implement the same dividing it to two types of indicators: indicative and imperative. The indicative KPIs correlate with the purposes and processes, viz., 'number of customer awareness programmes conducted in a week', etc. Indicative indicators can either be leading or lagging. Imperative (control) indicators are those which are created by the top management, and cascaded to different hierarchical levels, and its value matches with quantity or the targets fixed for each perspective of balanced scorecard. Aggregating the results obtained from different categories and sub-categories, organizations ultimately measure the extent of achievement of their business goals. Imperative indicators are lagging in nature, as it requires control from the top management to get results from down the line.

Performance Measures Through Productivity Metrics

Periodic monitoring and analysis of employees' performance can also be done through productivity metrics. Most commonly used measurement tools for employee productivity or performance are various productivity metrics. Before making use of such metrics, it is important to understand the purpose, method, and the desired outcome of any process that the organizations intend to implement. We need to get answers to the basic questions like why we want to measure? What could be our courses of action after measurement? What goals and objectives we have set for the organization? Answers to these questions can ultimately lead us to the solution of effective employee performance measurement through appropriate productivity indices. Goals and objectives of the organization are vision and mission aligned and concretized through identification of critical success factors (CSFs).

Successful identification of productivity metrics precedes understanding of contributing elements to productivity. Such elements not only ensure peripheral information, but also shape the scientific basis for performance measurement. After complete understanding of the productivity metrics, it is important to list those as under:

- Name of the metric.
- Metric description.
- Measurement procedure.
- Measurement frequency.
- Thresholds estimation.
- Current thresholds.
- Target value and units.

The first two elements identify what the organizations need to measure. Measurement procedure and frequency helps us to understand how the metric is to be measured and in what frequency such measurement has to be done. Thresholds estimation helps us to understand the process of calculating the thresholds, while the current thresholds clarify the current value range for the metrics that we consider essential. Finally, the target value is what we assign to the employees to achieve. Table 13.2 illustrates the process of developing the productivity metrics.

After successful identification of the key elements of any metric, best possible metrics are selected to track the rate of employees' productivity. To select the right productivity metric, it is important to identify at the outset the goals and objectives, and the key factors involved in identification of such goals and objectives. These key factors are the key performance indicators (KPIs). It is necessary for every organization to develop its own set of KPIs to measure productivity. A tentative performance metrics covering some of the critical areas can be illustrated as in Table 13.3.

By plotting the performance results (values) in relation to a median value, we can also get the statistical signal of performance trend. When the performance outputs are in statistical control, we call performance levels are in order. Further performance improvements from this level can only be achieved through systems and process improvement. Baldrige Award Examiners use this approach as a model. As it shows the performance trend data over a period of time, organizations can also benchmark such performance results with their competitors. In Figure 13.3, we are illustrating such much-used performance trend curve.

Therefore, it is evident, organizations can have wide choices in selecting the appropriate tools for performance measures. Which performance measures and why need to be answered by the organizations themselves, keeping in view the broader perspectives of organizational performance goals.

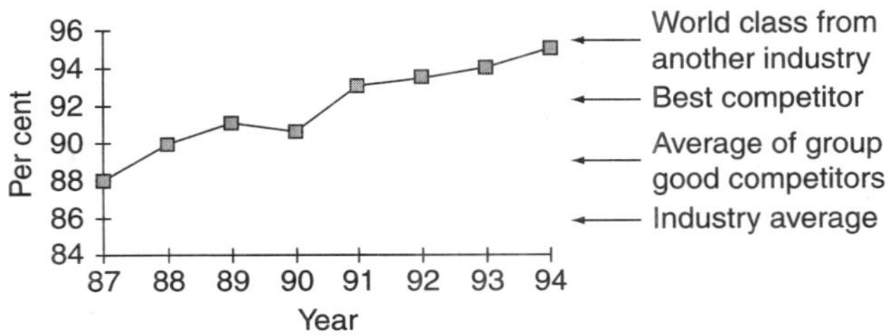

Figure 13.3 *Performance trend curve*

Table 13.2 *Process of developing the productivity metrics*

Name of the Metric	Metric Description	Measurement Procedure	Measurement Frequency	Thresholds Estimation	Current Thresholds	Target Value and Units
Sales performance metric	Contribution to sales growth	Number of sales made per person per day	Daily	Ten units per day	Eight units per day	Two units extra sales
Innovation metric	Contribution to new ideas	Number of new ideas per person per year	Yearly	Three ideas per year	One idea per year	Two ideas per year
Training metric	Contribution to new training design	Number of new training modules developed per month	Monthly	Two new training modules per month	One training module per month	One training module per month
Quality metric	Contribution to reduce unavoidable rate of rejection	Rate of rejection	Monthly	Two per cent reduction in rejection rate per month	Half per cent reduction in rejection rate per month	One-and-half per cent reduction in rejection

Table 13.3 *Tentative performance metrics*

Quality	Customer Satisfaction	Employee Satisfaction	Financial
Rework Discrepancies Mean time between failures Failures per hour/day/week/month Customer returns Customer complaints Mean time to repair Mean time to respond Requirement change rate	Number of complaints Customer returns Customer survey Referrals	Participation rates in company sponsored events Employee turnover rates Employee exit interviews or surveys Number of employee suggestions Productivity metrics Incidents of violence Revenue (or sales) per employee	ROI CPI SPI RONA ETC/EAC

SUMMARY

Performance measurement is the process of assigning numbers to various identified performance elements and key performance indicators (KPIs). Therefore, successful management of performance depends on a well-designed performance measurement system, which links organizational strategy and the behaviour of the employees. As the employees' performance relate to the performance of the processes, for developing effective performance measurement systems, it is necessary to understand the various process of the organizations. Processes are the sequence of cross-functional activities performed by people and machines, which combine valuable resources to convert inputs into outputs. Processes provide the link between organizational level goals and the work performed by employees. Measurement of processes depends on various aspects and attributes, which ultimately become the performance elements or the key performance indicators (KPIs). Developing KPIs need to be direct, and require both the enumerative and analytical studies. In this chapter we have discussed about various types of performance measurement methods, focusing on the inputs, outputs, and the outcomes. Depending on the specific organizational requirements, performance measurement can be qualitative or quantitative, may be based on observations or subjective, and may depend on the methods of collection of information. The chapter outlines all the important methods, leaving the choice before the organization to select the appropriate one, keeping pace with their specific requirements.

KEY WORDS

Production Counts—Production counts measure what a worker produces on the job. The worker with a higher production count is assumed to be a better worker. However, for many jobs, it may not be feasible to measure performance in terms of production counts. This is more applicable for managerial jobs. This apart, there is some possible dangers in production count method. It might change the behaviour of the worker. They may get pre-disposed to achieve higher results at the cost of job related stress, which in turn may be detrimental to decrease overall job performance.

Integrated Performance Measurement Systems—The process of combining different attributes of the organization within a hierarchical structure is called an integrated performance measurement framework (PMF). PMF establishes direct link between the top-level measures (such as shareholder value added (SVA) and the action plans of the entire organization. These collectively add up to the achievement of the established goals.

Control Charts—The control chart is a tool for on-line process control, widely used for the detection of assignable causes of variation. It is a graphical display of a sample quality measure versus sample number (or time). The chart shows a centre line that represents the average value of the quality characteristic corresponding to the in-control state. Two other parallel horizontal lines, called the upper control limit (UCL) and the lower control limit (LCL) are also shown on the chart.

Behaviourally Anchored Rating Scales—Behaviourally anchored rating scales (BARS) are 'descriptions provided on appraisal forms and surveys which describe a precise level of performance'. These are designed to reduce the rating errors of conventional scales. The scale includes number of performance dimensions like leadership, teamwork, communication, initiative, adaptability, etc. BARS were developed with the hope of improving rater accuracy by providing job-related behavioural anchors and altering the format of rating scales.

GENERAL REVIEW QUESTIONS

1. Explain various concepts of performance measurements.
2. Discuss how the performance measurement criteria are selected in an organization?
3. Define integrated performance measurement systems.
4. Explain the role of control charts in measuring performance.
5. What are the different scales used for performance measurement? Which scale you consider appropriate for measuring the performance quality of a operation manager?
6. Explain the concept of performance matrix. Also explain how the Baldrige model of excellence can be used in performance measurement of an organization?
7. Explain the difference between specific and general performance measures in an organization.
8. Define key performance indicators. How key performance indicators are developed? In what way key performance indicators become good performance measures for an organization?
9. Explain the concept of performance measurement through productivity indices.
10. Short Notes
    (a) Work Samples Methods
    (b) Control Charts
    (c) Process Capability
    (d) Response Scales

CRITICAL REVIEW QUESTION

11. Develop some important KPIs for software developers. Also indicate tentative measurement criteria for such KPIs. Present your information in a tabular form.

FURTHER READING

Bhattacharyya, D.K. (1995a), 'Corporate Body Builder—The Emerging Role of HRD Professional: A Prescriptive Model for Success', *Indian Journal for Training and Development*, (April–June).

Bhattacharyya, D.K. (1995b), 'Manpower Obsolescence—A study in Indian Ordnance Factories', (International Congress on Economic Transition with Human Face; Indian Industrial Relations Association, New Delhi, 3–6 September).

Bhattacharyya, D.K. (2000) 'Competency Mapping and Manpower Redundancy—Macro Level Study of Indian Organizations', *Management and Accounting Research*, (October–December) 4(2): 97–105.

Bhattacharyya, D.K. (2007), *Human Resource Research Methods* (New Delhi: Oxford University Press).

Bhattacharyya, D.K. (2010), *Industrial Management* (New Delhi: Vikas Publishing).

Brewster, C. and H. Scullion (1997), 'A Review and Agenda for Expatriate HRM', *Human Resource Management Journal*, (7)3: 32–41.

Brown, G. (1985) 'The Discovery of Expressed Emotion: Induction or Deduction?' in J. Leff and C. Vaughn (eds), *Expressed Emotion in Families* (New York, NY: Guilford Press), pp. 7–25.

Charles, Handy N. (1993), *Understanding Organizations*, 4th edition (New York, NY: Penguin).

Christiansen, James A. (2000), *Competitive Innovation Management* (London: Macmillan Business).

Dunning, J. (1998 [1958]), *American Investment in British Manufacturing*, revised and updated edition (London and New York, NY: Routledge).

Edwards, M.R., C.W. Borman and R.J. Sparoul (1985), 'Solving the Double-Bind in Performance Appraisal: A Saga of Sloths and Eagles', *Business Horizon*, 85: 59–68.

Gordon, Edward E. (2000), *Skill Wars, Winning the Battle for Productivity and Profit* (Boston, MA: Butterworth-Heinemann).

Gilbert, T.F. (1978), *Human Competence: Engineering Worthy Performance* (New York, NY: McGraw-Hill).

Hamel, G. and C.K. Prahalad (1990), 'The Core Competence of the Corporation', *Harvard Business Review*, (May-June) 68(8).

Jonne, Cesrani and Peter Greatwood (2001), *Innovation and Creativity* (New Delhi: Crest Publishing House).

Latham G.P. and K.N. Wexley (1981), *Increasing Productivity through Performance Appraisal* (Reading, MA: Addison-Wesley).

Nonka, Ikujoro and Hikjiro Takeuchi (1995), *The Knowledge Creating Company,* (New York, NY: Oxford University Press).

Paul, E. Plsek (1997), *Creativity, Innovation and Quality* (New York, NY: Quality Press).

Peterson R., N. Napier and W.S. Shim (1996), 'Expatriate Management: The Difference Role of National Multinational Corporation Ownership', *International Executive*, 38: 543–62.

Pollack, D.M. and L.J. Pollack (1996), 'Theory-Based Applications and Directions for Research', *Personnel Psychology*, 48: 803–39.

Rosenzweig, P.M. and N. Nohria (1994), 'Influences on Human Resource Management Practices in Multinational Corporations', *Journal of International Business Studies*, 25(2): 229–51.

Schmidt, F.L., J.E. Hunter, R.C. McKenzit and T.W. Muldrow (1979), 'Impact of Valid Selection Procedures on Work-Force Productivity', *Journal of Applied Psychology*, 64: 609–26.

Schmidt, F.L., J.E. Hunter and K. Pearlman (1982), 'Assessing the Economic Impact of Personnel Programs on Workforce Productivity, *Personnel Psychology*, 35(2): 333–48.

Shewhart, Walter A. (1931), *Economic Control of Quality of Manufactured Product* (New York, NY: D. Van Nostrand Company).

Stolovitch, H.D and J.G. Maurice (1998), 'Calculating the Return on Investment in Training: A Critical Analysis and Case Study', *Performance Improvement*, 37(8): 9–20.

Tahvanainen, M. (2000), 'Expatriate Performance Management: The Case of Nokia Telecommunications', *Human Resource Management*, (37)4: 267–75.

Trompenaars, F. and C. Hamden-Turner (1995), *Riding the Waves of Culture*, (New York, NY: McGraw-Hill).

Wright, P. (1994), 'Quality or Usability? Quality Writing Provokes Quality Reading', in M. Steehouder, C. Jansen, P. van der Poort and R. Verheijen (eds), *Quality of Technical Documentation* (Amsterdam: Editions Rodopi), pp. 7–38.

CASE STUDY

AutoMart Achieves Excellence Through Well-designed KPIs

Customer service, excellence in operations, and profitability are three core business objectives of Pune based automobile spares manufactures in India. With successive cross-country acquisition, the company is now in the forefront of global automobile spares market in the world. Name a car and you will find AutoMart's spares fitted with it. The company has now built its capacity for manufacturing spares of premium ranges of car, including its customized editions. Building capacity for customized cars cannot just be possible without the sincere efforts of ingenious engineers and technicians, not to talk about the level of technology requirements. With its global success, the company is now prepared to emerge as a global leader in automobile spares manufacturing. This requires the company to withstand the competition from German and US manufacturers, both in terms of price and quality. With strong focus on quality, the company is now close to six-sigma compliance. A strong culture of innovation and creativity literally makes it possible for the company to come out with new cost-effective designs. Using AutoMart's spares, automobile manufactures are able to reduce their cost of production significantly. Every new design attracts their attention, and they welcome the company for fitment trials on their vehicles. Such pace of activities gave the company the opportunity to get global recognition.

The company now realizes that their employees are their renewable and sustainable assets in a globally competitive market place, and the prime drivers for the company's success in customer service, operations, and profitability. To ensure employee retention, the company used the balanced scorecard and other human resource tools to affect significant and measurable increase in employee loyalty and satisfaction rates.

The company developed a set of metrics for all the perspectives, and for their obvious 'employees first' philosophy focused on improving the retention, satisfaction, and advancement rates among workers, to get their loyalty and performance excellence. To measure the areas of improvements in employee retention and satisfaction, financial growth, organizational efficiency and customer relationships, the company developed the KPIs aligning with all the four perspectives of the balanced score card. Goals were developed for each perspective, along with a series of measurements to help them determine how close they are to achieving each goal. Because employee engagement was considered to be the basis upon which excellence in each perspective was built, the learning innovation and growth perspective was prioritized, with a host of new tools created to engage employees and measure improvements in the workforce. These new measurement and engagement tools included:

- **Employee survey**—This survey lists series of employee benefits, and employees are required to first short-list these and prioritize. Management on studying the survey results, identify the commonalities, and based on the score values introduce those in the employees' benefits packages.

- **Birthday greetings and interview**—This is done by the respective supervisors, when they enquire employees' employment satisfaction levels, and accordingly make good the gaps, if any on the support services.
- **Leadership survey**—This survey gives opportunity to the employees to spell out the respect and support they receive from their supervisors.
- **Training and certification programme**—This encourages employees to renew, improve, and acquire new skill-sets, and in the process they make them capable to avail the career development opportunities.
- **Performance review meeting**—This ensures a thorough and holistic performance review, individual counseling, setting of future goals, enriching the personal and professional lives of the employees.

The balanced scorecard with suitable KPIs, focusing on people issues and more so on customer satisfaction, could help the company to measure the effectiveness, and to take stock of the situation to perpetuate their pursuit of customer service, excellence in operations, and profitability. In this process also the company exceeded their human resource goals, like high satisfaction, excellent performance, and increased level of retention.

Within three years of implementing a balanced scorecard with solid KPIs, AutoMart could achieve excellence in human resource goals.

CHAPTER 14

International Performance Management

Learning Objectives

After reading this chapter, you will be able to understand:

- Concepts and definitions of international performance management
- Structure and strategy of international performance management
- Expatriates' performance management
- Effect of culture
- Influences on performance appraisal
- Performance management in international assignment
- Globalization and international performance management practices
- Compensation and international performance management practices
- Appraising performance
- Managerial practices in China, Korea, and Japan

Cultural Congruent International PMSs

For business imperative an Indian paints major needs to establish its factories in eleven countries. For paints industry, market proximity is very important as paints shipment from far off manufacturing locations is not at all cost effective and even the quality of paints deteriorates. Even during the process of shipment companies suffer huge losses due to evaporation and normal wastage. The company is a pioneer in premium quality paints manufacturing and is the leader in India in this market segment. For the mass (low price) variety, however, it is in second position.

The company follows the traditional hybrid structure, which ensures the functional autonomy at each factory location, keeping administrative issues however within the domain of Mumbai-based *headquarters*. The human resource (HR) director of the company sits in Mumbai head office and enforces control in each unit of the group, located in eleven different countries. The performance management system (PMS) of the company is scorecard based. For every employee the company has developed key performance indicators (KPIs). The production system being highly automated, performance tracking with the use of KPIs can be done in quantitative terms. Employees with low performance scores are taken through the performance counselling session with their immediate supervisors and divisional heads.

> The company insists on achieving the performance goals and even arranges training for those who lag in performance results. In line with the global best practices in performance measurement systems of General Electric (GE) and Nestle Waters (NW), the company introduced integrated PMS organization wide. The idea behind was to follow the same approach in all business entities. The result, however, was not encouraging; rather it witnessed resistance in some of the countries from employees who took it as a threat to their jobs. Such apprehensions of the employees are tenable due to the obvious organizational practices prevalent in those countries, where a non-performer is shown the exit door in no time. To solve this problem, the company then started a culture congruent performance measurement system, which required the employees to come forward to explain his/her performance results, leaving to the management responsibilities limited to recording and taking corrective actions to remove performance blocks. When the employees continued to under perform even after removing the blocks, the company resorted to firing. The entire process was documented and communicated to the employees. The process worked well. Reducing the role of the manager to a listener in performance measurement process is a typical psychological syndrome of employees of Brazil, Mexico, and Portugal units of the company.

INTRODUCTION

Before the emergence of global competitiveness in business, demand used to exceed supply. Obviously in such a situation, management attention was more on efficient production processes and efficient resource utilization to achieve internal efficiency. During that era the financial control based PMSs were the prime focus. Organizational efficiency used to be defined in terms of objective financial results. Financial control based management system at General Motors in the industrialized economies (beginning in the 1970s), used to focus more and more on quality, differentiation, and customer satisfaction rather than only on cost/financial efficiency. The ability to create a positive effect for customers from their subjective perspective—and increasingly for other stakeholder groups that today have power over the 'license to operate' of an organization—became the critical success and survival factor for any business or non-profit organization (Daum, 2002). Efficiency, per se, cannot improve organizational performance. What is important is the effectiveness from the stakeholders' perspectives. Efficient performance emphasizes too much on quantitative performance details, that is, financial outcomes. In this process, it ignores the interests of the stakeholder. For this reason, performance management also needs to consider subjective evaluations, using different measurement scales, and to understand how it influences the interests of all stakeholders. For example, in the process of achieving high return on investment (ROI), organizations may meet the needs of the investors, but unless customers' interests are taken care of, they cannot sustain it in the long run. Performance improvement that leads to satisfaction of all parties—stakeholders, investors, and customers—can be achieved only when subjective as well quantitative measures are taken into account.

Others have very little knowledge about the performance appraisal system used by host country managers. These latter are usually isolated from their reporting bosses, and for obvious reasons experience difficulties in the conduct of the performance appraisal. Traditionally, performance appraisal process was influenced by bottom line results. However, international performance appraisal emphasizes on improving the bottom line results along with employee-supervisor relationships, giving due cognizance to the multinational's parent strategy, structure, and nationality. Managers of the host country often experience difficulties in performance appraisals for obvious lack of opportunities for career development and advancement in the organization. Such lack of opportunities naturally exerts influence in managing performance of the subsidiary. For this reason international PMSs emphasize on some modifications, to motivate the employees of the subsidiary to deliver better performance.

Apart from this, international PMSs also need to emphasize on managing the performance of expatriates. In such cases, performance dimensions need not be always job-related. PMSs extend to cross-cultural issues, responsiveness to the norms, laws, and customs, etc. Often the degree of adaptability to uncertainty and unpredictable conditions is construed as important determinant of performance. However, the degree varies with respect to the job profile of expatriates.

In a globalized business environment, multinational companies literally dominate the global competition, spreading their business across the world through their subsidiaries. For this reason, managers of the host country (HCMs) feel more responsible for employee performance along with their responsibility to strategically implement critical tasks. It is through these HCMs that multinational corporations (*MNC*s) exert control over their subsidiaries through the process of central integration (Chang and Taylor 1999). Through effective international performance management practices, an MNC continuously evaluates and improves individuals, subsidiary units and corporate performance against clearly defined preset objectives that are directly linked to the company strategy (Dowling, Welch, and Schuler 1999). Thus, effective international PMS ensures that the HCM and their overseas subsidiaries are acting in accordance with the parent MNC's interests. Any mismanagement of international PMS, primarily due to information asymmetry and goal incongruence between the parent company and its subsidiaries (Shen, 2005), leads to poor performance.

DEFINITIONS AND CONCEPTS

Dowling, et al (1999) observed that very little research was conducted on international PMSs. For this reason, it is difficult to understand the contributing factors underlying job satisfaction of employees of MNC subsidiaries. Major problems in international performance management are lack of understanding the criteria of performance measurement and identification of satisfactory and effective appraisal system. To a great extent international performance management depends on MNCs' nature of requirements. However, it is obvious that MNCs measure attributes and behavioural parameters of international employees more than those of parent country employees. Even though it is often criticized, it is also important for us to remember that performance dimensions of international employees in MNCs extend beyond the bottom line results. Some of the interesting findings of international performance management research suggest that qualitative criteria like the employees' attitude, adaptability and acceptance are more important. Also the effectiveness of international performance management depends on the degree of ratee (subordinate) satisfaction which largely depends on regular communication and positive relationship with the rater (supervisor). Such satisfaction may be achieved when the PMS ensures that both the subordinate and the supervisor clearly understand the purpose of the performance evaluation. In other words, not only should the subordinate's and supervisor's expectations be aligned, but also both need to be in congruence with the MNC's rationale for conducting the performance evaluation (Milliman et al., 1998; Shen, 2005).

Another important aspect of international performance systems is the feedback to employees. Employees of the subsidiaries often feel that they are unable to deliver results to their best performance level due to lack of opportunities to discuss their career goals, personal needs, views, and feelings. This occurs due to lack of performance feedback from their supervisors. Performance feedback, therefore, plays a vital role in the success of international management. It is seen as one of the important ways in which an MNC can extensively use and develop the talent of its diverse employees, as well provide a sense of direction (Milliman et al., 1998,). Interestingly, the reluctance to give feedback does not appear to lessen as managers become more experienced and work internationally. For example, Longenecker and Gioia (1992) illustrate this point by advancing the idea that the more a manager is promoted, the less likely will he/she provide quality feedback. When people receive feedback frequently, they perceive it to be more precise and timely (Milliman et al., 1998). Where a subordinate and supervisor are geographically distant, regular feedback has been found to be imperative (Cascio 2000, Milliman, et al. 1998). However, due to practical and logistical reasons, frequent, timely, and accurate feedback, particularly face to face feedback, may be challenging for the supervisor of the HCM. For instance, the HCM's supervisor in general looks after a large geographical territory (Harvey 1997), which usually demands extensive travelling for the supervisor.

STRUCTURE AND STRATEGY OF INTERNATIONAL PERFORMANCE MANAGEMENT

International performance management practices are influenced by the parent organization's HR strategy and structure (Ghoshal and Bartlett 1998). Parent organizations pursue the process of internationalization following certain stages. At the initial stage the subsidiaries are considered as extensions, specialized centres, or hubs for cost-effective manufacturing. Therefore, at this first stage, the same human resource management (HRM) policies and strategies continue to be followed (Ghoshal and Bartlett 1993). They tend to be centralized and inflexible. In the second stage, subsidiaries being considered as centres with specialized capabilities (like Germany's pharmaceutical companies' research and development centres in India), MNCs differentiate their HRM strategy and policies, making them subsidiary specific (Harvey et al., 2002). Finally when subsidiaries are considered as independent business entities, MNCs give more autonomy for HRM strategy and policies. Subsidiaries in such cases enjoy more autonomy and get full cooperation from the MNCs to run as independent business entities. The last case is more applicable for Hindustan Unilever and IBM. To accommodate such variations in HRM strategy and structure, performance management practices too vary.

Depending on the nature of internationalization, MNCs vary the pattern of structure and staff in subsidiaries. Here again we observe four different approaches in staffing and structure. MNCs that pursue ethnocentric approach do not give any autonomy to subsidiaries. In such subsidiaries (Mitsubishi Chemicals in India), MNCs man the key positions from expatriates from their own country. MNCs that pursue polycentric approach consider subsidiaries as separate business entities and accordingly give them decisional autonomy. Such subsidiaries can recruit the people on their own to form host country management (HCM) team, but MNCs never allow such persons to get elevated to the headquarters. With a geocentric approach, MNCs consider the subsidiaries as potential value adding centres, and recruit staff from the global pool of talent. With a region-centric approach, subsidiaries can enjoy region-specific autonomy in recruiting staff for managerial positions. Such differences in approach again greatly influence performance management practices.

Perceptions on structure and strategy issues of MNCs again vary widely. Birkinshaw and Hood (1998) observed that MNCs and transnational corporates frequently change their approach over time. From this perspective, the prevalent performance management practices in the MNCs also vary. Research work suggested that it is necessary for MNCs to understand the process of subsidiary evolution in order to better manage PMSs across their subsidiaries.

EXPATRIATES' PERFORMANCE MANAGEMENT

Expatriates are mostly poorly managed (Dowling et al., 1999; Tung, 1998); so also the expatriates' performance management, particularly in goal setting, training, feedback and development, and motivation

(Mabey and Salaman, 1995). Most of the studies on expatriates' performance management either focus on single organization or the culture of a single country. For example a number of studies have been conducted on Nokia's stand-alone performance management practices in a particular country. However, expatriates' performance management in the context of cultural variables is largely ignored by the researchers.

Therefore, it may be presumed that the performance management process becomes more complex in expatriate assignments. Performance management characteristics significantly change across national and cultural boundaries. Scholars like Black et al. (1999) and Caligiuri and Day (2000) observed that headquarters-based performance management practices in expatriate assignments often lead to incorrect and even misleading information. On the contrary, when in expatriate assignments local managers are involved in performance goal setting, its degree of acceptability become much higher. In expatriate performance management it is also important to provide feedback and train the managers to conduct the process. Training before the expatriates' assignment significantly minimizes the cultural shock and reduces problems. For example wide congruity in Indian and German managers' performance management practices could establish hardly any differences in expatriates. In both the cases, performance management is not only used as a tool to identify employee strengths and weaknesses but also as an important vehicle for employee development.

Another common area where performance management is used is compensation design. In India, though, it is apparently used more as an instrument to plan development activities. In this context, it is interesting to note that performance management use may differ from country to country. For example, while German managers use performance criteria for compensation decision, Indian managers use it primarily to assess employee promotion and development. Such perceptive differences basically lie in the respective countries' management practices, more specifically attributable to parent organization's culture.

EFFECT OF CULTURE

International performance management practices also vary with respect to the culture (Milliman, et al. 1998). For example when the subsidiary of an MNC is located in a country that pursues individualistic culture (Hofstede, 1980), the performance evaluation process pays adequate attention to employees' feelings. With cultural distance, subsidiaries therefore enjoy higher autonomy and benefit from the differentiated culture congruent performance management practices.

Again the performance management practices vary with respect to the MNC's country of origin. The reason is attributed to the specific HRM practices prevalent in the parent country (Hofstede, 1980; Ghoshal and Bartlett, 1993; Schuler et al., 1993; Harvey et al., 2000; Harzing, 2001; McGraw, 2002; Shen 2005). McGraw's study (2002) could observe variations between the HRM practices of USA and European countries. US-based multinationals are more likely to impose their HRM practices, while the European firms are not. Again there is a variation between Germany and other European countries. German MNCs emphasize on the traditional authority structure and value technical expertise, while France-based MNCs value employees' political and technical skills. The most elaborate study (200 MNCs in 23 different countries) on international HR practices was conducted by Harzing (2001). The study could identify variations in HR practices of MNCs headquartered in different European countries.

The aforementioned documented research applies to international HRM practices as well; based on the cultural differences of various countries international performance management practices also vary widely. Although for business imperatives, MNCs may try to enforce control, geographical dispersion and cultural incongruence often require MNCs to compromise with host countries' managerial abilities to conduct the performance evaluation process.

Influences on Performance Appraisals

The nature of MNCs' influence on HCMs varies in three respects. These influences naturally vary the performance management practices of MNC subsidiaries. The three are: MNCs' typical focus on the bottom line, employee relationship, and the nature of control. However, the bottom line effect is more important than other influences. This is why most of the MNCs in China focus more on enjoying the cost competitiveness, making effective use of the Chinese labour laws, which are yet far below International Labour Organization's (ILO) mandated standards.

PERFORMANCE MANAGEMENT IN INTERNATIONAL ASSIGNMENT

Variation in international performance management practices can also be related to the job context. The job context changes with respect to task, organization, culture, and development dimensions. However, in all international assignments, change in the job contexts may not be the same. When TCS deputes its software project managers on international assignments, it emphasizes more on cultural and developmental dimensions. But Nike in Thailand focuses more on tasks and organizational contexts. In the first case long-term sustainability is important, while in the second cost efficiency to improve the bottom line is more important.

Let us now review the different performance dimensions in international assignments. In most international assignments, technical performance receives the first priority. Technical performance is measured with respect to the specific assigned tasks given to the assignees. Here the performance measurement is specific to the task achievement. The assumption here is that the outcome of performance should be the same as has been mandated, irrespective of the cultural differences of the country where the assignees are asked to execute the task. Japan and China both emphasize more on this dimension of performance in international assignments.

Organizational performance, on the other hand, emphasizes on the broader aspects, that is, conformance to the safety norms, ethics, integrity, etc., in conformity with the organizational practices. Here the emphasis is more on leaving a positive impact rather than mere profitability.

Intercultural dimension of international performance assignment emphasizes on intercultural communication. In many cases, MNCs are required to form cross-country teams for new product launches, research and development activities, etc. Here intercultural dimension is more important as its effectiveness ultimately helps MNCs to realize their strategic intents.

Developmental dimension of international performance assignment focuses on knowledge acquisition, and understanding of the language and culture, so that assignees can be developed as global managers. For example, negotiating with the Chinese and Japanese would be seemingly difficult, unless the assignees acquire knowledge through real life cases. This dimension of performance literally helps the assignees to develop their competencies through international assignments.

It is very important to understand these performance dimensions as changes in the dimensions lead to changes in international PMSs and assignments.

GLOBALIZATION AND INTERNATIONAL PERFORMANCE MANAGEMENT

Globalization has brought about many changes in the landscape of business and non-business organizations across the world. Arguments are still persistent about the positive and negative effects of such changes. One such effect is the economic slowdown that has severely affected manufacturing and services. Higher education is no exception. The management of educational institutions today demand cost optimization and rigorous checks on the performance of every system and process. The use of standard models of PMS in such institutions is sparse, creating the need for a common platform which would provide an opportunity for management representatives to come together, ponder over, and prepare customized models for their respective institutions.

With globalization, MNCs focus more on collaboration and coordination among the HCMs located in different countries. The pre-cursor to collaboration and coordination is the formation of global work teams. Success of globalization is highly dependent on the success of teamwork. Teamwork among the HCMs in fact complicates the performance management process. This is because HCMs widely vary in their viewpoints on HR practices, encompassing areas like compensation plans, training, employee development, etc. Hewlett-Packard (HP) for example could successfully create a corporate culture to bind their HCMs and other employees across several countries. The basis of this conscious corporate culture of HP rests on three core philosophies, that is, respect for others, community feeling, and simple hard work (Fortune Magazine, May 15, 1995). HP is able to sustain conscious corporate culture through extensive training of all cross-sections of employees. The company's lesson in binding the corporate culture despite their globalization plans is unique.

Another illustration of corporate culture is Southwest Airlines. It is one of the most profit making airlines in the USA Southwest's CEO, Herb Kelleher, defines the airline culture in the following words:

> Well, first of all, it starts with hiring... If you start with the type of person you want to hire, presumably you can build a work force that is prepared for the culture you desire. Another important thing is to spend a lot of time with your people and to communicate with them in a variety of ways. …the way you appear and the way you act—is a form of communication. We want our people to feel fulfilled and to be happy, and we want our management to radiate …that we are proud of our people, we are interested in them as individuals and we are interested in them outside the work force, including the good and bad things that happen to them as individuals.

Likewise there is also the case of Dresden (East Germany) based Advanced Micro Devices (AMD). AMD is the configuration of three cultures, that is, American, West and East German. These countries are culturally apart. To create the conscious corporate culture AMD blended together the go-getter American, analytic West German, and innovative East German cultures. Such cultural convergence could help AMD to achieve global success. The specific strategy followed by AMD was to make the employees believe that no one should take defences, rather focus on mutual learning, keeping aside the ethic issues. Lessons of AMD have developed the Dilemma Theory (Trompenaars, F., Hampden-Turner, C., 1998), which is also known as THT Theory. The basic premise of this theory is that insidious culture clashes and changes our habit strengths. Such cultural clashes help to reach a consensus.

Another example of global congruence of corporate culture is the case of Sears. Sears globally pursues a 3 C philosophy, that is, the compelling place to work, compelling place to shop, and compelling place to invest. In the process of pursuing this 3 C philosophy, Sears achieves growth and stability, which among others also require Sears to follow uniform PMSs in alignment with 3 Cs. Likewise Wal-Mart and McDonald also could achieve culture congruence for their specific corporate practices.

Wal-Mart believes in total empowerment of their employees (they call them associates), even to the extent of sharing strategic information. McDonald with their uniformity in quality and service also could achieve the consensus culture.

All these international examples, illustrate how successfully managing the culture of an organization, it is possible to become effective in international operations, and in international performance management.

Indian conglomerate like Aditya Birla Group could also metamorphoses itself into multi-cultural transnational with more than 72,000 people spread over 20 different countries.

They also illustrate how a conscious culture in the work place can contribute to the growth and prosperity of a global organization. PMSs of all these organizations being culturally congruent; they hardly encounter any problems in their globally dispersed units.

To illustrate further we site the example of Jack Welch, CEO, GE, who created a new corporate culture to meet the business objectives. Key elements of GE's corporate culture are as follows:

- Re-designing the role of the leader in the new economy, creating followers through communicating a vision, and establishing open, caring relations with every employee.
- Creating an open, collaborative workplace where everyone's opinion is welcome.
- Empowering senior executives to run far-flung businesses in entrepreneurial fashion.
- Liberating the workforce; making everybody a participant through improving vertical communication and employee empowerment.

COMPENSATION AND INTERNATIONAL PERFORMANCE MANAGEMENT PRACTICES

Multinational organizations' compensation management practices vis-à-vis their relation with the performance management are one of the key issues in international performance management practices. While it is a common trend for every organization to align their performance management practices with compensation plans, such practices vary from organization to organization. This variation is mostly attributable to the organization-specific strategic focus on HRM practices, more specifically on the corporate culture. Compensation design in alignment with the performance management practices is primarily viewed by the MNCs, as their important vehicle for deriving international competitive advantages (Rosenzweig and Nohria, 1994).

Nationality of ownership has been seen as a major factor influencing the kind of pay and performance (P&P) policies that MNCs adopt. American companies, for example, have long been regarded as HR 'innovators' in such aspects of P&P as productivity related pay bargaining, individual performance appraisal, performance-related pay, and employee share ownership (e.g. Dunning, 1998). National influences stem from the characteristics of the parent-country business system; the USA, for instance, has had a long history of pay innovation. This can be traced to the attempts of organizations to deter unionization by providing innovative terms and conditions to employees, and by linking pay to individual performance. In Japan, by contrast, large firms have typically linked pay to seniority. In Germany, sectoral pay bargaining and company-level employee representation through work councils has traditionally limited the scope for individually-focused forms of pay and appraisal systems. In recent years forms of performance-related pay have become more widespread in German firms. Due to the absence of statutory regulation on compensation systems, and taking advantage of equal opportunities and minimum wage legislation, foreign subsidiaries in the UK have the choice to reflect parent-country practices or to adapt to local (or other) norms. Most of the UK organizations experiment with the compensation systems, and are not averse to embrace even the practices of low-compensation cost countries for their migrant workers.

In UK too, except for foreign subsidiaries, organizational size, sectoral dimension, adherence to the principles of payment by results, and group-based performance-related pay are major influencers in compensation management practices in alignment with the PMSs. In general, international structure plays a very crucial role.

New PMS for an International Retailer

Many multinationals today prefer enterprise performance management (EPM) systems for optimizing their global performance. Numerous vendors develop IT enabled EPM systems and automate their PMSs globally. The same was the case of an Indian retail major, which has recently gone for globalized operation. Retailing is a structured job process, and mostly documented in the company's standard operating process (SOP). The company systematically trains its employees on SOP for gaining uniformity in performance results globally. Being automated, performance results of the employees are traceable in specific quantitative terms. Every performance laggard is taken through the rigorous process of counselling and specific action plans for improving performance are suggested. Even after successive counselling some employees continued to underperform despite their presence in the stores, and attention to the customers. To understand the nature of performance problems with more specificity, the company then started video-recording employee actions and dealings with the customers. The selected performance laggards' video clippings were then extensively studied to map their attitude and suggest ways to help them focus on change. Although there was no intention to intrude upon employee privacy, the move was opposed by employees particularly those located in the American and European countries, alleging snooping to intrude privacy. The lesson from this case is that performance systems need to be culturally congruent.

APPRAISING PERFORMANCE

While the expatriate is on assignment, the individual performance must be appraised (Dowling, Welch and Schuler 1999; Tahvanainen 2000). Many comparative research studies on British, German, Japanese, and US multinationals established that expatriate performance appraisal systems are different from the parent countries' systems. Performance appraisal mechanisms varied from quantitative (e.g. graphic scale) to qualitative (e.g. MBO or narrative). Depending on the nature of expatriate assignments, job performance dimensions varied widely. Multinational organizations, with respect to the expatriate assignment, need to evaluate such performance dimensions which need not always be job-related. They may concern issues such as cross-cultural interpersonal qualities, sensitivity to foreign norms, laws, and customs, adaptability to uncertain and unpredictable conditions, and the degree of integration of host country's unit with the multinationals.

However, for short-term assignments, such as special technical projects, performance management approach for the expatriates essentially becomes operational and task focused. Large multinational organizations pursue different strategic missions for the expatriates, within the constraints of different legal conditions and competitive situations. This requires MNCs to keep pace with differing environmental conditions while adopting performance management practices. Designing a suitable performance appraisal format that accommodates situational differences can benefit the MNCs to track, evaluate, and compare the performance of expatriates.

To increase the international competitiveness leveraging human resources, we can draw lessons from the success of Japanese automobile and electronic manufacturers of the 1970s and 1980s. Japanese employers embrace HR practices, which substantially enhance labour productivity and foster innovation at the same time. Large Japanese multinationals like Toyota and Matsushita primarily owe their success to such HR practices. Some of the characteristics of Japanese HRM practices are:

- Emphasis on rigorous selection and recruitment.
- Increased focus on training (both induction and on the job).
- Emphasis on teamwork.
- Continuous skill upgradation and multi-skilling.
- Free flow of communication between the management and workers.
- Motivating employees to participate in small group activities (quality circles).
- Promoting innovation.
- Encouraging employee suggestions.
- Removing hierarchical barriers in sharing common services.

All these HRM practices in Japan created the organizational culture which allowed workers to identify their own success with that of the corporation. This is how organizational culture became instrumental in enhancing employee performance. Achieving organizational excellence through employee performance is now an established observation globally (Peters and Waterman, 1982).

> Human resource functions of Morris India underwent sea change for expansion of its activities in the USA and European countries. It has now become imperative for the company to depute their Indian employees to overseas assignments, and also to transfer US and European employees on short-term basis to Indian units of Morris. While cultural sensitivity in both the cases is most important, the company in its HR practice encountered a major problem in compensation planning and design, particularly in cases of deputations abroad. The Indian employees started complaining that they are facing financial stricture in their foreign assignments, while their counterparts from USA and other European countries, in their India assignments, get doubly benefited due to the difference in currency valuation. Morris then decided that for all foreign assignments, employees will continue to get their home country salaries while getting additional allowances to ensure their standard of living. It means when Indian executives are posted in the USA, the befitting standard of living of the Indian executives in India would be protected. This arrangement ultimately settled the impasse. Thus was changed the Morris compensation policy for overseas assignments.
>
> This is a typical example of resolving international HRM issues.

INTERNATIONAL PERFORMANCE MANAGEMENT PRACTICES

Globally PMSs focus on improvement in internal performance, and to extend support to the management to achieve business goals. Effective performance management also increases organizational responsiveness to change. Australia for example embraced performance management to improve public services. Counties like Canada, Denmark, and Finland use performance management to build organizational capabilities and to bring desired cultural changes. In the USA and several European countries, performance management is more focused on controlling employee performance rather than on employee and capability development. We observe a similar trend in China and Korea. Japan, however, emphasizes on team performance, and lets the team compel members to achieve results. The Japanese perception of people makes them believe that all employees are capable of delivering. In India and Germany, performance is used more as a tool to understand the relative strengths and weaknesses of employees, and their relative abilities in goal achievement. In Germany, the trend is to use performance management for compensation decisions and employee promotion. In all countries, performance management is by and large used as a vehicle for enforcing accountability and control. With clear definition of objectives and performance targets, members of the organization are urged to achieve results; when they fail, they are provided training to develop and deliver. PMS is also widely used for effective salary administration.

Now let us focus on three Asian countries, which have made their vibrant presence felt globally. China has become a member of the World Trade Organization (WTO) in 2001 and since then opened its economy to MNCs. To reap the advantages of the Chinese market and also to gain cost competitiveness, many organizations (including several Indian) have now relocated their manufacturing hubs to China.

After the liberalization move, private sector participation in China has increased. Chinese global majors such as Legend, Haier, China Mobile, etc. are large enough to compete with any multinationals across the globe. Corporatization of Chinese industry has compelled it to embrace professional management practices. PMSs in China, however, are still in a nascent stage. The primary reason for this can be attributed to the Chinese management system, wherein managers work more as employees of the organization rather than as entrepreneurs. Ownership and control are distinctly separated. Chinese organizations treat management practices, including performance management practices, as mere legal compliance tools.

Korea, however, is worth examining. Unlike the Chinese economy, the Korean economy embraced professional management practices after witnessing the economic crisis of the late 1990s. Greater emphasis on promoting positive organizational culture and structural change reinforced HRM practices in Korea. Korean companies emphasize on individual performance measurement rather than on team or collective performance measurement. This is because of the typical Korean social system. But for this exception, Korean organizations follow professional management practices.

Japan is known for its emphasis on social collectivism. After losing their business ground in global markets in the early 1990s, Japan started focusing on strategies and embracing western managerial practices. Haslam et al. (1996) could document stupendous performance in Japanese organizations in the 1970s and 1980s. To keep pace with international competition, Japan has become more innovative in HRM practices. More focus on product reengineering rather than processes alone, unparalleled inventory management systems (which literally leads to zero inventory holding), teamwork, etc., could put Japan back on track in business performance. As in production, Japan follows participative approach in deciding performance goals. A consensual decision-making system makes every stakeholder accountable for achieving results.

SUMMARY

International performance management is a critical business tool for MNCs in translating strategy into results. PMSs, per se, influence critical organizational outcomes, such as financial performance, productivity, product or service quality, customer satisfaction, and employee job satisfaction. All these are equally applicable to international performance management. Additionally, international PMSs need to be flexible enough to accommodate cross-country cultural issues. For this reason, managers are required to be trained in international PMSs. Internationally it is observed that MNCs with effective performance measurement systems can anticipate the future and are likely to lead in the changing business environment. Success of international performance management depends on the degree of agreement on strategy, clarity of communication, focus on alignment of efforts, and finally organizational culture. Strategic alignment is a business imperative, as it ensures realising of objectives. Communication ensures a clear message and provides a common language for all. Alignment of efforts ensures that individual performance matches the performance of business units and that of the organization as a whole. Finally, promoting a strong organizational culture with focus on cooperation and teamwork promotes self-monitoring of individual performance and enhances the employee willingness to take risks. International performance management practices, though following more or less generic performance management practices, may vary widely from country to country and also from organization to organization. Particular HRM strategies of MNCs and their subsidiaries are the major determinants of international PMSs. While it is common for MNCs to adopt a universal approach in managing the performance of cross-country employees, we also have a couple of examples of MNCs who adopt subsidiary-specific PMSs. This chapter discusses the core issues of international performance management.

KEY WORDS

Expatriates' Performance Management—Expatriates' performance management considers the context of cultural variables. Particularly in the context of goal setting, training, feedback and development, and motivation, expatriates' performance management is crucial.

Performance Management in International Assignment—Performance management in international assignment is a job context and not a job description. Most international assignees' performance dimensions are considered within four broad categories: task, organizational, intercultural, and developmental dimensions.

Developmental Performance—This dimension of international performance is not always an organizationally-desired outcome of the assignment. Developmental dimensions may be knowledge-based, such as language acquisition or understanding the worldwide structure of the organization. They may be ability-based, such as learning how to lead a team, negotiating, conducting a meeting or a product launch, instituting a process in another country.

Structure of MNCs—Multinational corporations structure and staff their subsidiaries in four different ways. When an ethnocentric approach is adopted, subsidiaries have little autonomy and key positions are filled by expatriates from the parent country; in a polycentric approach, the subsidiary is treated as a distinct entity with some decision-making autonomy, but the HCM is rarely promoted to the head office; in a geocentric approach, the company recognizes the unique contribution of each subsidiary and managerial positions are filled from its worldwide pool of employees; a region-centric approach provides subsidiaries with some autonomy within their region and uses employees from within the region to fill managerial roles.

GENERAL REVIEW QUESTIONS

1. Define the concept of international performance management. How is it different from national level performance management?
2. Explain how international performance management is different in the contexts of structure and strategy.
3. Explain the concept of expatriate performance management.
4. What are the important cultural effects on international performance management?
5. Discuss the changes in the international performance management practices in the context of globalization.

6. Discuss the differences in international performance management practices with respect to compensation management practices.
7. Write short notes on the following:
   (a) Inter-cultural performance management
   (b) International assignment
   (c) Performance management in China
   (d) Performance management in Korea

CRITICAL REVIEW QUESTION

8. Essex is a noted US-based R&D organization, which outsources its research projects to India under contract research programme. Contract research outsourcing is different from other conventional low skill job outsourcing. Essex needs to maintain close contacts with the Indian scientists, who perform the research work. Based on their annual performance review, Essex requires to plan the compensation packages, which the Indian outsource agent needs to comply with. However, of late, it is observed that there exists a wide incongruity in Essex's performance evaluation process. Indian scientists are highly disgruntled with the system and resigned. At this stage, Essex hired you to suggest a performance management model for Indian scientists. Suggest your action plan.

REFERENCES

Bhattacharyya, D.K. (2009), *Compensation Management—Text and Cases* (New Delhi: Oxford University Press).

Bhattacharyya, D.K. (2010), *Cross-cultural Management* (New Delhi: PHI Learning).

Birkinshaw, J. and N. Hood (1998), 'Multinational Subsidiary Evolution: Capability & Charter in Foreign-Subsidiary Companies', *The Academy of Management Review*, 23(4): 773–95.

Black, J.S., H.B. Gregersen, M.E. Mendenhall and L.K. Stroh (1999), *Globalizing People through International Assignment* (New York, NY: Addison-Wesley, Longman).

Caligiuri, P.M. and D.V. Day (2000), 'Effects of Self-Monitoring on Technical, Contextual, and Assignment-Specific Performance', *Group and Organization Management*, 25(2): 154–74.

Cascio, W.F. (2000), Managing a virtual work place. Academy of Management Executive, 12(3), 81–91.

Chang, E. and S. Taylor (1999), 'Control in MNCs: The Case of Korean Manufacturing Subsidiaries', *Journal of Management*, 25(4): 541–65.

Daum, J.H. (2002), *Intangible Assets and Value Creation* (Chichester: John Wiley).

Dowling, P., D. Welch and R. Schuler (1999), *International Dimensions of Human Resources* (Cincinnati, OH: South Western College Publishing).

Dunning, J. (1998 [1958]), *American Investment in British Manufacturing*, revised and updated edition (London and New York, NY: Routledge).

Ghoshal, S. and C.A. Bartlett (1988), 'Creation, Adoption and Diffusion of Innovations by Subsidiaries of Multinational Corporations', *Journal of International Business Studies*, 19(3): 365–88.

Ghoshal, S. and N. Nohria (1993), 'Horses for Courses: Organizational Forms for Multinational Corporations', *Strategic Management Journal*,14: 23–34

Guest, D.E. (1997), 'Human Resource Management and Performance: A Review and Research Agenda', *International Journal of Human Resource Management*, 8(3): 263–76.

Harvey, M. (1997), 'Focusing on International Performance Appraisal Process', *Human Resource Development Quarterly*, 8(1): 41–62.

Harvey, M. and M. Novicevic (1999), 'Inpatriate Managers: How to Increase Their Probability of Success', *Human Resource Management Review*, 9(1): 51–81.

Harvey, M., M. Novicevic and C. Speier (2000), 'Strategic Global Human Resource Management: The Role of Inpatriate Managers', *Human Resource Management Review*, 10(2): 153–75.

Harvey, M., C. Speier and M. Novicevic (2001), 'A Theory-Based Framework for Strategic Global Human Resource Staffing Policies and Practices', *Human Resource Management*, 12(6): 898–915.

Harvey, M., C. Speier and M. Novicevic (2002), 'The Evolution of SHRM Systems & Their Application in a Foreign Subsidiary Context', *Asian Pacific Journal of Human Resources*, 40(3): 284–300.

Harzing, A.W. (2001), 'An Empirical Study of Executive Staffing Practices in Foreign Subsidiaries', *Human Resource Management*, 40(2): 139–58.

Harzing, A.W. (2005), 'Geographical Distance and the Role of Management of the Subsidiaries: The Case of Subsidiaries Down Under', *Asian Pacific Journal of Management*, 23(2): 167–85.

Hofstede G. (1991), *Culture's Consequences: International Differences in Work-Related Values* (London, Sage).

Hofstede, G. (1995), 'The Business of International Business in Culture', in T. Jackson (ed.), *Cross-cultural Management* (London, Butterworth).

Longenecker, C.O. and D.A. Gioia (1992), 'The Executive Appraisal', *Academy of Management Executive*, 6(2): 18–22.

Mabey, C. and G. Salaman (1995), *Strategic Human Resource Management* (Oxford: Blackwell).

McGraw, P. (2002), 'Human Resources Function in Local & Overseas Firms', *Asian Pacific Journal of Human Resources*, 40(2): 205–27.

Milliman, J., S. Nason, E. Gallagher, P. Huo, M.A. Von Glinow and K.B. Lowe (1998), 'The Impact of National Culture of Human Resource Management Practices: The Case of Performance Appraisal', *Advances in International Comparative Management*, 12: 157–83.

Peters, J. and D. Waterman (1982), *In Search of Excellence* (New York, NY: Harper and Row).

Porter, M. (1996), 'What Is Strategy?', *Harvard Business Review* (November), 70–81

Rosenzweig, P.M. and N. Nohria (1994), 'Influences on Human Resource Management Practices in Multinational Corporations', *Journal of International Business Studies*, 25(2) 229–51.

Schuler, R., P. Dowling and H. De Cieri (1993), 'Integration Framework of SIHRM', *Journal of Management*, 19(2): 419–49.

Shen, J. (2005), 'Effective International Performance Appraisals: Easily Said, Hard To Do', *Compensation and Benefits Review*, 27(1): 70–80.

Tahvanainen, M. (1998), *Expatriate Performance Management*, (Helsinki: Helsinki School of Economics Press).

Tahvanainen, M. (2000), 'Expatriate Performance Management: The Case of Nokia Telecommunications', *Human Resource Management*, 37(4): 267–75.

Trompenaars, F. and C. Hamden-Turner (1995), *Riding the Waves of Culture* (New York, NY: McGraw-Hill).

Trompenaars, F. and P. Wooliams (2003), Business across Cultures (Oxford, Capstone).

Tung, R.L. (1998), 'A Contingency Work of Selection and Training of Expatriate Revisited', *Human Resource Management Review*, 8(1): 23–37.

CASE STUDY

Developing a High Performance Work Culture: A Study on Siemens AG

Siemens AG is a global major in electrical and electronics goods with a turnover of £60 billion and more than half a million people on the payroll. Based in Munich, Germany, Siemens has business presence all over the world. Today Siemens is inseparable from our lives, as its product lines extend from traffic signal lights to MRI scanning machines. Due to its global presence, Siemens needs to address cross-cultural issues and include them in its management practices. Siemens high performance work culture is shared by everyone from top to down the line. High-performance culture is a way of working and a set of values which Siemens nurtures to encourage people to achieve high results.

For its sophisticated range of products, Siemens employs people with high level of competency. Some of the skill-sets required by Siemens are not even available in the market easily. For example, information technology specialists, researchers, new product developers, etc., who are available do not easily fit the Siemens manpower requirements. However, because of high employer branding and prevalence of performance culture, Siemens could edge over other competitors in sourcing the requisite skills.

To sustain performance culture, Siemens adopts HR development strategy and helps people to fulfill it at work. The choice for development is given to the people. They are encouraged to identify ways to improve their careers, attend training programmes, do interesting work and maintain better work–life balance.

Siemens believes total engagement of people in the workplace develops the commitment towards organization. People become the citizen of the company. When people are managed well, they feel motivated autonomously and do a good job! This is Siemens core value on HRM. Siemens refers its plan as business strategy, which among others emphasizes on performance, operational excellence and responsibility towards the organization. With specific reference to people management areas, Siemens emphasizes on people excellence, building and sustaining culture of high performance. People can achieve excellence when they are given the responsibility. The sense of responsibility motivates them, and they feel their efforts are valued. A strong sense of loyalty and belongingness, even in a technology intensive organization like Siemens, made their employees innovative. Innovation and creativity of employees today are Siemens' greatest competitive advantages. The increasing sense of value and engagement of people can be best ensured by sustaining a high-performance work culture.

Engagement both as a feeling and as a reality is possible through teamwork. Siemens' teamwork culture is very strong, as all operations are assigned to various teams. Siemens expects true involvement of all cross-sections of people in the business of the organization. A high-performance team is one in which all members of the team work towards shared responsibility to achieve results. Siemens HR development strategy is drawn around the following four main areas:

- Achieving a high performance culture
- Increasing the global talent pool
- Strengthening expert careers
- Siemens' Leadership Excellence Programme (SLE)

A high-performance culture is the way of working at Siemens and it involves everyone. The global talent pool is made up of all Siemens employees. Within Siemens everyone has the opportunity to develop their own specialization and to acquire further expertise. The SLE provides the highest calibre leadership and management training. Siemens' talent management philosophy involves making sure that every employee is provided with the guidance and support to achieve his/her full potential. This aids them to do their best, every day. Everyone works together to achieve the organization's objectives as well as meeting their own personal goals. Everyone shares the same vision and dreams. Within this culture they are able to progress and take on greater responsibility within the company. People excellence involves developing everybody who works for the organization—not just the high-fliers. Everyone has talent. For Siemens, matching talent with tasks produces competitive advantage. Each individual at Siemens can make best use of their talents, whatever they may be. Talent management enables both:

- Job enrichment, where individuals are encouraged to take on extra tasks and responsibilities within an existing job role to make work more rewarding, and
- Job enlargement, where the scope of the existing job is extended to give a broader range of responsibility, plus extra knowledge and skills development.

Talent management is a global philosophy that is the key to all supporting elements of Siemens' business strategy. Talent management enables Siemens' managers to engage and motivate employees throughout the organization. By applying talent management to all staff:

- All customer-facing staff are engaged, so all customers benefit
- Everyone has the opportunity and choices to achieve their full potential
- The pipeline of high-fliers is sustained.

Siemens has created a standard process for managing the performance and development of all employees. This is referred to as the Performance Management Process. The process creates a direct link between the strategy of the whole organization and plans for each individual. Every individual is given targets based on their role and responsibility within the organization. It is through meeting personal targets that the individual is best able to help the organization to achieve its targets. Performance management is a systematic process that creates trust and open communication by:

- Setting objectives
- Monitoring progress made
- Creating an ongoing dialogue between each team member and his/her manager
- Enabling forthright discussion

Performance management in Siemens is the engine that drives talent management. It is the cornerstone of its high performance culture. When carried out in a consistent way, this system makes sure that everyone is told honestly about their performance. Employees are clear about the impact of their performance and what the consequences are for their development. Everyone within the organization is pulling together to achieve the business strategy.

Question: Write a detailed note on performance management practices at Siemens.

Source: Adapted from www.siemens.co.uk, www.thetimes100.co.uk

CHAPTER 15

Performance Audit, Human Resource Valuation, Accounting, and Audit

Learning Objectives

After reading this chapter, you will be able to understand:

- Concept of performance management and its scope
- Differences between performance appraisal and performance audit
- Structure of performance audit
- Steps in performance audit
- Methods and techniques of performance audit
- Process of human resource valuation
- Human resource accounting
- Various aspects of human resource audit
- Relation between HR audit and HR personnel record keeping

Tracking Performance Excellence Through Performance Audit

Performance audit examines the function, operation, or the management systems and procedures of an organization to assess whether it is achieving economy, efficiency, and effectiveness in its resource utilization. Worldwide, we have many institutional templates for undertaking performance audit. However, these are more applicable for government organizations, where bound audit procedure protocol is very important. In business organizations, however, performance audit methods need to be customized, keeping pace with the individualized needs and expectations. Many software vendors have now come out with the e-performance management systems, which can better facilitate the performance audit functions. E-performance management, apart from conducting the performance audit and tracking the performance records also helps in implementing HR strategies, policies, and practices in organizations, making effective use of web-based technology. E-performance management is often offered as a separate module under e-HRM package. However, in many cases it is a stand-alone solution for the organization. E-HRM solutions can be operational, relational, or transformational. Operational e-HRM solutions facilitate maintenance or administrative functions of HRM like payroll, employees' personal record keeping, etc. Relational e-HRM solution, on the other hand facilitates development and some support functions of HR like; training, recruitment, performance management, etc. Finally, transformational e-HRM is concerned with strategic HR activities such as knowledge management, strategic re-orientation, etc.

Summarized features of e-performance management are the automation of performance management process, accommodation of performance measures and key performance indicators assigning values to each indicator, keeping pace with the organizational goals and needs, and customizing the workflow to manage its execution. Through real-time reports and information, e-performance management solutions facilitate the organizational decision-making, strategy framing while leveraging the employee-related information.

INTRODUCTION TO PERFORMANCE MANAGEMENT AUDIT

Performance management systems manage the entire workforce of an organization to ensure optimum performance. It is the process of evaluation of employees' performance, in alignment with the organizational strategy and business goals, benchmarking with the best practices. Performance audit ensures development, management, and retention of talent in the organization. The scope of performance management audit, among others emphasize on formal performance evaluations, incentive assessment, career development programme assessment, succession planning programme assessment, goal setting assessment of the organization, assessment of coaching and mentoring programme of the organization, work environmental issues assessment, etc. It helps the organizations to diagnose the major issues of bottleneck in employees' performance. Using a participative approach, performance management audit process can successfully track the issues and areas of organizational performance improvement. Performance audit process and its results become more credible when it makes use of questionnaire, scaled comparison method, and when these can be reliable and valid statistically. Administering a questionnaire, performance audit can be conducted in a more cost-effective and time efficient manner. It can either be conducted using a traditional paper pencil mode or on-line. Thus, the performance audit is a systematic performance measurement approach to identify the best performance improvement opportunities within the organization. Apart from the sales and revenues figures, performance audit should look at quality and so also the quantity. For example, organizational performance occurs at different hierarchical, functional, and divisional levels. It considers total sales and other revenues, production, purchase, and so also individual level specific tasks achievement.

Successful performance audit facilitates in prudent business decision-making. Using the scalable information, performance audit can provide information in measurable terms. With the dashboards and the balanced score card, such audit information even become more authentic. For example, IBM's cognos is a performance management solution, used by organizations.

SCOPE OF PERFORMANCE MANAGEMENT AUDIT

Among other the performance management systems consider issues like:

- Performance expectations.
- Frequency of performance evaluations.

- Participative goal setting.
- Job-profile matching, keeping pace with the skill of people.
- Promotion of team work and group activities.
- Practice of performance-based promotions.
- Career development through succession planning.
- Assessment of performance.
- Introduction of fair performance appraisal process.
- Practicing performance-based compensation design.

A comprehensive performance management audit assesses the degree of economy, efficiency, and effectiveness in the use of human, financial, and material resources at individual employee's level, at the group or team level, departmental level, division level, and finally at the level of the organization. Unlike financial audit, it is not statutorily required, but organizations need to undertake such internal audit for assessment of their current situation and for designing the possible action plans for future development. Aligning the performance audit with the organizational strategies, and business goals, organizations can gain substantially, as it sets the direction for the people and so also for the organization as a whole.

DIFFERENCES BETWEEN THE PERFORMANCE AUDIT AND FINANCIAL AUDIT

Although procedurally, performance audit and the financial audit have many things in common, they are not alike. Basic difference between the two, while the performance audit focuses on efficiency measurements, financial audit focuses on the accuracy and correctness of accounts. Other areas of difference between the two can be listed as under:

- Financial audit is a routine job. It does not focus on any specific problem. Performance audit, on the other hand focuses on problems and the process of identification of its causes.
- In financial audit, attention is more on figures, in performance audit, however, the attention is more on people, and other resources.
- For obvious focus on specific requirements and expectations, financial audit is having a narrow focus, while performance audit is essentially broader and more elaborate for judgement and interpretation.
- Financial audit is conducted for a specific financial period, while performance audit is on-going and it can even extend over a cycle of several years. However, organizations may also carry out performance audit annually, matching with their financial year results. But such approach to performance audit is rather narrow, and time specific.
- Unlike financial audit results, performance audit reports are more elaborate, diverse and interpretative.
- Performance audit requires more detailed preliminary surveys, for developing the actual audit plan. In financial audit, however, this is not required.
- Financial audit is more protocol-bound, while the financial audit is not.

Performance audits measure efficiency of an organization, processes and elements, to determine whether inputs are reflected into outputs in an optimal way, considering, particularly the costs. The final performance audit assesses the real value of outputs, comparison of outputs against the identified standards, and finally the overall effectiveness of the organization.

Some of the common terms of performance audit are input, objective, effect, output, economy, efficiency, effectiveness, purposefulness, targets, results, feedback, performance standards, unit costs, benchmarking, etc. All these terms we are already familiar with, save and except the term effect, which indicates the outcome or consequence of performance measures, as a whole.

CHECKLIST OF PERFORMANCE AUDIT

It is difficult to design any universal checklists for performance audit, as the process is highly organization specific. Performance checklists determine whether the employees deserve incentives, promotions, rewards, areas of their performance improvement, quality of their work, employees' willingness to undertake the work assignments, errors in terms of performed work duties, etc. Also a job performance checklist is prepared on general attendance, tardiness, more use of sick leave, propensity to leave work early and increase the time of lunch break, etc. Job performance checklist considers the general work performance of the employees, like conforming to general operating procedures, adherence to the safety measures, implementing the training knowledge, complying with the previous suggestions to improve the work performance, etc. The job performance checklists, therefore helps the organization to assess how employees perform, and so also the degree of compatibility of the organization with the employees' needs and expectations.

STRUCTURE OF PERFORMANCE AUDIT

Depending on the scope of performance audit in organization, it can be structured as under:

- Measuring the degree of professionalism.
- Measuring the efficiency.
- Measuring the economy.

Professionalism audit emphasize on the identification of any possible lapses in terms of personal bias and methodological issues while conducting the audit. Efficiency audit emphasizes on the objective achievement and effectiveness measurement. While the economy audit measures the economy or cost effectiveness of performance.

Professionalism in performance audit is understood in terms of quantification and actual definition of performance results, considering various alternatives. It is understood measuring whether performance measures help in achieving the goals, or changing the status quo, whether the time frame for implementing the measures is reasonable, and adequately explained, the extent of data availability to conduct the performance audit, to what extent such information can be rated, etc. It can be understood answering the following questions:

- What is the degree of professionalism in designing the performance audit process?
- What are the deficiencies that exist in preparing the performance measures?
- With such deficiencies can the performance audit be carried out?
- Are the performance indicators adequate and auditable?

Efficiency audit consists of audit of achievement of goal, and the audit of effects or the causality. Audit of goal achievement can be done answering the following questions:

- Was the defined goal achieved?
- To what extent was the defined goal achieved?
- To what extent the comparison of planned results or goals with the achievement actual results or goals can be made?

Audit of effects or causality answers the following questions:

- Can the goal be achieved with the adopted performance measures?
- To what extent performance measures are the right fit for achieving the performance goals?
- Apart from the adopted performance measures, what else could influence the circumstances that facilitated in achieving the performance goals?
- Are there any other effects (especially the adverse one) in audited performance measures?
- What is the degree of actual effects with the planned ones?

For better results it is always advisable to adopt multiple methods like empirical and economic, while conducting the performance audit. With the application of more than one method, results of performance measurement can be correlated and subjected to statistical tests for its reliability and validity.

Economy audit evaluates the costs incurred in measuring the performance of the individual and the organization. Capitalized value methods like the net present value, internal rate of return, etc. are the important areas of consideration for economy audit in performance management. Also the economy audit identifies whether any unnecessary expenses incurred during the process of performance audit.

STEPS IN PERFORMANCE AUDIT

Performance audit process in any organization follow certain steps. Most commonly used steps are indicated below:

- Development of assessment criteria.
- Preparation schedule.
- The choice of audit tasks.
- The choice of audit objectives.
- Preparatory work.
- Performance audit planning.

While developing the performance assessment criteria it is important to consider the aspects of economy, efficiency, and effectiveness. Accordingly, it needs to be translated into specific assessment criteria to facilitate the measurement of the organizational performance. While developing the assessment criteria, it is also important to conform to the test of relevancy, operative, and consistent. In the next step, preparing the schedule of performance is important. Performance schedule guides us the process of gathering information, determination of the audit tasks, and decision on when to begin the audit, and at what frequency, etc. The choice of audit tasks or the scope of performance audit depends on the specific requirements of the organization. Similarly, choosing of performance audit objectives, preparatory work like review of information availability, financial information like trend analysis, ratio analysis, predictive analysis, i.e., operating data to predict the sales volume, etc., need to be organization-specific. The final step in performance audit is the planning, that requires collection of relevant background information. Assessment of the presence of relevant management and control systems to guard against the performance irregularities, etc.

METHODS AND TECHNIQUES OF PERFORMANCE AUDIT

Methods are the ways and procedures that lead to achieving the goals of performance audits. Techniques are the tools used to measure the achieved performance goals. Performance audit methods could be an analysis, synthesis, sorting, comparison, or a generalization. The process of analysis is defined as the method of breaking down the whole performance goals and objectives into different parts, and then examining each part separately. Through analysis we can get into the root of a given fact. Analysis reveals the nature of the managed processes, pinpointing the causes behind the variances from the desired state. As the process of analysis reveals the substance of audit facts and then explains the links and relations, it is considered as the most important method of performance audit. Analysis also facilitates the benchmarking duly comparing the performance achievement of one organization with another.

The process of synthesis starts after the analysis ends. Synthesis combines the parts and elements with the overall performance of the organization. Synthesis assesses how the results relate to causes and helps in designing the effective measures to correct the deviations and so also to establish the preventive conditions to achieve the desired results in future. Sorting enables us to better the facts explored and reveal their interrelations. Sorting could be both quantitative and qualitative. Quantitative sorting can be expressed in numbers, while the qualitative sorting helps us to establish the logical interrelations based on facts. Based on these results we can make comparison of the performance data. Generalization makes it possible to capture the extent of certain action in terms of ratio. It is closely related to the methods of sorting and synthesis. Yet, the other terms used to define the performance audit methods are statistical, accounting, mathematical, etc. The commonly used statistical methods for performance audit are Index, time series, mean values, probabilities, and correlation. Accounting method is the basic audit method used to perform the audit function. Mathematic methods help in detecting the undesirable facts and in tracking the trends.

Performance audit techniques, as already explained above are the tools used to measure the degree of performance goal achievement. Such techniques could be observation, simple document study, interviewing, and questionnaire administration. Observation is a planned and targeted analysis of material aspects of an activity. The document study examines facts in flow, the study of all available records on a given fact is both vital and effective, and the audit would be inconceivable without it. The nature of the documents studied depends on the aim of the audit. Interview is an auxiliary technique to understand the issue with the interview results clues. Finally, the questionnaire is the structured approach to track the performance information based on the responses of the respondents.

PERFORMANCE DATA RELIABILITY AUDIT (DRA)

Data Reliability Audit (DRA) is basically performance audit to ensure accuracy and precession level of observations. Performance audit assesses the degree of economy, efficiency, and effectiveness in the use of human, financial, and material resources at a level of organization unit, organization, or certain actions. This type of internal audit examines processes and systems of an auditee in particular.

Performance audit and financial audit have much in common. These two types of audit may involve the same kind of tasks, namely, the measuring and explanation of the performance of an auditee. They also rely on similar data collection methods. While performance auditors have their sights on efficiency, financial auditors focus on the accuracy and correctness of accounts. However, there are some differences between performance audit and financial audit as well. These differences we have already explained. Using the DRA, performance audit also fulfils the requirements and the correctness of performance measurement results.

HUMAN RESOURCE VALUATION, ACCOUNTING, AND AUDIT

A resource is defined as an object which can provide expected future services. Hence, objects which do not have expected future service potential cannot by definition, be resources. People being capable of rendering future services, such potential services constitute a form of capital. Human Resource Accounting (HRA) is the process of identifying, measuring, and communicating data about human resources. Flamhoitz (1974) defined HRA as 'Accounting for people as an organizational resource. It involves measuring the costs incurred by business firms and other organizations to recruit, select, hire, train and develop human assets. It also involves measuring the economic value of people to the organization'. HRA, therefore, shows how the organization makes investment in its people and how the value of the people changes over time. Value of the employees increases by training (the core HRD activity) and experience over a time period. Such information on human resources facilitates effective management within an organization.

According to Likert (1971), HRA benefits organization in the following ways:

- It furnishes cost value information to facilitate the management to take effective decisions on manpower acquisition, allocation development, and retention to sustain cost-effective competitiveness in the organization.
- It ensures effective utilization of human resources.
- It facilitates human assets control duly tracking its appreciation or depreciation.
- It helps in the development of management principles.
- This method attaches money estimates in the value of manpower of an organization. The process is somewhat like estimating the goodwill value and can be appraised by developing a procedure to undertake periodic measurement of certain variables. Such variables are either categorized as key variables or intervening variables. Key variables are policies and decisions of an organization, its leadership strategies, skills, behaviour of an employee, etc. Intervening variables are loyalties, attitudes, motivations, interpersonal relations, communication, and decision-making. Measuring such variables over several years, quantification of human assets are difficult for the obvious problem in developing the accounting procedure. It is not a very popular method of performance appraisal. However, this system is more appropriately used for evaluating the collective performance of an organization, rather than individual appraisal of an employee. This method is useful for organizational development, as it helps in identifying the changed areas more scientifically than any other method. We have discussed this method in a separate chapter. HR is the valuable asset and HR accounting helps to understand the relative value of HR. While doing the HR accounting, it is important to account for quantitative value of employees' performance. From such determined

quantitative value, all forms of employees' costs are deducted, to accurately understand the value addition by the employees. This forms the basis of human resource accounting.

- Certain information on the human capital can be reported by an organization in their annual reports. In the process of developing such information, organizations can address to the requirements of HRP integrating their HRIS. Information pertaining to employees can be listed under the following broad heads as mentioned in Table 15.1.

However, the extent of disclosure of such information depends on the respective organizational practices. For example, Engineers India Ltd. (EIL) widely disclosed information on its human capital on all the areas mentioned above and reported the human valuation during 1998–99 in Table 15.2 and 15.3.

Table 15.1 *HRIS information*

Basic Information About Human Resource	HR Acquisition	HR Development	HR Maintenance	HR Separation
Number of employees, categories, grades Total value of human resource and value per employee	Number of employees acquired during the year Cost of acquisition Levels for which they were acquired	All information pertaining to HRD activities of the organization	Cost related to HR maintenance	Cost related to HR separation, attrition rate Details of benefits provided to the employees

Table 15.2 *Employee details of EIL*

Category	No. of Employees as on 31 March 1999
Senior manager and above executives up to the manager level	613
Technical	2097
Non-technical	295
Supporting staff	719
Total	3724

Table 15.3 *Human valuation of EIL*

Category	Human Valuation During 1998–99 (Rupees in lakhs)	
	Category-wise total HR Value	Value per employee
Senior manager and above executives up to the manager level	24151	39.39
Technical	65007	31.00
Non-technical	9145	—
Supporting staff	16264	22.62

Source: Annual report of EIL

VARIOUS METHODS OF VALUATING HUMAN RESOURCES

Different approaches to the valuation of human resources may be broadly grouped under two categories:

- Non-monetary measurement
- Monetary measurement

Non-monetary Measurement

Such methods involve the classification of human resources in terms of skills (skills inventory), performance evaluations, potentiality for developments and promotions, attitude surveys, and subjective values.

Skill is a coordinated series of actions to attain some goal. Operationally, skills are defined widely as overt responses and controlled stimulation. Overt responses may either be verbal, motor, or perceptual. Verbal response typically stresses on speaking (which requires memorization of words). Motor responses stress on movements of limbs and body while Perceptual responses stress on understanding of sensory responses. Controlled stimulation, on the other hand, are energy inputs to the workers which is expressed in units of frequency, length, time, and weight.

Basic concepts of rest of the method have already been introduced in relevant chapters, excepting the 'subjective value'. 'Subjective value method indicates a subjective evaluation of approximation of the likelihood of an event'.

Monetary Measurement

There are number of monetary measurement techniques. Each such technique has its relative advantages and disadvantages. Here we will discuss such techniques very briefly as under:

Capitalization of Historical Costs Method: This method was developed by Likert. It capitalizes all costs of recruitment, hiring, training, and other initial costs involved in developing of human resources, i.e., the employees. The amount so capitalized is written off over aperiod an employee remains with the organization. If he leaves before the expected service period, the amount remaining as an asset is written off in its entirety in the year of leaving.

Replacement Cost Method: This method measures the cost to replace an organization's existing human resource. It indicates what it would cost the concern to recruit, hire, train, and develop human resources to match the present level of efficiency.

Opportunity Cost Method: Under this methods, the value of human resources is determined on the basis of the value of an individual employee in an alternative use. If an employee can be hired easily externally, there is no opportunity cost for him.

Economic Value Method: Under this method, human resources are valued on the basis of the contribution they are likely to make to the organization during the period of their employment. The remuneration to be paid to an employee is estimated and discounted appropriately to arrive at the current estimated value.

Present Value Method: This method measures human resources; measuring by attributing employee's value to the organization as an equivalent to the present value of his remaining earnings. Organizations like MMTC, ONGC, BHEL, ACC, Neyvell Lignite Corporate, etc., have already adopted this concept.

From HRD point of view, human resources accounting helps to understand many pertinent issues like developing skill inventory, performance appraisal, assessing the individual's capacity for development, attitude surveys, and subjective appraisal, as discussed above. Hence, for designing a human resource information system (HRIS), we need to consider the following factors:

Personal Profile: This includes name, sex, range, age, marital status, address and phone number, service date, etc.

Career Profile: Education, training, certificates, licenses, degrees, skills, hobbies, requisite training, interests, etc., are combined in the skill profile.

Benefits Profile: Insurance coverage, disability provisions, pension, profit-sharing, vacation, holidays, sick leave, etc., are covered in the benefits profile.

Practice Assignment

Visit any organization and study how they assess their human resource value. (Note: Not many organizations do human resource valuation. Hence recommend visiting Web sites like BHEL, TCS, and Infosys, and study their method of human resource valuation).

HR AUDIT

Personnel/Human Resources or HRD audit is a systematic survey and analysis of different HR functions with a summarized statement of findings and recommendations for correction of deficiencies. Basically, it examines and evaluates policies, procedures, and practices to determine the effectiveness of HR function in an organization. HR audit ensures that sound and cost effective policies are implemented. However, purposes and objectives of HR audit can be listed as follows:

Objectives of HR Audit

1. To determine the effectiveness of management programmes, which facilitate management to develop, allocate and monitor human resources.
2. To analyse the factors involved in HR and develop a statement of findings with recommendations for correcting deviations, if any, on the following issues:
   (a) The extent of deviation from HR policies.
   (b) To what extent objectives are spelt out.
   (c) To what extent performance standards have been established.
3. To seek explanations, information, and answers to the above questions such as: What happened? Why did it happen?
4. To study the extent to which line managers have complied with HR policies and as such the operational problems in implementing the existing HR policies.
5. To study the current manpower inventory and identify shortfall or excess, if any.

Job/Role of HR Auditor

From the above stated objectives, the job of HR Auditor can be enumerated as follows:

1. To get the current facts.
2. To study the effectiveness of the present system by answering the following issues:
   (a) Why was the practice introduced?
   (b) What would be the result if the practice is discontinued?
   (c) What were the needs intended to be fulfilled and have those been fulfilled or not?
   (d) What could be the best possible alternative for fulfilling such needs?
   (e) What changes can improve effectiveness of existing practice?
   (f) Are such intended changes economically and operationally viable?
   (g) Are such changes sustainable from union's point of view?
   (h) What should be the time frame for introducing the change?

Importance of HR Audit

To keep pace with the changing environment, importance of periodic HR audit has increased in recent years. Recent economic restructuring programme of the Government of India, as discussed earlier, prompted the need for restructuring of the organization, which, inter alia, calls for restructuring of production, manpower, strategies, management practices, philosophies, etc. All such possible reasons for periodic HR audit can be enumerated as follows:

- Technological changes, inter alia, are calling for renewal of knowledge and skills of existing manpower. Training function, therefore, has assumed importance. Periodic HR audit can help to identify the changing training needs and development of new training modules for effective utilization of manpower.
- To keep pace with the environmental changes, management philosophy and practices at the organizational level also need to be changed, like participative management (through quality circles and value engineering teams), employee empowerment, total Eemployee involvement, etc. The need for all these can be understood only when we periodically undertake HR audit.

  Similarly, changing role of trade unions (which is now more pro-active than reactive), government (which is now more liberal than restrictive), emergence of new working class (who are more enlightened than their predecessors), emergence of international quality system requirements (which calls for scientific documentation of different corporate functions and infuse attitudinal changes), changing expectations of customers (which calls for more customer orientation), new statutory requirements (pollution control), etc., are now influencing HR functions at the corporate level, the effectiveness of which can only be understood by periodic HR audit.

Records Used for HR Audit

Records provide ready reference and serve as future reference and guide. Reports, on the other hand, describe an incident, event, or situation. Depending upon the organization, the following records/reports are usually checked for HR Audit. Time study records and time standards, cost records, records on scores obtained in test and other examination, medical and accident reports, attitudinal survey reports, grievance reports, turnover reports, data on work stoppages, performance reports, payroll data, labour costs data, etc.

Methods and Techniques of HR Audit

HR audit can be carried out either by attitudinal survey or by interpreting data. Details of attitudinal survey have already been explained in a separate chapter. Interpretation of data can be done either by simple comparison over a period or by ratio analysis or by graphical or pictorial displays. The following examples illustrate the data interpretation method.

Checklists for HR Audit

T.V. Rao and Udai Pareek (1996), to measure the effectiveness of people management, developed a set of 20 questions mostly to suggest linking of HR to the corporate objectives, goals, and strategies; effectiveness of free flow of HR information down the ranks; application of knowledge of behavioural science; industrial psychology for HR, etc.

For other HR sub-systems too, they have developed similar sets of questionnaire, adding responses, which can help an organization to audit their HR activities. However, using same general checklists for all organizations may not be very effective to audit human resources for its obvious uniqueness in functional practices and philosophies.

HUMAN RESOURCE RECORDS

Human resource records, also called personnel files, are recorded information about employees, which are kept by an employer, usually in the form of and under the name 'personal files'.

Information is one of the most important inputs for an organization. A boundary spanning sub-system of open organization collects information inputs from outside the organization, to bring changes in technical and managerial sub-system. This process enables an organization to remain competitive in the market. In-house information, more particularly those pertaining to employees, also serves as a valuable input for decision-making. Some of the personnel records are maintained more for statutory reasons. However, true benefits of maintaining personnel records can be derived, only when these are used for both routine and strategic decision-making. Personnel records can be maintained in one of the following basic systems:

- Manually (in file cabinets without a computer).
- With an integrated payroll/human resources system.
- With a standalone human resource information system (HRIS).
- Any combination of the three.

Manual personnel record systems exist in almost all companies. Organizations, which are not fully computerized, integrate such manual personnel record system in conformity with the computer systems requirements. This type of organizations maintains their integrated computerized payroll or HR systems. Some organizations, however, maintain stand-alone human resource information systems, to ensure that HR information become effective input for routine and strategic HR decisions.

Personnel records thus include all information collected, assembled, or maintained by the organization and relevant to the employment relationship of the individual with the organization. Organizations maintain personnel files for individual employees to record and document relevant events and discussions with the employees regarding performance, recognition, promotion, demotion, compensation, leave, absence, disciplinary issues, training, and conduct. Routine documentation in personnel files pertains to personal demographics of the employees. Maintaining some personnel records are statutory and such records need to be preserved for a longer time frame. While some other personnel records may be voluntarily maintained by an organization to derive the benefit of strategic decisions like succession planning, competency mapping, etc.

LIST OF PERSONNEL RECORDS

For organizational convenience, a tabular list of personnel records, which should be maintained in employees' personnel file, is reproduced here.

Personnel File Contents	**Document/File**
a. Application Details	Yes/No
Application for employment form Employee CV Employee I.D. document or permanent residency (Photostat) Employee driver's license (Photostat) Interviewing notes Interview correspondence Offer of employment Employee acceptance Employee orientation checklist Employee contact numbers, address, and next of kin	
b. Salary Details	Yes/No
Employee salary advice Monthly salary advices Complaints of indebtedness Stop Order and other salary deduction authorization forms Retirement fund and medical aid membership forms Beneficiary forms	
c. Leave Record	Yes/No
Leave schedules Annual Casual Sick Study/sabbatical Others	

d. Performance and Development	Yes/No
Position descriptions Training records, including formal training plans Performance plans Performance ratings	
e. Disciplinary Procedures	Yes/No
Pending personnel actions, awards recommendations, etc. Disciplinary/adverse action backup materials Disciplinary file documentation checklist *Objective:* To provide a clear audit trail of all actions taken and leading up to a formal disciplinary action. Copies of notice of proposed action Employee response (or notation that no written response made) Summary of response when made orally (including employee's or representative's signature as to accuracy of memorandum) Notice of decision and reasoning behind decision (specifically addressing Douglas factors) *Supporting documentation such as:* 1. Witness statements 2. Affidavits 3. Documents 4. Investigative reports or extracts of them 5. Pertinent regulations 6. Personnel actions 7. Reports on personal interviews/group meetings • Evidence of delivery of notice letters • Completed case sheets, with all items filled in (noting 'N/A' if necessary)	
f. Grievance Procedures	Yes/No
Objective: To provide a clear audit trail on all actions taken and leading up to a final decision on each grievance. This checklist applies to both negotiated and administrative grievances. Written grievance Designation of representative Witness statements Memos on discussions with grievant/supervisor/rep/witnesses All grievance forms and notices Chairperson (all levels) report of findings and recommendations Union letter invoking dispute	

Request for arbitration or application to Labour Court (Memos regarding meetings with union to select arbitrator/schedule arbitration, etc.) Brief Arbitration notes Post-hearing brief Arbitrator's or Labour Court decision Record of implementation of arbitrator's decision *Other supporting documentation such as:* Applicable regulations Official documents (e.g., performance plans, performance ratings) Documentation regarding requests for and approval of extensions/waivers of any steps in the process.	
g. Personal Medical Information	Yes/No
Note: Medical documentation, including injury compensation forms, suitability and/or security information should not be maintained in this folder. Other official folders must be established for this purpose.	

Recommendations for Personnel Record Keeping

Some of the recommendations for personnel record keeping are presented below:

- Review applicable laws with regard to required records.
- Review employment application forms, evaluation forms, and other similar documents to be sure they are non-discriminatory.
- Review with supervisors the kind of disciplinary documentation, which should be maintained in all employee files.
- Know to what extent state laws mandates employee access to personnel files and establish a system for controlling such access.
- Do not disclose information on employees except to those who have a legitimate need to know the information.
- Do not discuss charges or complaints against individual employees with more people than absolutely necessary.
- Get consent before disclosure where possible.
- Have one person responsible for all disclosures to ensure consistency of treatment.
- Provide 'neutral' references for former employees.
- Maintain adequate security over all employment records.

Use of Human Resource Information System (HRIS) for Maintaining Personnel Records

An HRIS is a systematic procedure for collecting, storing, maintaining, retrieving, and validating data needed by an organization about its resources. The HRIS is usually a part of the organization's larger management information system (MIS). The HRIS need not be complex or even computerized. But computerization has its own advantage of providing more accurate and timely data for decision-making. Thus, human resource information systems (HRIS) are defined as the range of computerized technology that is used to store, record, and link, analyse, and present data about the human element within the business. Connections to the external environment through the Internet are significant in this definition, as are Intranets, which allow organizations the potential to communicate from within more rapidly and effectively. HRIS will assist in the provision of high-level customer focus and lowering an organization's operational costs. Although HRIS includes hardware and software, it also includes people form, policies, procedures, and data. The areas of application of HRIS are many. Some of them include training management, risk management, turnover analysis, succession planning, flexible benefits, compliance with government and legal requirements, attendance with governments and legal requirements, attendance reporting and analysis, HRP, accident reporting and prevention, strategic planning, financial planning, and other related areas.

Application of computers in modern organizations can help in processing organizational data, job data, and personnel (people) data. Organizational data include market for competitive information, e.g., the life cycle of a company's products, the mission, and values, strategy of the company, its structure and culture, management style, employee attitudes, and its output results. Job data include the proposed duties and responsibilities, performance standards, compensable factors, and competency requirements. People or personnel data may include current and potential employees' demographic information, work history education levels, training and development history, competency assessments, performance appraisal data, and career path.

Practice Assignment

Visit an organization that has adopted computerized human resource information system (HRIS). Study their personnel record keeping.

SCOPE OF HR AUDIT

For integration of personnel management with HR functions, HR audit now encompasses all the areas like review and integration of corporate mission, goals, policies and objectives, manpower planning, career planning and development, promotion and transfer policies, performance appraisal systems, training and development functions, recruitment and selection, etc.

The audit will take stock of the degree to which HR delivers its four key roles. The following information indicates the aspects to be audited for each role. The sequence in which this information is presented also approximates the sequence in which the audit needs to be conducted. Each step in the process will produce information and conclusions about HR that is used as an input to guide each succeeding phase of the stock-taking.

Audit of the Functional Role of HR: A model was formulated for the American Society for Training and Development by a task team headed by Patricia Mclagan in 1990. This model was used to develop an audit questionnaire to assess the following four functional areas defined below.

Human Resource Development Systems and Procedures (HRD): Audit whether there is the integrated use of training and development, organization development, and career development to improve individual, group, and organizational effectiveness. These three areas use development as their primary process.

Training and Development: Identifying, assuring, and—through planned learning—helping develop the key competencies that enable individuals to perform current or future jobs

Organization Development: Assuring healthy inter- and intra-unit relationships and helping groups initiate and manage change

Career Development: Alignment of individual career plans with the organizational career-management processes to achieve an optimal match of individual and organizational needs.

PURPOSES OF HR AUDIT

Dave Ulrich (1996) and his associates chalked out the methodology of HR audit based on four key principles. Primary purposes of personnel audit can be aligned with existing HR systems and procedures of an organization, keeping in view, however, that HR systems and procedures are line manager-friendly, accommodate various labour laws and procedures, in line with the HR strategy and the entire process runs at optimal cost. All these assumptions Ulrich and his associates translated into some critical roles that HR professionals must play if they wish to be seen to make a real contribution to a business' success.

Human Resource Management (HRM)

Audit whether the HRD systems and procedures are aligned with the HRM systems and procedures to promote staff competence, confidence, and performance standards. These areas are closely related to the three primary HRD areas. In them, development is important, but it is not the primary orientation or process.

Organization Job Design: Defining how tasks, authority, and systems will be organized and integrated across organizational units and in individual jobs.

Human Resource Planning: Determining the organization's major human resource needs, strategies, and philosophies.

Performance Management Systems: Assuring individual and organization goals are linked and what individuals do every day supports the organizational goals.

Selection and Staffing: Matching people and their career needs and capabilities with jobs and career paths.

HR Information Systems (HIRS)

Audit whether these areas support the achievement of results in the area of HRD and HRM; audit whether HR maintains performance indicators that help management keep track of HR costs and benefits.

Compensation and Benefits: Assuring compensation and benefits fairness and consistency.

Employee Assistance: Providing personal problem-solving and counselling to individual employees.

Union/Labour Relations: Assuring healthy union/organization relationships.

HR Research and Information Systems: Assuring an HR information base is in place that provides on time management information assuring HR functional performance indicators are in place.

Table 15.4 *Framework for audit of the service role of HR*

Service Role Dimensions of HR	
Tangibles/ Appearance	The appearance of physical facilities, equipment, personnel, and communication materials the HR function uses/supplies.
Reliability	Ability to perform HR functions and service dependably and accurately.
Responsiveness	Willingness to help line/employees and provide prompt service.
Assurance	Knowledge and courtesy of HR staff and their ability to inspire trust and confidence.
Empathy	Caring individualized attention the HR function provides its customers (line and employees).

Audit of the Service Role of HR

Human resource functions have traditionally played a service role to compliment their functional activities. Therefore, any audit, to be complete needs to examine the service responsiveness of HR. Although we have different models for service role dimensions of HR, here we are discussing a very commonly applicable service role model, keeping in view of the common organizational practices in Table 15.4.

Audit of the Compliance Role of HR

In our country, we have many labour laws to regulate employment relations. These apart, we have several rules and regulations. All these put great deal of pressure on employers to improve the standard of their people management policies, practices, and procedures. Compliance with the labour laws is now a business imperative and this requires periodic audit to optimize the risk of violation, which not only make employers liable for penalty (and even imprisonment in some cases), but also affect the organizational image. The main thrust of this part of the audit will be to assess whether the required policies, practices, and procedures exist, and to what extent management and labour have been trained to enact these codes of best practice.

Audit of the Strategic Role of HR

Each has an implicit or explicit people management strategy to increase the value of employees to the business. This strategy is to a large degree implemented through the major HR functional available to management and HR. The choice of workforce strategy may also be tempered by the leadership and management skills within each organization. Hence, auditing these functions enables an organization to understand whether the implicit or explicit human resource strategy is appropriate for the organization and whether the HR policies, systems, and procedures are aligned to achieve business plan results, and workforce strategy. Organizations need to mandate a particular HR strategy, aligning their management, leadership, and HR practices/workforce strategy to support the achievement of the business plan mission, goals, and values.

Audit of the Financial Management Role of HR (Financial Ratios)

A comprehensive audit of HR systems and procedures needs to go beyond the 'check and tick/inspection' level. Basic financial ratios/scorecard measures appropriate for a staff function like HR need to be put in place to audit the efficiency of the various functions. Different functions of HR act as a system of levers for optimizing employee, team, and organizational performance results over time. Organizations can select from the following list of customer, financial, business process, and growth and learning measures that will be calculated to round off the audit.

Planning and staffing	**Special recruitment programmes (e.g. universities)** Interviewing costs Special event analysis (Rush assignments) Response time analysis (Speed) Time to fill analysis (Quality) Job posting response rate (Internal) Job posting hire rate **Internal cost per hire/make** Internal hire rate Interviewing time **External cost per hire/buy** Source cost Staff time Management time Processing cost Travel and relocation
Recruitment efficiency	Interview time (internal and external appointments Recruitment agency costs
Recruitment effectiveness	**Staff requisitions** Requisitions opened Requisitions filled **Optimizing staff levels** Actual versus projected staff levels (by function/department)
Compensation measures	Cost control Distribution patterns relative to evaluation of performance Employee pay Attitudes Benefits Total cost
Orientation cost per employee	Departmental orientation cost (Personal walk through by mentor)
Counselling/disciplinary costs (early warning measure)	Departmental counseling factor Counseling topic factor Counseling topic time
Lost time costs	Absence rate Absenteeism cost Negotiation time cost factor Strike/downtime cost factor
Turnover rates	Length of service Transfer cost (internally across departments/functions) Termination by department or job category/reason for leaving

Training and development costs/ measures	Cost per learner (classroom) Cost per learner (on-job-training) Knowledge change benefit Skill change benefit Performance change benefit
Organization development measures	Satisfaction Adaptiveness Development Risk taking Creativity/learning Job stress Job flexibility/multiskilling Leader behaviours Commitment measures

BENEFITS OF HR AUDIT

From our foregoing discussions, it is thus clear that HR audit in any organization provides many benefits. However, here we are discussing only some of those benefit points:

- It helps to find out the proper contribution of the HR department towards the organization.
- Development of the professional image of the HR department of the organization.
- Reduce the HR cost.
- Motivation of the HR personnel.
- Find out the problems and solve them smoothly.
- Provides timely legal requirement.
- Sound performance appraisal systems.
- Systematic job analysis.
- Smooth adoption of the changing mindset.

Practice Assignment

You have understood the personnel or HR audit process. Collect one HR audit report and relate the same with your learned theories.

SUMMARY

Performance audit assesses the degree of economy, efficiency, and effectiveness in the use of human, financial, and material resources at individual, unit, departmental, divisional, and finally at the organizational level. This internal audit examines processes and systems through some kind of tasks to measure and explain the performance of an organization, as a whole. Although performance audit has certain similarities with the financial audit, these two are different in terms of their scope and areas of investigation.

In addition to the performance audit, this chapter elaborates on several HR application areas in an organization for a holistic understanding of the audit functions. For a HR manager, understanding organizational environment both in the context of internal and task related issues, and external environmental issues are now considered very important. Organizational environment, per se, affect the performance and productivity of the employees, hence its effective management is now an important priority for HR managers. Many organization environmental issues (more particularly task related), contributes to employees' fatigue, monotony, boredom, accidents, safety, morale, and grievances. As HR manager, each such micro-effect needs to be managed, or else organizations will lose its business focus and nurture unproductive and demotivated workforce, which only add to the financial burden of the organization. The chapter finally concludes with elaborate discussions on personnel record keeping, duly focusing on both from statutory and voluntary perspectives. Personnel audit, HRIS, and human resource accounting are some other important areas discussed in this chapter to add value to HR managers to understand how all these contribute to effective decision-making.

KEY WORDS

HRIS—Human Resource Information System, used by an organization primarily with computer support to utlize such information for strategic and routine HR decisions.

Human Resource Accounting—Valuation of employees and understanding their potentiality to suit present and future organizational requirements.

Replacement Cost—Cost incurred for manpower replacement.

Performance Data Reliability Audit (DRA)—Data Reliability Audit (DRA) is basically performance audit to ensure accuracy and precession level of observations.

Personnel/HR Audit—Systematic evaluation of personnel or HR functions to understand how it contributes to organizational business goals and meet statutory compliance.

Opportunity Cost—Cost of foregone opportunities.

Skill Development—Developing the skill to meet the changing job requirement.

Synthesis of Performance Data—Synthesis combines the parts and elements with the overall performance of the organization. Synthesis assesses how the results relate to causes and helps in designing the effective measures to correct the deviations and so also to establish the preventive conditions to achieve the desired results in future.

GENERAL REVIEW QUESTIONS

1. Explain the concept of performance management audit. How is performance management audit different from the financial audit?
2. Discuss the structure and the steps involved in performance audit.
3. What are the different methods and techniques used in performance audit? Select some specific methods and techniques (with justification) for carrying out the performance audit in a knowledge intensive R&D organization.
4. Define human resource accounting. For designing human resource accounting system, what are the factors needed to be considered?
5. Define HR audit. What are its objectives and importance?

6. What is the scope of HR audit? What are the records needed for it?
7. Briefly explain methods and techniques of personnel audit.
8. Explain the nature of HR records. What type of HR records will you recommend for an organization?
9. Short Notes
   (a) HR audit
   (b) Career profile
   (c) Present value method
   (d) Sorting
   (e) Economy audit

CRITICAL REVIEW QUESTION

10. To conduct performance audit in a manufacturing organization mainly for operation level employees (executives, supervisors, and workers), develop your action plans with checklists with adequate logic.

REFERENCES

Bhattacharyya, D.K. (2007), *Human Resource Research Methods* (New Delhi: Oxford University Press).

Davenport, T.O. (2000), 'Workers Are Not Assets, Across the Board', 37(6): 30–34.

Flamholtz, Eric G. (1999), *Human Resource Accounting: Advances in Concepts, Methods and Applications*, 3rd edition (AA Dordrecht, The Netherlands: Kulwer Academic Publishers).

Grossman, R.J. (2000), 'Measuring Up', *HR Magazine*, 45(1): 28–35.

Head, G.E. (1985), *Training Cost Analysis* (Washington, DC: Marlin Press).

Lepak, D.P. and S.A. Snell (1998), 'Virtual HR: Strategic Human Resource Management in the 21st Century', *Human Resource Management Review*, 8(3): 215–34.

Likert R. (1971), 'Human Organizational Measurements: Key to Financial Success', *Michigan Business Review* (May) pp. 1–5

Strohmeier, S. (2007). 'Research in e-HRM: Review and Implications', *Human Resource Management Review*, 17(1): 19–37.

Swanson, R.A. and D.B. Gradous (1988), *Forecasting the Financial Benefits of Human Resource Development* (San Francisco, CA: Jossey-Bass).

Ulrich, D. (1996), *Human Resource Champions: The New Agenda for Adding Value and Delivering Results* (Boston, MA: Harvard Business School Press).

Walker, J.W. (1998), 'Are We Using the Right Human Resource Measures?', *Human Resource Planning*, 21(2): 7–8.

CASE STUDY

Valuing Human Resources—The Infosys Way

The human resource accounting concept was pioneered by the Indian public sector companies. It was first introduced by two public sector majors, i.e., Bharat Heavy Electricals Limited (BHEL) and Steel Authority of India Ltd (SAIL) in the 1970s. At Infosys, the concept was started in the year 1995–96. Infosys basically utilized the Lev & Schwartz Model of human resource accounting. Later with the acceptance by Infosys, started under the initiative of Shri Narayan Murthy, the then Chairman of the company, human resource accounting started gaining importance in India.

Infosys' HRA model was based on the present value of the employees' future earnings with the following assumptions:

- An employee's salary package included all benefits, whether direct or otherwise, earned both in India and in a foreign nations.
- The additional earnings on the basis of age and group were also taken into account.

To calculate the value of its human assets in 1995–96, all the 1,172 employees of Infosys were divided into five groups, based on their average age. Each group's average compensation was calculated. Infosys also calculated the compensation of each employee at retirement by using an average rate of increment.

Human resource accounting information for Infosys for the current year is reproduced below:

Human Resource Accounting Information of *TCS*

	2010	2009
General Efficiency		
Sales per support staff		
$ million	0.84	0.94
Rs crore	4.00	4.35
General and admin expenses/revenue (%)	7.15	7.51
Average proportion of support staff (%)	5.36	5.04
Stability		
Average age of support staff (years)	30.4	29.6

Competence—Our people

	2010	2009
Growth/renewal		
Total employees	1,13,796	1,04,850
Added during the year		
Gross	27,639	28,231
Net	8,946	13,663
Laterals added	4,895	5,796
Staff education index	2,96,586	2,72,644
Employees–Number of nationalities	83	76
Gender classification (%)		
Male	66.5	66.6
Female	33.5	33.4
Number of non-Indian national employees	6,064	4,698
Efficiency		
Value-added/employee (Rs crore)		
Software professionals	0.21	0.20
Total employees	0.20	0.19
Value-added/employee ($ million)		
Software professionals	0.04	0.04

Total employees	0.04	0.04
Stability		
Average age of employees (years)	27	26
Attrition—excluding subsidiaries (%)	13.4	11.1
Attrition—excluding involuntary separation (%)	10.4	9.1

Note: The above figures are based on consolidated financial statements (Annual Reports of TCS).

At Infosys, it is always believed that information asymmetry between the management and shareholders should be minimized. Accordingly, the company is in the forefront in practicing progressive and transparent disclosures. Infosys is the first in India to adopt the US Generally Accepted Accounting Principles (US GAAP). Further, the company is the first foreign–private issuer in India to file primary financial statements with Securities and Exchange Commission (SEC) in accordance with the International Financial Reporting Standards (IFRS) as issued by International Accounting Standards Board. Thereafter, the company rapidly progressed to additional disclosures that give deeper insights to the way the company runs their business and into their value creation. The company continues to provide additional information even though it is not mandated by law because the company believes that it will enable the investors to make more informed choices about their performance.

CHAPTER 16

Ethical and Legal Issues of Performance Management

Learning Objectives

After reading this chapter, you will be able to understand:

- Concepts of ethical and legal issues involved in performance management systems
- Ethical perspectives in performance appraisal systems
- Objectives of performance management ethics
- Code of ethics and code of conduct
- Benefits of ethical practices in organizations
- Implementing code of ethics in workplaces
- Ethical dilemmas in performance management
- Legal aspects of performance management

Code of Ethics on Corporate Governance of Infosys, India

Infosys is one of the pioneers in information technology in India. The company is recognized for ethical compliance and always emphasizes on achieving performance with integrity. Known internationally for its best practices in corporate governance, Infosys always put endeavours to respect minority rights in all its business decisions.

The company's corporate governance philosophy is based on the following principles:

- Satisfy the spirit of the law and not just the letter of the law. Corporate governance standards should go beyond the law.
- Be transparent and maintain a high degree of disclosure levels. When in doubt, disclose.
- Make a clear distinction between personal conveniences and corporate resources.
- Communicate externally, in a truthful manner, about how the company is run internally.
- Comply with the laws in all the countries in which the company operates.
- Have a simple and transparent corporate structure driven solely by business needs.
- Management is the trustee of the shareholders' capital and not the owner.

As a part of commitment to follow global best practices, the company complies with the Euro shareholders Corporate Governance Guidelines 2000, and the recommendations of the Conference Board Commission on Public Trusts and Private Enterprises in the USA. The performance management systems at Infosys are considered to be one of the best in the country, for its transparency and employees acceptance.
Adapted from: http://www.infosys.com/investor/corporategovernance.asp.

INTRODUCTION

Compliance with the ethical issues by any organization is possible when they balance the bottom-line and the social welfare. Such a process of balancing may not always be without conflict, because of the differences in the stakeholders' interest. Obviously for this reason, organizations feel constrained in the process of balancing opposing objectives. Being multi-dimensional, an organization has to meet such opposing expectations of stakeholders, who even encompass society, culture, religion, diversity issues, religions, socio-politico-economic issues, or for that matter any possible issues which may have direct or indirect linkages with the organizational activities. Ethical practices cascade to compliance with the corporate social responsibility (CSR). Today CSR has become the managerial responsibility; it is in-built with the organizational effiiciency. In practice, many organizations show their concern for social responsibilities, but indulge in generating profits only. Therefore, organizations need to get a model which can make a trade-off between the profit, ethics, and social responsibility. While doing such trade-offs, it is often difficult for the organization to quantify the direct impact of social responsibility vis-à-vis profit motive.

A mid-sized pharmaceutical company in India, started by an entrepreneur was trying to introduce performance culture to weed out the deadwoods and non-performers and reward the good performers. The company initially started as a family business, but for subsequent business expansion had to go for professional management practices, hiring professional managers and employees. The owner CEO gradually distanced himself from the nitty-gritty of day-to-day work, to play the figure-head role in the organization. In the process of introducing the performance culture, the organization could identify serious ethical issues involving the marketing team members who in the name of achieving the sales targets, indulged in unethical and even illegal means. While the business performance is achieved, adding to the bottom-line of the company, the organization faced with the dilemma whether to comply with the legal and ethical issues, or just keep quite to allow the things to continue to achieve the results. At this stage, the owner CEO of the company, keeping in view the long-term perspectives, developed the code of ethics in compliance with the law of the land. The CEO then ordered for listing of the issues involving managerial ethics and challenges to ensure its compliance. To do so, the first attempt was made to list the factors, which contribute to the compliance of ethical behaviour, and then develop the suitable mechanisms for ethical control and compliance.

An ethical organization can achieve better business results. This maxim is now making more and more corporate leaders accept their social responsibilities and organizational ethics. Organizations indulging in unethical business practices or in unethical dealings with their employees are now quickly identified and become globally transparent in this era of technology-intensive communication systems. Organizational activities require redesigning and updating, keeping pace with public expectations and ever-rising standards. The pattern of organizational behaviour, injustice, corporate dishonesty, exploitation, and negligence being more visible, and attracting public opinion and criticism, ethical violations are carefully avoided. We all know City Toy's case, which used to manufacture toys, using child labour in China to offer it as gift item to the customers of McDonald. It was subjected to criticism internationally to such an extent that McDonald had to withdraw the practice. The Indian carpet industry and Bangladesh garment industry faced similar predicaments in terms of export restrictions for using child labour. Even suppressing facts on products and services become an ethical violation from customers' point of view.

For organizations, ethical issues encompass every citizen of the world. The definition of stakeholder is no longer limited to shareholders, investors, and partners. Stakeholder is any group, which has an interest in, involvement with, dependence on, contribution to, or is affected by the organization. A stakeholder is any individual or group who could lose or gain something because of the actions of the organization.

Unethical corporate practices can be classified into immoral category, that is, a deliberate violation of ethical issues to harm the stakeholders. This apart; there may be unknowing violations of ethics by the organization, which we can be categorized in amoral type. Negative consequences of unethical corporate cultures in human resource management or organizational behaviour pervade selection and staffing, performance appraisal, compensation, and retention decisions. Thus, human resource systems and ethical corporate cultures should be considered partners in the process of creating competitive advantages for organizations. According to Zadek (1997), while complying with the ethical issues in the organizations, managers must also be able to get the flexibility in aligning performance, ethics, and accountability.

DEFINITION AND CONCEPTS

Ethics are moral principles about what is good, defensible, and right. Although operationally ethics need to be integrated with our behaviour and actions, we often treat ethics as an afterthought. Ethics and ethical reflection need to be integrated through all organizational practices. A common philosophical definition of ethics is the science of conduct or values of management. Moral values such as respect, honesty, fairness, and responsibility are important constructs of ethics. Application of such ethics is ensured by organizations by adopting some code of ethics. Thus, ethics includes the fundamental ground rules and organizations give an informed choice to the employees to understand whether something is right or wrong and then take decisions making the right choice. Ethics, therefore, is the framework of values for moral behaviour. It is a social glue to ensure that an organized society prospers and everybody's interest is served. The Ten Commandments of the Christians or the teachings of the Bhagwad Gita for Hindus are sources of directions for ethical behaviour in life. Today, we are concerned with the issue of ethics in two aspects of life, namely, business and profession. Business represents the entrepreneurs and profession represents those who are employed in an organization or who work for an employer. In other words, ethics are equally applicable for the employers and the employees. In India, we find reference to ethics in the Bhagwad Gita. Our traditional guild systems laid down the ethics of business or profession. This sacred text emphasizes the need for internalization of the ethical codes by the individuals, so that they can reflect the same through their behaviour. Organizations can benefit in the best way when they make their people internalize the ethical codes and values. However, external forces now also compel organizations to comply with ethical issues. External forces always need not be the regulatory authorities alone, they could even be stakeholders, whose changing expectations require organizations to step up their ethical standards and conducts. In the case of a profession, it could be the professional association or the guild and in the case of a society where there is a government, it is the government agency, which ensures that the laws are obeyed. In fact, in a secular society, it is the law that lays down what is acceptable conduct and what is not. Acceptable conduct would be encouraged and unacceptable conduct would be considered illegal and punishment meted out.

When performance management systems are abused in organizations, we call it a violation of ethics. It not only speaks on poor corporate governance, but also creates unhealthy work environment, where every employee feels demoralized. Reduced performance and productivity, and employees' dissension even ultimately weakens the organizational competitive strength. It is necessary to ensure transparency in performance evaluation process and communicate to employees, whose interests get prejudiced for any performance aligned decisions like promotions, transfer, salary raise or increments, training, etc. Some organizations even ask the poor performers to quit. Violation of ethics in performance management systems may not always be deliberate for the managers. It may be just for their self-understanding of the process in the absence of any guidelines. Managers often feel they are skillful and knowledgeable enough to rationally use the performance management process.

Sometimes, major miscommunications occur in performance review sessions due to basic differences in ethical orientation. For example, the reviewer may say, 'Reviewing the employees' performance is a requirement, and we need to follow the rules of the organization'. The person being reviewed may reply, 'I contribute to the organization very significantly, but I don't get the rewards or appreciation. I am being treated equally like my other colleagues who underperform. The reviewer is concerned with decisions and actions that conform to basic principles and rules (adherence). The employee appears to be oriented towards the outcome, the ends justify the means (results). They are talking on two different, non-connecting planes. Unless the employee and the reviewer are successful in negotiating an ethical balance, each may view the other as taking unfair shots—and the battleground will be the performance review process.

ETHICAL PERSPECTIVE IN PERFORMANCE APPRAISAL SYSTEM

The *American Heritage Dictionary* elaborates the term ethics as certain set of principles of right conduct, moral values, philosophy, and rules or standards that govern the conduct of a person or the members of a profession. Ethical issues become more challenging in human resource management issue, which encompasses performance management as well. Performance evaluation, generally, consists of multiple factors like punctuality, attitude, conforming to dress codes, good interpersonal relations with the customers, peers, and subordinates, language, neatness, congeniality, and finally the performance output, among other things. The evaluation process will be considerably different between service and production employees and between general employees and professional employees. The ethical challenge arises when, after all the factors have been considered, the decision is made on a factor or factors other than those by which all the employees have been evaluated.

Performance appraisal processes is susceptible to ethical issues. Ethical violation occurs when performance evaluation is done based on biased observation and judgement. Even at times of appraisals, managers often emphasize on unrelated factors like race, religion, argumentative, etc. Ethical performance review is the most important aspect of the performance evaluation process. It requires managers to conduct the review process with honesty and mutuality. Honesty requires honest assessment of performance, while mutuality requires mutual development of performance plans that can ensure improvement of performance.

OBJECTIVES OF PERFORMANCE MANAGEMENT ETHICS

The overall objective of performance appraisal is to provide an honest assessment of performance and to mutually develop a plan to improve the individual's effectiveness. Prerequisites for the same are to make people understand where they stand in terms of their performance achievement. To ensure compliance with the performance ethics, structured performance objectives are laid down, keeping the following points in the backdrop:

- Adequate definitions of the objectives and the purpose of the organization.
- Issues of priority, like values or achievement of performance goals.
- How the employees contribute to the achievement of organizational results.
- Focus of the organization in terms of achieving the performance results like individual, group, or organizational.
- Degree of compatibility of employees with the job position.

Many effective, high-ethics managers invite such inputs to ensure that performance management process becomes ethic complaints. Managers help the employees to understand how their contribution leads to mutually beneficial performance outcomes. Often during the process of performance review, managers face the paradoxical situation, where the employees allege their performance review is meaningless as they see no future in the organization and hence they have made an informed decision to leave the organization. In such cases, most of the managers commit the blunder of immediate recommendation for promotion, even going to the extent of tampering of performance results for the retention of the employees when they feel employees are valuable for the organization. However, ideally in such cases, managers instead of insisting the employees to stay need to allow the normal separation, despite the fact that such separation is painful.

Some managers again, while reviewing the performance of employees, emphasize on conformance with legal aspects. They nurture this impression wrongly, as legal compliance is not the adequate taste of ethical performance evaluation process. Adhering to the rules and regulations and documentation of the entire performance review results may put them in perceptive secured and defensible position, but may make them liable for ethical violation. Managers need to appreciate that the performance review process is not just an annual ritual, but rather a human resource development initiative in terms of injecting the spirit which enables the individuals to recognize and strive for performance improvement.

Again a mechanical performance review process may not violate the ethical requirements, but may imbibe feelings in the minds of the employees being reviewed, that their feelings are ignored. Employees with such feelings lose their personal worth. Again the managers' propensity to stereotype the performance review process is not desirable, as managers in such cases often try to please the subordinates with overrating, without considering the differences in their performance levels. Such erroneous performance review, in reality, make the organization prone to high turnover of best performers. Therefore, performance appraisal process needs to balance between the ethical, legal, and business issues. Without the proper trade-off, the process is meaningless. Self-esteem of employees is the most critical issue. The review process should not damage the self-esteem of the employees for the coercive behaviour of the managers.

Contrarily, when the performance appraisal process helps employees to understand how their contributions relate to the overall objectives of the organizations, they perform better and with proper feedback, they can even autonomously develop themselves and renew their capabilities to improve their future performance levels. With such continuous development of employees, organizations can achieve long-term sustainability and a high degree of competitiveness.

Thus, the primary objective of the performance appraisal process is to develop the employees, and through employees' development and capability enhancement to gain the competitive strength. Ethical consideration of the managers becomes evident from the explicit understanding that making people understand their self-worth autonomously make them deliver better performance results.

CODE OF ETHICS AND CODE OF CONDUCT

Code of ethics and code of conduct specify the ethical standards that a group (e.g., staff or a professional group) should follow in order to continue as a member of the group. They are generally formally stated and members are required to accept them as part of their membership of the group while accepting employment/membership. Values vary between individuals and across cultures. Hofstede's four value dimensions (1980) help us understand cultural value clashes. Long-term versus short-term values affect many aspects of organizational life. The four key ethical principles are egalitarianism, utilitarianism, individual right, and distributive justice. Organizations following the utilitarianism approach in ethics make decisions based on their outcomes and consequences. Ethical behaviour is influenced by moral intensity, ethical sensitivity, and the situation. A code of ethics serves a number of key roles.

A code of ethics is different from a code of conduct. Code of ethics for an organization or for a profession is developed more in the form of statement of values and beliefs that defines an organization or a group. Value statements are aspirational, while rules or principles are the beliefs, which individual members of an organization should subscribe to in order to continue as members of the organization. These are listed in different sections in the code, regarding specific relationships with employees, customers, shareholders, suppliers, and competitors, as well as the society in general. Because of the increasing importance of ethical compliance, professional organizations emphasize on imparting training on ethics.

The code of conduct, on the other hand, translates the values (documented in the code of ethics) into specific behavioural standards, keeping in mind the possible reflection on the stakeholders' interest. It outlines a fundamental set of principles, explains why members of an organization should behave in a certain way, what actions are prohibited, and also how to determine which action is ethical or unethical. Therefore, codes of ethics are general guides to operational values and decisions, while codes of conduct are more specific or formal statements of the values and practices of a business. Codes of conduct for any organization are better understood through the mission statement of the organization.

A common philosophical definition of ethics is the science of conducts or values of management. Moral values are respect, honesty, fairness, and responsibility, and these values are translated into a code of ethics, according to Carter McNamara (2002), a Minneapolis consultant, specializing in leadership development and strategic planning ethics 'includes the fundamental ground rules by which we live our lives'. As it pertains to business, ethics is generally considered the act of learning what is right and what is wrong in the workplace and then making the decision to do the right thing.

Benefits of Code of Ethics

It is now clear that merely having by default a code of ethics or conduct will not solve the ethical problems. However, having a developed code of ethics will certainly be beneficial to the organization and to the society as a whole. For the organization, a clear code of ethics or standards provides concrete guidelines necessary to deal with situations both within the company as well as in external relations. Internal ethical dilemmas always need not be straight and simple; it may be complex, requiring well-defined policies to facilitate fairness and moral management. In external relations with suppliers, customers, and shareholders, a solid code is the best way to avoid decisions that can lead, in extreme cases, to governmental intervention and prosecution.

A clear statement of ethics policy of an organization also helps employees to align their personal values with those of the organization, creating a stronger workplace bond with both fellow workers and company leaders. Also, a code of ethics provides individual workers with security that protects them from possible violation of ethical practices by unscrupulous organizations. Society also benefits when the organizations comply with the ethical codes. Some such areas may be organizations' decision to comply with environmental hazards, and improving the quality of work life (apart from the benefit to the people who work with the organization, it also benefits the society through improved infrastructural facilities). Also, a code of ethics benefits future corporate leaders, as these prospects can improve their moral standards right from the beginning, to rise to the future expectations of ethical standards in their higher role positions.

Hence, a developed code of ethics benefits all types of organizations and businesses, irrespective of their size and nature of activities. Such a code not only transcends business practices, but also encourages employees to be upfront about problems, which they may encounter in the workplace.

Benefits of Ethical Practices in Organizations

By behaving ethically, organizations can derive huge advantages. Even though the primary constructs of ethical practices are humanity and compassion for the stakeholders, it can provide the following advantages to organizations:

- **Competitive advantage**—Customers favour those organizations which are known for their ethical practices. Hence, ethical violation reduces the market share, reduces their sales and revenues, and ultimately adversely affects the bottom line of the organization.
- **Better staff attraction and retention**—Ethics compliant organizations also develop their brand image and such employer branding helps them to attract and retain the best people, which eventually contribute to their sustainable competitive advantage. On the contrary, ethical violation means high attrition rate of employees, recruitment of average performers, and overall cost inefficiency.
- **Investment**—Ethics compliant organizations can also attract investors as people repose their confidence only on those who show integrity, a sense of responsibility, and who are trustworthy.
- **Morale and culture**—Ethics-compliant organizations also create a workplace, where employees feel compelled to work. Ethical organizations develop high integrity, become socially responsible, and globally considerate. All these, make such organizations less prone to stress, attrition, and dissatisfaction. Therefore, complying with the ethics, organizations develop a work culture, free from stress, which makes employees feel happier and become more productive.
- **Reputation**—Building organizational reputation takes years of efforts and ruining it hardly requires one violation. Ethically responsible organizations are less prone to scandals and disasters. They become more sensitive to any such practices, which may adversely affect the reputation of the organization.
- **Legal and regulatory reasons**—Even though compliance with ethics still now voluntary and organizations comply with these for their long-term business interests, globally ethical issues are likely to come under legal and regulatory norms, making it compulsory for organizations to comply with

the same. Hence, early preparedness of the organization will benefit them in the long run, when ethical issues become legally enforceable.

- **Legacy**—It is human nature to be good. Ethical consideration changing our percept of legacy, which is not to pile up money at the cost of others' sufferings, but decisions and business practices which are beneficial to mankind. Hence, organizations believe the test of real legacy is ethical decision-making.

IMPLEMENTING CODE OF ETHICS IN THE WORKPLACE

Once a decision is made to develop a code ethics or a code of conduct for an organization, the next step is to decide what it will include, what it will aim at, and who will prepare it. Carter McNamara, in the guidebook, *The Ethics Toolkit for Managers*, points out 'codes should not be developed out of the human resource or legal departments alone, as is too often done'. Rather, he says, 'All staff must see the ethics programme being driven by top management'.

The Institute of Business Ethics recommends these general steps to be followed in the initial planning phase:

- Find a champion—preferably a very senior level management person.
- Get endorsement from the chairman and the board.
- Find out what bothers people—talk to both employees and management to find out topics that are sensitive issues or require guidance.
- Pick a well-tested model, looking to other organizations' codes to develop ideas and to understand what could be appropriate for meeting own organizational needs.
- Develop your own organization's code of conduct, document it with due care to customization to deal with the problems that are likely to arise in all areas of organizational relations.
- Pilot test it both within and outside the organization to understand its suitability.
- Issue the code—publish the code and make sure it gets sent directly to all employees, shareholders, suppliers, and customers. It's also a good idea to post it on the company's Web site.
- Introduce examples of the code in action into company's training programmes.
- Enforce the code and regularly review it, and assess whether it continues to remain a good fit for your needs.

Ben and Jerry's (1978) code begins with a mission statement: The code goes on to state the company's mission, relating to the product quality, economic mission, and the social mission of the organization. Similarly, Gap Inc's (1998) code contains specific statements for each group with whom the company has relationship, viz., 'commitment to ethical sourcing', 'code of vendor conduct', 'code for global compliance team', etc. Such elaborate codes for specific groups, the company feels, are necessary because of globally expanded operations and outsourcing.

ETHICAL DILEMMA IN PERFORMANCE MANAGEMENT

In the process of performance evaluation, the following ethical dilemmas are experienced by performance reviewers.

- Emphasis on trait-oriented and subjective performance evaluation criteria, which are difficult to quantify—It is always desirable to use objective criteria for performance evaluation. Subjective evaluation often becomes discriminatory. Using the SMART approach, and so also BARS (behaviourally anchored rating scales), many subjective performance attributes can be quantified (Barrett, 1966, Campbell et al., 1970, and Smith and Kendall, 1963).
- Ambiguous performance standards and KPIs—This restraints accurate assessment of performance. Performance standards need to be quantitative; time bound, realistic, and job related. Such standards need to be developed by the managers in such a way, so that it can encapsulate the critical performance dimensions of the job. Again while developing performance standards, managers also need to understand that too much emphasis on quantitative performance criteria may not help them to track the important qualitative skills of the employees that facilitate them to manipulate a situation to get the results, without, however, ethical violation. More careful approach of the managers in writing the performance standards may reduce the errors.
- Simultaneous use of different performance appraisal tools—Often, managers to reduce the rating errors use this approach of multiple uses of performance appraisal tools. But this practice may lead to ambiguous performance results, as different raters for their different use of performance appraisal tools, may come out to different rating results for the same individual, leading to the problem of consolidation.
- Difference in approach in using the performance results—Essentially, performance management system is an employee development tool. It must facilitate the human resource development, which includes succession planning, promotions, compensation design, training, human resource planning, etc. Arbitrary use of performance results information is detrimental to the interests of the employees only, and ultimately makes the performance management process incredible to the employees. Gradually for this performance management systems in an organization loses its sanctity.
- Non-participative approach in developing performance standards—Ideally, managers need to adopt the practice of mutuality in terms of discussing the performance standards with the employees. If required, managers also need to make changes in the performance standards, based on the inputs of the employees. Employees' participation in performance goal setting, designing the performance standards and the KPIs, substantially enhances their level of performance commitment and facilitates the organizations to achieve the business goals. Once it is ethically agreed by the managers to involve employees in the performance appraisal process, the scope of employees participation can be extended to performance goals setting, performance standards development, performance criteria development, data collection, self-rating, problem solving, and feedback (DeVries et al. 1980). Form of such participation may be in terms of mutual problem solving (Maier, 1958), in MBO process (Meyer et al., 1965), and 'rap session' formats (Meyer, 1977).

LEGAL ASPECTS OF PERFORMANCE MANAGEMENT

Performance management and decisions thereupon, per se, is the prerogative of management, unless it prejudices the interest of the appraisee. Prejudicing of interest occurs when decisions on promotions, pay raises, and other career development of the employees are taken by the organizations, affecting their interests. The premise of prejudicing the interest of employees, however, is the perception of the employees. Hence legally, it is the onus of employees to substantiate that their interests have been prejudiced. In India, we have many labour law provisions to enforce the mandatory requirements that the performance evaluations, or for that matter any work-related behaviour be based on objective, job-related criteria, to ensure that mangers are free from biases. Biases in performance evaluation of employees affect the interests of the employees and become a legal issue. Therefore, legal consideration is one of the most important aspects of performance evaluation systems.

Performance evaluation results are used to select present employees for merit pay, promotion, training, retention, transfer, discipline, demotion, or termination. The nature of the employment relationship, as well as the nature of the employment decision, must be considered to determine the potential for performance evaluations. Where there are no express contract terms that govern performance appraisals, courts have allowed employers a good deal of latitude to determine how to evaluate their employees (Gomez-Mejia et al.1995). However, even in an *employment at will* relationship, under which either the employer or the employee may terminate the employment relationship at any time, an employer's discretion is not entirely without limits. As Keys et al. (1987) have pointed out, courts vary by jurisdiction in their recognition of the *at will* doctrine as a matter of state contract and labour law. Moreover, courts have found employers liable under numerous exceptions to the doctrine. These exceptions include implied contract (as where an obligation to terminate only for just cause arises based on verbal promises or those contained in an employee handbook) and violation of public policy (as where an employee is terminated after complaining of harassment or accusing the employer of other misconduct). Potential liability for defamation or negligence also may restrict, in practical terms, the manner in which employers can manage and appraise performance. As the following examples illustrate, performance appraisals also may figure in determining the very nature of the employment relationship.

Some of the legal principles that may govern the performance appraisals and the nature of employment relatiónsips, based on the global trend can be listed as under:

Employment at Will—It indicates the employer or the employee may terminate the employment relationship at any point of time, viz., in India in the letter of appointment, many organizations endorse the statement, 'This employment may be terminated from either side giving one-month notice, or one-month pay in lieu of notice, without assigning any reason'. In such a situation, the employer gets considerable latitude in determining whether, when, and how to appraise the performance of employees.

Implied Contract—Such assumptions in employment relationship restrict the employer to appraise the performance with a structured and documented approach with adequate transparency. Employment termination decision, based on the performance results, often becomes the litigation issue. Hence, performance evaluation process needs to be considered by the managers very carefully.

Violation of Public Policy—Determination that given action is adverse to the public welfare and is, therefore, prohibited. Public policy may restrict the manner in which an employer can use appraisal results (e.g., may prevent retaliation for reporting illegal conduct by employer).

Negligence—Breach of duty to conduct performance appraisals with due care. Potential liability may require employer to inform employee of poor performance and provide opportunity to improve.

Defamation—Disclosure of untrue unfavourable performance information that damages an employee's reputation. Potential liability may restrict the manner in which negative performance information can be communicated to others.

Misrepresentation—Disclosure of untrue favourable performance information that causes risk of harm to others. Potential liability may restrict willingness of employer to provide references altogether, even for good former employees.

Labour Standards—Employment relationships in India and in other countries are largely governed by various laws and regulations. All these impose obligations to the employers in matters of termination, even when performance level may not be up to the mark.

Some of the important suggestions while drafting the appointment letter, employees' handbooks, employment standing orders, human resource management policy manuals, which can minimize the problem of future litigation, alleging biased performance evaluation can be listed as under:

- That employment is understood to be *at will.*
- That the employer expressly reserves the right to discharge the employee at any time for any reason with or without any cause and with or without any notice.
- That nothing in the employer's policies, practices, or procedures, including performance appraisals, should be construed to confer any right upon the employee to continued employment.
- That the employer expressly reserves the right to unilaterally alter the terms and conditions of employment, including the manner in which performance is or is not appraised.
- That the employer is under no obligation to appraise performance.
- That neither the fact that appraisals are or are not conducted, nor the manner in which they may be conducted, should be construed to give rise to a 'just cause' requirement for terminating the employment relationship.
- That performance appraisals and other evaluation procedures should in no way be considered in any other manner in determining the existence or nature of any employment relationship that may be found to exist between the parties.

Some of the legal aspects of the performance evaluation systems are listed as under:

- Punitive or retaliatory attitude of managers while evaluation of employees' performance. This problem occurs when managers fail to become impersonal, and even a trivial disagreement with the employees occupies their mind, while they make the performance evaluation of employees.
- Disregard of diversity issues while evaluating the performance of employees. Managers while performing their duties of performance evaluation, often discriminate employees on the basis of race, religion, age, gender, disability, culture, etc.
- Doing performance evaluation of employees without adequate backup or evidences. While taking decisions based on poor performance evaluation reports, it is important for managers to keep backup support; else it may affect the morale and the motivation level of employees. For example, in 360-degree performance appraisal systems, peers views may be recorded as evidence to avoid any future litigation.
- It is important to give adequate cognizance to the employees' views. This can be done by giving adequate opportunities to the employees to express their feelings, while commenting on their performance appraisal reports.
- Hundred per cent weight, or absolute performance-based decision on promotion, compensation, transfer, career development opportunities, and even termination, to the extent possible should be avoided by the managers, else such decisions may become legal issues, particularly when it affects the interests of the employees. Many organizations while appreciating the performance-based or for those matter merit-based decisions, also give importance to other multiple factors, for holistic study of the employees.

- Employees with poor performance need to be given fair chance to improve the performance. If, however, the employees continue to underperform, they can then be asked to leave.
- Sharing of performance feedback with the employees, time to time, and giving them the guidance through the performance counseling sessions, make the performance appraisal process more credible, and can avoid litigation.
- Retention of performance records to avoid future litigation is important. Charges of discriminatory performance appraisal can be mooted by the employees, even afterwards.
- Auditing of performance evaluation results by outside experts for validation may be necessary to avoid any possible litigation.
- Performance evaluation needs to be specific to job requirements, hence it must be written in dispassionate style.
- Training the managers and supervisors, on the nitty-gritty of performance evaluation systems, can reduce the rating errors and make the process immune from litigation.
- Records and reports on performance appraisal need to be kept in secured condition. This ensures zero tampering of performance records, and minimizes the chances of litigation.

Keeping in view the legal complications involved, performance appraisal criteria need to conform to the following:

- Should be objective rather than subjective.
- Should be job-related or based on job analysis.
- Should be based on behaviours rather than traits.
- Should be within the control of the ratee.
- Should relate to specific functions, not global assessments.
- Should be communicated to the employee.

Procedural recommendations for legally sound performance appraisals need to conform to:

- Should be standardized and uniform for all employees within a job group.
- Should be formally communicated to employees.
- Should provide notice of performance deficiencies, and opportunities to correct them.
- Should provide access for employees to review appraisal results.
- Should provide formal appeal mechanisms that allows for employee input.
- Should use multiple, diverse, and unbiased raters.
- Should provide written instructions and training for raters.
- Should require thorough and consistent documentation across raters that includes specific examples of performance based on personal knowledge.
- Should establish a system to detect potentially discriminatory effects or abuses of the system overall.

Nevertheless there are principles of equity and fairness that should be upheld in any good performance evaluation process.

SUMMARY

Performance management is a systematic data-based approach to manage human behaviour in the workplace. It is systematic as it emphasizes on the laws of behaviour, i.e., the lawful relation between the employees' performance behaviour and the environment. In the process of complying with the laws of behaviour, employees also need to conform to the ethical issues. Effective performance management process needs to balance legal and ethical issues to conform to the social and environmental principles to deliver the best performance results. Organizations adopting a code of ethics pursue activities ethically while conducting their business.

Now-a-days, conforming to ethical and legal issues in managing the performance of employees, organizations can not only achieve the business results, but also earn the respects and social prestige, which goes a long way in employer branding. With a properly designed code of ethics, organizations encourage ethical practices in all spheres of its activities, including the performance management process.

This chapter introduces the basics of legal and ethical aspects in performance management, adhering to which managers need to do the performance assessment, to conform to the social, environmental, and legal norms, while at the same time address the business needs.

KEY WORDS

Code of ethics—Specify the ethical standards that a group (e.g., staff or a professional group) should follow in order to stay as a member of the group. They are generally formally stated and members are required to accept them as part of their membership of the group while accepting employment.

Ethical decision-making—Decision making in compliance with the ethical issues, providing transparency, effect, and fairness.

Ethical culture—The ethical environment of an organization, which influences ethical or unethical behaviour of the members of an organization.

Ethics of intellectual property, knowledge and skills—Organizations while doing business, need to comply with these. Even though these are difficult ownable objects, ethical violations can drag the organization into a difficult phase. Ethical violation in these areas may come from patent infringement, copyright infringement, and trademark infringement.

CONCEPT REVIEW QUESTIONS

1. Discuss the ethical perspectives of performance appraisal systems.
2. What are the important points of consideration for developing performance ethics? Discuss some of the paradoxical situations that managers face while pursuing the performance objectives.
3. Discuss the benefits of code of ethics and the ethical practices in organization.
4. Discuss the steps involved in implementing workplace ethics.
5. What are the important ethical dilemmas faced by the managers in evaluating the performance of employees? How can such dilemmas be addressed?
6. What are the important legal aspects of performance management systems? List some of the legal principles that govern the performance appraisal systems and employment relations in organizations.
7. Short Notes
   (a) Moral and culture
   (b) Legacy
   (c) Code of ethics
   (d) Employment at will

CRITICAL REVIEW QUESTION

8. Visit some recent press reports on ethical violation in performance appraisal systems of any organizations. Critically examine those and suggest what could be the possible courses of action for your chosen organization to avoid such ethical violation. Study any ethical compliance report of an Indian organization. Relate their degree of compliance with their business achievement along with your comments and observations.

REFERENCES

American Heritage Talking Dictionary (1997), electronic edition (The Learning Company, Inc.).

Barrett, R.S. (1966), *Performance Rating* (Chicago, IL: Science Research Associates).

Bhattacharyya, D.K. (2007), *Human Resource Research Methods* (New Delhi: Oxford University Press).

Bhattacharyya, D.K. (2009), *Organizational Behaviour—Concepts and Applications* (New Delhi: Oxford University Press).

Bowie, Norman (1982), *Business Ethics* (Englewood Cliffs, NJ: Prentice-Hall, Inc.).

Campbell, J.P., M.D. Dunnette, E.E. Lawler and K.E. Weick (1970), *Managerial Behavior, Performance and Effectiveness* (New York, NY: McGraw-Hill).

Carter, McNamara (2002), 'An Ethical Toolkit for Managers', *Journal of Business Ethics*, 35(1): 35–49.

DeVries, D.L., A.M. Morrison, S.L. Shullman and M.L. Gerlach (1980), *Performance Appraisal on the Line* (Greensboro, NC: Center for Creative Leadership).

Gap Inc's Code of Ethics (1978), www.gapinc.com, accessed on 7 July 2007. The company created these codes in 1978.

Gomez-Mejia, L.R., D.B. Balkin and R.L. Cardy (1995), *Managing Human Resources* (Englewood Cliffs, NJ: Prentice Hall).

Hofstede, G. (1980), *Cultural Consequences: International Differences in Work-Related Values* (Beverly Hillls, CA: Sage).

Jerry, White (1978), *Honesty, Morality and Conscience* (Colorado Springs, CO: Nav Press).

Key, D.J., S. Briggs and J. Grenig (1987), 'State Court Disparity on Employment-at-Will', *Personnel Psychology*, 40: 565–77.

Maier, N.R.F. (1958), *The Appraisal Interview: Objectives, Methods, and Skills* (London: Wiley).

Meyer, H.H. (1977), 'The Annual Performance Review Discussion... Making It Constructive', *Personnel Journal*, 56: 508–11.

Meyer, H.H., E. Kay and J.R.P. French Jr. (1965), 'Split Roles in Performance Appraisal', *Harvard Business Review*, 43: 123–29.

Smith, P.C. and L.M. Kendall (1963), 'Retranslation of Expectations: An Approach to the Construction of Unambiguous Anchors for Rating Scales', *Journal of Applied Psychology Al*, 149–55.

Zadek, S. (1997), 'Balancing Performance Ethics and Accountability: Emerging Practices of Social Ethical Accounting, Auditing, and Reporting', available at http://dnwe.unirostock.de/e97wza.htm

CASE STUDY

United Technologies Corporation (UTC)

UTC is a global conglomerate with multiple business units like Carrier Corporation, Hamilton Sundstrand, Otis Elevator, Pratt & Whitney, Sikorsky, UTC Power, and the Chubb. With more than 2.5 lakh employees, UTC has presence in 4,000 locations, spread across 62 countries. UTC's most challenging role is to orient its new recruits on its global ethics programme. Integrating the global ethics programme in cross-cultural and cross-country work environment literally made UTC design the programme that conforms to the global workplace. Most of UTC's business units are almost a century old. UTC's business presence being ranges from aircraft engines, helicopters, security and fire protection, air control systems, detector lock, machine tools, etc. compliance with ethical issues are especially important, as many regulatory norms embrace UTC's manufacturing ventures. As a major vendor to US Government Department of Defense in the 1980s, in one of the UTC units, there was serious allegation of ethical violation, which was like making super-normal profit in defense contracts.

All these prompted UTC to increase there self-regulating through formal Code of Ethics, which UTC had adopted since 1990. UTC's code of ethics articulates standards of conduct surpassing even the legal requirements. UTC could successfully embrace the code of ethics into their corporate culture and business practices.

Documented Code of Ethics of UTC

UTC's code of ethics encompasses certain generic principles and philosophies, within the ambit of which the activities of the organizations are managed and controlled.

Corporate Principles

United Technologies commit to high ethical standards that encompass the overall business conduct and the company's relationship with all the stakeholders, including their own employees. These ethical standards show the commitments and the responsibilities of the company, covering the following areas:

Customers

Lawful and ethical dealing with customers, commitment for highest quality value, fair prices, and honesty in transaction are the ethical codes of the UTC.

Employees

UTC is committed to fair employment practices, respecting equal employment opportunity, valuing diversity, and offering safe and healthy working conditions.

Suppliers

Commitment to fair dealing with suppliers for long-term business relationships.

Shareowners

Commitment to provide higher returns to the shareowners to protect and improve the value of their investment, conforming to legal and ethical conduct of business.

Competitors

Commitment to fair competition putting all business efforts on merits.

Communities

Commitment to become a law-abiding corporate citizen for national and global communities, with emphasis on improving their well-being. Encourage and promote employees' participation in civic affairs.

Standards of Conduct

In UTC, the code of ethics governs their business decisions and actions. It represents the fundamental values, which form the basis of decisional framework. The company communicates and explains the code of ethics through circulars and corporate policy manuals. For UTC, business results are the outcome of ethical actions of all members of the organization. Each UTC member is made personally responsible for ethical compliance.

Performance: In performance management, UTC believes in emphasizing on customer feedback and calibrate the employees' performance extending all support to them.

Pioneering Innovation: UIC believes in innovation and research and development activities. The company promotes the culture of seeking and sharing ideas and encourages diversity of experience and opinion.

Personal Development: The company emphasizes on employees' development through lifelong learning to constantly renew their knowledge and capabilities.

Social Responsibility: UTC is committed to social responsibility maintaining highest ethical, environmental, and safety standards.

Question: Study the code of ethics of UTC, one of the stable globally diversified conglomerates, having business presence in some of the areas over more than a century. Relate the company's code of ethics with the performance management systems (collect input visiting their Web site information), and explain how with these sets of code of ethics, the company would be able to comply with their performance ethics.

CHAPTER 17

Contemporary Issues in Performance Management

Learning Objectives

After reading this chapter, you will be able to understand:

- Various contemporary organizational improvement tools as drivers of performance management systems
- Business process reengineering
- Lean management practices
- Toyota production system
- Quick response manufacturing
- Total quality management
- Six-sigma practices
- Innovation and creativity

General Electric—Achieving Excellence Through Six-sigma

General Electric Company (GE) is one of the largest diversified companies in the world. Even some of GE's strategic business units (SBUs), because of their size and volume of activities, can independently figure out among Fortune 500 companies. With business volume of almost $150 million, the company operates in more than 100 countries, and has over 250 manufacturing facilities across the globe. With diversified product portfolio ranging from plastics to locomotives, GE could also transform into the business of services and solutions. GE, a quality in name itself, is powered by the world's largest scientists' pool, whose R&D work continuously give GE the edge over other competitors. GE's R&D is the centre point for strategic cost effective technical innovations. Jack Welch the legendary ex-CEO of the company never used to believe in quality programmes, branding it as theoretical. His quality philosophy rather was more deep-rooted, as he used to consider quality an integral part of any business. However, Motorola's six-sigma quality initiatives impressed him and for obvious opportunity of objective assessment of achieved quality level, he had embraced the six-sigma practices in the company in 1995.

Six-sigma, per se, is a structured data-driven approach to eliminate defects, wastage, etc. recreating the process. While recreating the process, six-sigma emphasizes on factors critical to quality as perceived by the customers. Primarily, it is based on a combination of statistical quality control techniques, assuming that the output of most of the physical processes follows a normal distribution, with the processes centred at the mean. Theoretically, any process would have a natural spread of three sigma (standard deviation) from the normal distribution mean on either side of the centre.

This spread contains 99.9999998 per cent of the process output. Thus, only 0.002 parts per million are out of the design specification. At six-sigma level, defects get reduced to 3.4 per million opportunities.

While introducing six-sigma in GE's operations, it was observed that GE could achieve 3–4 sigma level, i.e., about 35,000 defects per million opportunities, which per se indicates that almost $7–10 billion are avoidable expenditure for the company, which can be saved introducing six-sigma.

However, GE's premise for implementation of six-sigma was getting ready from 1988 onwards for its 'Work Out' programme. Even though it was not theoretically known as six-sigma, this programme gave every employee the opportunity to influence and improve GE's operations. Among others, GE's 'work out' programmes emphasized on building trust, employee empowerment, etc. Therefore six-sigma implementation in GE was relatively much hassle free.

Within few years of six-sigma implementation, GE's annual savings went up to $2.5 billion, and above all GE could achieve customer satisfaction and improve the stakeholders' value.

INTRODUCTION

In today's complex business environment, performance improvement is the most challenging task for any organization. In this concluding chapter, we have discussed various contemporary performance improvement tools. The major drivers for organizational performance improvement are business process re-engineering (BPR), Toyota production system (TPS) and lean management, six-sigma, total quality management (TQM), and quick response manufacturing (QRM). Successful use of these tools depends on the specific requirements of the organizations. Business process reengineering (BPR) in organizations is now considered essential to keep pace with global competition. Among others, BPR requires organizations to align with change, which altogether requires them to revisit their missions and reinvent with the changing business focus. When Dell reengineered themselves from a computer-renting business to a reseller with their K-12 workforce, everybody was skeptical if Dell would be able to run the show with the same soldiers! Today, Dell is a success story, so much so that IBM was unable to withstand the price competition and had to change its business focus, withdrawing from desktop manufacturing and selling. But all these are not so simple and linear. Most of the organizations fail in their BPR because of their overfocus on issues concerning structure and process. BPR, among others, involves adoption of new strategies, redesigning of organizational structures, management style, and external relationships. But, more importantly, the culture of an organization has to be considered, as BPR also requires people to change. Globally, we have many examples of organizations which have failed in theprocess of transformation for not adequately addressing people's issues. We all know the case of the collapse of the more than 200-year old legacy of *Encyclopedia Britannica*. Resistance from their employees could not allow them to redesign their product (from printed volumes to CD version of Encyclopedia) to respond to Microsoft's Encarta. Or, for that matter, consider the case of Phillips in India. They hived off their business (TV and other consumer electronics divisions in Kolkata, West Bengal) selling their stake to Videocon. Today Phillips is planning to re-enter the Indian market. For Videocon, putting back erstwhile Phillips employees to business was not so easy. It was a sustained cultural alignment initiative, which ultimately could make them a right-fit to pursue Videocon's business objectives.

All these, therefore, justify that any performance improvement initiative, be it through BPR or any other initiatives, would not be a success unless we also suitably address the cultural issues. McKinsey's 7S model (Henley, 1991) provides a generic model of organizations. The 7S model has shared values at its heart. If BPR has significant impact on all of the other six dimensions, then it would be reasonable to conclude that BPR involves significant organizational change through performance improvement and that it has a significant impact on, or dependency on, organizational culture.

The introductory discussion, therefore, substantiates that performance management systems of any organization, among others, also depend on practicing a number of organizational change tools and techniques, in addition to its core focus on basic issues. The chapter, therefore, introduces these concepts with a brief discussion on its application related to performance management issues.

BUSINESS PROCESS REENGINEERING—CONCEPTS AND DEFINITIONS

People and processes are the two cornerstones for any organization. Making people to work hard alone cannot increase the business performance. It requires simultaneous restructuring of the business processes too. Globally, it is now proved that BPR can dramatically improve the organizational performance. Through BPR, organizations achieve radical improvement in productivity, cycle times, and quality, all by redesigning the business processes. With a customer-centric approach, BPR eliminates unproductive activities, introducing the culture of cross-functional teams and using the technology supported information dissemination for better decision-making.

To understand BPR, at the outset, we need to understand the business process. In line with Davenport and Short (1990), we can understand it as some 'logically related tasks' that helps the organization to achieve defined business results. A process, per se, is a certain set of activities. Davenport and Short considered three dimensions of a business process: entities, objects, and activities. While doing BPR in any organization, all these dimensions need to be taken care of. Organizational entities could be inter-organizational, inter-functional, or inter-personal. Objects may be both physical and informational, while the activities are managerial and operational. For successful reengineering of the business processes, Hammer and Champy (1993) suggest introduction of teamwork and employee empowerment. These, among others, require bringing the change in the culture of the organization.

For achieving improved organizational performance through BPR, it requires organizations to take the following major steps:

- Redefining the organizational strategy to meet customer needs.
- Redesigning business processes to achieve performance improvement.
- Supporting restructuring process with information technology.
- Developing cross-functional teams for improved performance.
- Rethinking core organizational and people issues.
- Holistic improvement of business processes across the organization.

Empirical studies indicate that globally organizations can get incremental results in performance through BPR. Such performance improvement could exert positive impact on customers. Also by implementing BPR, organizations can reduce costs and cycle time by eliminating unproductive activities and the people who do such activities. BPR is constructed as a process without human face for making people redundant who perform unproductive activities. But BPR never reduces manpower who is engaged in productive activities. By reorganizing the work structure and introducing team culture, BPR paves the way for lean management practices, enhances the flow of information, reduces quality problems and avoids rework. All these significantly improve organizational performance.

BPR practices were earlier considered generic by its major proponents like Hammer (1990), Hammer and Champy (1993), Earl (1994), Davenport (1995), Kettinger and Grover (1995), Stoddard and Jarvenpaa (1995), and Harkness et al., (1996), as the one and same across various organizations, irrespective of their size, nature of activities, etc. However, Kettinger et al. (1997) observed the variation in BPR practices with respect to the nature of BPR projects that varies with the nature of organization.

Although for business imperatives, and so also for performance improvement, organizations today feel compelled to do BPR, organizational approaches to BPR may vary in terms of three different elements: quick hits, incremental improvement, and reengineering. Organizations with quick hits approach focus on achieving immediate results through BPR. Hence, such organizations select those areas of restructuring which are relatively simple to address and results are immediately achievable. Incremental improvement approach also focus on immediate results with BPR efforts. But characteristically it is different from quick hits as it addresses the small issues on specific performance gaps. It is only reengineering which emphasizes on achieving dramatic business results. Reengineering is more focused on total organizational change for holistic organizational development and performance improvement.

Two global organizations, Ford Motor Company and Proctor and Gamble Corporation (P&G), could achieve excellence in business performance through business process reengineering.

Ford's reengineering process helped them to manufacture quality cars only. This could help the company to save substantially on recalls and warranty repairs. Ford reengineered the car manufacturing process by introducing bar codes to trace any missing parts in the assembled cars. A foolproof reengineered process helped Ford to offer unparallel extended warranty of 3 years.

Procter and Gamble Corporation reengineered their brand management activity by introducing selective innovative brands pacing with the market demand. Also the company introduced the digital scorecard to perform R&D in virtual mode. This substantially reduced the response time for new product design, after the selection of innovative ideas.

McKINSEY 7S FRAMEWORK

McKinsey 7S framework developed by Tom Peters and Robert Waterman also helps the organization to improve performance. The framework also helps the organization to examine the effect of future changes for mergers and acquisitions or any other changes per se. The central focus of the model is shared values. With shared values, organizations can achieve business excellence, i.e., improvement of overall performance. The typical shape of the model (Figure 17.1) illustrates the interrelatedness of all the seven items, indicating any change in either of the item or items can bring change in the organization. McKinsey's 7S model helps the organization to pull the people together to achieve performance goals. Each item of 7S model is explained as:

- **Strategy:** It defines the scope of organizational activities to manage the situation of uncertainty. Also through strategy organization allocates scarce resources. Based on the strategy, organizations draw specific action plans to achieve performance goals.
- **Structure:** It distributes the activities of the organization into hierarchical levels, and also illustrates how the authority flows from top to down the line in the organization.
- **Systems:** Defines various processes and procedures of the organization.
- **Staff:** Defines the people and groups to undertake the tasks of the organization.

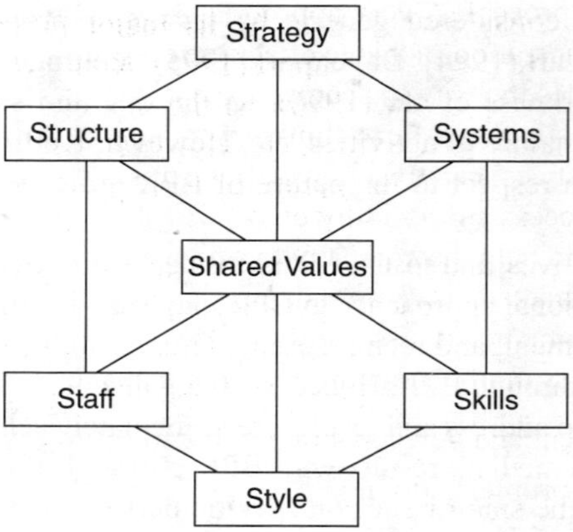

Figure 17.1 *7S model*

- **Style:** Defines the way the managers must behave to achieve the performance goals.
- **Super-ordinate goals (shared vision):** Guides the people of the organization to pursue the common performance goals.
- **Skills:** Determines the abilities of people for achieving the performance goals.

The concept of 8S has now been introduced, which includes streaming. Streaming directly or indirectly influences all the 7S, i.e., through streaming, change in any of the 7 S can be brought to order.

Peters and Waterman (1982) the proponents of 7S model suggested certain specific performance improvement plans that can help the organizations to achieve the excellence. These are explained as

- Bias for action.
- Customer proximity.
- Autonomy and entrepreneurship.
- Productivity.
- Value-driven management.
- Stick to the knitting (dealing with strength).
- Lean staff.
- Simultaneous loose–tight properties (decentralize but enforce strict control).

TOYOTA PRODUCTION SYSTEM (TPS) AND LEAN MANAGEMENT

Two global organizations, Toyota and Tesco, successfully implemented lean management to achieve quality and efficiency in their business processes. Lean management practices aim to achieve effectiveness through efficient systems and processes. Very appropriately we can define efficiency as how to do the things correctly, while the organizations achieve effectiveness doing the things correctly. From that perspective, while efficiency guides the way to achieve excellence through its successful implementation, organizations achieve the effectiveness. Lean thinking is the efficient way of thinking to improve the business process and lean practices lead to achieve effective results. Toyota by introducing a standardized yet adaptive and agile process successfully embedded their lean management practices into their organizational DNA. This could help the company to achieve excellence. So from the operational point of view, we can define lean management as an 'adaptive continuous improvement' process.

Toyota's lean management practice is also known as Toyota Production System (TPS). The company adopts the following approaches in implementing the lean management:

- Analyse the biggest problem and develop strategy-based solution path to solve the problem.
- Achieve stability through problem solving.
- Ensure continuous flow through interconnected processes.
- Assign meaningful work to all (*Jidoka*).
- Make standardized yet adaptive (to change) work and workplace.
- Level production (*Heijunka*).
- Introduce demand pull manufacturing.
- Ensure material and information flow through value stream mapping.

TPS is based on two main premises, i.e., 'Just-in-time' and '*Jidoka*', which advocates the philosophy that 'good thinking means good product'. Some of the commonly used terms in lean management are:

Andon

Visual displays of present status of work, indicating alarming situation, if any, various work instructions, progress of job, etc. It acts as a control device and is used as one of the major tools of Jidoka.

Genchi Genbutsu

The basic principle is 'see the problem to know the problem.' It means experiencing a job is more important that understanding the job theoretically.

Heijunka

It is leveling of production schedule for just-in-time delivery.

Hoshin

It means setting goals pacing with the business priorities, i.e., leveling performance to achieve growth.

Jidoka

It is one of the major pillars of TPS. It is the process of stopping production to avoid quality problem. It requires identification or fixing of quality problems for reasons likemalfunctioning of machines, late work, etc. and correct the problems and build in quality in the production process.

Jishuken

It is a management-driven initiative to stimulate Kaizen activity for continuous improvement and spreading its awareness to all members of the organization.

Just-in-Time

It is another major pillar of TPS. It requires organizations to produce keeping in pace with real-time demand. The key control of just-in-time production is *Kanban*. *Kanban*, the small sign, gives instruction for production, checks irregular production, and identifies irregular speed of processing.

Kaizen

It is a system of continuous improvement eliminating the *Muda* (wastage). It simultaneously improves the performance and minimizes the costs. We can define Muda as non-value-adding activities which in reality adds to waste. Muda may be for overproduction, waiting, conveyance, processing, inventory, motion, and time for correction.

Nemawashi

It indicates cross-functional and cross-sectional participation in discussions to address the common issues and policies.

Pokayoke

It supports *Jidoka* preventing production of defective parts through mistake-proof method.

The TPS or lean management practices, therefore, ensure efficient organizing of the production sequence without any *Muda* using three elements, i.e., Takt-time, working sequence, and standard in-process stock. Takt-time decides the monthly production schedule considering 100 per cent operating efficiency with full working hours. It also permits flexible response to change in sales position. It is decided by dividing work time with the required number of production based on demand. Working sequence is the sequence of operations in a single process to produce quality goods reducing overburden and maintaining the security and safety of workers. Standard in-process stock is maintaining of minimum stock for ongoing processing and between different sub-processes. TPS requires implementation in all areas of organizational activities, known as *Yokoten*. The literal meaning of *Yokoten* is 'across everywhere'.

PERFORMANCE IMPROVEMENT THROUGH QUALITY MANAGEMENT PRACTICES

Organizations can also improve performance through quality management practices. To understand quality management practices, at the outset, we need to understand the concept of quality. Quality is now defined as the totality of features and characteristics of products or services which satisfy stated or implied needs of customers. It means for today's organizations, customers define the quality. The traditional percept of quality was to consider conformance to defined standards. Modern concept discards this and considers quality as in-built features of products and services that customers only can understand while they use the same. To achieve performance improvement, organizations focus on quality management practices that encompass cost reduction, productivity, teamwork, communication, training on problem-solving, decision-making, organizational dynamics, and interpersonal skills development. All these can significantly bring positive changes in the organization, and thereby can contribute to performance improvement. Quality management practices can give better performance results when aligned with the organizational goals. For performance improvement, quality management programmes emphasize on developing the capability of people to troubleshoot quality problem and to develop quality as an essential in-built attribute of products and services. The concept of total quality management (TQM) has now become an accepted principle for achieving quality improvement in organization. A literal definition of TQM, among others, is that it considers an organizational improvement strategy through development of people. Therefore, quality is intertwined with the people development activities of an organization.

To institutionalize quality management, almost every organization declares in their mission statements that achieving quality is their important priority to grow in a globally competitive market. To establish their quality icon, organizations are now getting International Organization for Standardisation (ISO) Certification. Although ISO certification alone cannot bring positive changes in the business results, but in the process of getting it, organizations bring many positive changes in the way they work by revisiting their processes and systems, and understanding their priorities for quality management practices.

Performance Improvement Through Quality

Organizations achieve performance improvement through quality from different perspectives. The first obviously is achieving customer satisfaction, which increases customer retention and future churning of customers for better business results. A satisfied customer becomes a captive customer and he/she has compelling reasons to buy again and again. Such repeat buying obviously benefits organizations. Moreover, one satisfied customer can influence new customers through referrals. Quality management practices can also improve performance through enormous savings in the cost of quality. By waste minimization, process simplification, and customer-focused approach it can exert many performance improvement issues and thereby achieve increased business results. Over and above, as quality management prioritizes the development of people, with renewed capabilities, people can also perform better.

Cost of Quality

To analyse the cost of quality, it is necessary to first classify the nature of cost under three sub-headings as follows:

Cost of Failure: Quality may fail either internally (within the organization) or externally, i.e., within the customers' premises (outside the organization). Therefore, failure cost can be grouped either as internal failure cost or external failure cost. Cost of re-work, cost for additional raw-materials, additional payments required to be made to workmen, eventual scrap arising, etc. can be accounted under internal failure cost. In case of external failure, we also consider the cost incurred for re-transportation, re-packaging, servicing and handling of customer complaints,and cost for loss of goodwill, in addition to the cost to be incurred for internal failure. Experience shows cost of failure itself absorbs 70 per cent of the total cost of quality.

Cost of Appraisal: For verification of quality, organization has to incur expenses toward inspection, for maintaining an inspection team. Also for carrying out inspection, certain inspection gadgets and tools are required. All the expenses incurred toward this account are considered as cost of appraisal. On this account usually organization spends between 28 and 29 per cent of the total quality cost.

Cost of Prevention: This type of quality cost is incurred to reduce the other two quality costs indicated above. Such expenses are amount spent for Research & Development and Human Resource Development. Expenses on this account normally vary between 1 and 2 per cent.

Although in Indian organizations, we are yet to make serious study about computing cost of quality, from international perspective, it is seen that such cost, even though not accounted under any separate head, is as high as 40 per cent of the cost of production. In Indian organizations, we typically assume that in the normal manufacturing process we are supposed to have some natural rejection, which may be as high as 22 per cent (at least in some cases), which we call as unavoidable rejection rate (UAR). Contrarily, in developed countries, more particularly in Japan, they are subscribing to the philosophy of zero defects.

Experience shows that a mere 1–2 per cent more expenditure on cost of prevention can substantially reduce the expenditure on other two sub-heads of cost of quality. In fact, the rate of such incremental cost benefit is as high as 70–80 per cent for a mere additional of 1–2 per cent expenses on cost of prevention.

Thus, it is evident that cost of quality, even though not apparent from the books of accounts, is a significant wasteful cost factor, which can be reduced substantially to increase the profitability of an organization. In fact, ISO documentation process helps to prune cost of quality in addition to augment internal efficiency of an organization. It also helps to achieve total quality management in a phased manner.

Quality Management Principles

With growing global competition, quality management is becoming increasingly important to the leadership and management of all organizations. Quality management principles provide understanding and guidance on the application of quality management. By applying the following eight quality management principles, organizations can produce benefits for all its stakeholders.

- Customer-focused organization.
- Leadership.
- Involvement of people.
- Process approach.
- System approach to management.
- Continual improvement.
- Factual approach to decision-making.
- Mutually beneficial supplier relationships.

Teamwork Through Quality Management

Quality management practices can institutionalize teamwork. When TQM is successful, employees at every level participate in decisions affecting their work. The most common vehicle for employee participation is a team. Teams range in scope and responsibility from problem-solving groups to self-managed work teams that schedule work, assign jobs, hire members, and set standards and volume of output. A participative work culture is encouraged when quality becomes everybody's responsibility.

Employee involvement practices in any organization may differ in terms of organizational policies and strategies. Common employee involvement practices are:

- Suggestion system.
- Survey feedback.
- Quality circles.
- Formation of quality of work life team.
- Job redesign.
- Formation of self-managed teams.
- Formation of TQM team.

Participative management is used as the most important approach for introducing TQM culture in any organization.

Employee Empowerment

Employee empowerment means to confer legitimate right to employees, irrespective of their nature of job and hierarchical level to make judgements, to take decisions on their own. Hence employee empowerment can facilitate development of problem solving abilities of the employeesand in the process enhance their performance ability. Operationally, in organizations, we empower employees first by developing their capabilities and second by giving them indulgence to commit mistakes. Unlike other quality management approach, empowerment not only calls for employee participation in the operational area, but also allows them to participate in corporate level decision-making, so that employees emerge as a total man. An empowered employee, in other words, is not a mere seller of his time and labour for a contracted sum of money. The empowered employee acquires necessary skill and authority to own. Employee empowerment, involvement, and participative management as important corporate practices have been experimented in several multi-national and national organizations. In all these cases, it was identified that the employee ownership and commitment (which is possible through employee empowerment) are the two ingredients that achieved efficiency and productivity. Some organizations are even empowering their employees at the strategic level rather than confining their involvement only to limited operational activity. With full empowerment, organizations achieve excellence in performance.

Quality of Work Life (QWL)

QWL is most conventionally defined as those perceived important personal needs, which an individual tries to satisfy by working in an organization. Its conceptual foundations, though laid by a host of behavioural scientists, were in reality advocated by Chris Argyris (1975) in his famous work on *Personality and Organization*. The socio-technical Systems Theory, pioneered by Tavistock Institute of Human Relations, London during the 1960s is considered as an important QWL construct. Basic conceptual criteria for QWL consider growth and security as important personal needs for an individual. The possibility of furthering one's career within the organization has, therefore, been identified as one of the important criteria for QWL. Although common QWL strategists emphasize more on job re-design, formation of autonomous work groups, and worker participation in management, there exists wide differences among the pioneers in this area as to what should be construed as QWL factors. The process of QWL can be explained with the help of the following criteria:

- Adequate and fair compensation.
- Safe and healthy working conditions.
- Immediate opportunity to use and develop human capacities.
- Future opportunity for continued growth and security.
- Social integration in the work organization.
- Work and total life space.
- Social relevance of working life.

Based on studies carried out both in India and abroad, it is evident that the essence of QWL is the opportunity for employees, at all levels, to have substantial influence over their work environment. This is the result of their participating in the decision-making process relating to their work, thereby enhancing their self-esteem and the overall satisfaction from their work. Hence, QWL calls for an open style of management, i.e., sharing of information and genuinely encouraging the efforts relating to the improvement of the organization. This makes it amply clear that QWL, in fact, is an important managerial activity to develop employees of an organization. The success of TQM programmes largely depend on appropriate HRD interventions like emphasis on continuous training and development activity, encouraging participation in management through small group forums, increasing employee motivation, looking after the career development of employees, employee empowerment, and infusing attitudinal changes at the top (like accepting a flatter organization structure, following an democratic approach, becoming receptive to changes on a continuous basis, supporting group performance, etc.).

PERFORMANCE IMPROVEMENT THROUGH SIX-SIGMA PRACTICES

The literal meaning of six-sigma is six standard deviations from mean. The word 'sigma' is a Greek term indicating standard deviation. Essentially, it helps in process improvement by making use of statistics as a tool to identify and address performance management issues. It was first started in Motorola and then gradually became a globally accepted tool to improve organizational performance. The underlying philosophy of six-sigma is that no process is error free. Hence organizations should continuously focus on achieving excellence through process improvement by recreating it every time. Using the DMAIC cycle, i.e., define opportunities, measure performance, analyse opportunities, improve performance, and control performance, the six-sigma approach constantly reviews a process to recreate it again and again to achieve error-free performance results. Six-sigma is essentially a customer-centric break-through process improvement approach for business results. Improvement in processes lead to error-free production and so also services, achieve cost effectiveness, earn customer satisfaction, which ultimately cascade to increased profitability and improved business results. Higher sigma value indicates better business results.

For performance improvement, six-sigma is now widely accepted in organizations globally. To introduce six-sigma in organizations, certain sequence of activities need to be followed, as enumerated below:

Emphasis on training and learning: Take all cross-sections of employees through this. Make them understand the importance of achieving quality. The emphasis at this stage should be to embed in the minds of the people the need and imperativeness of six-sigma with a customer-centric approach and take employees through the intricacies of the processes. Class room training should be further extended to hands-on practices in small projects.

Collection of data and consolidation of information: Help the employees to understand the process of data collection with detailed checklists for a process. Also employees should understand how to translate data to information and interpret the same. Such information processing will gradually educate employees to learn what is important and what is not.

Understanding the customer needs: Employees must also understand what customers want. Six-sigma is essentially a customer-driven approach. The benchmark of quality in six-sigma language is customers' satisfaction. Critical to quality (CTQs) are decided by the customers. With the list of CTQs, it is possible to understand better the deviation areas in a process.

Thorough understanding of the inputs of a process: It is very important for employees to understand what constitutes the input of a process. If required, employees need to be helped to go through a detailed work breakdown structure analysis (WBS) to understand the process.

Six-sigma Implementation

Six-sigma implementation process, at the outset, focuses on improvement in areas like process, products and services, investor relationship, design, vendor relationship, recruitment, training and development, and performance management systems. A typical six-sigma structure to achieve breakthrough improvement strategy can be presented as in Figure 17.2.

The inverted pyramidal structure shows at the top the management who extend support to balance the six-sigma implementation. Champions are the executives who select leaders to make them understand the key functions and how these can be connected to six-sigma projects. Champions select the master black belts and make them the catalyst to disseminate information on identified six-sigma projects, train people selected as black belts and green belts, organize them, conduct cross-functional experiments, coordinate, collect, and organize information. Master black belts select the black belts and facilitate them to apply six-sigma to specific selected areas of improvement. Green belts are the employees at the

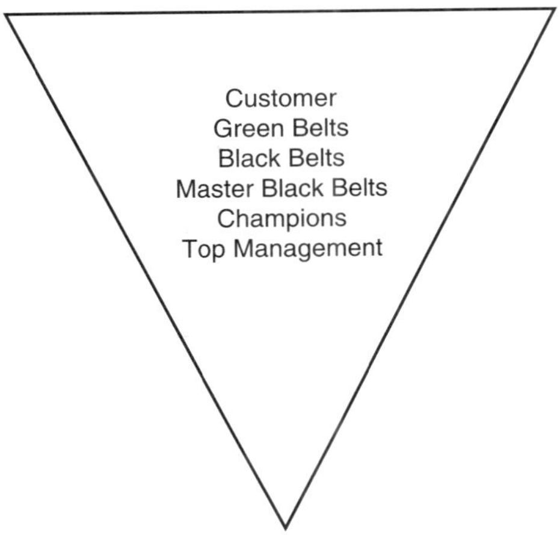

Figure 17.2 *Six-sigma implementation*

ground level who are directly involved in the six-sigma implementation in their jobs and projects. Six-sigma is implemented by the following eight steps in line with the DMAIC cycle:

- Recognize
- Define
- Measure
- Analyse
- Improve
- Control
- Standardize
- Integrate

For the sake of our understanding, the six-sigma implementation stages are presented in Table 17.1. The tabular information is self-explanatory. However, as six-sigma process makes use of statistical information, performance managers should be made clear about the calculation process to understand the level of sigma achieved through the six-sigma initiatives.

To calculate six-sigma, we make use of defects per million opportunities (DPMO) formula. The DPMO formula helps us to translate customers' perceived critical to quality (CTQ) factors into sigma level which can be verified from the six-sigma table. For doing so, we need quantitative data on number of units, number of defects as perceived by the customers, and the number of opportunity for errors, i.e., the chance for the occurrence of defects. With the above discrete information, we then use the following formula:

$$\frac{\textit{Number of Defects}}{\textit{Number of Opportunities} \times \textit{Number of Units}} X^{1,00,000}$$

Table 17.1 *Implementation stages of six-sigma*

Stages	Strategy Phase	Objectives	Responsibilities
Identification	Recognize and define	To understand key business issues and documenting the same	Master black belts with support from the champions.
Characterization	Measure and analyse	To understand and document the level of current performance	Black belts with help and support from the master black belts
Optimization	Improve and control	To start the improvement exercises	Black belts
Institutionalization	Standardize and integrate	To transform day-to-day activities in accordance with the six-sigma practices	Black belts

For performance management, employees are the internal customers to the organization. It is the employees who define the CTQ. Let us assume that employees of an organization perceive four CTQs in their performance management systems, as follows:

- Poor performance feedback.
- Stretched performance goals.
- Poor support for development.
- Poor recognition for achieving performance excellence.

These CTQs then make four opportunities for error in the performance management systems. Let us now consider the discrete data on number of units as the number of performance evaluations done in a particular period for their employees. For this purpose, let us assume it as 2,500, i.e., the number of employees for whom the performance measurements have been done. Now we need to understand the number of defects. For this purpose let us assume that the employees (customers) have reported 10 defective performance evaluations for stretched goals and 5 for poor performance feedback. This, therefore, makes the total number of defects as 15. Now, using the DPMO formula, we can understand the present sigma level of the hypothetical organization's performance management systems. The calculation in this case would be as follows:

$$\frac{15}{2\times 2500} X^{1,000,000} = 3,000 \text{ DPMO}$$

3,000 defects per million opportunities represent 4.25 sigma levels in the performance management systems of the company. At six-sigma level, it should have been only 3.4 defects. Therefore, this suggests enormous flaws in the performance management system of the organization, which they need to study and correct to achieve higher sigma level.

Most of the organizations now make extensive use of six-sigma practices in their human resource management practices to develop their employees for gaining sustainable competitive advantages. In all HR areas, six-sigma can be implemented to align HR benefits for achieving organizational business goals. With six-sigma compliant performance management systems, the process becomes much more effective, as performance management itself can address many areas of employee needs like development, motivation, matching compensation, and improved work culture. A partial six-sigma value table is presented as Table 17.2.

Table 17.2 *Partial six-sigma*

Defects per million	Table value of sigma
3000	4.25
2,560	4.30
1,350	4.5
233	5.0
5	5.9
3.4	6

Therefore, to improve performance management systems and so also the overall business performance of the organization, it is necessary to understand the process, then train people to transform the performance improvement project to a six-sigma project and periodically measure the levels of achievement.

PERFORMANCE IMPROVEMENT THROUGH INNOVATION AND CREATIVITY

Innovation is another important tool for achieving business results. Innovation can encompass products/services, process, managerial styles, and even performance management systems. Innovation in performance management can be either technology push or demand pull. Technology push innovation in performance management indicates introduction of e-performance management systems for total transparency of information and enforcing control so that organizations can sustain the performance level. Many vendors now make available computer enabled balanced score cards, performance dash boards, etc. which can quickly assess the employees' performance level and guide them to meet the shortfalls in performance, if any, when they fail to achieve the desired performance. Many organizations institutionalize innovation to survive in competition. Innovation becomes more effective when it is customer focused and aligned with the organizational needs. It is not a specific documented practice; rather it means those practices, which require lateral thinking to improve the performance in organizations. For that matter reengineering, lean management, total quality management, six-sigma, etc. are innovative practices adopted by organizations to achieve performance excellence. Ford Motor's innovative bar coding system to trace missing spares in assembled cars could help them to achieve performance excellence and extend the same to customers in the form of 3 year 100,000 km free maintenance plan. This signal of in-built quality could help the company to gain customers' confidence and increased sales of cars. Organizations aspiring to achieve innovation in performance management practices need to map customer needs (internal customers) and align the same to the desired innovation initiative, which among others require them to bring positive changes in work environment and promote inter-organizational cooperation through teamwork.

QUICK RESPONSE MANUFACTURING (QRM)

Quick response manufacturing (QRM) is another lean management practice that originated in the 1980s, which focuses on lead time optimization to enhance productivity. It is an extension of just-in-time (JIT) concept that emphasizes on customer satisfaction by quickly responding to customer's requirements. QRM reduces lead times in all activities of the organization by analysing various processes using step-by-step approach. At the outset, it requires understanding of the whole organization, and its parts, and then focusing on those that particularly affect the lead time.

Lead time always need not be attributable to manufacturing processes. It may be for many non-manufacturing activities like purchase and materials management function, back office function, dispatch, finance, planning, and human resource management functions. This is why it plays a very crucial role for performance improvement.

SUMMARY

To achieve performance improvement, globally, organizations are now adopting various contemporary performance improvement practices, explained in this chapter. In performance improvement, BPR, lean management, six sigma, TQM, TPS, QRM, QWL, innovation and creativity, etc. play a pivotal role. In this chapter, we have discussed all these tools as important drivers of performance management systems. However, improved performance management with the use of these tools can be achieved only through simultaneous transformation of the organization culture. This chapter discussed all these tools and, drawing lessons from the corporate world, illustrated how using such tools organizations could achieve performance excellence. The chapter will serve as an important guideline for organizations to embrace contemporary performance improvement tools and its successful implementation for better business results.

KEY WORDS

BPR—BPR is fundamental rethinking and redesign of business processes of an organization, addressing technological, human, and internal way of functioning of the organization, keeping pace with the changes, to achieve success in critical performance areas, like cost, quality, service, and delivery.

McKinsey's 7S Framework—McKinsey's 7S framework identified seven independent organizational factors that need to be managed by today's managers. These are strategy, structure, systems, staff, styles, skills, and finally the shared values. Any change in any S factor may result in adjustment of other S factors.

TPS—It was based on two primary concepts: the manufacturing production system of Henry Ford and the Ford Motor, and the supermarket operations in the United States. TPS incorporated the Just-In-Time (JIT) production and *Jidoka* techniques to optimize time and human assets in the manufacturing environment. TPS later became the basis for lean production and the 'lean enterprise' movements beginning in the early 1990s.

Balanced Scorecard—It helps in quantification of performance results of the employees from four major perspectives, i.e., learning and growth, internal processes, customer, and finance. Irrespective of their functional areas, and hierarchical level, each employee contributes to these four areas. Keeping a track on employees' performance to understand their performance dynamics scientifically is necessary in lean management practices or else organizations won't be able to track the incremental changes, after its implementation.

Process Innovation—It requires new thinking. It requires challenging the existing process, and managing the operations altogether from different perspectives.

DMAIC—It is the structured model of problem investigation and resolution, which we use in organizational improvement strategy through six-sigma. DMAIC stand for: Define, Measure, Analyse, Improve, and Control. This structured approach helps us identify problems and also to evolve its solution for successful implementation of lean management practices in organizations.

CTQs—CTQs are customers' perceived critical to quality (CTQ) factors, and are considered as opportunities for error, while we compute the sigma level achieved by any organization in quality.

Kaizen—*Kaizen* ensures continuous improvement of entire value stream or an individual process adding more value with less waste. System or flow, *Kaizen* focuses on the overall value stream, and process *Kaizen* focuses on individual process. Both the levels of *Kaizen* benefit the organization, achieving the efficiency.

CONCEPT REVIEW QUESTIONS

1. Explain the concepts and definitions of BPR. How does BPR exert impact on the culture of an organization?
2. Explain briefly BPR experiences of any organization, specifically in the Indian context.
3. Why is BPR often criticized? Do you think such criticisms are always valid?
4. Explain the conept of lean management and its relationship with the culture of any organization.
5. What are the principles of TQM? Does TQM differ from BPR?
6. It is often said quality management practices are culture centric! Do you believe in this statement? Justify your answer.
7. Explain the concept of six-sigma. How does six-sigma relate to the culture of an organization?
8. Short notes:
   (a) Quick response manufacturing
   (b) Streaming
   (c) Four perspectives of balanced scorecard
   (d) JIT

CRITICAL REVIEW QUESTION

9. You have been retained by an organization who wants to implement six-sigma in their design and development function. The company is engaged in manufacturing of desktops, where price and non-price (say, quality and services) competitions are fierce. The company follows a traditional hierarchical structure. The design and development function of the company undertakes most of the R&D work in virtual mode, and hardly require any physical validation, excepting in cases, where chips, etc. are used for sourcing from vendors other than their validated one. Understand the functioning of the R&D division of any desktop manufacturer. Identify at least one functional area. Study its details and draw your six-sigma implementation plan to ensure the performance of the function is totally error free.

REFERENCES

Bhattacharyya, D.K. (2000), 'Competency Mapping and Manpower Redundancy—A Macro Level Study of Indian Organizations', *Management and Accounting Research*, (October–December) 4(2): 97–105.

Bhattacharyya, D.K. (2009), *Organizational Behaviour—Concepts and Applications* (New Delhi: Oxford University Press).

Bhattacharyya, D.K. (2010a), *Cross-cultural Management—Text and Cases* (New Delhi: PHI Learning).

Bhattacharyya, D.K. (2010b), *Industrial Management* (New Delhi: Vikas Publishing).

Champy, J. (1995), *Reengineering Management* (New York: Harper Business Books).

Davenport, Thomas (1993), *Process Innovation: Reengineering Work through Information Technology* (Boston, MA: Harvard Business School Press).

Davenport, Thomas and J. Short (1990), 'The New Industrial Engineering: Information Technology and Business Process Redesign', *Sloan Management Review*, (Summer) 11–27.

Drucker, Peter (1972), 'Work and Tools', in W. Kranzberg and W.H. Davenport (eds), *Technology and Culture*, (New York, NY: Schocken Books).

George, Eckes (2001), *The Six sigma Revolution* (New York, NY: John Wiley and Sons Inc.).

Hammer, Michael (1990), 'Reengineering Work: Don't Automate, Obliterate', *Harvard Business Review*, (July/August) 104–12

Hammer, Michael and James Champy (1993), *Reengineering the Corporation: A Manifesto for Business Revolution* (New York, NY: Harper Business Books).

Hammer, M. and S. Stanton (1995). *The Reengineering Revolution* (London: Harper Collins).

Johansson, Henry J., et al. (1993), *Business Process Reengineering: Break Point Strategies for Market Dominance* (New York, NY: John Wiley & Sons).

Leavitt, H.J. (1965), 'Applied Organizational Change in Industry: Structural, Technological and Humanistic Approaches', in James March (ed.), *Handbook of Organizations* (Chicago, IL: Rand McNally).

Mikel, Harry and Schroeder Richard (2000), *Six Sigma* (New York, NY: Currency).

Richard, C.H. Chua (2001), 'Six Sigma: A Pursuit of Excellence and Dramatic Results', *Today's Manager* (August–September) 43–45.

CASE STUDY

Total Quality Management—Experience of Nissan

Nissan embedded the total quality management (TQM) practices in their work systems. Nissan's TQM, apart from improving the internal processes, emphasizes on customer satisfaction on a priority basis. With such a customer-centric approach, Nissan directs all their activities, focussing on high quality. Perhaps, Nissan has adopted the most effective way of institutionalizing TQM, as with customer-centric approach, they could achieve both high quality and at the same time enhanced business, through customer satisfaction. To excel in TQM through customer-centric approach, Nissan focused on the following aspects:

- Basic understanding of customer requirements.
- Analysis of process requirements to meet customer perceived quality.
- Standardizing processes to meet the customer perceived quality.
- Building employees' capabilities to work in accordance with the standardized process, etc.

With the above focus, Nissan could make TQM an ongoing quality improvement process. Also, in all performance improvement initiatives, Nissan embraces customers' expectations, making it their cultural DNA. The culture of improvement at Nissan is transparent, and every cross-section of employees of Nissan can understand and measure their contribution towards the improved culture. In the process, employees of Nissan also feel motivated, as they can understand their worth, and how they could help the organization to achieve excellence in performance. The performance improvement culture, addressing the customer perceived quality requirements, is now so deeprooted in the minds of Nissan employees that they now volunteer to develop their capabilities and achieve business results. Nissan's example now teaches us how, by institutionalizing customer-centric TQM practices, organizations can benefit from performance improvement and enhanced profitability.

To make TQM work, Nissan embedded the cycle of plan, do, check, action (PDCA) in the thought process of every employee, which gradually cascaded to their work processes in conformity with Nissan's way of working. Nissan's success in TQM is the outcome of balanced focus on people and process-centric approach addressing customer' requirements. Moreover, Nissan could achieve performance excellence by building employees' problem-solving capabilities.

Question: Study the case of Nissan and compare it with Maruti India to understand the degree of compatibility in effective use of total quality management practices to effect the performance improvement of employees.

Index

Q

R

S